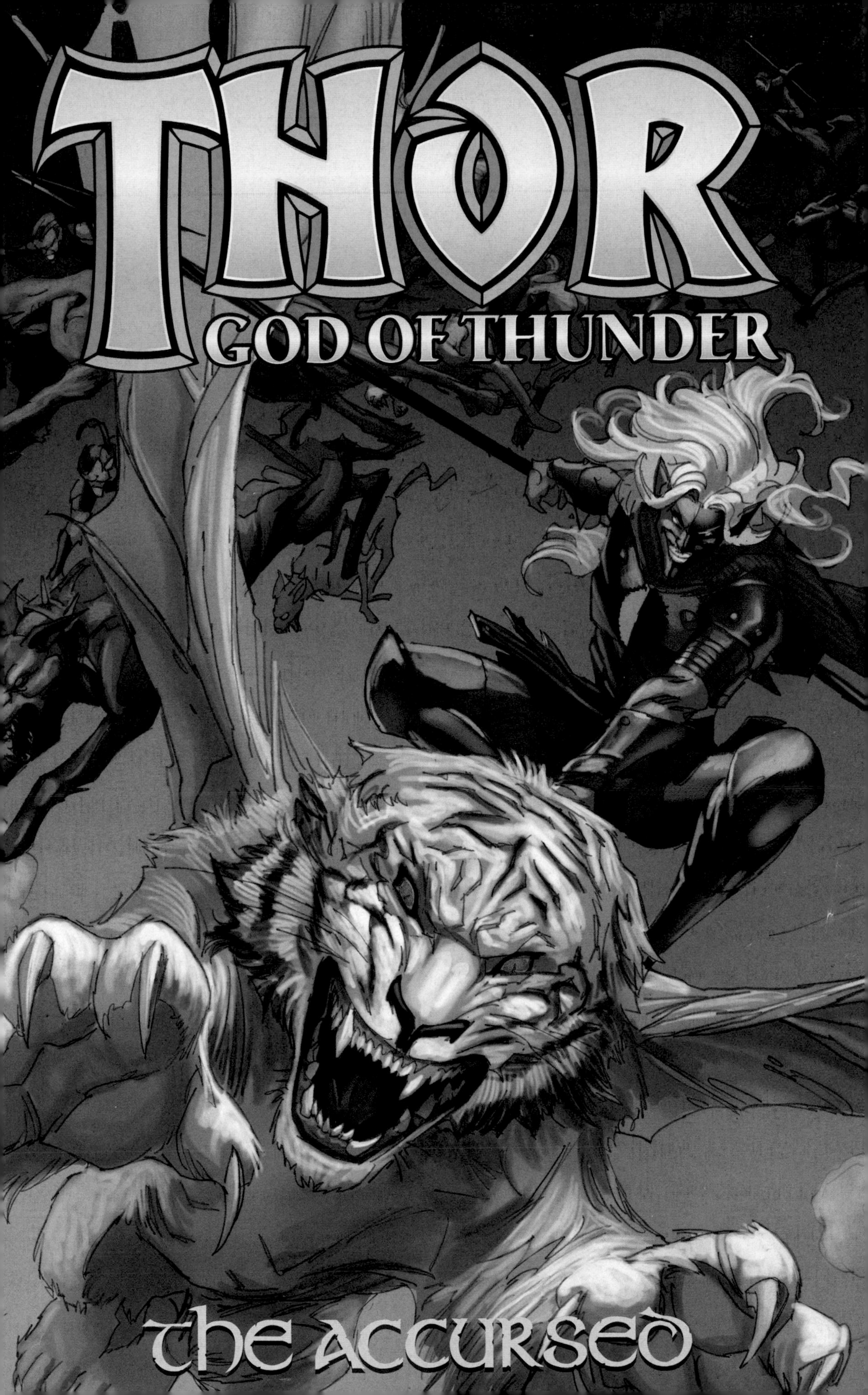
THOR
GOD OF THUNDER
THE ACCURSED

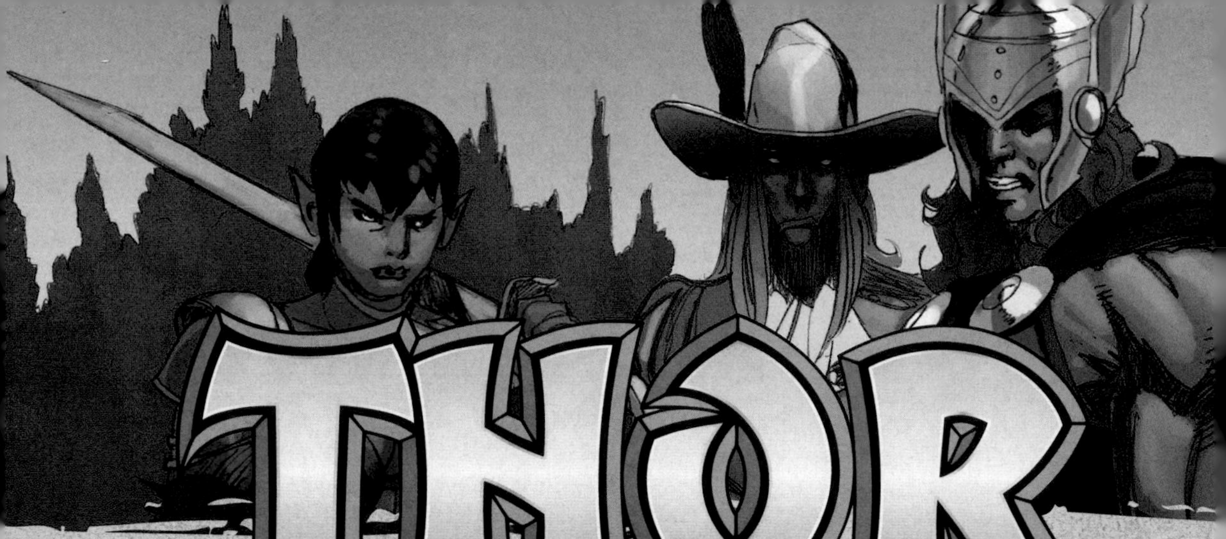

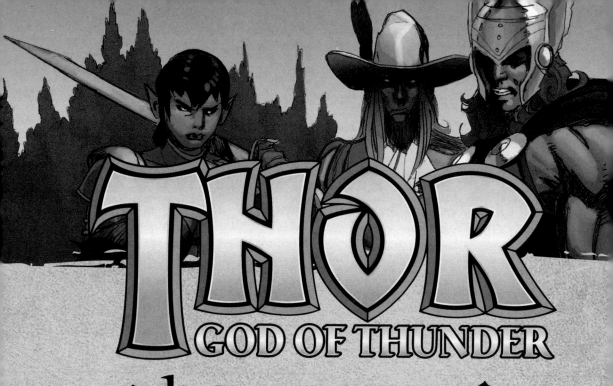

THOR
GOD OF THUNDER
THE ACCURSED

WRITER
JASON AARON

ISSUE #12
ARTIST: **NIC KLEIN**

ISSUE #18
ARTIST: **DAS PASTORAS**

ISSUES #13-17
ARTIST: **RON GARNEY** WITH **EMANUELA LUPACCHINO** (#16-17)
COLOR ARTIST: **IVE SVORCINA** WITH **LEE LOUGHRIDGE** (#17)

COVER ART
ESAD RIBIC (#12 & #16-18) AND **RON GARNEY** & **IVE SVORCINA** (#13-15)

LETTERER
VC'S JOE SABINO

ASSISTANT EDITOR
JON MOISAN

EDITOR
LAUREN SANKOVITCH

Collection Editor: **Jennifer Grünwald** • Associate Managing Editor: **Alex Starbuck** • Editor, Special Projects: **Mark D. Beazley**
Senior Editor, Special Projects: **Jeff Youngquist** • SVP Print, Sales & Marketing: **David Gabriel** • Book Design: **Jeff Powell**

Editor in Chief: **Axel Alonso** • Chief Creative Officer: **Joe Quesada**
Publisher: **Dan Buckley** • Executive Producer: **Alan Fine**

THOR: GOD OF THUNDER VOL. 3 — THE ACCURSED. Contains material originally published in magazine form as THOR: GOD OF THUNDER #12-18. First printing 2014. ISBN# 978-0-7851-8555-0. Published by MARVEL WORLDWIDE, INC., a subsidiary of MARVEL ENTERTAINMENT, LLC. OFFICE OF PUBLICATION: 135 West 50th Street, New York, NY 10020. **Printed in the U.S.A.** ALAN FINE, EVP - Office of the President, Marvel Worldwide, Inc. and EVP & CMO Marvel Characters B.V.; DAN BUCKLEY, Publisher & President - Print, Animation & Digital Divisions; JOE QUESADA, Chief Creative Officer; TOM BREVOORT, SVP of Publishing; DAVID BOGART, SVP of Operations & Procurement, Publishing; C.B. CEBULSKI, SVP of Creator & Content Development; DAVID GABRIEL, SVP of Print & Digital Publishing Sales; JIM O'KEEFE, VP of Operations & Logistics; DAN CARR, Executive Director of Publishing Technology; SUSAN CRESPI, Editorial Operations Manager; ALEX MORALES, Publishing Operations Manager; STAN LEE, Chairman Emeritus. For information regarding advertising in Marvel Comics or on Marvel.com, please contact Niza Disla, Director of Marvel Partnerships, at ndisla@marvel.com. For Marvel subscription inquiries, please call 800-217-9158. **Manufactured between 1/10/2014 and 2/24/2014 by R.R. DONNELLEY, INC., SALEM, VA, USA.**

10 9 8 7 6 5 4 3 2 1

PREVIOUSLY

With the bloody shadow of the God Butcher gone
forever, the three Thors returned to their homes: Young
Thor to the battle-hungry Vikings of an earlier age, Thor
the Avenger to Midgard of the present and Old King
Thor to rebuild Asgard that was in the far future.

Due to the strange nature of their travels through time,
none will remember their adventures together for long.

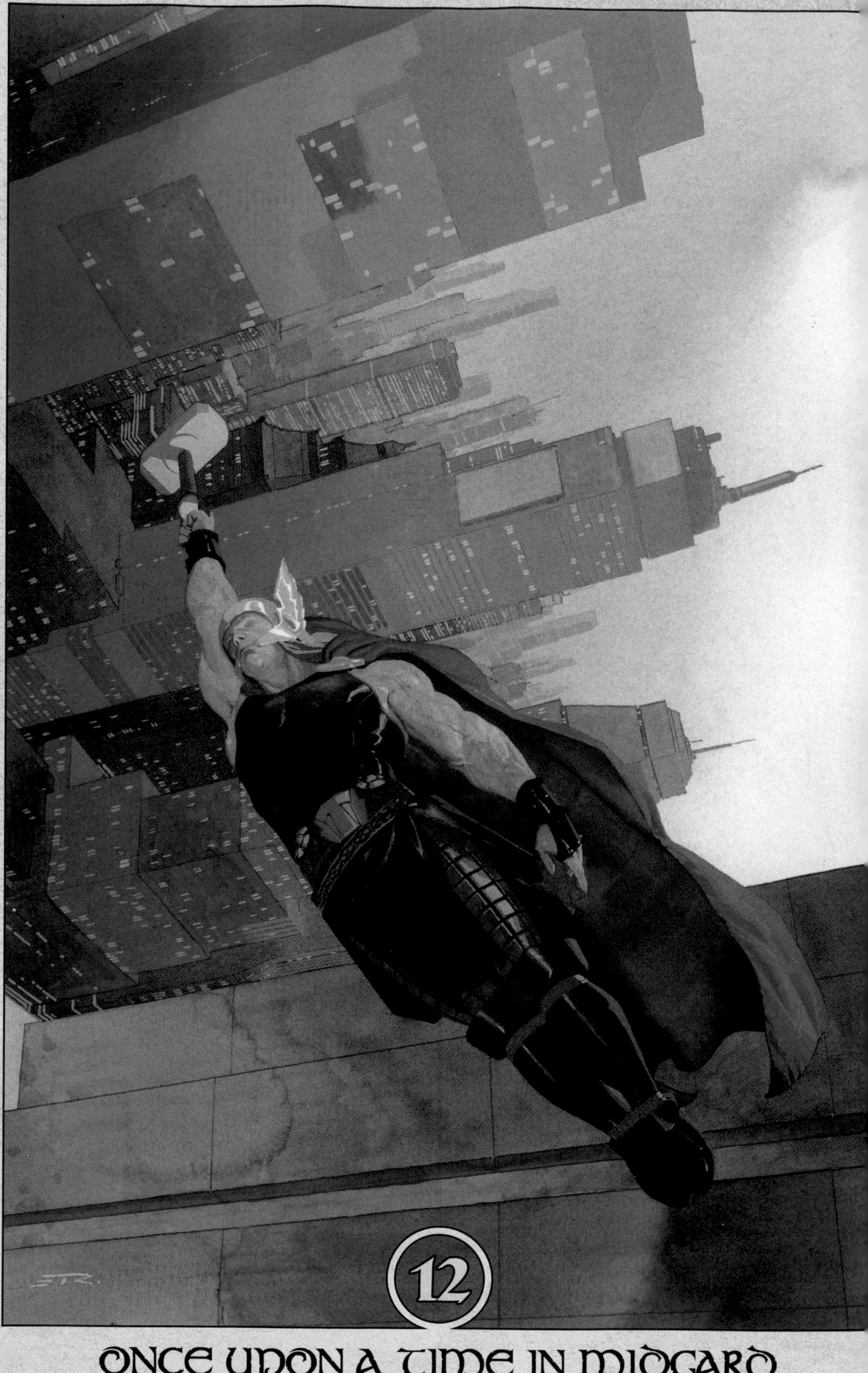

12

ONCE UPON A TIME IN MIDGARD

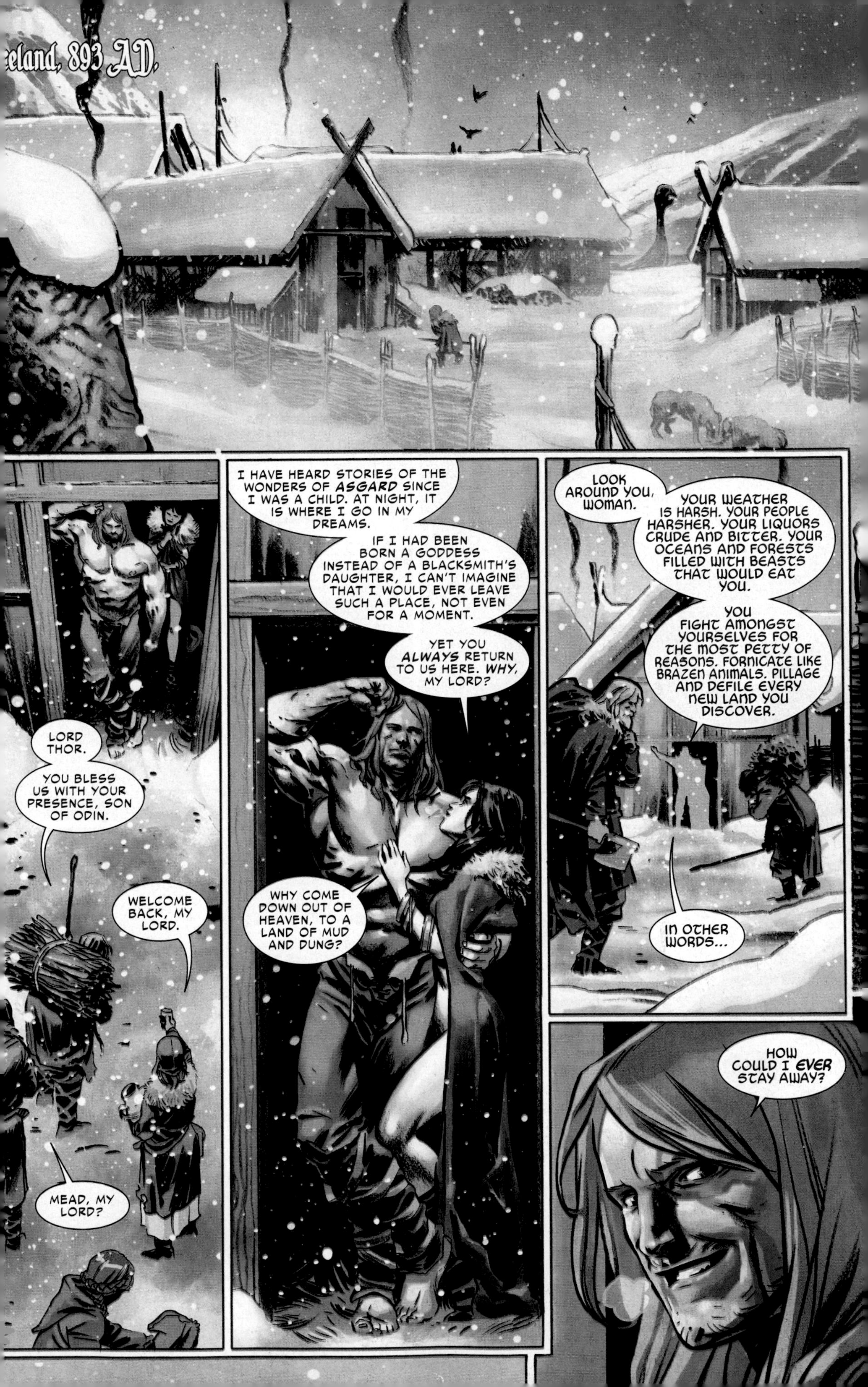

eland, 893 A.D.
LORD THOR.
YOU BLESS US WITH YOUR PRESENCE, SON OF ODIN.
WELCOME BACK, MY LORD.
MEAD, MY LORD?
I HAVE HEARD STORIES OF THE WONDERS OF ASGARD SINCE I WAS A CHILD. AT NIGHT, IT IS WHERE I GO IN MY DREAMS.
IF I HAD BEEN BORN A GODDESS INSTEAD OF A BLACKSMITH'S DAUGHTER, I CAN'T IMAGINE THAT I WOULD EVER LEAVE SUCH A PLACE, NOT EVEN FOR A MOMENT.
YET YOU ALWAYS RETURN TO US HERE. WHY, MY LORD?
WHY COME DOWN OUT OF HEAVEN, TO A LAND OF MUD AND DUNG?
LOOK AROUND YOU, WOMAN.
YOUR WEATHER IS HARSH. YOUR PEOPLE HARSHER. YOUR LIQUORS CRUDE AND BITTER. YOUR OCEANS AND FORESTS FILLED WITH BEASTS THAT WOULD EAT YOU.
YOU FIGHT AMONGST YOURSELVES FOR THE MOST PETTY OF REASONS. FORNICATE LIKE BRAZEN ANIMALS. PILLAGE AND DEFILE EVERY NEW LAND YOU DISCOVER.
IN OTHER WORDS...
HOW COULD I EVER STAY AWAY?

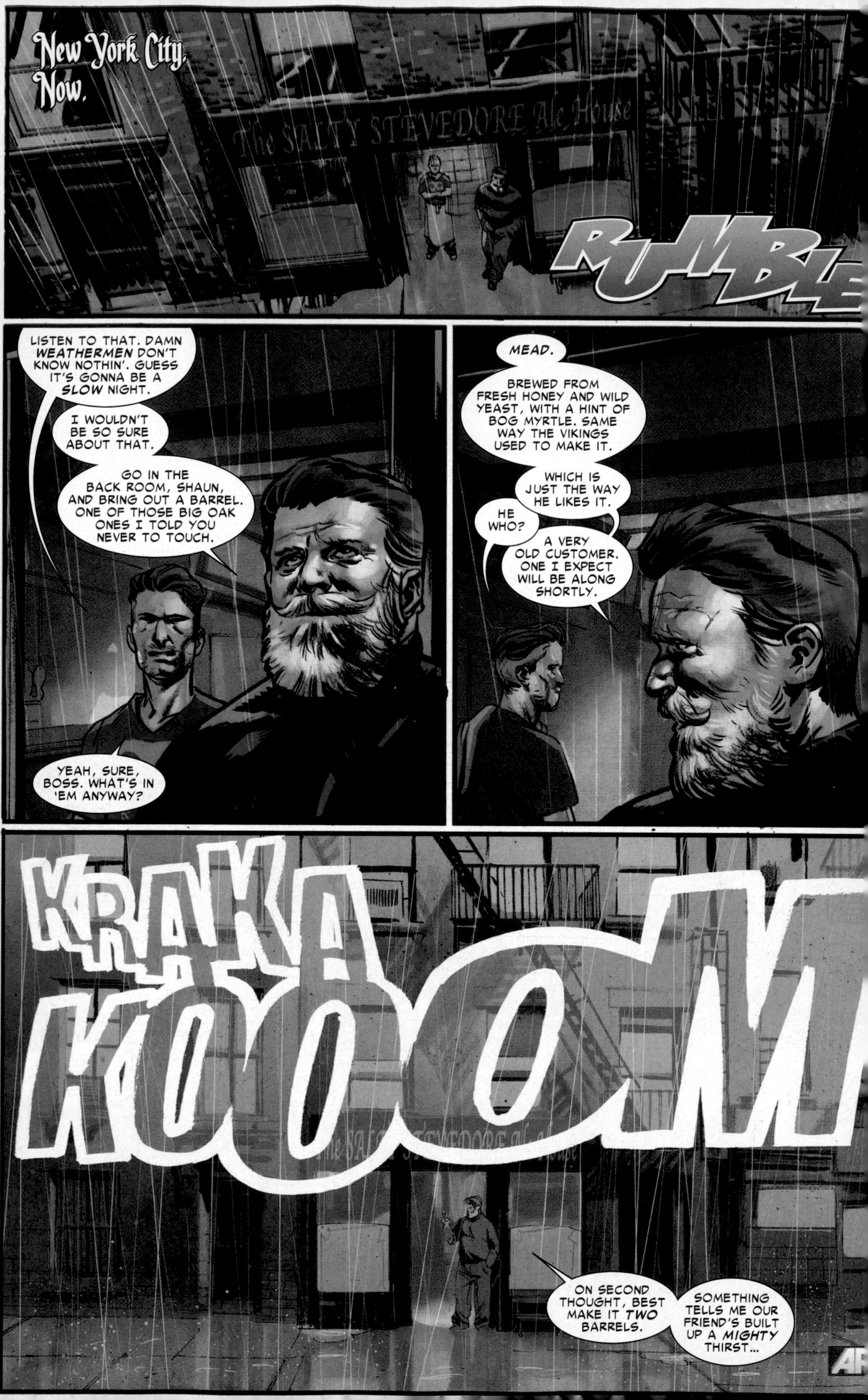
New York City, Now.
The SALTY STEVEDORE Ale House
RUMBLE
LISTEN TO THAT. DAMN WEATHERMEN DON'T KNOW NOTHIN'. GUESS IT'S GONNA BE A SLOW NIGHT.
I WOULDN'T BE SO SURE ABOUT THAT.
GO IN THE BACK ROOM, SHAUN, AND BRING OUT A BARREL. ONE OF THOSE BIG OAK ONES I TOLD YOU NEVER TO TOUCH.
YEAH, SURE, BOSS. WHAT'S IN 'EM ANYWAY?
MEAD.
BREWED FROM FRESH HONEY AND WILD YEAST, WITH A HINT OF BOG MYRTLE. SAME WAY THE VIKINGS USED TO MAKE IT.
WHICH IS JUST THE WAY HE LIKES IT.
HE WHO?
A VERY OLD CUSTOMER. ONE I EXPECT WILL BE ALONG SHORTLY.
KRAKA KOOOM
ON SECOND THOUGHT, BEST MAKE IT TWO BARRELS.
SOMETHING TELLS ME OUR FRIEND'S BUILT UP A MIGHTY THIRST...

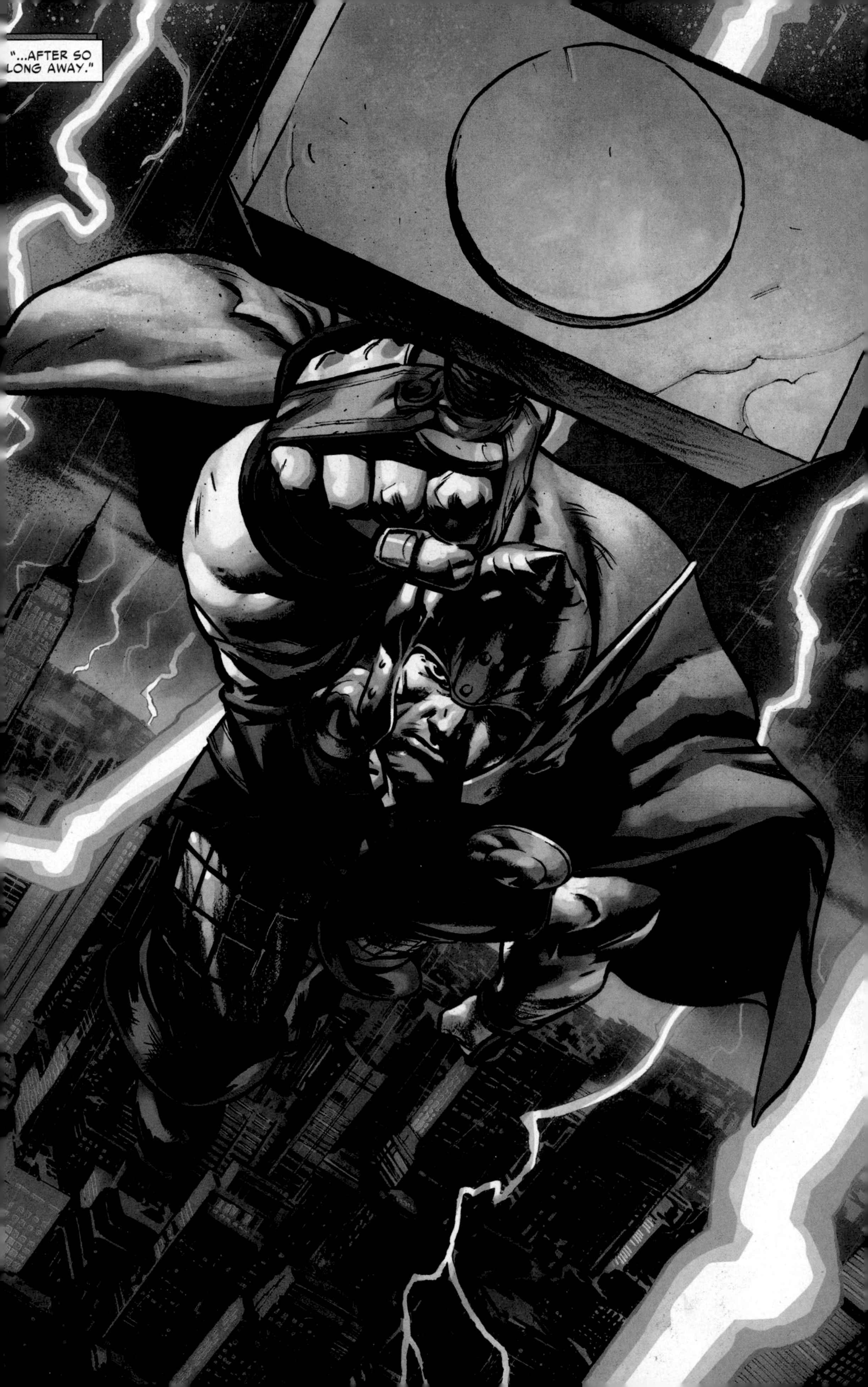
"...AFTER SO LONG AWAY."

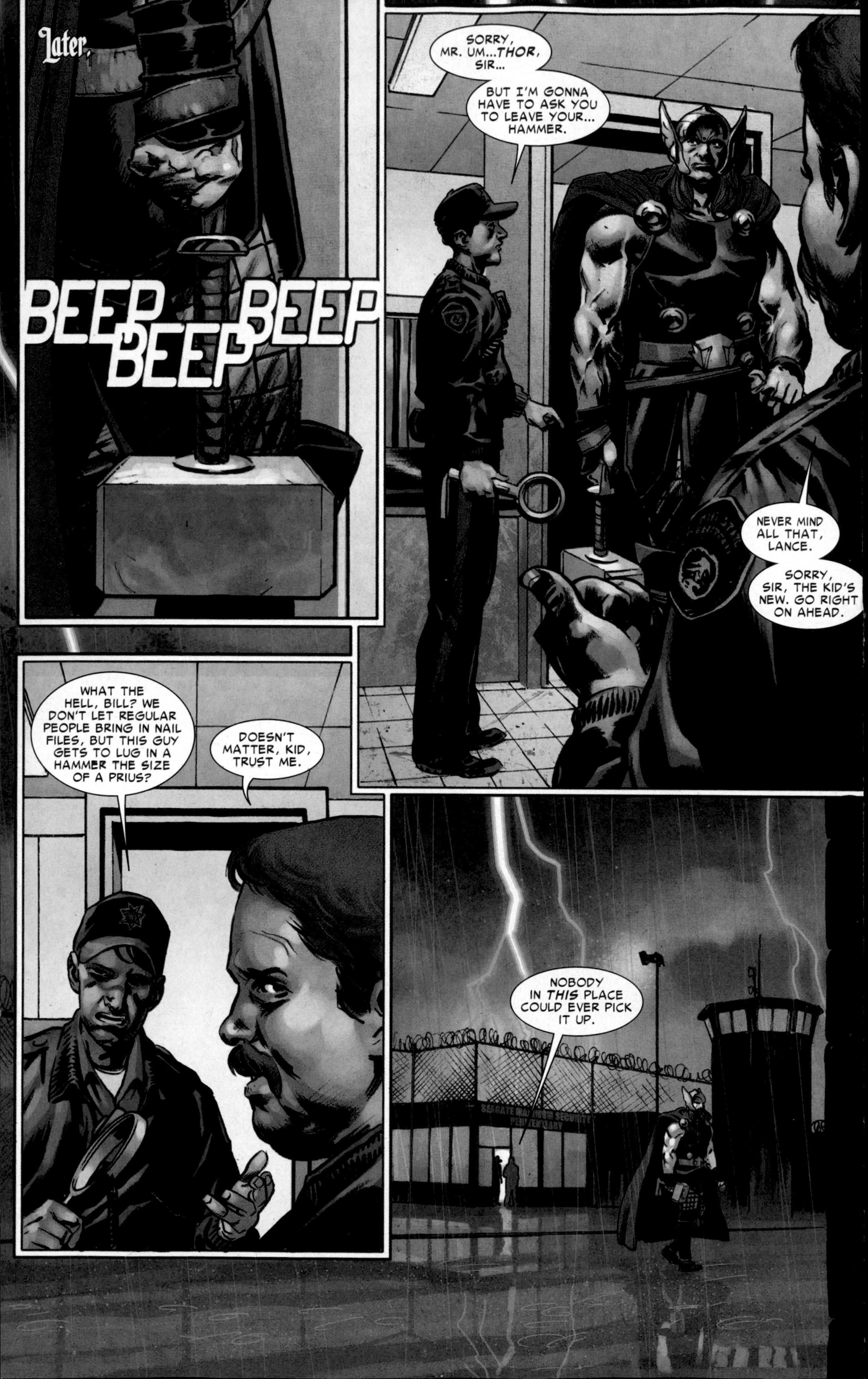
Later,
BEEP BEEP BEEP
SORRY, MR. UM...THOR, SIR...
BUT I'M GONNA HAVE TO ASK YOU TO LEAVE YOUR... HAMMER.
NEVER MIND ALL THAT, LANCE.
SORRY, SIR, THE KID'S NEW. GO RIGHT ON AHEAD.
WHAT THE HELL, BILL? WE DON'T LET REGULAR PEOPLE BRING IN NAIL FILES, BUT THIS GUY GETS TO LUG IN A HAMMER THE SIZE OF A PRIUS?
DOESN'T MATTER, KID, TRUST ME.
NOBODY IN THIS PLACE COULD EVER PICK IT UP.

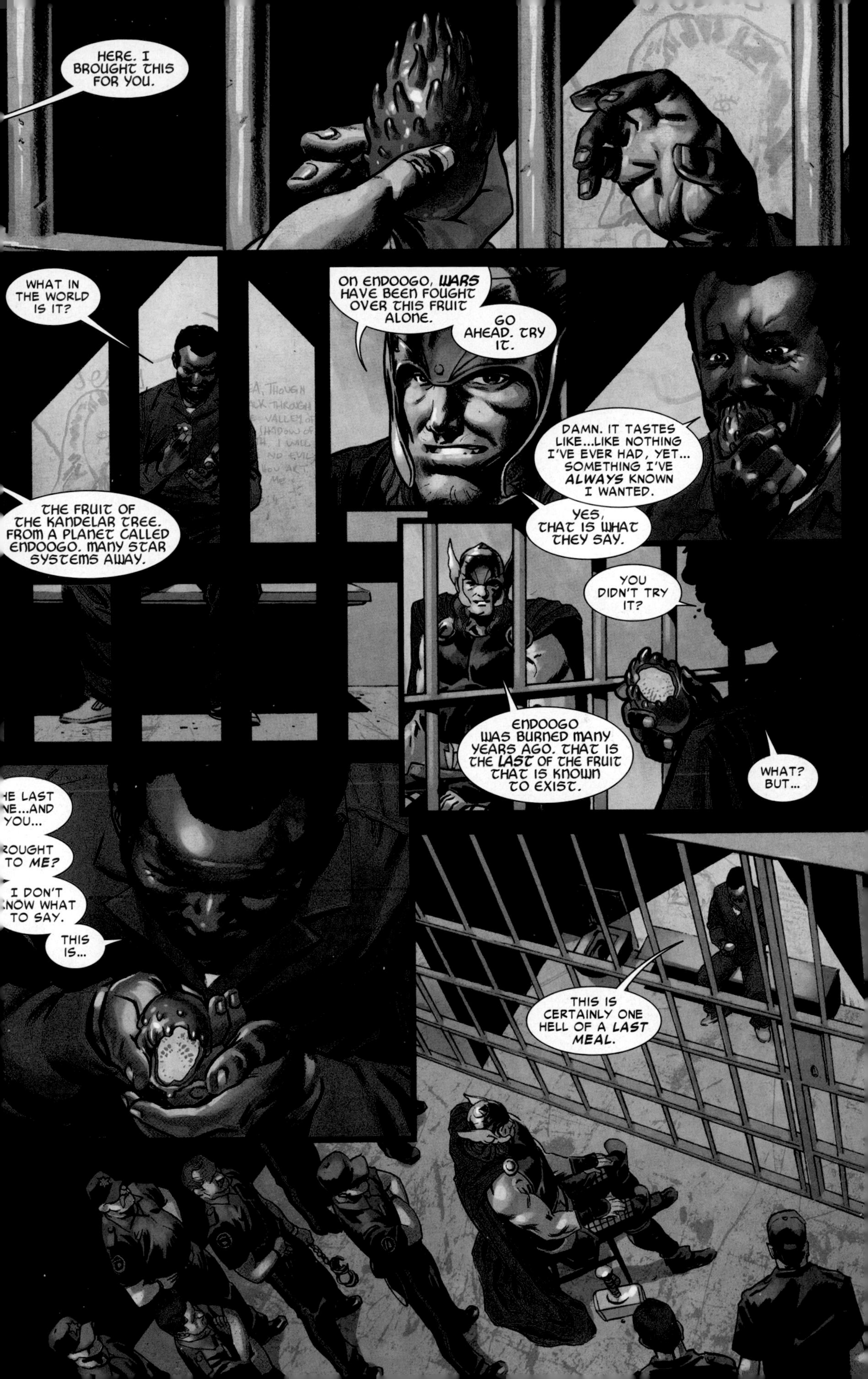
HERE. I BROUGHT THIS FOR YOU.
WHAT IN THE WORLD IS IT?
THE FRUIT OF THE KANDELAR TREE. FROM A PLANET CALLED ENDOOGO. MANY STAR SYSTEMS AWAY.
ON ENDOOGO, WARS HAVE BEEN FOUGHT OVER THIS FRUIT ALONE.
GO AHEAD. TRY IT.
DAMN. IT TASTES LIKE...LIKE NOTHING I'VE EVER HAD, YET... SOMETHING I'VE ALWAYS KNOWN I WANTED.
YES, THAT IS WHAT THEY SAY.
YOU DIDN'T TRY IT?
ENDOOGO WAS BURNED MANY YEARS AGO. THAT IS THE LAST OF THE FRUIT THAT IS KNOWN TO EXIST.
WHAT? BUT...
HE LAST NE...AND YOU...
ROUGHT TO ME?
I DON'T NOW WHAT TO SAY.
THIS IS...
THIS IS CERTAINLY ONE HELL OF A LAST MEAL.

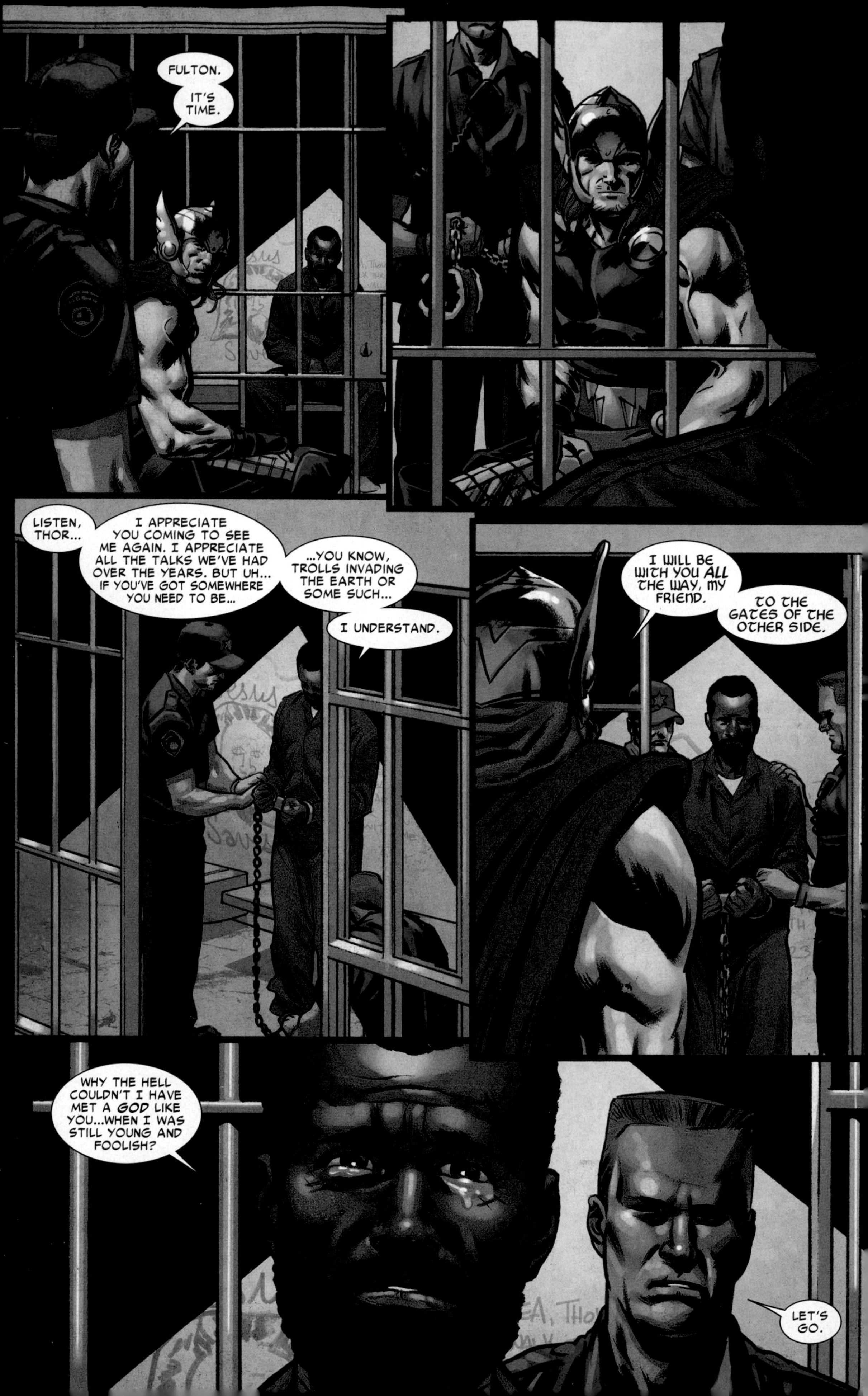
FULTON.
IT'S TIME.
LISTEN, THOR...
I APPRECIATE YOU COMING TO SEE ME AGAIN. I APPRECIATE ALL THE TALKS WE'VE HAD OVER THE YEARS. BUT UH... IF YOU'VE GOT SOMEWHERE YOU NEED TO BE...
...YOU KNOW, TROLLS INVADING THE EARTH OR SOME SUCH...
I UNDERSTAND.
I WILL BE WITH YOU ALL THE WAY, MY FRIEND.
TO THE GATES OF THE OTHER SIDE.
WHY THE HELL COULDN'T I HAVE MET A GOD LIKE YOU...WHEN I WAS STILL YOUNG AND FOOLISH?
LET'S GO.

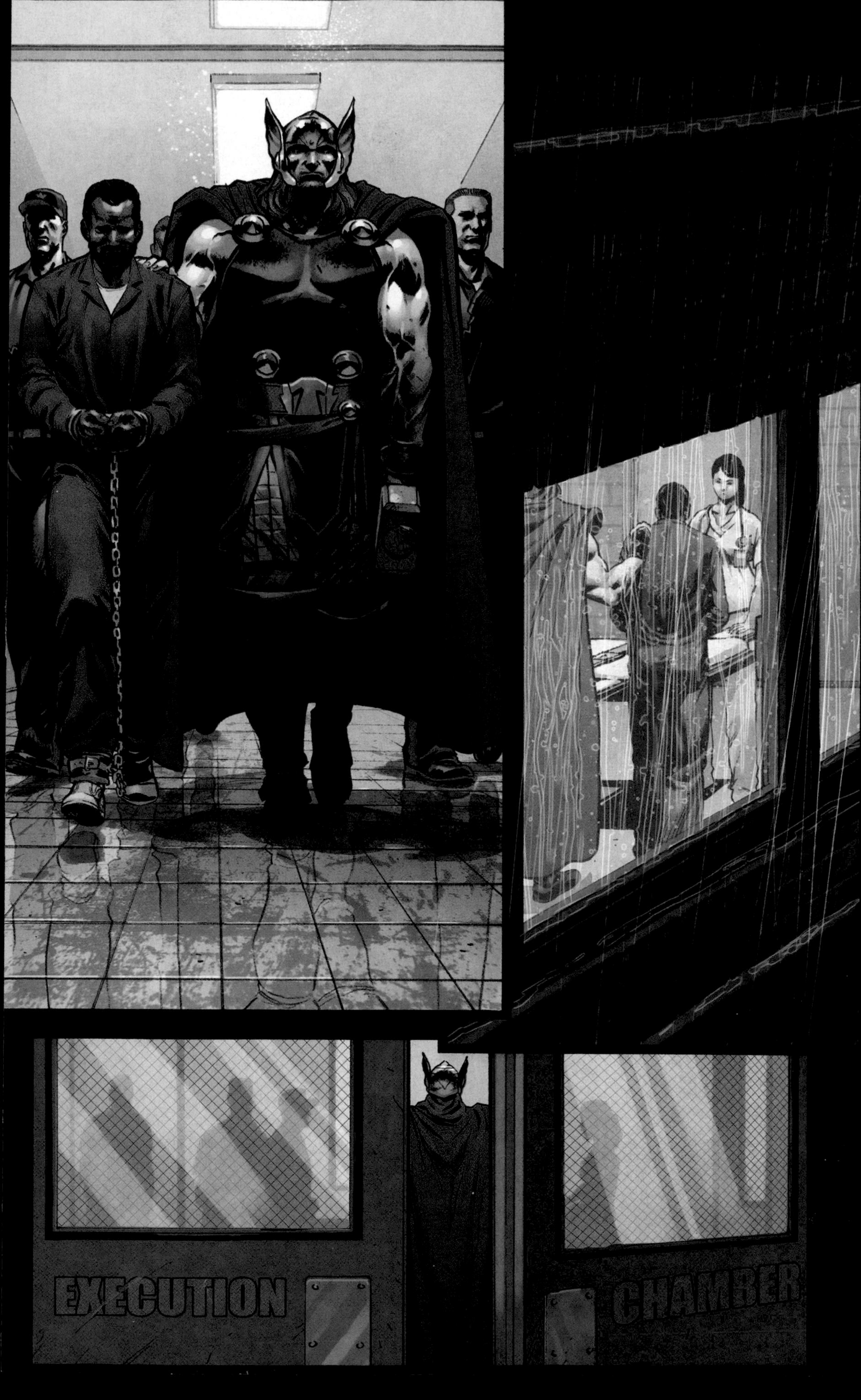
EXECUTION
CHAMBER

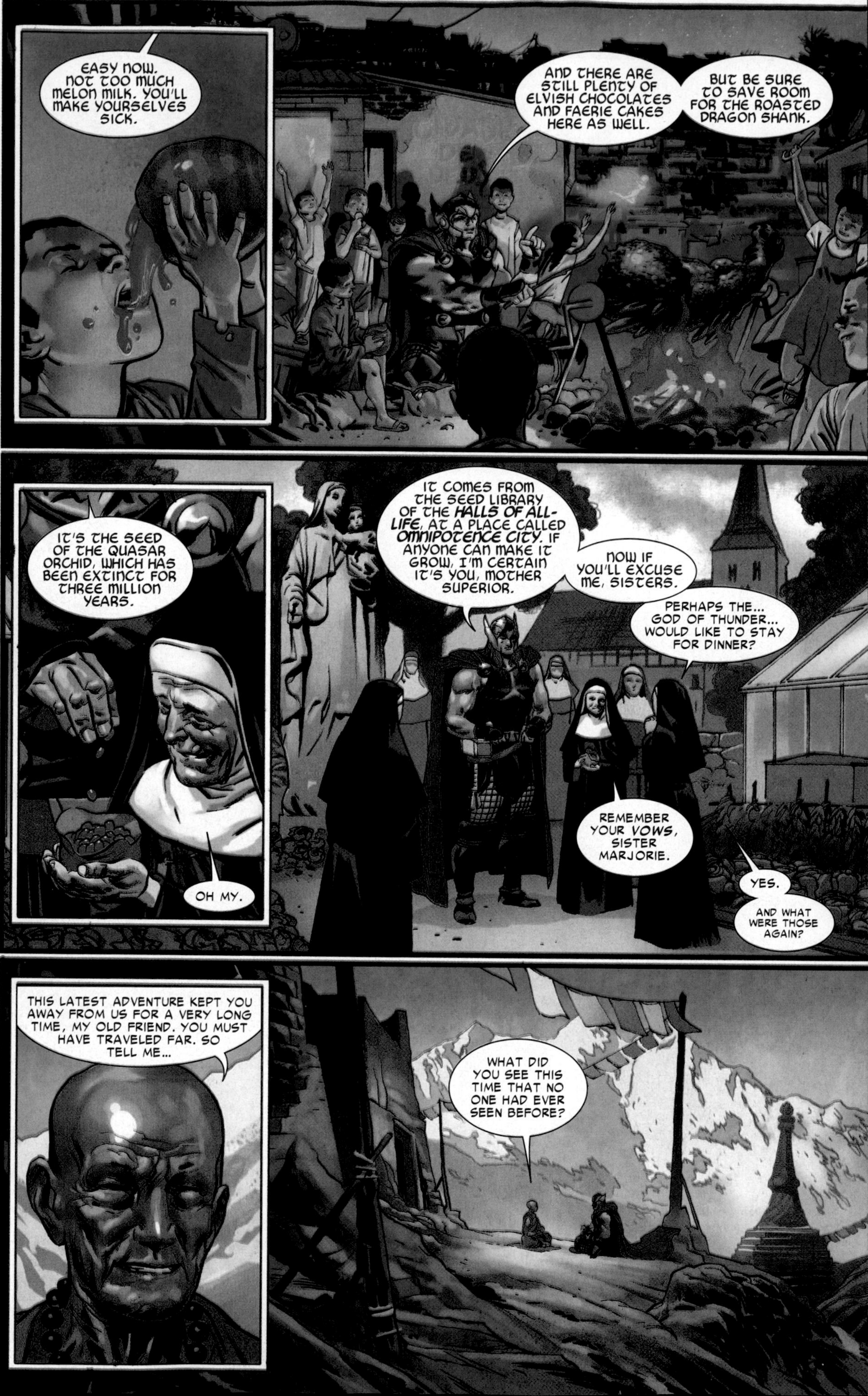
EASY NOW. NOT TOO MUCH MELON MILK. YOU'LL MAKE YOURSELVES SICK.
AND THERE ARE STILL PLENTY OF ELVISH CHOCOLATES AND FAERIE CAKES HERE AS WELL.
BUT BE SURE TO SAVE ROOM FOR THE ROASTED DRAGON SHANK.
IT'S THE SEED OF THE QUASAR ORCHID, WHICH HAS BEEN EXTINCT FOR THREE MILLION YEARS.
OH MY.
IT COMES FROM THE SEED LIBRARY OF THE HALLS OF ALL-LIFE, AT A PLACE CALLED OMNIPOTENCE CITY. IF ANYONE CAN MAKE IT GROW, I'M CERTAIN IT'S YOU, MOTHER SUPERIOR.
NOW IF YOU'LL EXCUSE ME, SISTERS.
PERHAPS THE... GOD OF THUNDER... WOULD LIKE TO STAY FOR DINNER?
REMEMBER YOUR VOWS, SISTER MARJORIE.
YES.
AND WHAT WERE THOSE AGAIN?
THIS LATEST ADVENTURE KEPT YOU AWAY FROM US FOR A VERY LONG TIME, MY OLD FRIEND. YOU MUST HAVE TRAVELED FAR. SO TELL ME...
WHAT DID YOU SEE THIS TIME THAT NO ONE HAD EVER SEEN BEFORE?

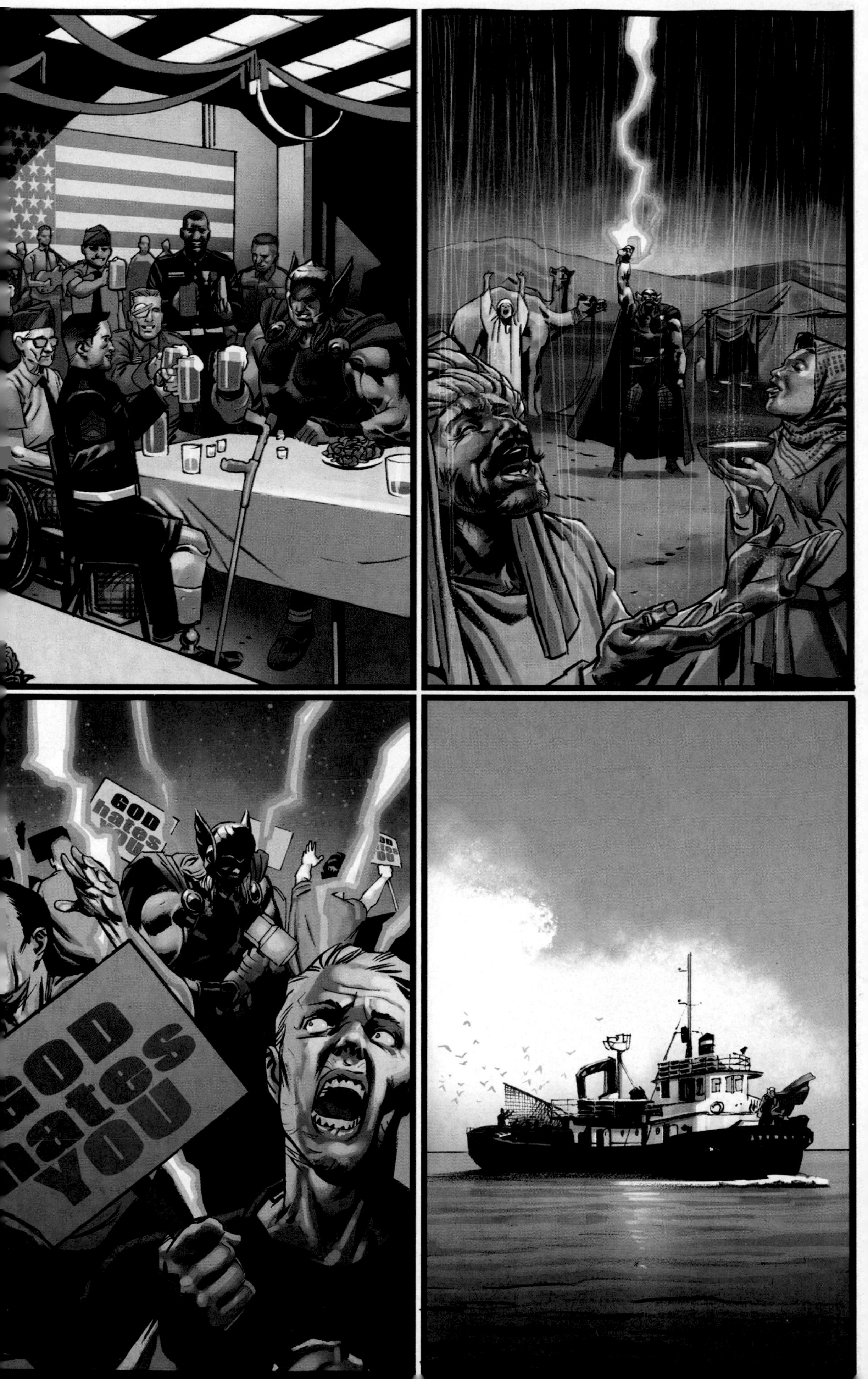
GOD hates YOU
GOD hates YOU
GOD hates YOU

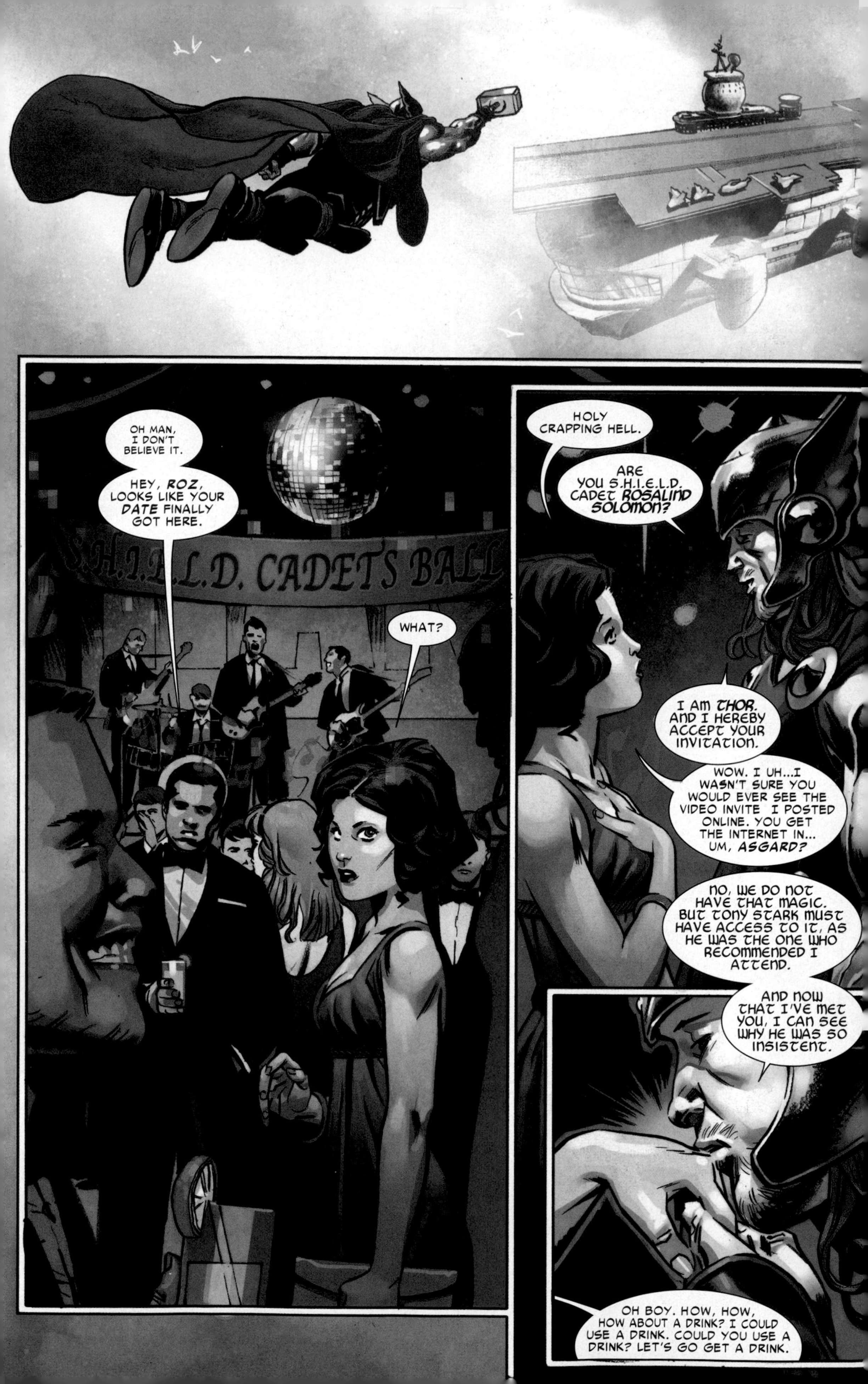

OH MAN, I DON'T BELIEVE IT.
HEY, ROZ, LOOKS LIKE YOUR DATE FINALLY GOT HERE.
S.H.I.E.L.D. CADETS BALL
WHAT?
HOLY CRAPPING HELL.
ARE YOU S.H.I.E.L.D. CADET ROSALIND SOLOMON?
I AM THOR. AND I HEREBY ACCEPT YOUR INVITATION.
WOW. I UH...I WASN'T SURE YOU WOULD EVER SEE THE VIDEO INVITE I POSTED ONLINE. YOU GET THE INTERNET IN... UM, ASGARD?
NO, WE DO NOT HAVE THAT MAGIC. BUT TONY STARK MUST HAVE ACCESS TO IT, AS HE WAS THE ONE WHO RECOMMENDED I ATTEND.
AND NOW THAT I'VE MET YOU, I CAN SEE WHY HE WAS SO INSISTENT.
OH BOY. HOW, HOW, HOW ABOUT A DRINK? I COULD USE A DRINK. COULD YOU USE A DRINK? LET'S GO GET A DRINK.

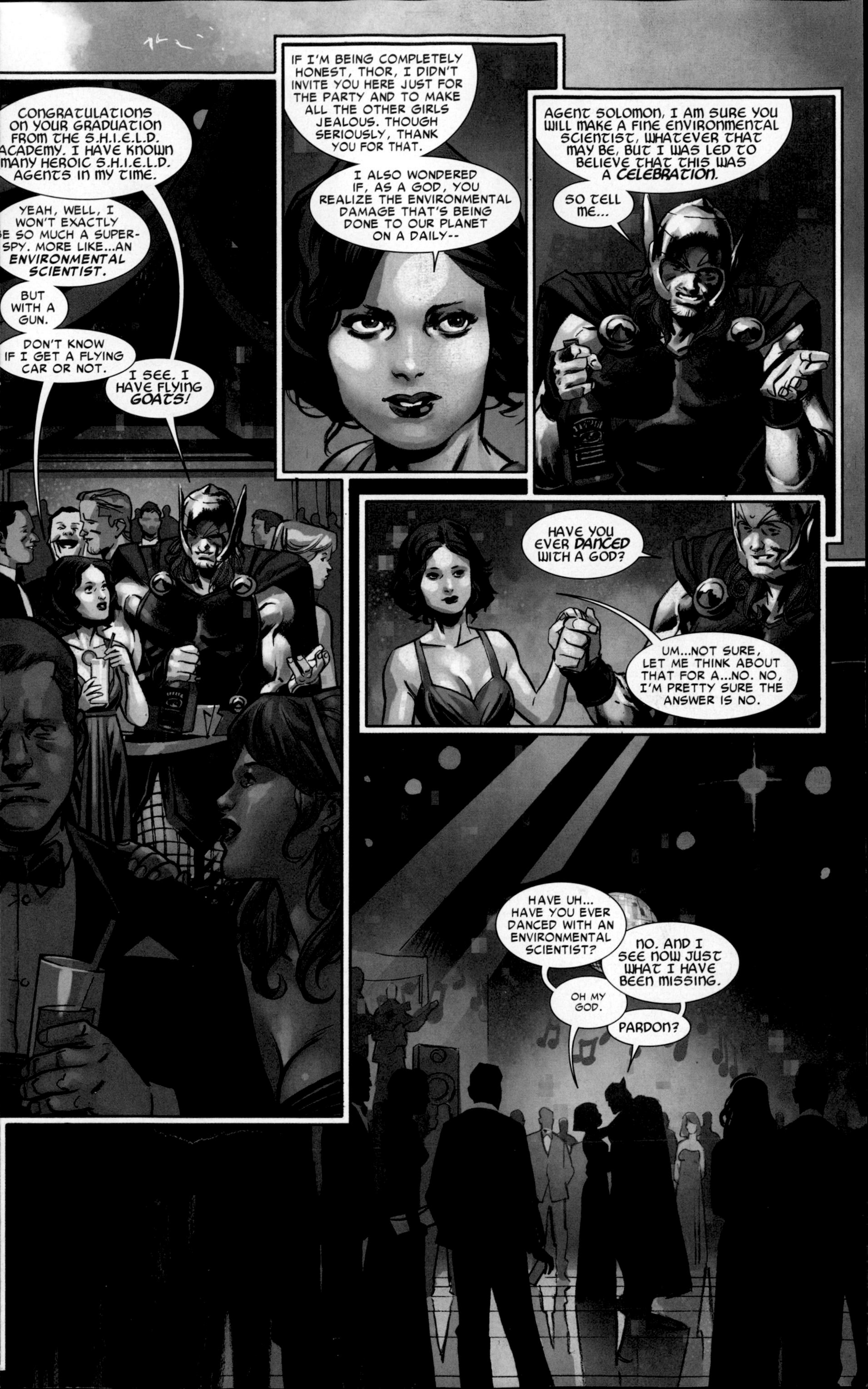
CONGRATULATIONS ON YOUR GRADUATION FROM THE S.H.I.E.L.D. ACADEMY. I HAVE KNOWN MANY HEROIC S.H.I.E.L.D. AGENTS IN MY TIME.
YEAH, WELL, I WON'T EXACTLY BE SO MUCH A SUPER-SPY. MORE LIKE...AN ENVIRONMENTAL SCIENTIST.
BUT WITH A GUN.
DON'T KNOW IF I GET A FLYING CAR OR NOT.
I SEE. I HAVE FLYING GOATS!
IF I'M BEING COMPLETELY HONEST, THOR, I DIDN'T INVITE YOU HERE JUST FOR THE PARTY AND TO MAKE ALL THE OTHER GIRLS JEALOUS. THOUGH SERIOUSLY, THANK YOU FOR THAT.
I ALSO WONDERED IF, AS A GOD, YOU REALIZE THE ENVIRONMENTAL DAMAGE THAT'S BEING DONE TO OUR PLANET ON A DAILY--
AGENT SOLOMON, I AM SURE YOU WILL MAKE A FINE ENVIRONMENTAL SCIENTIST, WHATEVER THAT MAY BE, BUT I WAS LED TO BELIEVE THAT THIS WAS A CELEBRATION.
SO TELL ME...
HAVE YOU EVER DANCED WITH A GOD?
UM...NOT SURE, LET ME THINK ABOUT THAT FOR A...NO. NO, I'M PRETTY SURE THE ANSWER IS NO.
HAVE UH... HAVE YOU EVER DANCED WITH AN ENVIRONMENTAL SCIENTIST?
NO. AND I SEE NOW JUST WHAT I HAVE BEEN MISSING.
OH MY GOD.
PARDON?

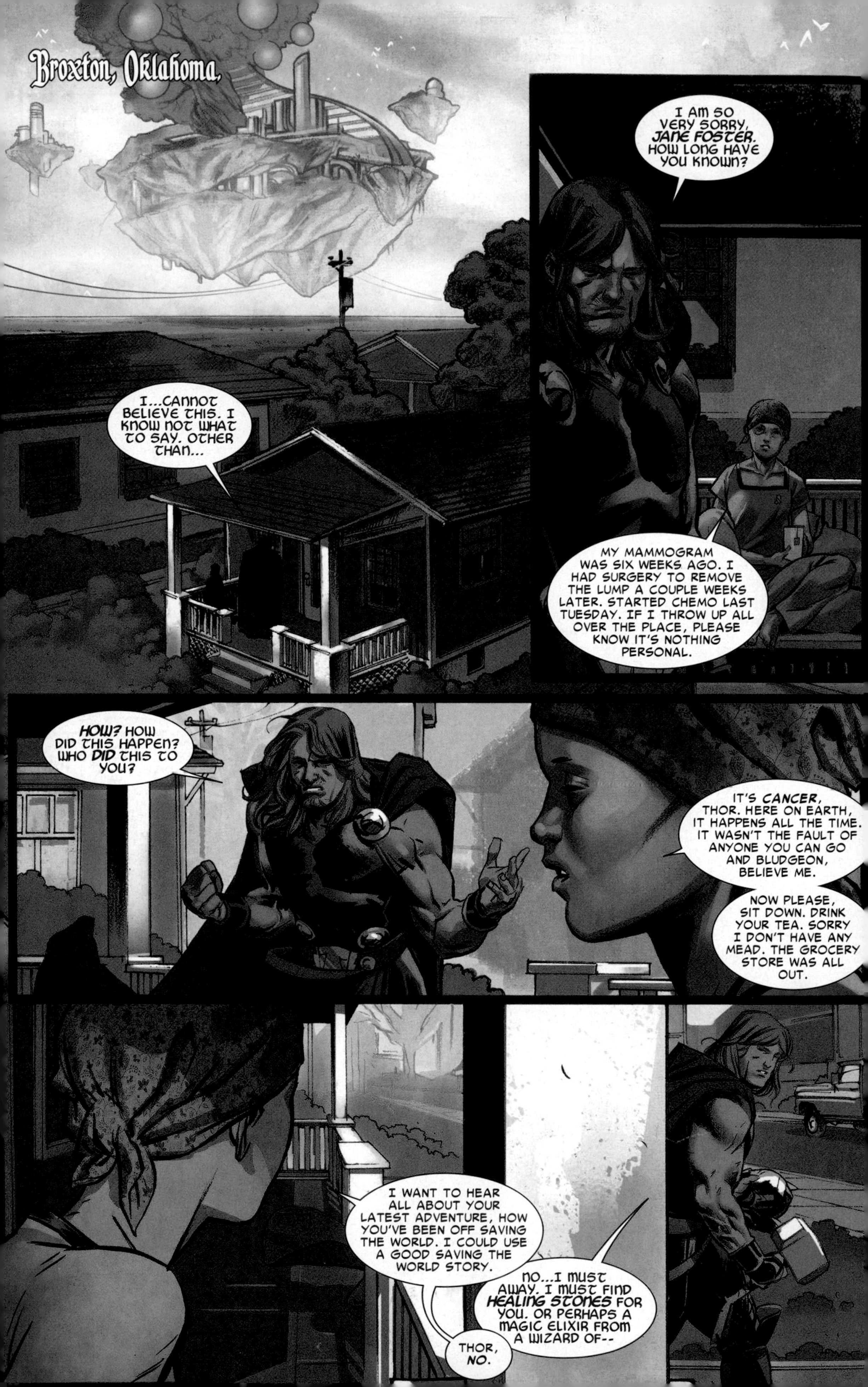

Broxton, Oklahoma.
I...CANNOT BELIEVE THIS. I KNOW NOT WHAT TO SAY. OTHER THAN...
I AM SO VERY SORRY, JANE FOSTER. HOW LONG HAVE YOU KNOWN?
MY MAMMOGRAM WAS SIX WEEKS AGO. I HAD SURGERY TO REMOVE THE LUMP A COUPLE WEEKS LATER. STARTED CHEMO LAST TUESDAY. IF I THROW UP ALL OVER THE PLACE, PLEASE KNOW IT'S NOTHING PERSONAL.
HOW? HOW DID THIS HAPPEN? WHO DID THIS TO YOU?
IT'S CANCER, THOR. HERE ON EARTH, IT HAPPENS ALL THE TIME. IT WASN'T THE FAULT OF ANYONE YOU CAN GO AND BLUDGEON, BELIEVE ME.
NOW PLEASE, SIT DOWN. DRINK YOUR TEA. SORRY I DON'T HAVE ANY MEAD. THE GROCERY STORE WAS ALL OUT.
I WANT TO HEAR ALL ABOUT YOUR LATEST ADVENTURE, HOW YOU'VE BEEN OFF SAVING THE WORLD. I COULD USE A GOOD SAVING THE WORLD STORY.
NO...I MUST AWAY. I MUST FIND HEALING STONES FOR YOU. OR PERHAPS A MAGIC ELIXIR FROM A WIZARD OF--
THOR, NO.

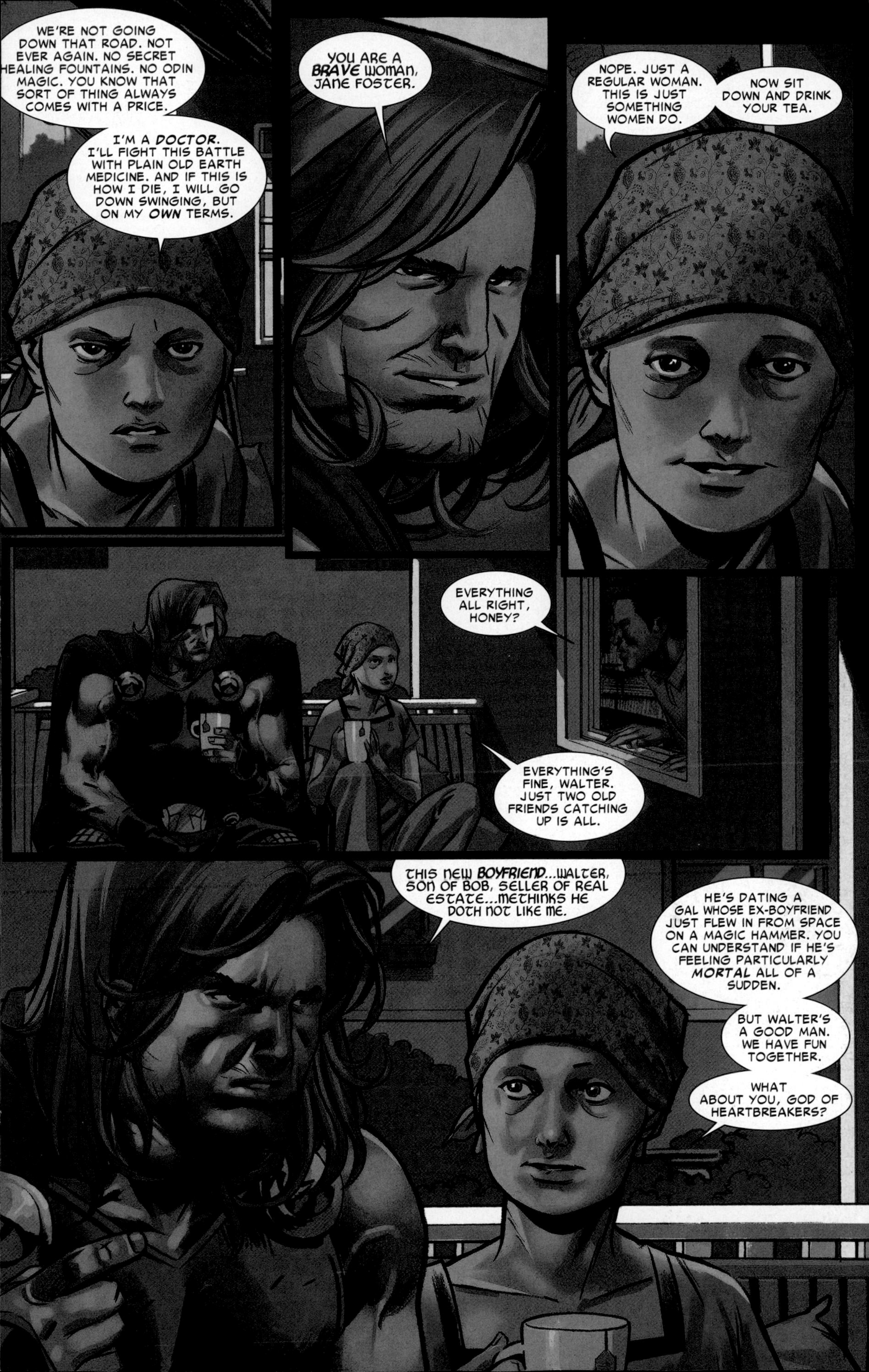

WE'RE NOT GOING DOWN THAT ROAD. NOT EVER AGAIN. NO SECRET HEALING FOUNTAINS. NO ODIN MAGIC. YOU KNOW THAT SORT OF THING ALWAYS COMES WITH A PRICE.
I'M A DOCTOR. I'LL FIGHT THIS BATTLE WITH PLAIN OLD EARTH MEDICINE. AND IF THIS IS HOW I DIE, I WILL GO DOWN SWINGING, BUT ON MY OWN TERMS.
YOU ARE A BRAVE WOMAN, JANE FOSTER.
NOPE. JUST A REGULAR WOMAN. THIS IS JUST SOMETHING WOMEN DO.
NOW SIT DOWN AND DRINK YOUR TEA.
EVERYTHING ALL RIGHT, HONEY?
EVERYTHING'S FINE, WALTER. JUST TWO OLD FRIENDS CATCHING UP IS ALL.
THIS NEW BOYFRIEND...WALTER, SON OF BOB, SELLER OF REAL ESTATE...METHINKS HE DOTH NOT LIKE ME.
HE'S DATING A GAL WHOSE EX-BOYFRIEND JUST FLEW IN FROM SPACE ON A MAGIC HAMMER. YOU CAN UNDERSTAND IF HE'S FEELING PARTICULARLY MORTAL ALL OF A SUDDEN.
BUT WALTER'S A GOOD MAN. WE HAVE FUN TOGETHER.
WHAT ABOUT YOU, GOD OF HEARTBREAKERS?

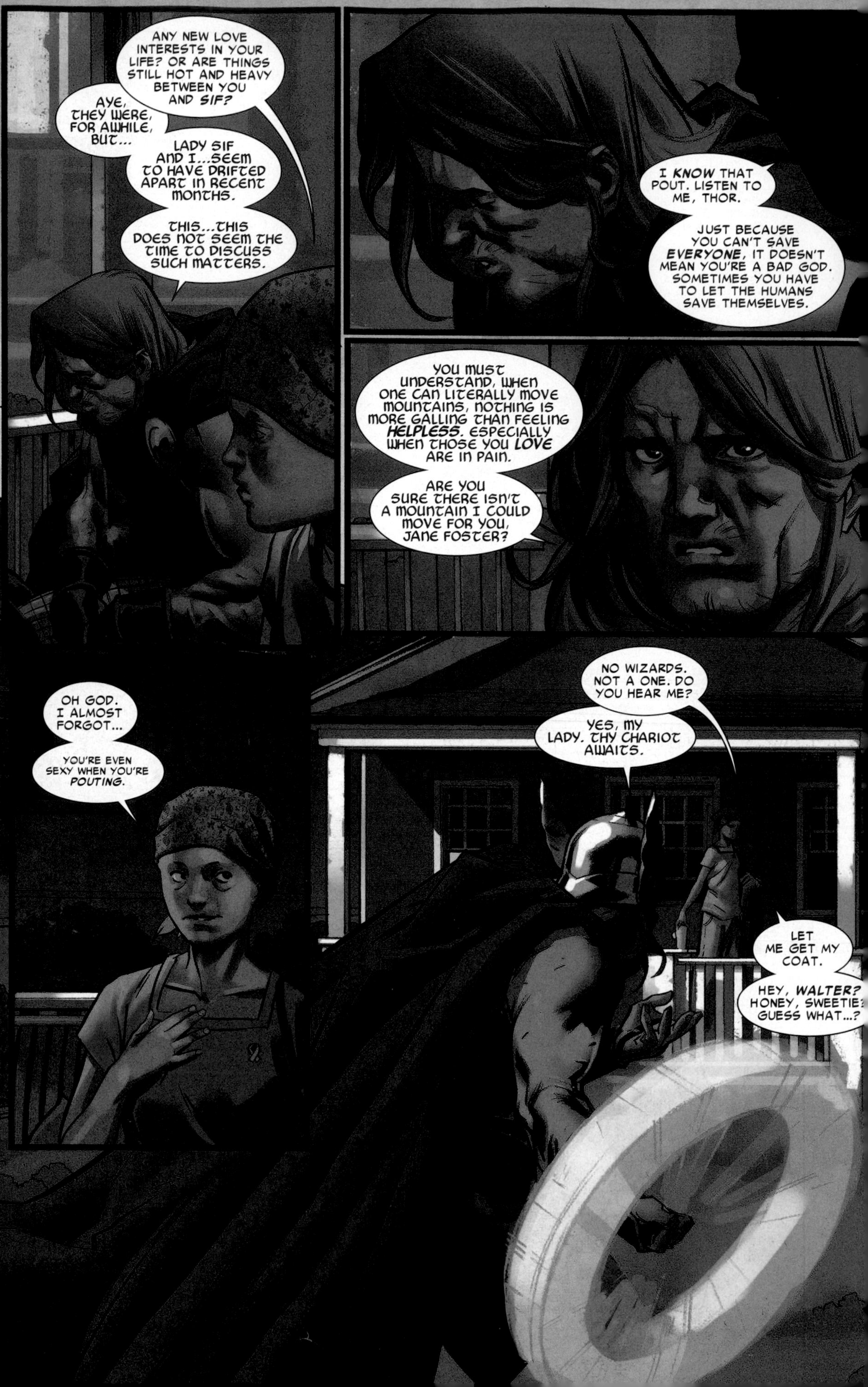
ANY NEW LOVE INTERESTS IN YOUR LIFE? OR ARE THINGS STILL HOT AND HEAVY BETWEEN YOU AND SIF?
AYE, THEY WERE, FOR AWHILE, BUT...
LADY SIF AND I...SEEM TO HAVE DRIFTED APART IN RECENT MONTHS.
THIS...THIS DOES NOT SEEM THE TIME TO DISCUSS SUCH MATTERS.
I KNOW THAT POUT. LISTEN TO ME, THOR.
JUST BECAUSE YOU CAN'T SAVE EVERYONE, IT DOESN'T MEAN YOU'RE A BAD GOD. SOMETIMES YOU HAVE TO LET THE HUMANS SAVE THEMSELVES.
YOU MUST UNDERSTAND, WHEN ONE CAN LITERALLY MOVE MOUNTAINS, NOTHING IS MORE GALLING THAN FEELING HELPLESS. ESPECIALLY WHEN THOSE YOU LOVE ARE IN PAIN.
ARE YOU SURE THERE ISN'T A MOUNTAIN I COULD MOVE FOR YOU, JANE FOSTER?
OH GOD. I ALMOST FORGOT...
YOU'RE EVEN SEXY WHEN YOU'RE POUTING.
NO WIZARDS. NOT A ONE. DO YOU HEAR ME?
YES, MY LADY. THY CHARIOT AWAITS.
LET ME GET MY COAT.
HEY, WALTER? HONEY, SWEETIE? GUESS WHAT...?

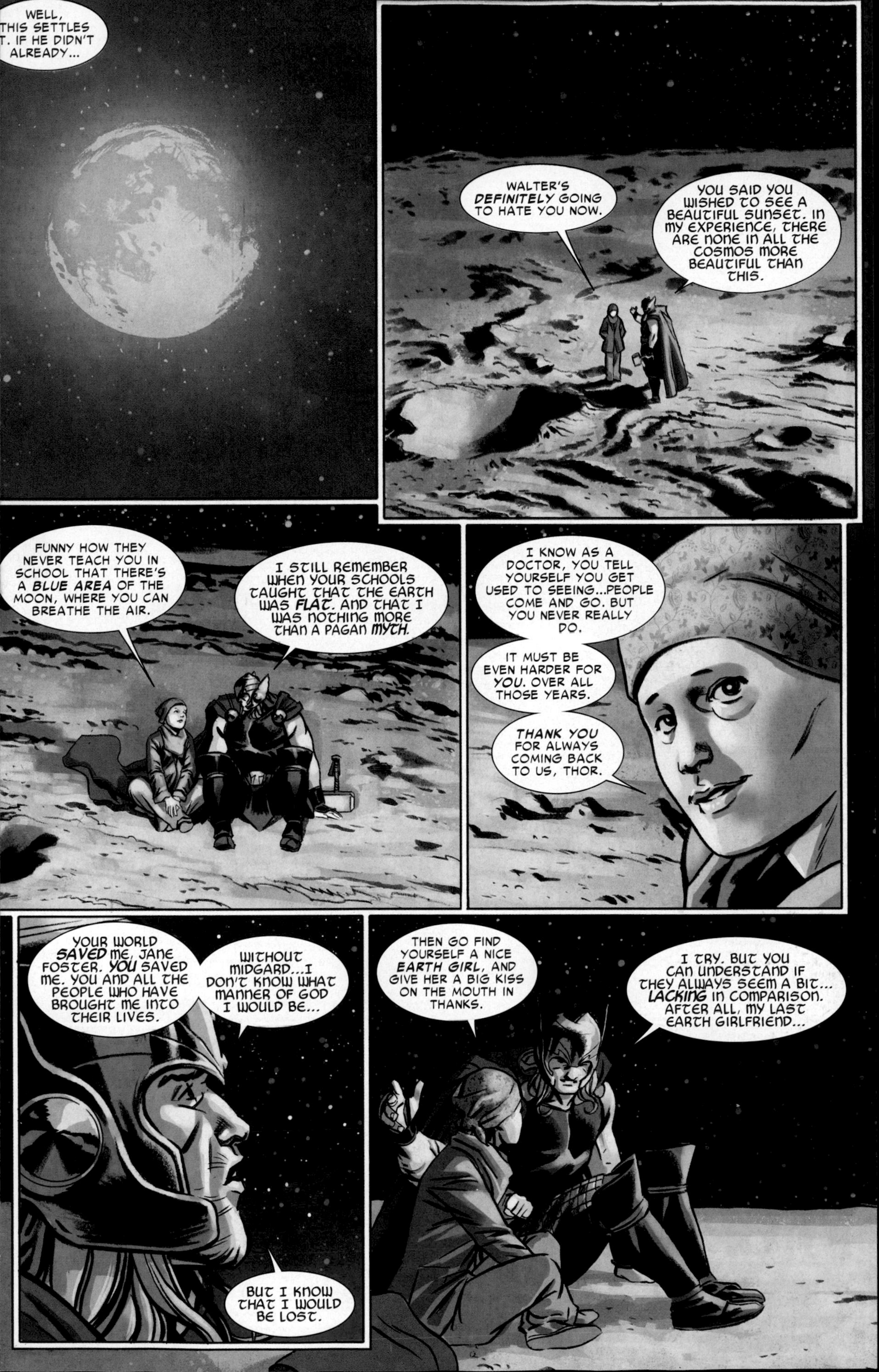
WELL, THIS SETTLES IT. IF HE DIDN'T ALREADY...
WALTER'S DEFINITELY GOING TO HATE YOU NOW.
YOU SAID YOU WISHED TO SEE A BEAUTIFUL SUNSET. IN MY EXPERIENCE, THERE ARE NONE IN ALL THE COSMOS MORE BEAUTIFUL THAN THIS.
FUNNY HOW THEY NEVER TEACH YOU IN SCHOOL THAT THERE'S A BLUE AREA OF THE MOON, WHERE YOU CAN BREATHE THE AIR.
I STILL REMEMBER WHEN YOUR SCHOOLS TAUGHT THAT THE EARTH WAS FLAT. AND THAT I WAS NOTHING MORE THAN A PAGAN MYTH.
I KNOW AS A DOCTOR, YOU TELL YOURSELF YOU GET USED TO SEEING...PEOPLE COME AND GO. BUT YOU NEVER REALLY DO.
IT MUST BE EVEN HARDER FOR YOU. OVER ALL THOSE YEARS.
THANK YOU FOR ALWAYS COMING BACK TO US, THOR.
YOUR WORLD SAVED ME, JANE FOSTER. YOU SAVED ME. YOU AND ALL THE PEOPLE WHO HAVE BROUGHT ME INTO THEIR LIVES.
WITHOUT MIDGARD...I DON'T KNOW WHAT MANNER OF GOD I WOULD BE...
BUT I KNOW THAT I WOULD BE LOST.
THEN GO FIND YOURSELF A NICE EARTH GIRL, AND GIVE HER A BIG KISS ON THE MOUTH IN THANKS.
I TRY. BUT YOU CAN UNDERSTAND IF THEY ALWAYS SEEM A BIT... LACKING IN COMPARISON. AFTER ALL, MY LAST EARTH GIRLFRIEND...

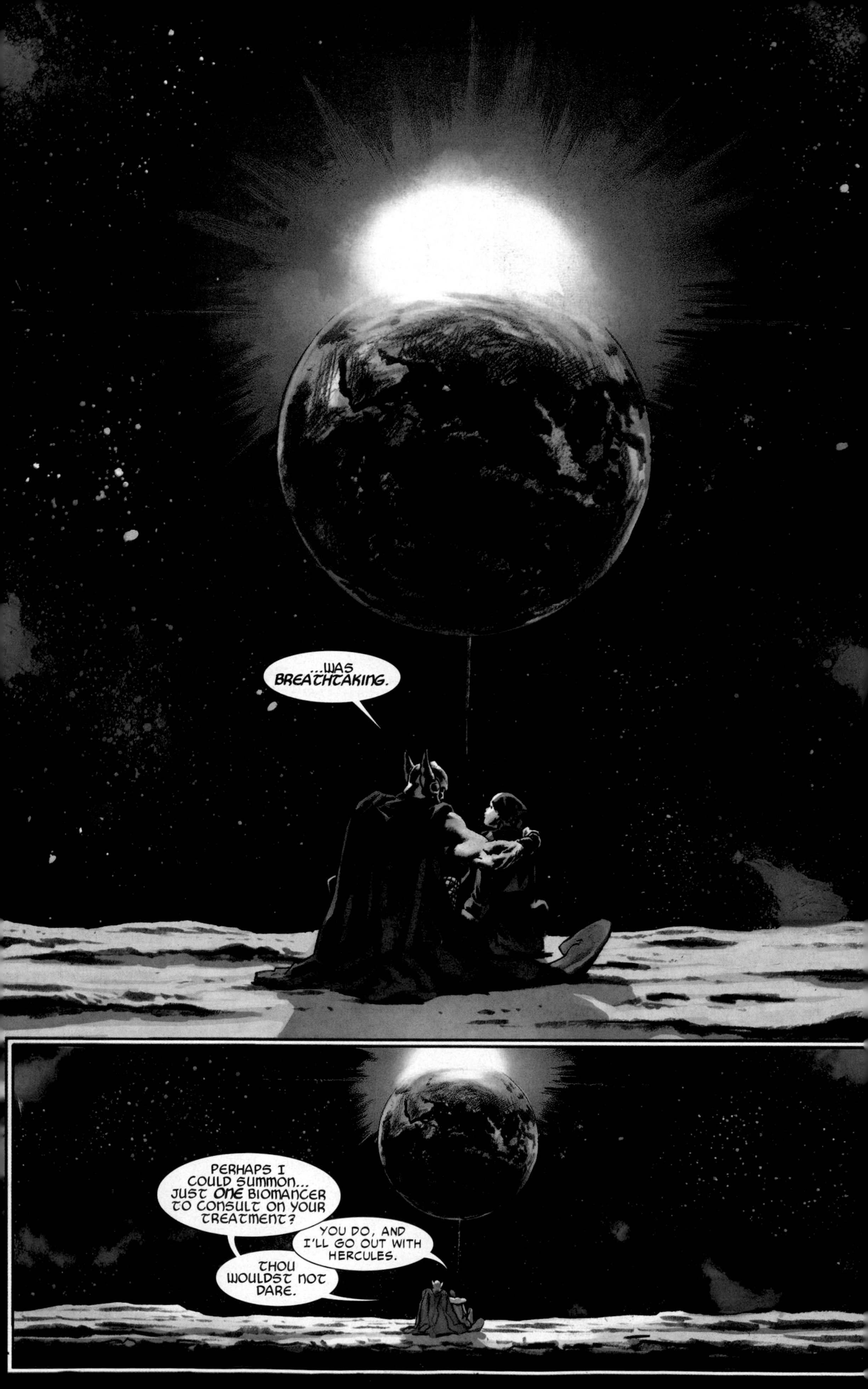
...WAS BREATHTAKING.
PERHAPS I COULD SUMMON... JUST ONE BIOMANCER TO CONSULT ON YOUR TREATMENT?
THOU WOULDST NOT DARE.
YOU DO, AND I'LL GO OUT WITH HERCULES.

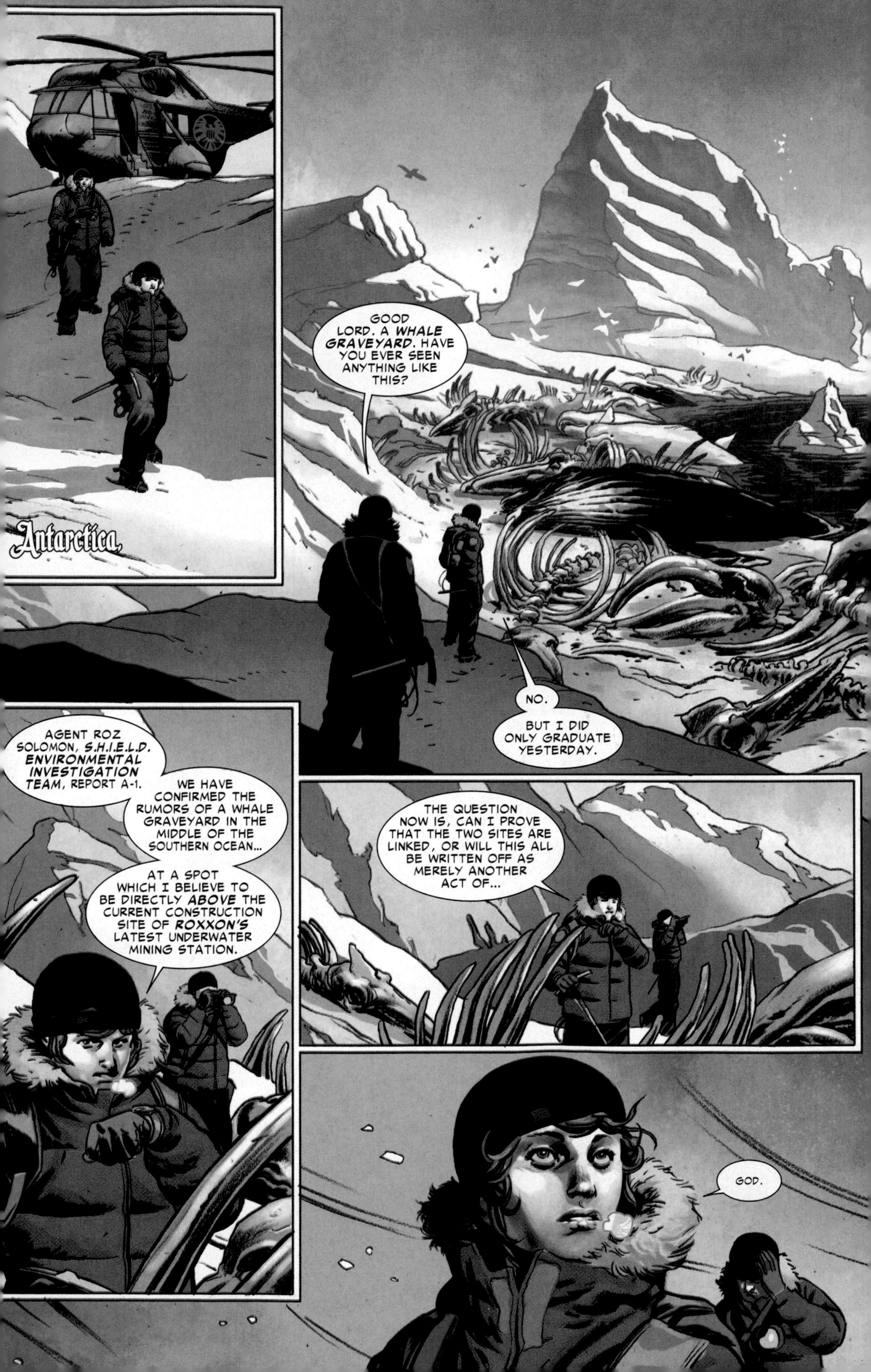
Antarctica.
GOOD LORD. A WHALE GRAVEYARD. HAVE YOU EVER SEEN ANYTHING LIKE THIS?
NO.
BUT I DID ONLY GRADUATE YESTERDAY.
AGENT ROZ SOLOMON, S.H.I.E.L.D. ENVIRONMENTAL INVESTIGATION TEAM, REPORT A-1.
WE HAVE CONFIRMED THE RUMORS OF A WHALE GRAVEYARD IN THE MIDDLE OF THE SOUTHERN OCEAN...
AT A SPOT WHICH I BELIEVE TO BE DIRECTLY ABOVE THE CURRENT CONSTRUCTION SITE OF ROXXON'S LATEST UNDERWATER MINING STATION.
THE QUESTION NOW IS, CAN I PROVE THAT THE TWO SITES ARE LINKED, OR WILL THIS ALL BE WRITTEN OFF AS MERELY ANOTHER ACT OF...
GOD.

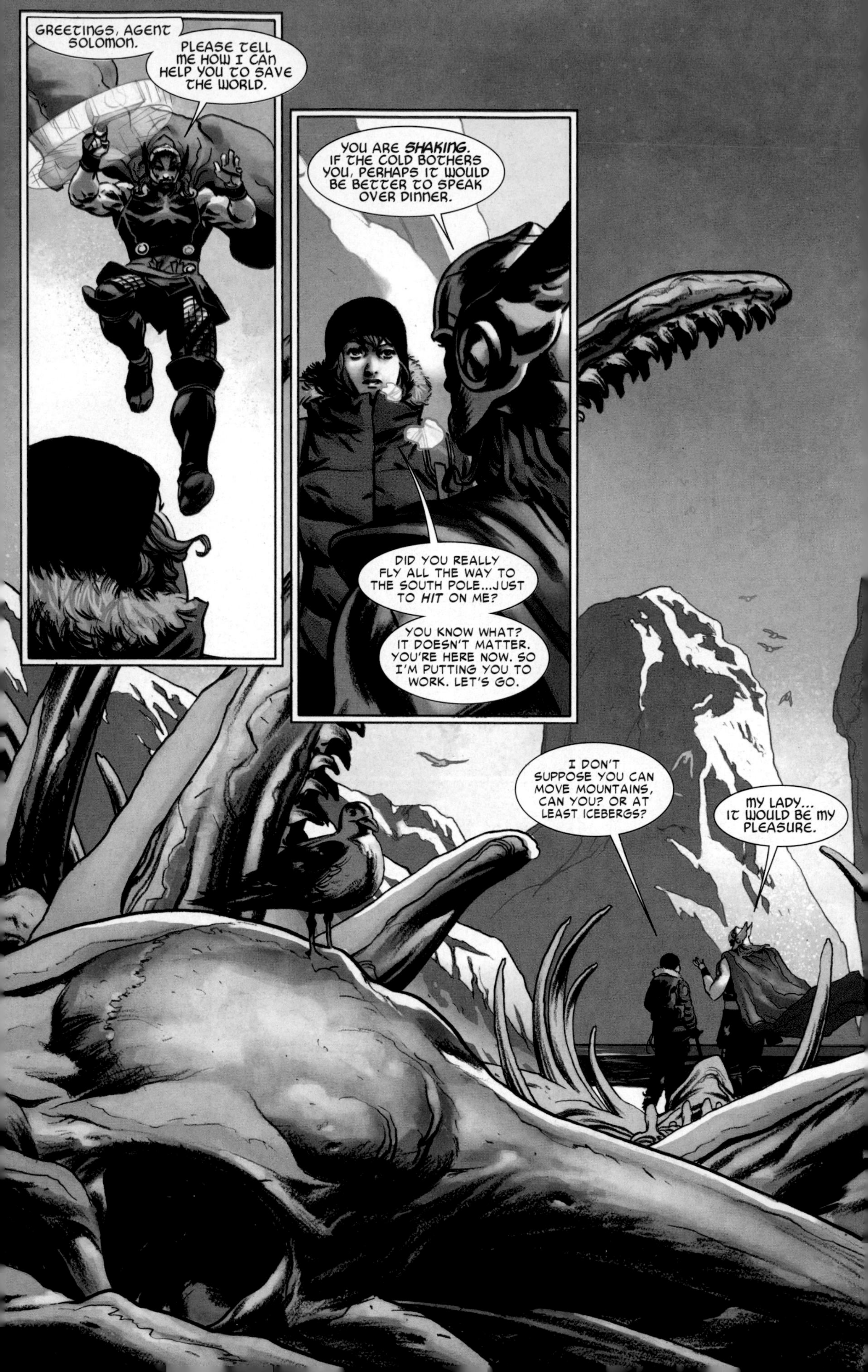
GREETINGS, AGENT SOLOMON.
PLEASE TELL ME HOW I CAN HELP YOU TO SAVE THE WORLD.
YOU ARE SHAKING. IF THE COLD BOTHERS YOU, PERHAPS IT WOULD BE BETTER TO SPEAK OVER DINNER.
DID YOU REALLY FLY ALL THE WAY TO THE SOUTH POLE...JUST TO HIT ON ME?
YOU KNOW WHAT? IT DOESN'T MATTER. YOU'RE HERE NOW. SO I'M PUTTING YOU TO WORK. LET'S GO.
I DON'T SUPPOSE YOU CAN MOVE MOUNTAINS, CAN YOU? OR AT LEAST ICEBERGS?
MY LADY... IT WOULD BE MY PLEASURE.

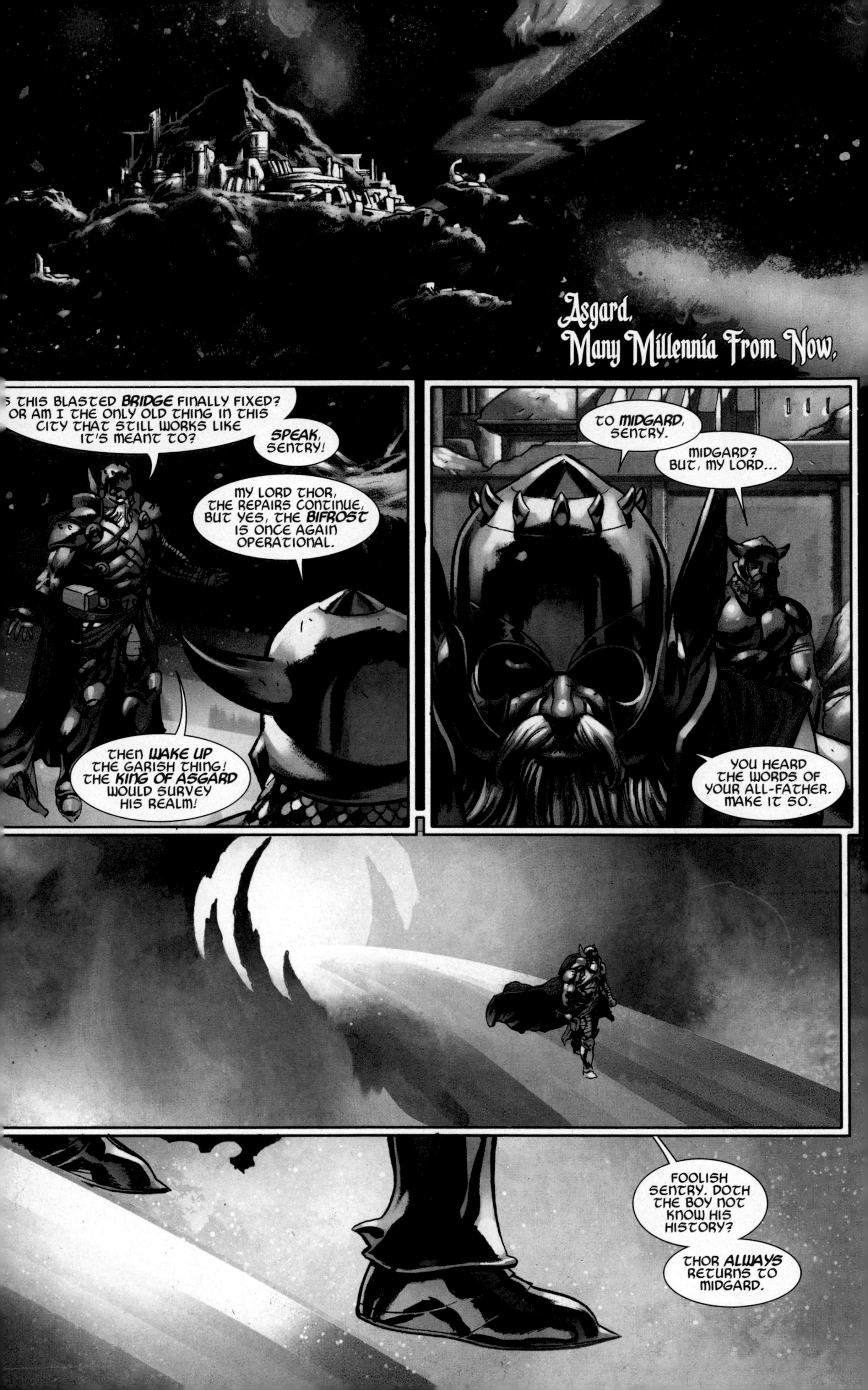

Asgard,
Many Millennia From Now.
S THIS BLASTED BRIDGE FINALLY FIXED? OR AM I THE ONLY OLD THING IN THIS CITY THAT STILL WORKS LIKE IT'S MEANT TO?
SPEAK, SENTRY!
MY LORD THOR, THE REPAIRS CONTINUE, BUT YES, THE BIFROST IS ONCE AGAIN OPERATIONAL.
THEN WAKE UP THE GARISH THING! THE KING OF ASGARD WOULD SURVEY HIS REALM!
TO MIDGARD, SENTRY.
MIDGARD? BUT, MY LORD...
YOU HEARD THE WORDS OF YOUR ALL-FATHER. MAKE IT SO.
FOOLISH SENTRY. DOTH THE BOY NOT KNOW HIS HISTORY?
THOR ALWAYS RETURNS TO MIDGARD.

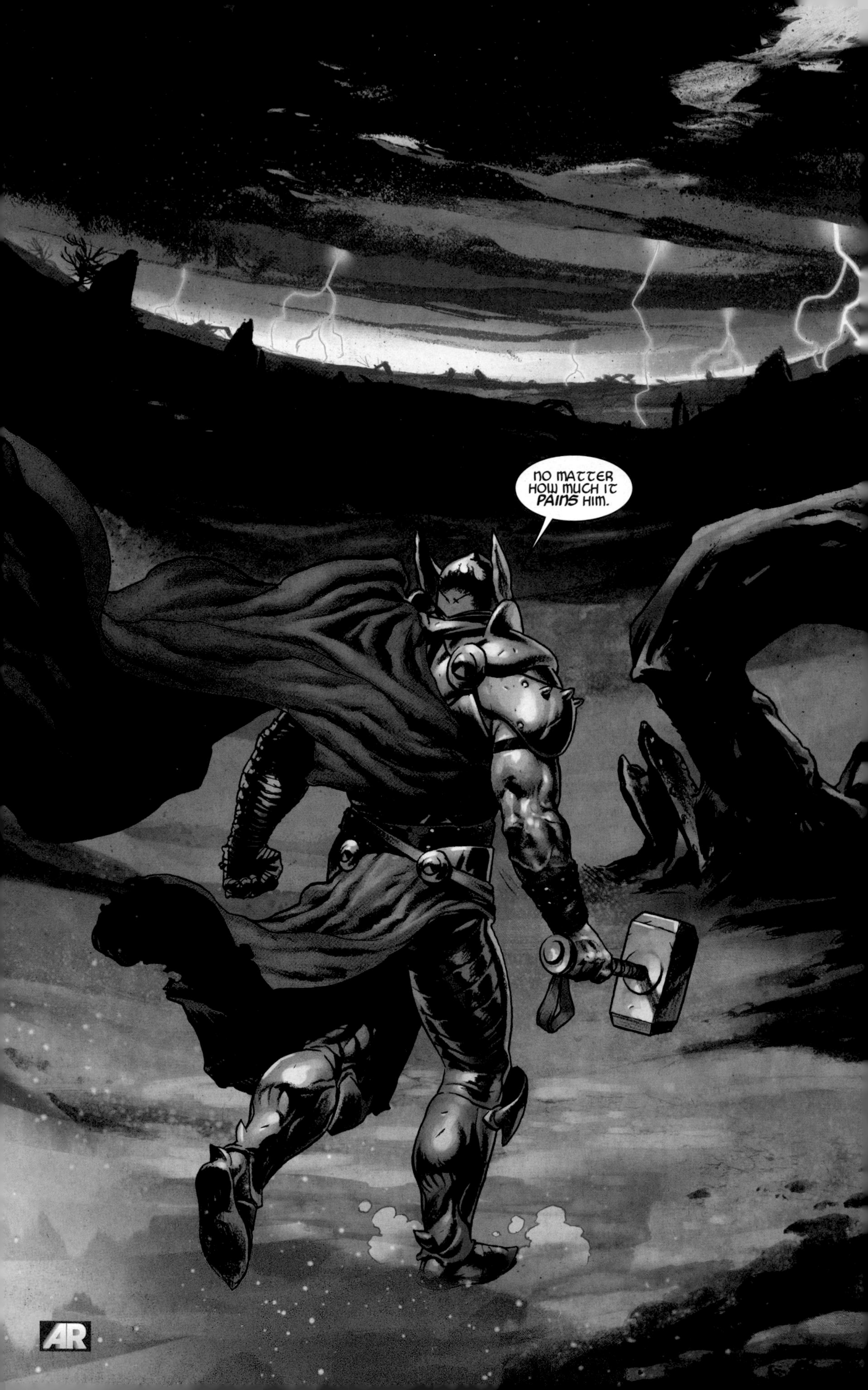
NO MATTER HOW MUCH IT PAINS HIM.

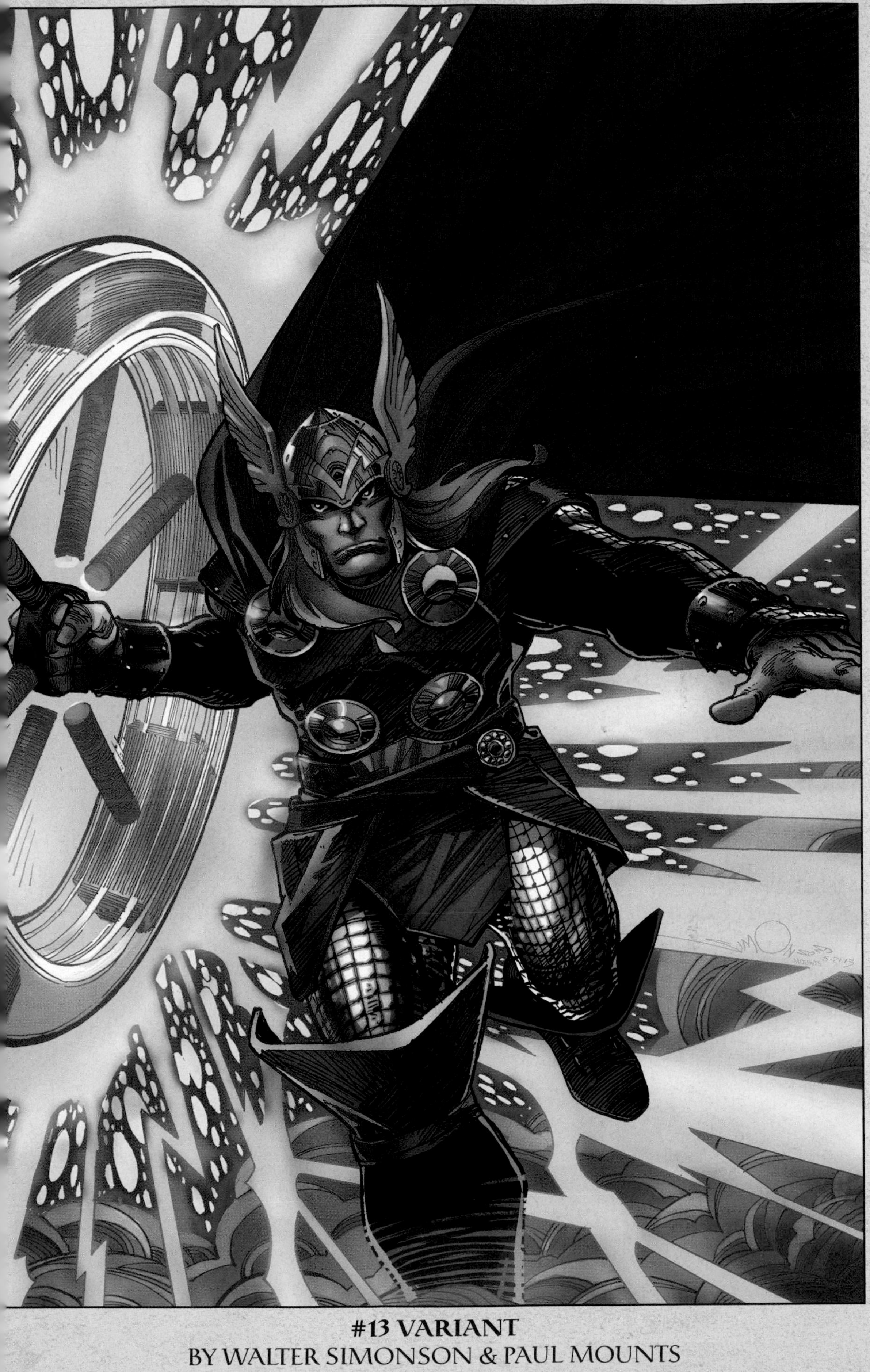

#13 VARIANT
BY WALTER SIMONSON & PAUL MOUNTS

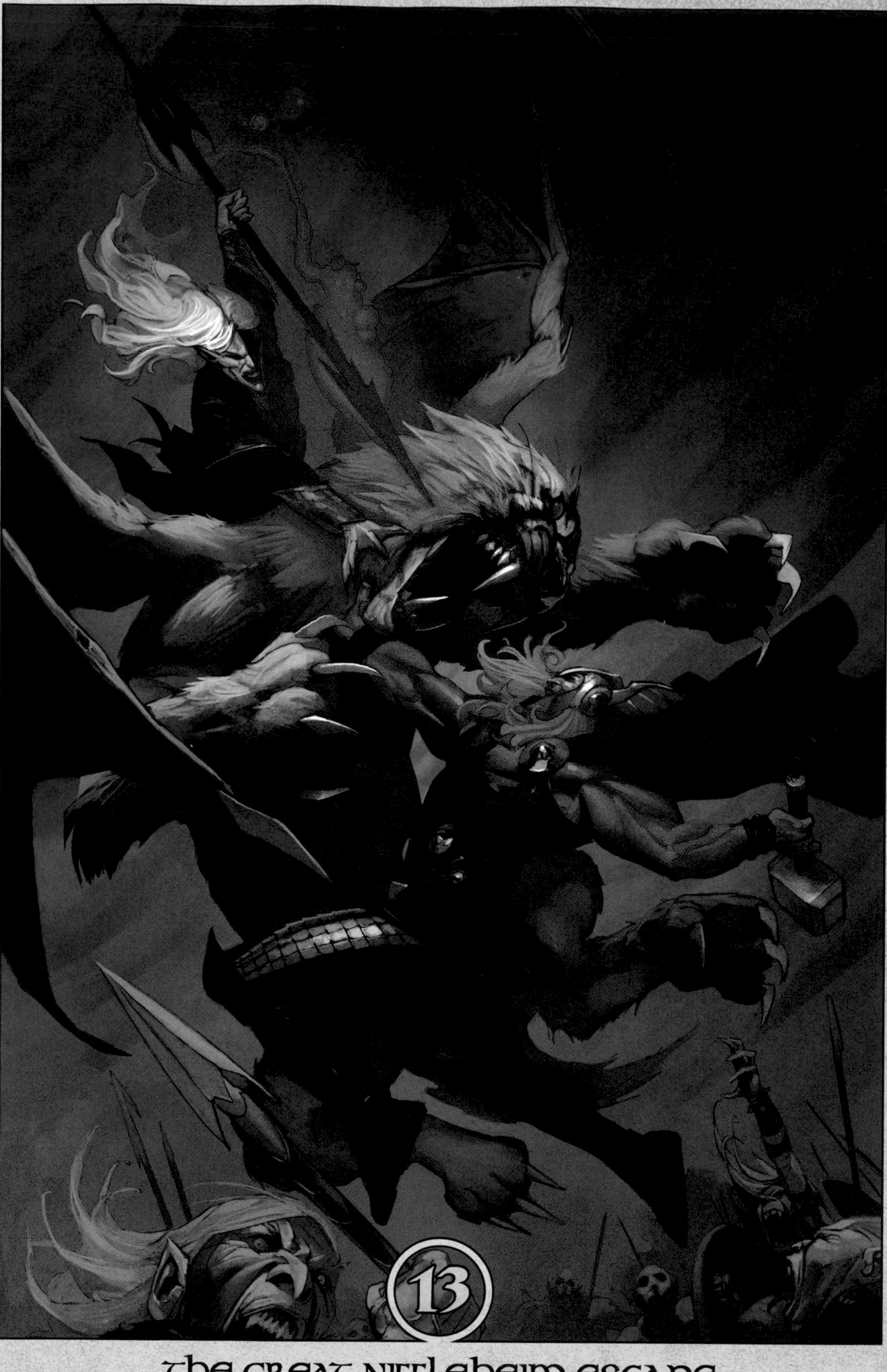
13

THE GREAT NIFFLEHEIM ESCAPE
OR
THE SVARTALFHEIM MASSACRE

*IN THE BEGINNING,
THERE WAS
DARKNESS.*

*AND THEN FROM THE
SOUTH CAME FIRE,
AND FROM THE NORTH,
COLD AND MIST.*

*AND WHERE THE TWO
FORCES MET IN THE
YAWNING VOID, LIFE
WAS BORN.*

*GODS AND GIANTS.
DWARVES AND ELVES.
TROLLS AND MEN.*

*AND WORLDS WERE
MADE FOR EACH OF
THEM. NINE IN TOTAL.*

*EACH WITH ITS OWN PLACE
ALONG THE TREE OF LIFE.
EACH WITH ITS OWN
WONDERS AND TERRORS.*

*THIS IS THE STORY OF
THOSE NINE WORLDS.*

*AND OF THE ONE MIGHTY
GOD WHO BESTRODE
THEM ALL.*

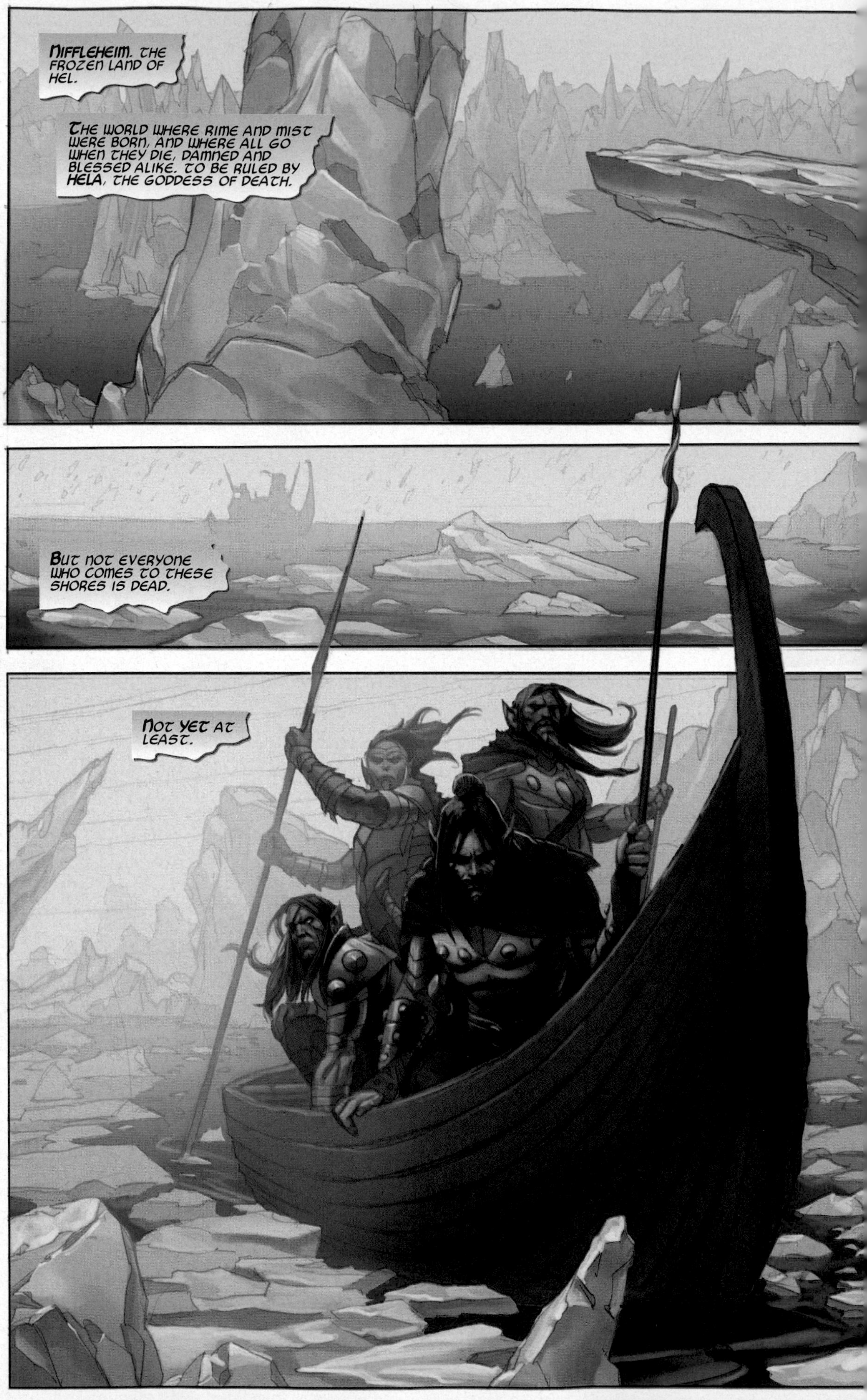
NIFFLEHEIM. THE FROZEN LAND OF HEL.
THE WORLD WHERE RIME AND MIST WERE BORN, AND WHERE ALL GO WHEN THEY DIE, DAMNED AND BLESSED ALIKE. TO BE RULED BY HELA, THE GODDESS OF DEATH.
BUT NOT EVERYONE WHO COMES TO THESE SHORES IS DEAD.
NOT YET AT LEAST.

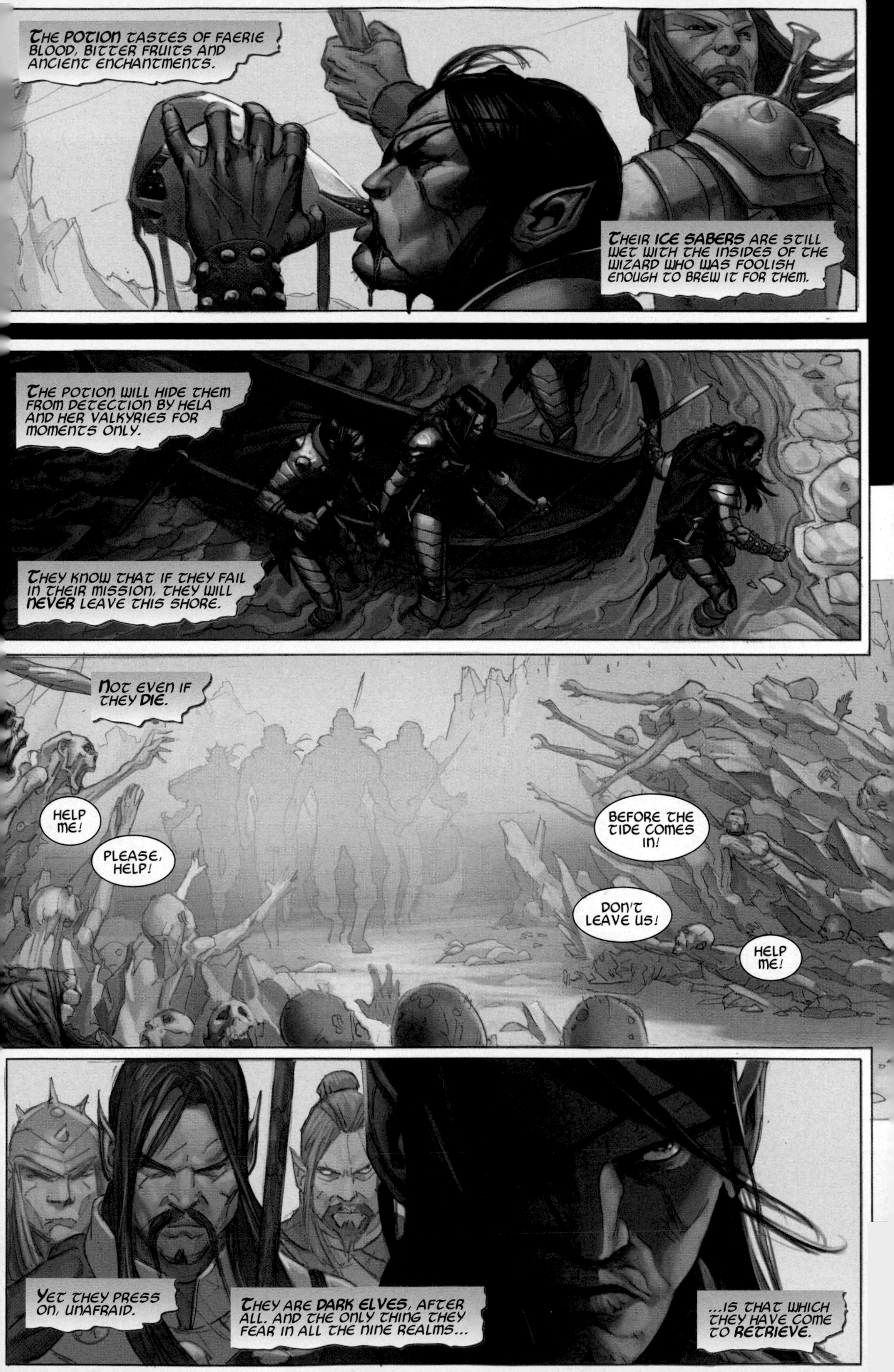
THE POTION TASTES OF FAERIE BLOOD, BITTER FRUITS AND ANCIENT ENCHANTMENTS.
THEIR ICE SABERS ARE STILL WET WITH THE INSIDES OF THE WIZARD WHO WAS FOOLISH ENOUGH TO BREW IT FOR THEM.
THE POTION WILL HIDE THEM FROM DETECTION BY HELA AND HER VALKYRIES FOR MOMENTS ONLY.
THEY KNOW THAT IF THEY FAIL IN THEIR MISSION, THEY WILL NEVER LEAVE THIS SHORE.
NOT EVEN IF THEY DIE.
HELP ME!
PLEASE, HELP!
BEFORE THE TIDE COMES IN!
DON'T LEAVE US!
HELP ME!
YET THEY PRESS ON, UNAFRAID.
THEY ARE DARK ELVES, AFTER ALL. AND THE ONLY THING THEY FEAR IN ALL THE NINE REALMS...
...IS THAT WHICH THEY HAVE COME TO RETRIEVE.

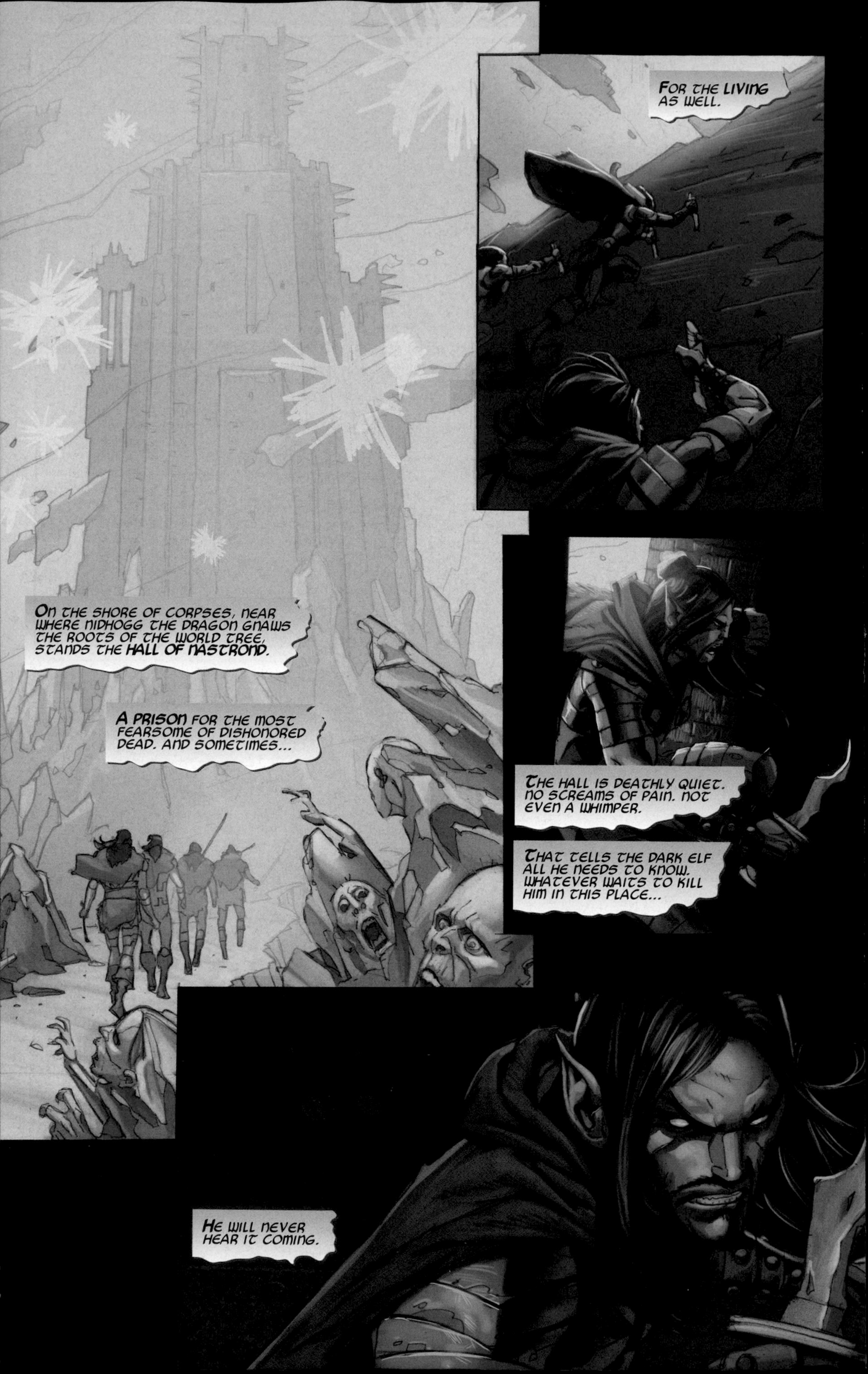
On the shore of corpses, near where Nidhogg the dragon gnaws the roots of the world tree, stands the HALL OF NASTROND.
A PRISON for the most fearsome of dishonored dead. And sometimes...
For the LIVING as well.
The hall is deathly quiet. No screams of pain. Not even a whimper.
That tells the dark elf all he needs to know. Whatever waits to kill him in this place...
He will never hear it coming.

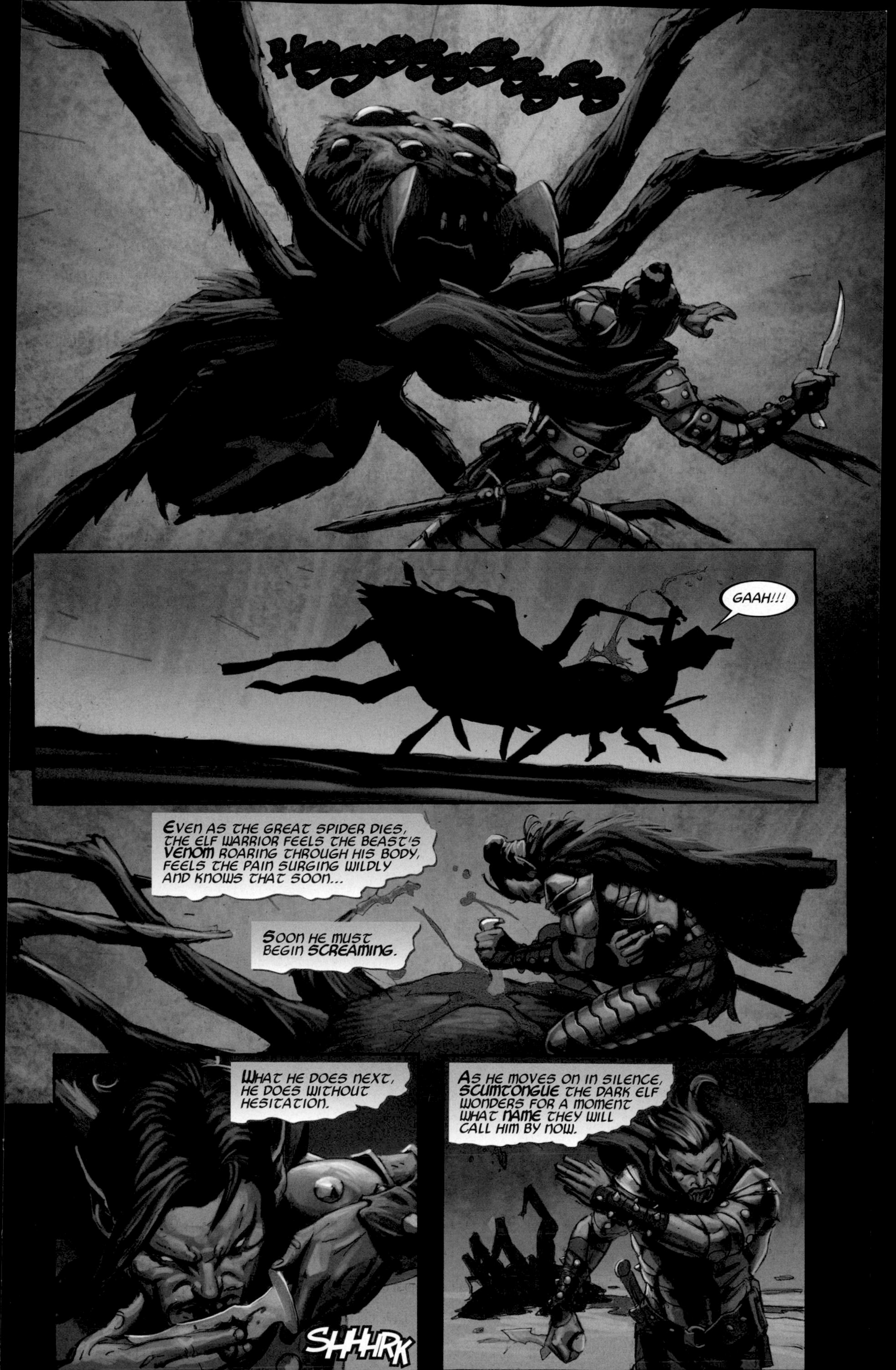
GAAH!!!
EVEN AS THE GREAT SPIDER DIES, THE ELF WARRIOR FEELS THE BEAST'S VENOM ROARING THROUGH HIS BODY, FEELS THE PAIN SURGING WILDLY AND KNOWS THAT SOON...
SOON HE MUST BEGIN SCREAMING.
WHAT HE DOES NEXT, HE DOES WITHOUT HESITATION.
SHHHRK
AS HE MOVES ON IN SILENCE, SCUMTONGUE THE DARK ELF WONDERS FOR A MOMENT WHAT NAME THEY WILL CALL HIM BY NOW.

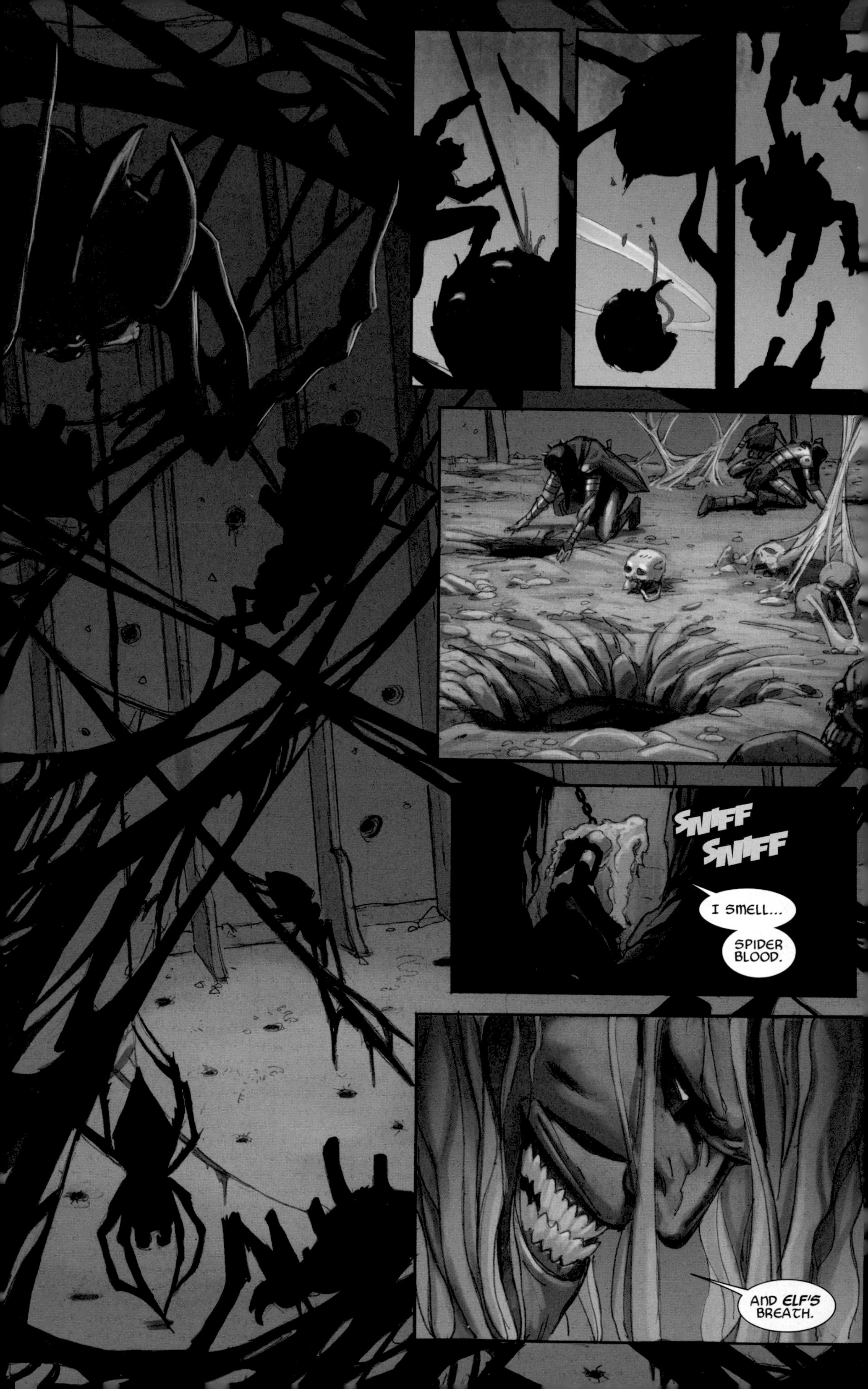
SNIFF
SNIFF
I SMELL...
SPIDER BLOOD.
AND ELF'S BREATH.

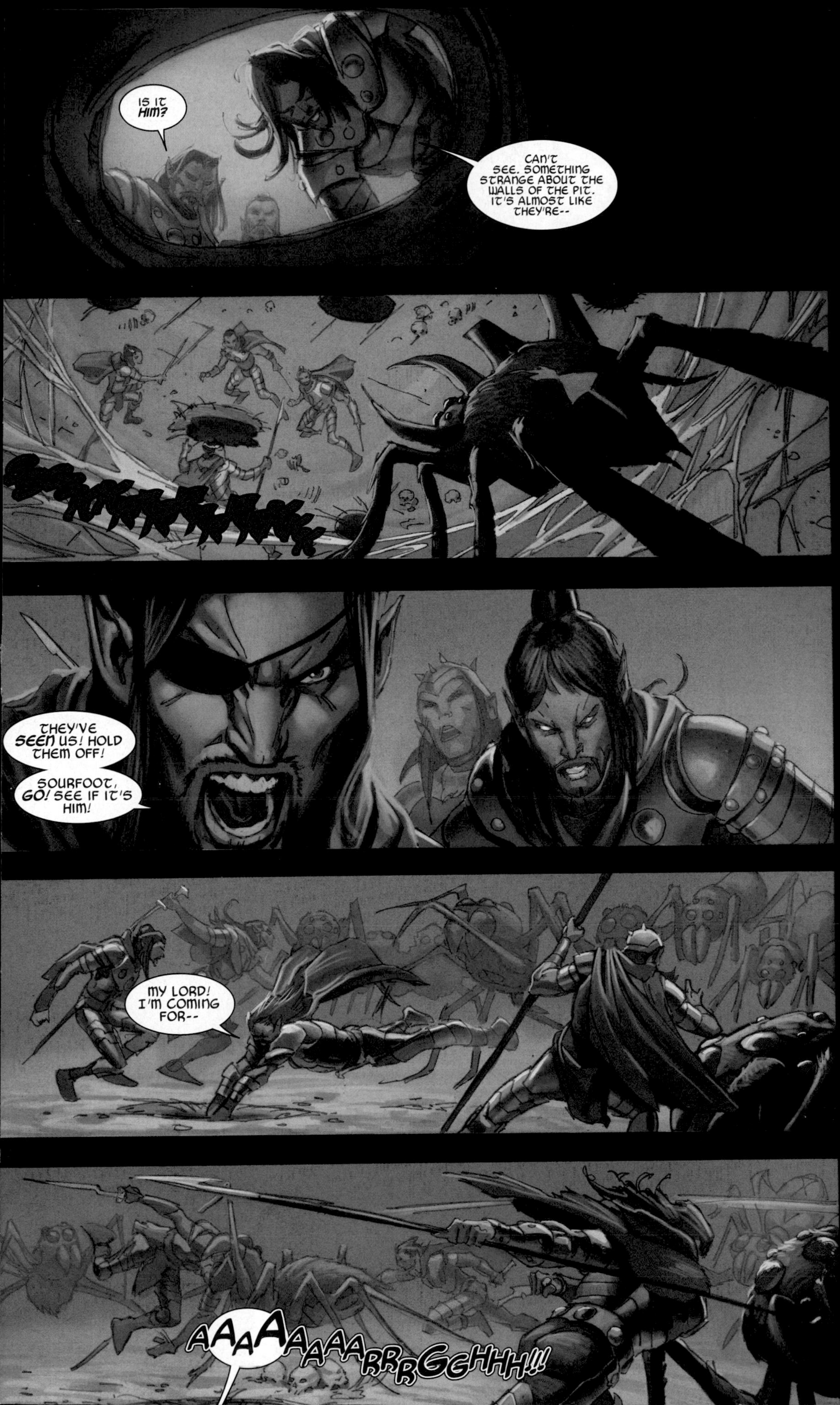
IS IT HIM?
CAN'T SEE. SOMETHING STRANGE ABOUT THE WALLS OF THE PIT. IT'S ALMOST LIKE THEY'RE--
THEY'VE SEEN US! HOLD THEM OFF!
SOURFOOT, GO! SEE IF IT'S HIM!
MY LORD! I'M COMING FOR--
AAAAAAAARRRRGGHHH!!!

SOURFOOT? IS THAT YOU, YOU BEAUTIFUL ELF?
YES, MY LORD...THOUGH IT APPEARS...
GAAARGGH!!!
IT APPEARS I AM RATHER STUCK!
YES, VICIOUS LITTLE CREATURES, THOSE HEL-SNAKES.
YOU WON'T LAST LONG NOW, I'M AFRAID. THEIR VENOM WILL BURN THROUGH YOU LIKE A FLAMING SWORD THROUGH TALLOW.
HERE, MY LORD!
TAKE MY DAGGER! HACK YOUR WAY TO FREEDOM! PLEASE!
YES, OF COURSE.
BUT AH... YOU DO SEEM TO BE IN THE WAY.
USE MY FLESH AND BONES AS YOUR LADDER, MY LORD. I...I GLADLY GIVE MY ALL TO THEE.
GODS, THE PAIN.
AND I GLADLY ACCEPT.
EYES OPEN WIDE NOW, SOURFOOT, SON OF SVARTALFHEIM. YOU WILL WANT TO SEE THIS CLEARLY, AS WITH THIS DAGGER...
I CARVE YOUR NAME INTO HISTORY.

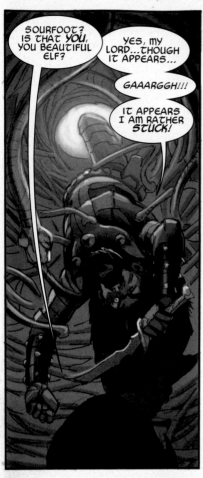

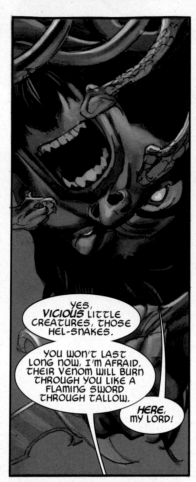

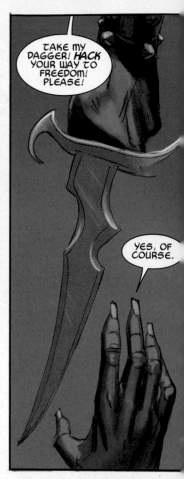

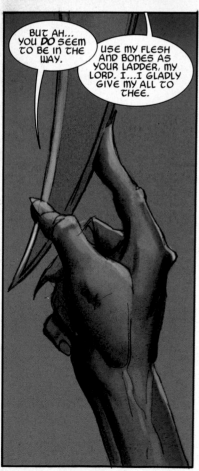

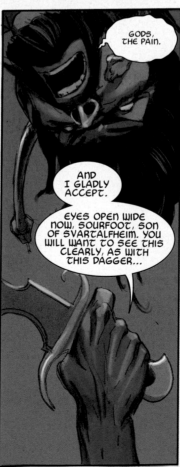

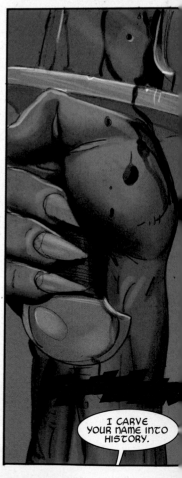

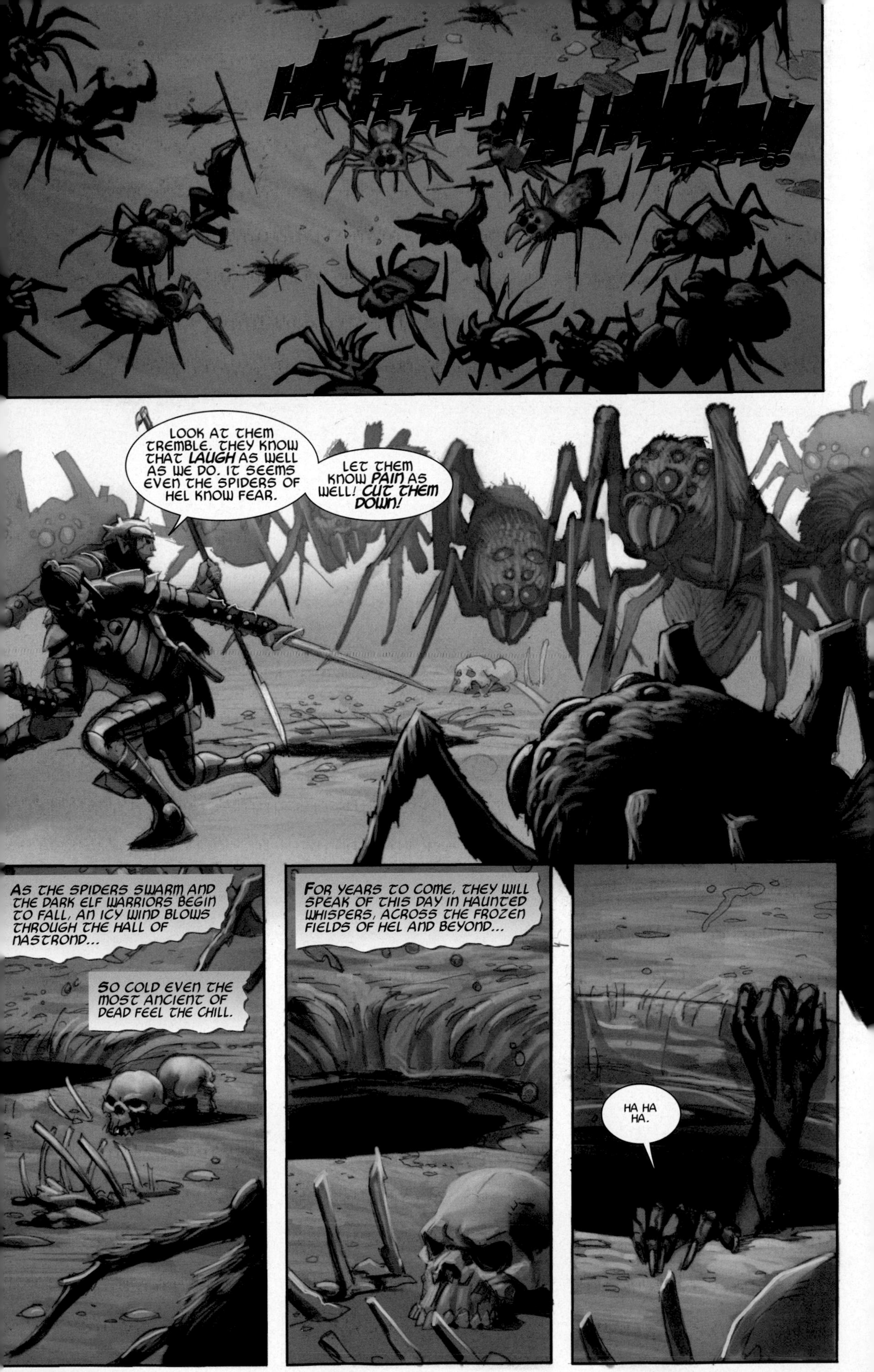
LOOK AT THEM TREMBLE. THEY KNOW THAT LAUGH AS WELL AS WE DO. IT SEEMS EVEN THE SPIDERS OF HEL KNOW FEAR.
LET THEM KNOW PAIN AS WELL! CUT THEM DOWN!
AS THE SPIDERS SWARM AND THE DARK ELF WARRIORS BEGIN TO FALL, AN ICY WIND BLOWS THROUGH THE HALL OF NASTROND...
SO COLD EVEN THE MOST ANCIENT OF DEAD FEEL THE CHILL.
FOR YEARS TO COME, THEY WILL SPEAK OF THIS DAY IN HAUNTED WHISPERS, ACROSS THE FROZEN FIELDS OF HEL AND BEYOND...
HA HA HA.

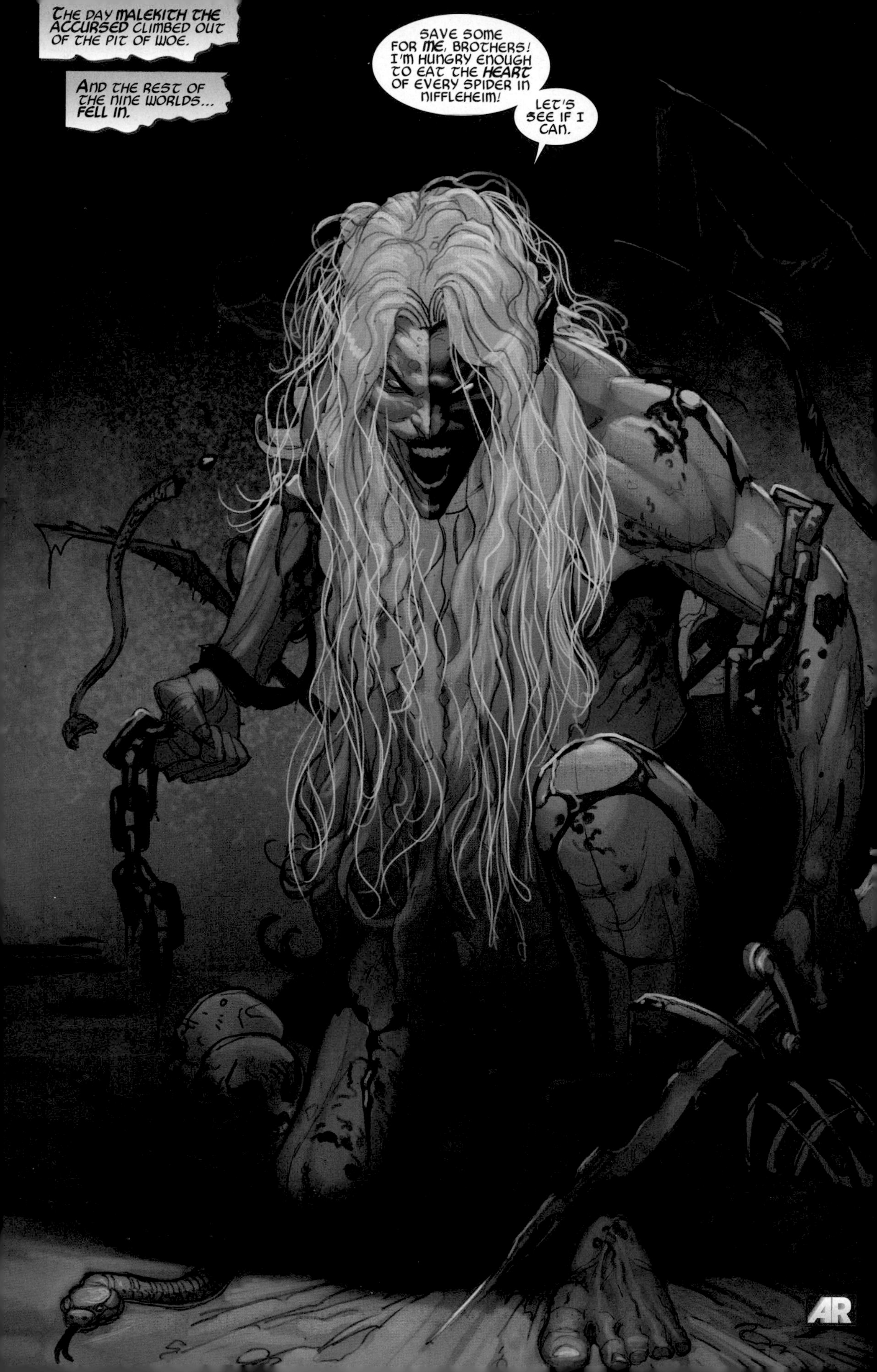

THE DAY MALEKITH THE ACCURSED CLIMBED OUT OF THE PIT OF WOE.
AND THE REST OF THE NINE WORLDS... FELL IN.
SAVE SOME FOR ME, BROTHERS! I'M HUNGRY ENOUGH TO EAT THE HEART OF EVERY SPIDER IN NIFFLEHEIM!
LET'S SEE IF I CAN.
AR

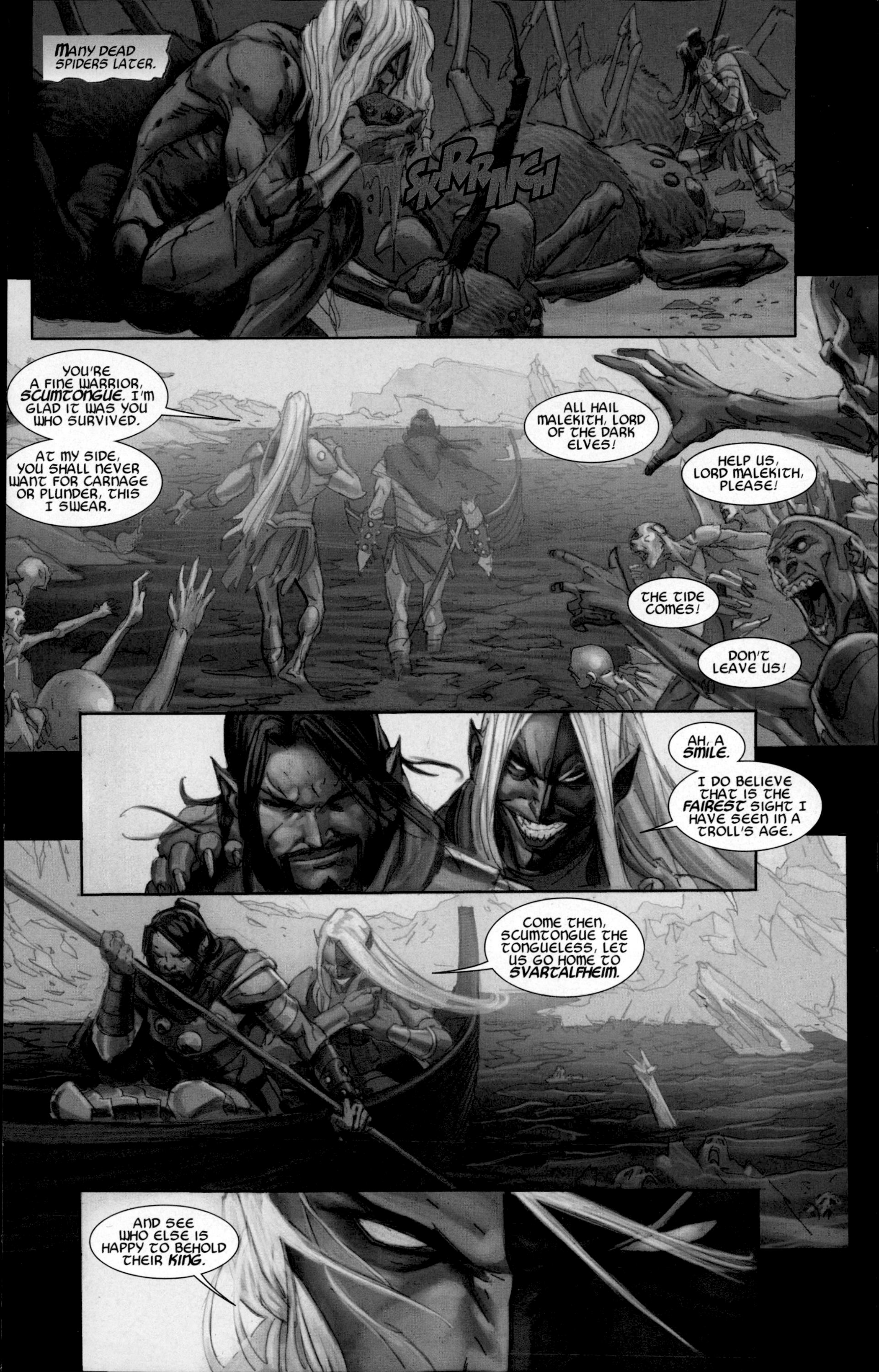
MANY DEAD SPIDERS LATER.
SKRRRUNCH
YOU'RE A FINE WARRIOR, SCUMTONGUE. I'M GLAD IT WAS YOU WHO SURVIVED.
AT MY SIDE, YOU SHALL NEVER WANT FOR CARNAGE OR PLUNDER, THIS I SWEAR.
ALL HAIL MALEKITH, LORD OF THE DARK ELVES!
HELP US, LORD MALEKITH, PLEASE!
THE TIDE COMES!
DON'T LEAVE US!
AH, A SMILE.
I DO BELIEVE THAT IS THE FAIREST SIGHT I HAVE SEEN IN A TROLL'S AGE.
COME THEN, SCUMTONGUE THE TONGUELESS, LET US GO HOME TO SVARTALFHEIM.
AND SEE WHO ELSE IS HAPPY TO BEHOLD THEIR KING.

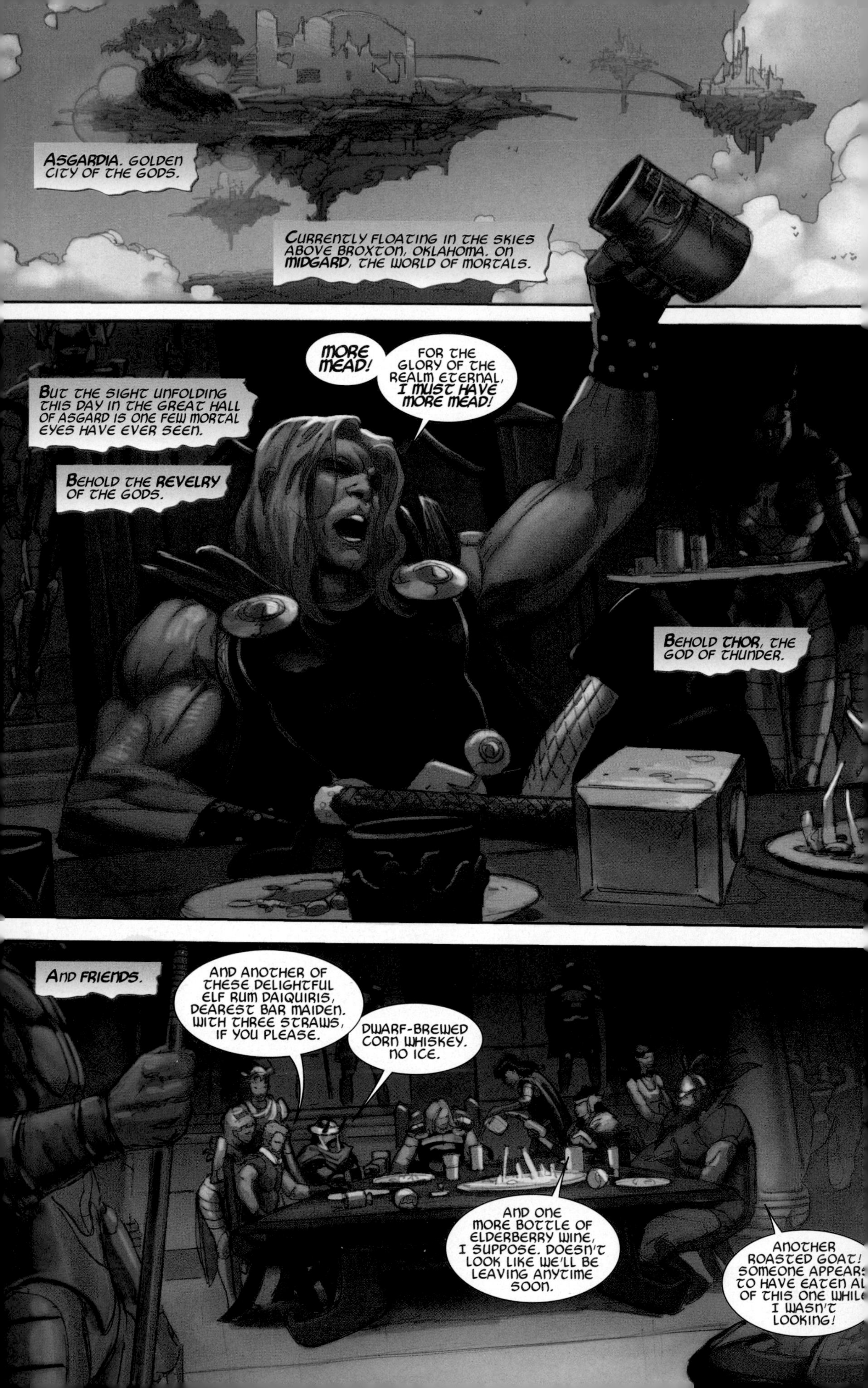
ASGARDIA. GOLDEN CITY OF THE GODS.
CURRENTLY FLOATING IN THE SKIES ABOVE BROXTON, OKLAHOMA. ON MIDGARD, THE WORLD OF MORTALS.
BUT THE SIGHT UNFOLDING THIS DAY IN THE GREAT HALL OF ASGARD IS ONE FEW MORTAL EYES HAVE EVER SEEN.
BEHOLD THE REVELRY OF THE GODS.
MORE MEAD!
FOR THE GLORY OF THE REALM ETERNAL, I MUST HAVE MORE MEAD!
BEHOLD THOR, THE GOD OF THUNDER.
AND FRIENDS.
AND ANOTHER OF THESE DELIGHTFUL ELF RUM DAIQUIRIS, DEAREST BAR MAIDEN. WITH THREE STRAWS, IF YOU PLEASE.
DWARF-BREWED CORN WHISKEY. NO ICE.
AND ONE MORE BOTTLE OF ELDERBERRY WINE, I SUPPOSE. DOESN'T LOOK LIKE WE'LL BE LEAVING ANYTIME SOON.
ANOTHER ROASTED GOAT! SOMEONE APPEARS TO HAVE EATEN AL OF THIS ONE WHIL I WASN'T LOOKING!

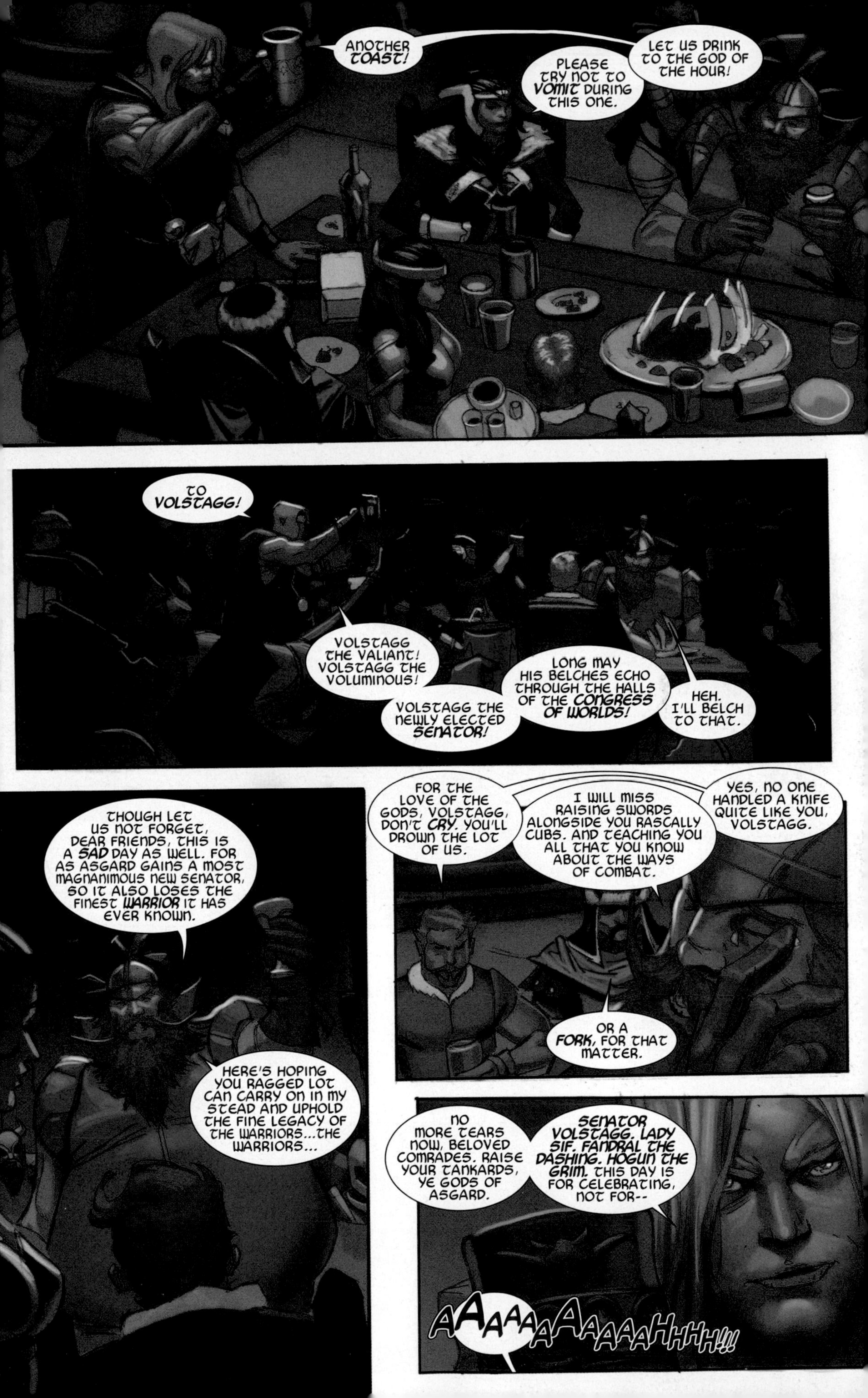
ANOTHER TOAST!
LET US DRINK TO THE GOD OF THE HOUR!
PLEASE TRY NOT TO VOMIT DURING THIS ONE.
TO VOLSTAGG!
VOLSTAGG THE VALIANT! VOLSTAGG THE VOLUMINOUS!
VOLSTAGG THE NEWLY ELECTED SENATOR!
LONG MAY HIS BELCHES ECHO THROUGH THE HALLS OF THE CONGRESS OF WORLDS!
HEH. I'LL BELCH TO THAT.
THOUGH LET US NOT FORGET, DEAR FRIENDS, THIS IS A SAD DAY AS WELL. FOR AS ASGARD GAINS A MOST MAGNANIMOUS NEW SENATOR, SO IT ALSO LOSES THE FINEST WARRIOR IT HAS EVER KNOWN.
HERE'S HOPING YOU RAGGED LOT CAN CARRY ON IN MY STEAD AND UPHOLD THE FINE LEGACY OF THE WARRIORS...THE WARRIORS...
FOR THE LOVE OF THE GODS, VOLSTAGG, DON'T CRY. YOU'LL DROWN THE LOT OF US.
I WILL MISS RAISING SWORDS ALONGSIDE YOU RASCALLY CUBS. AND TEACHING YOU ALL THAT YOU KNOW ABOUT THE WAYS OF COMBAT.
YES, NO ONE HANDLED A KNIFE QUITE LIKE YOU, VOLSTAGG.
OR A FORK, FOR THAT MATTER.
NO MORE TEARS NOW, BELOVED COMRADES. RAISE YOUR TANKARDS, YE GODS OF ASGARD.
SENATOR VOLSTAGG. LADY SIF. FANDRAL THE DASHING. HOGUN THE GRIM. THIS DAY IS FOR CELEBRATING, NOT FOR--
AAAAAAAAAAAAHHHH!!!

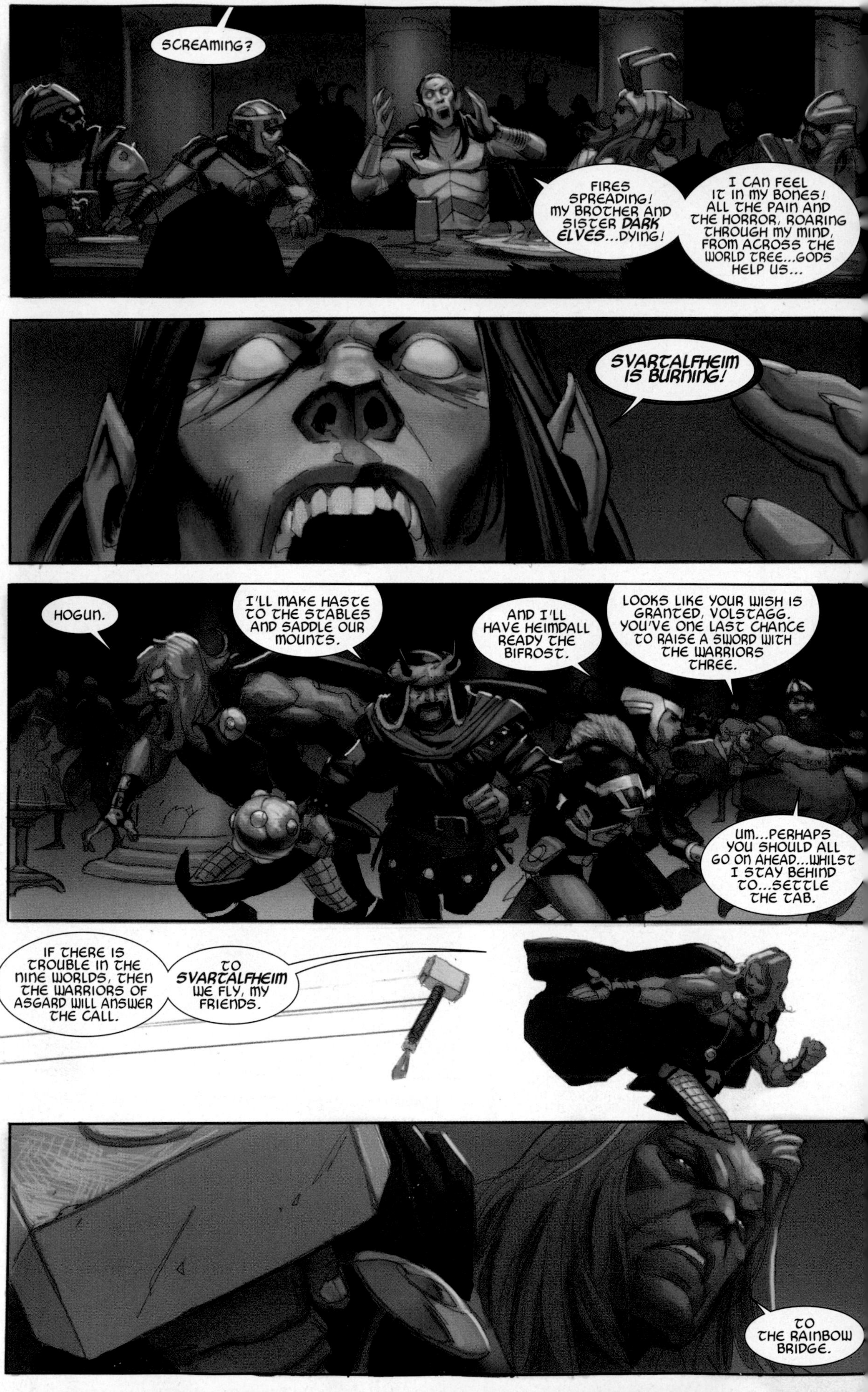
SCREAMING?
FIRES SPREADING! MY BROTHER AND SISTER DARK ELVES...DYING!
I CAN FEEL IT IN MY BONES! ALL THE PAIN AND THE HORROR, ROARING THROUGH MY MIND, FROM ACROSS THE WORLD TREE...GODS HELP US...
SVARTALFHEIM IS BURNING!
HOGUN.
I'LL MAKE HASTE TO THE STABLES AND SADDLE OUR MOUNTS.
AND I'LL HAVE HEIMDALL READY THE BIFROST.
LOOKS LIKE YOUR WISH IS GRANTED, VOLSTAGG. YOU'VE ONE LAST CHANCE TO RAISE A SWORD WITH THE WARRIORS THREE.
UM...PERHAPS YOU SHOULD ALL GO ON AHEAD...WHILST I STAY BEHIND TO...SETTLE THE TAB.
IF THERE IS TROUBLE IN THE NINE WORLDS, THEN THE WARRIORS OF ASGARD WILL ANSWER THE CALL.
TO SVARTALFHEIM WE FLY, MY FRIENDS.
TO THE RAINBOW BRIDGE.

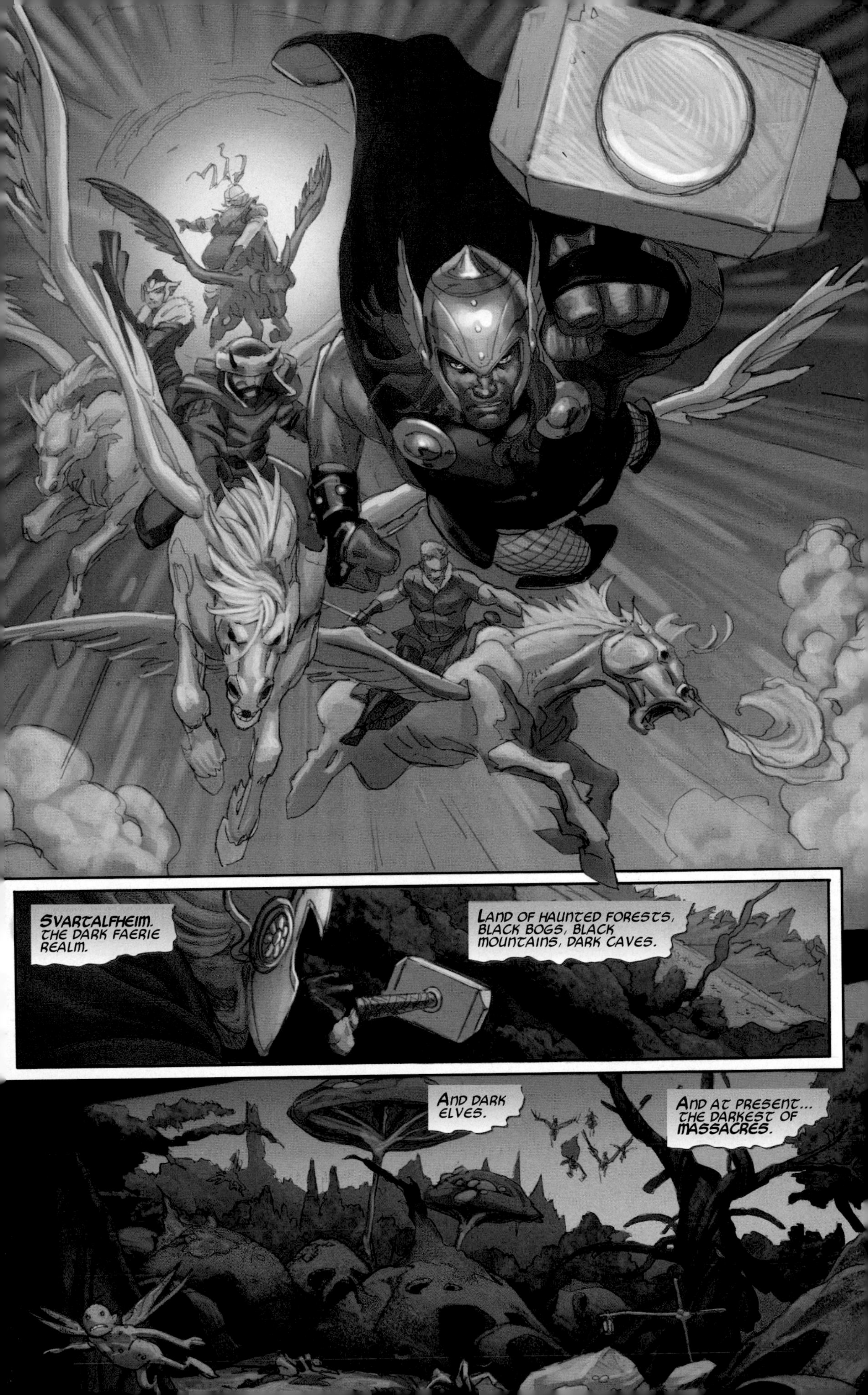
Svartalfheim. The dark faerie realm.
Land of haunted forests, black bogs, black mountains, dark caves.
And dark elves.
And at present... the darkest of massacres.

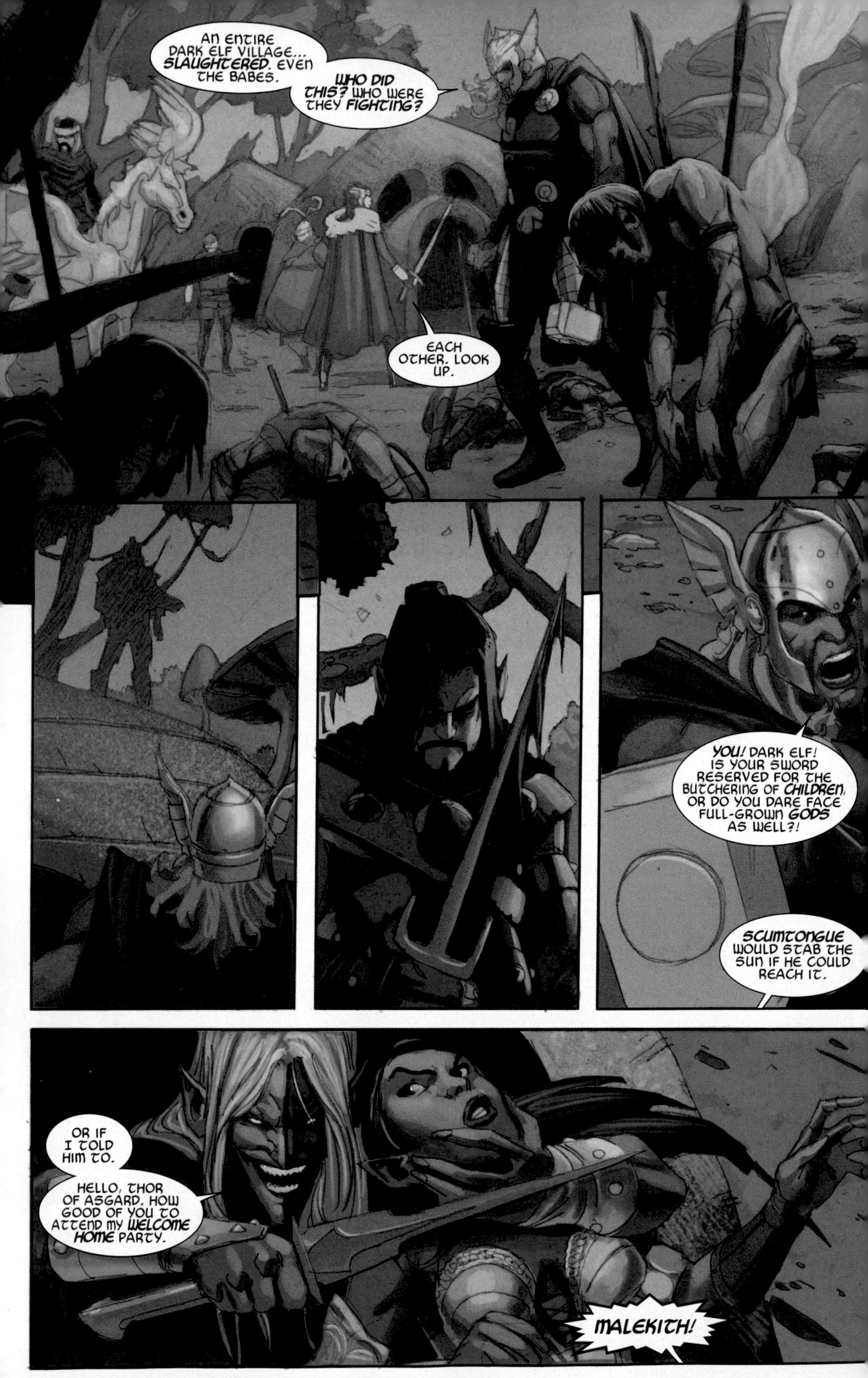

AN ENTIRE DARK ELF VILLAGE... SLAUGHTERED. EVEN THE BABES.
WHO DID THIS? WHO WERE THEY FIGHTING?
EACH OTHER. LOOK UP.
YOU! DARK ELF! IS YOUR SWORD RESERVED FOR THE BUTCHERING OF CHILDREN, OR DO YOU DARE FACE FULL-GROWN GODS AS WELL?!
SCUMTONGUE WOULD STAB THE SUN IF HE COULD REACH IT.
OR IF I TOLD HIM TO.
HELLO, THOR OF ASGARD. HOW GOOD OF YOU TO ATTEND MY WELCOME HOME PARTY.
MALEKITH!

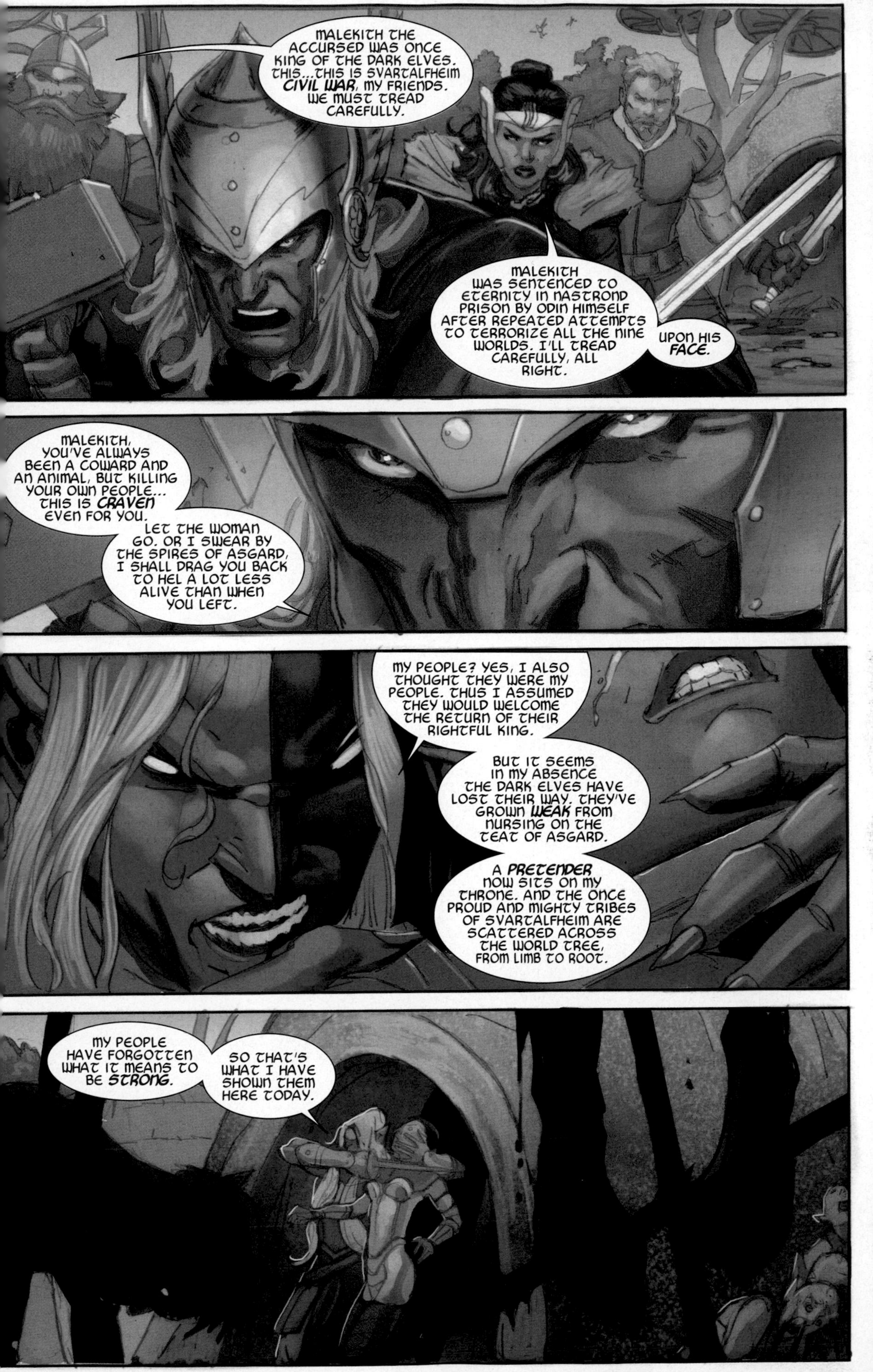
MALEKITH THE ACCURSED WAS ONCE KING OF THE DARK ELVES. THIS...THIS IS SVARTALFHEIM CIVIL WAR, MY FRIENDS. WE MUST TREAD CAREFULLY.
MALEKITH WAS SENTENCED TO ETERNITY IN NASTROND PRISON BY ODIN HIMSELF AFTER REPEATED ATTEMPTS TO TERRORIZE ALL THE NINE WORLDS. I'LL TREAD CAREFULLY, ALL RIGHT.
UPON HIS FACE.
MALEKITH, YOU'VE ALWAYS BEEN A COWARD AND AN ANIMAL, BUT KILLING YOUR OWN PEOPLE... THIS IS CRAVEN EVEN FOR YOU.
LET THE WOMAN GO. OR I SWEAR BY THE SPIRES OF ASGARD, I SHALL DRAG YOU BACK TO HEL A LOT LESS ALIVE THAN WHEN YOU LEFT.
MY PEOPLE? YES, I ALSO THOUGHT THEY WERE MY PEOPLE. THUS I ASSUMED THEY WOULD WELCOME THE RETURN OF THEIR RIGHTFUL KING.
BUT IT SEEMS IN MY ABSENCE THE DARK ELVES HAVE LOST THEIR WAY. THEY'VE GROWN WEAK FROM NURSING ON THE TEAT OF ASGARD.
A PRETENDER NOW SITS ON MY THRONE. AND THE ONCE PROUD AND MIGHTY TRIBES OF SVARTALFHEIM ARE SCATTERED ACROSS THE WORLD TREE, FROM LIMB TO ROOT.
MY PEOPLE HAVE FORGOTTEN WHAT IT MEANS TO BE STRONG.
SO THAT'S WHAT I HAVE SHOWN THEM HERE TODAY.

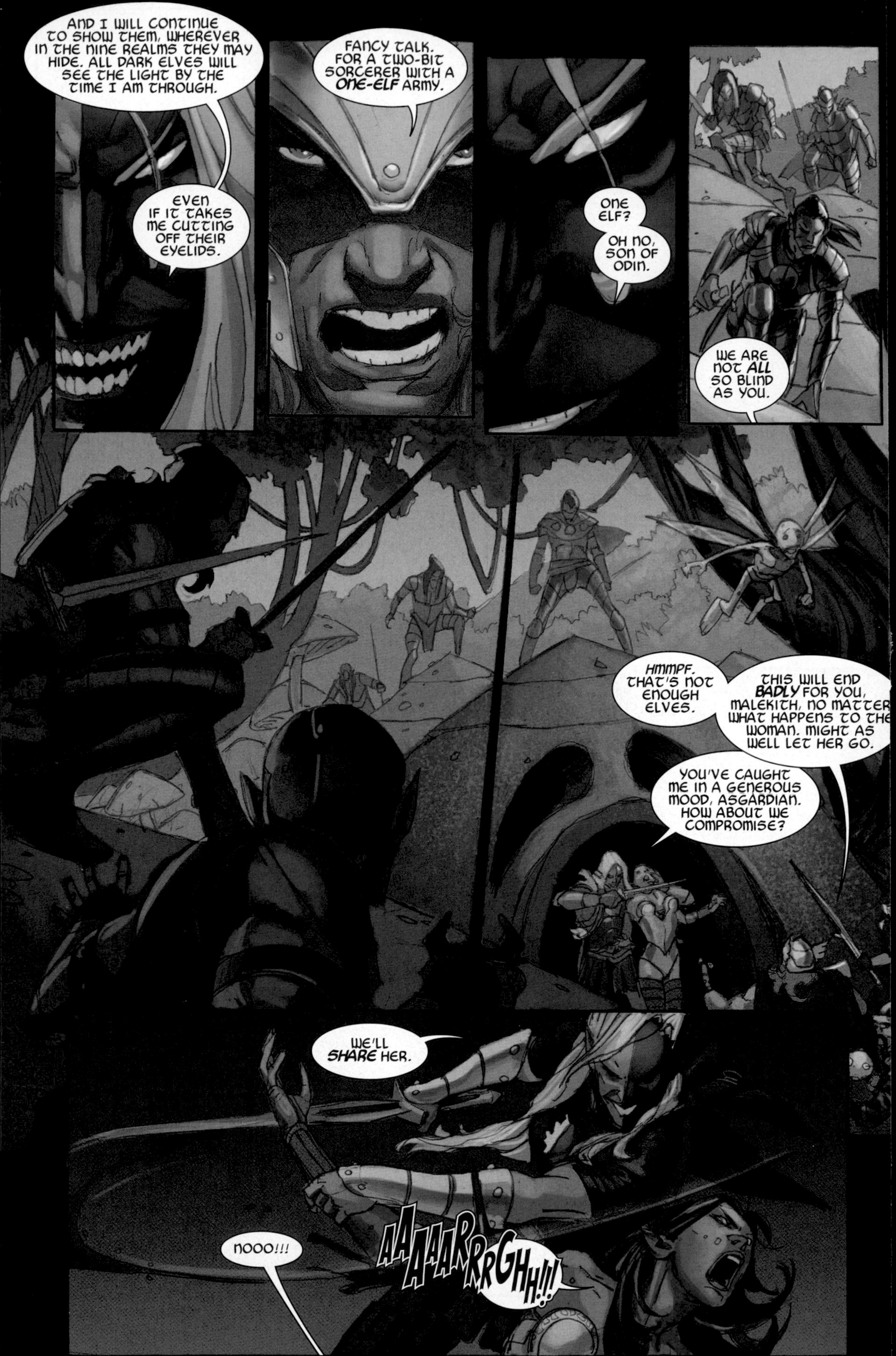
AND I WILL CONTINUE TO SHOW THEM, WHEREVER IN THE NINE REALMS THEY MAY HIDE. ALL DARK ELVES WILL SEE THE LIGHT BY THE TIME I AM THROUGH.
EVEN IF IT TAKES ME CUTTING OFF THEIR EYELIDS.
FANCY TALK. FOR A TWO-BIT SORCERER WITH A ONE-ELF ARMY.
ONE ELF?
OH NO, SON OF ODIN.
WE ARE NOT ALL SO BLIND AS YOU.
HMMPF. THAT'S NOT ENOUGH ELVES.
THIS WILL END BADLY FOR YOU, MALEKITH, NO MATTER WHAT HAPPENS TO THE WOMAN. MIGHT AS WELL LET HER GO.
YOU'VE CAUGHT ME IN A GENEROUS MOOD, ASGARDIAN. HOW ABOUT WE COMPROMISE?
WE'LL SHARE HER.
NOOO!!!
AAAAARRRGHH!!!

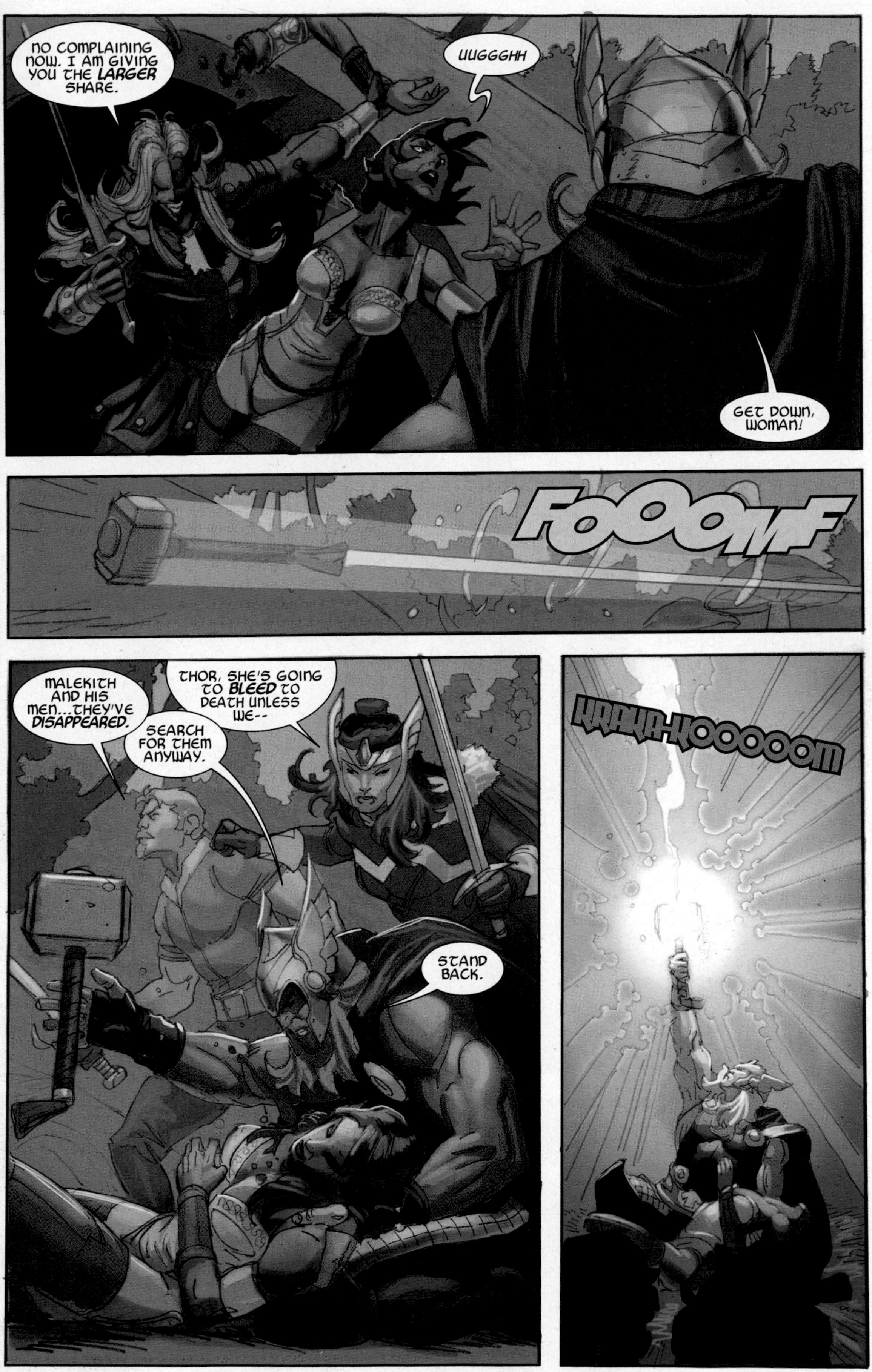
NO COMPLAINING NOW. I AM GIVING YOU THE LARGER SHARE.
UUGGGHH
GET DOWN, WOMAN!
FOOOOMF
MALEKITH AND HIS MEN...THEY'VE DISAPPEARED.
THOR, SHE'S GOING TO BLEED TO DEATH UNLESS WE--
SEARCH FOR THEM ANYWAY.
STAND BACK.
KRAKA-KOOOOOM

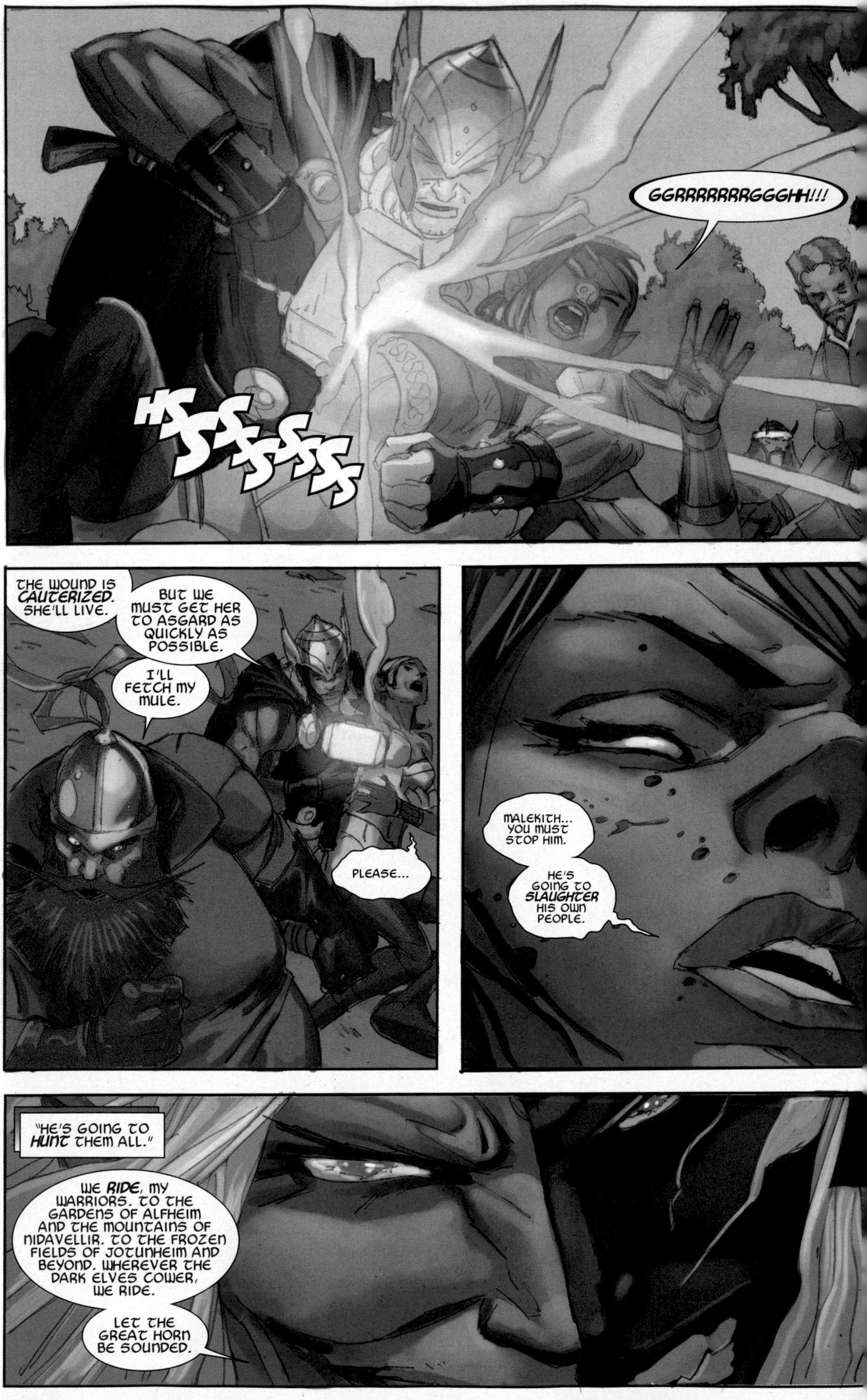
GGRRRRRRRGGGHH!!!
HSSSSSSSSS
THE WOUND IS CAUTERIZED. SHE'LL LIVE.
BUT WE MUST GET HER TO ASGARD AS QUICKLY AS POSSIBLE.
I'LL FETCH MY MULE.
PLEASE...
MALEKITH... YOU MUST STOP HIM.
HE'S GOING TO SLAUGHTER HIS OWN PEOPLE.
"HE'S GOING TO HUNT THEM ALL."
WE RIDE, MY WARRIORS. TO THE GARDENS OF ALFHEIM AND THE MOUNTAINS OF NIDAVELLIR. TO THE FROZEN FIELDS OF JOTUNHEIM AND BEYOND. WHEREVER THE DARK ELVES COWER, WE RIDE.
LET THE GREAT HORN BE SOUNDED.

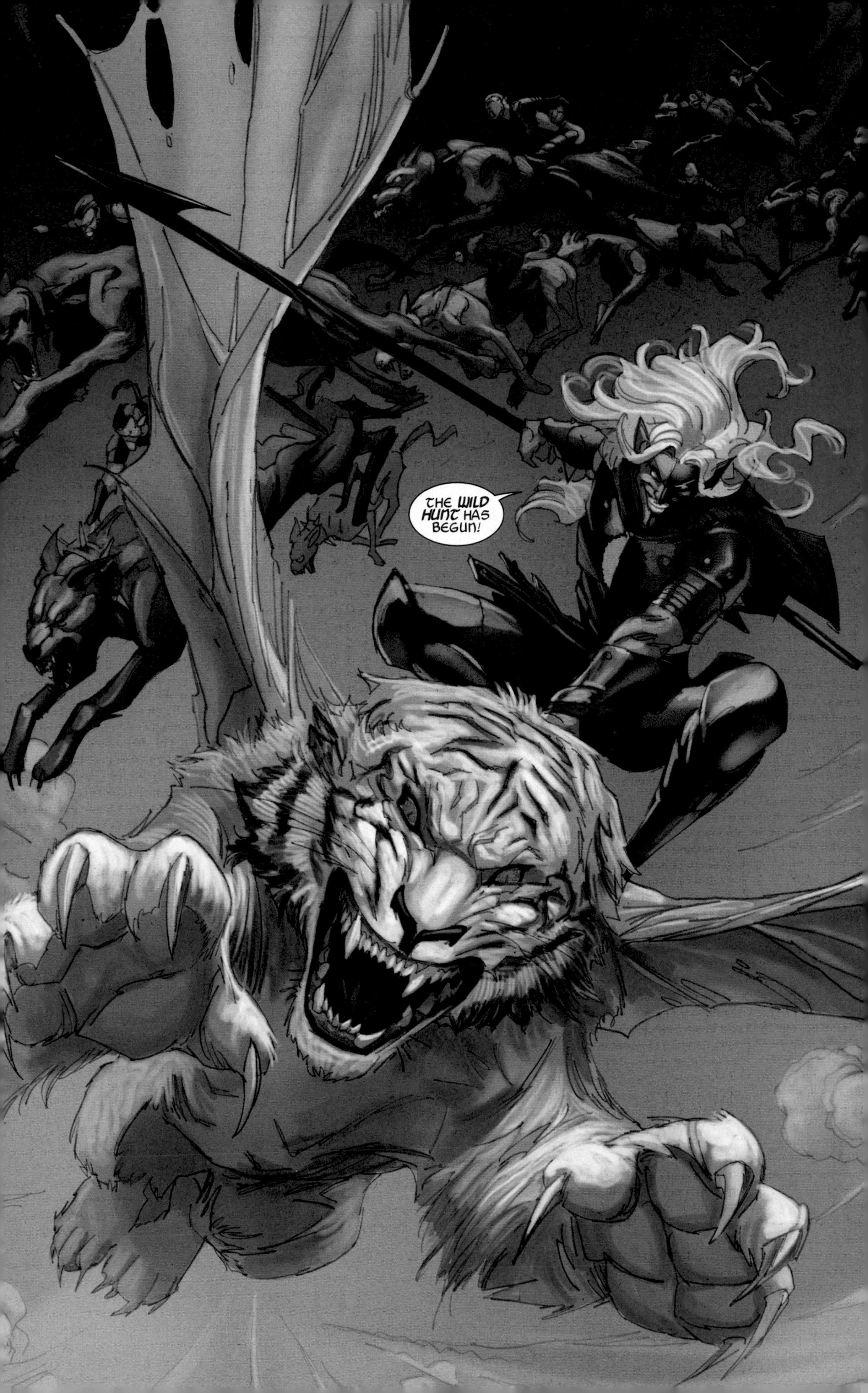
THE WILD HUNT HAS BEGUN!

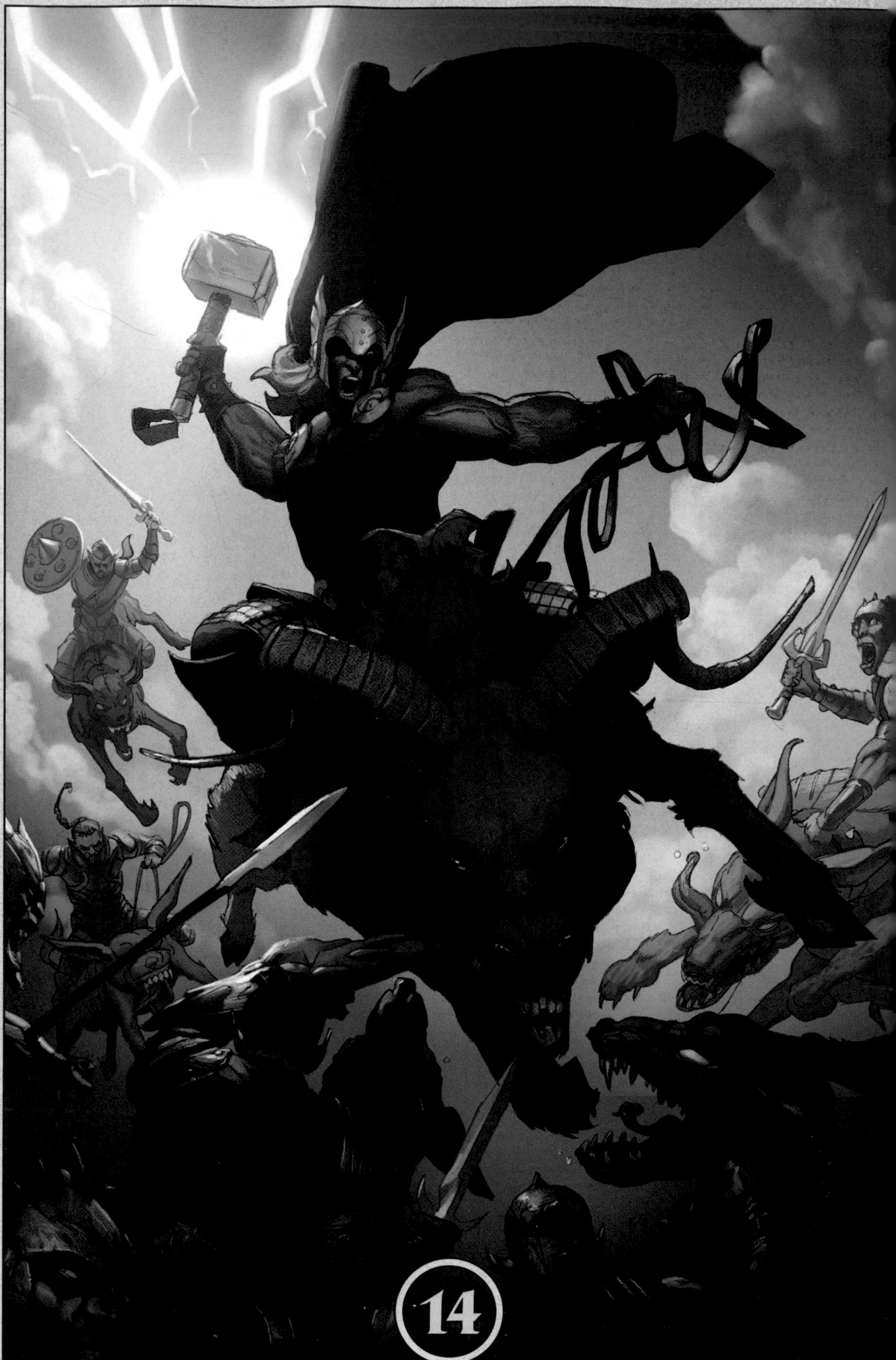

14
THE LEAGUE OF REALMS

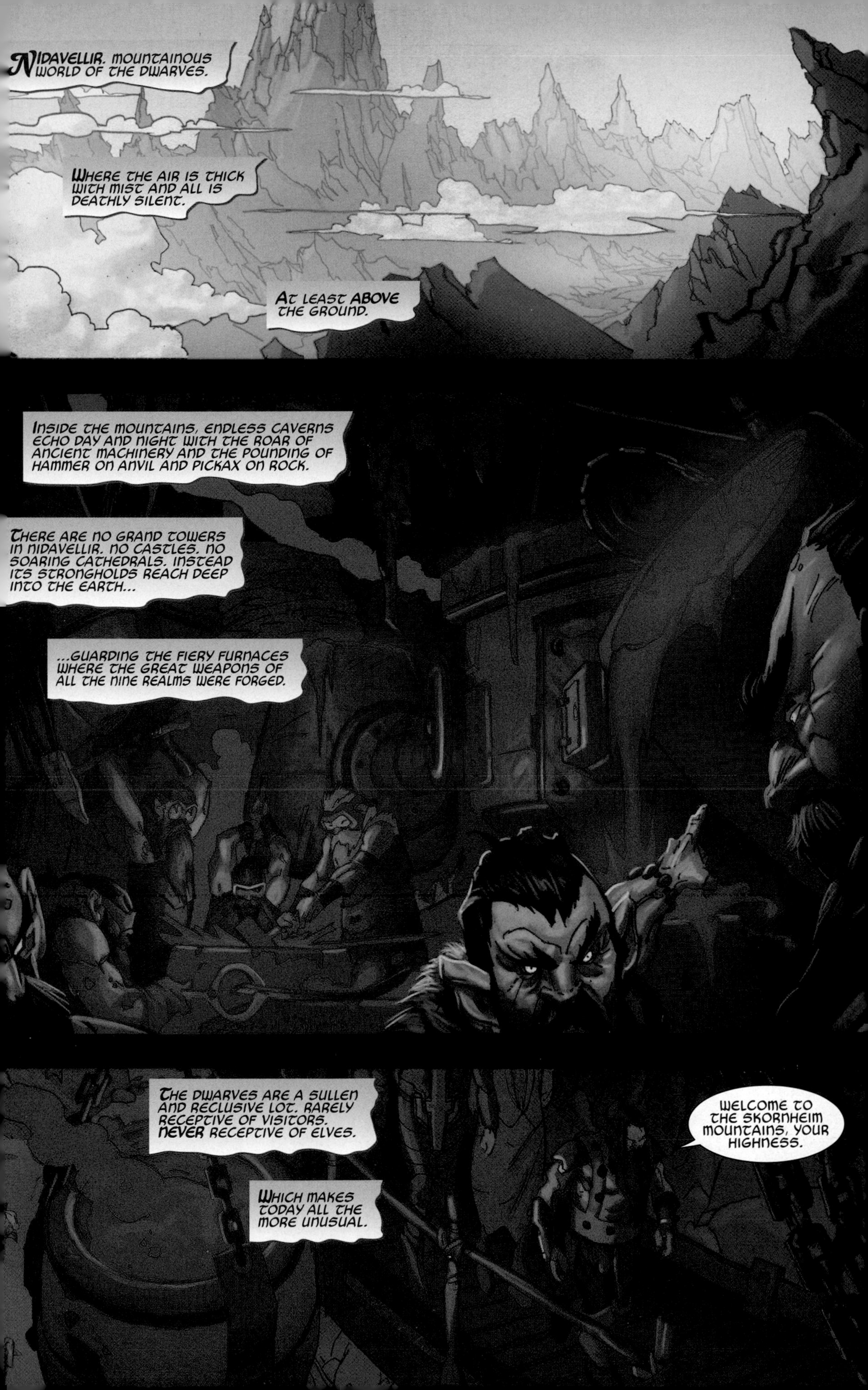
NIDAVELLIR. MOUNTAINOUS WORLD OF THE DWARVES.
WHERE THE AIR IS THICK WITH MIST AND ALL IS DEATHLY SILENT.
AT LEAST ABOVE THE GROUND.
INSIDE THE MOUNTAINS, ENDLESS CAVERNS ECHO DAY AND NIGHT WITH THE ROAR OF ANCIENT MACHINERY AND THE POUNDING OF HAMMER ON ANVIL AND PICKAX ON ROCK.
THERE ARE NO GRAND TOWERS IN NIDAVELLIR. NO CASTLES. NO SOARING CATHEDRALS. INSTEAD ITS STRONGHOLDS REACH DEEP INTO THE EARTH...
...GUARDING THE FIERY FURNACES WHERE THE GREAT WEAPONS OF ALL THE NINE REALMS WERE FORGED.
THE DWARVES ARE A SULLEN AND RECLUSIVE LOT. RARELY RECEPTIVE OF VISITORS. NEVER RECEPTIVE OF ELVES.
WHICH MAKES TODAY ALL THE MORE UNUSUAL.
WELCOME TO THE SKORNHEIM MOUNTAINS, YOUR HIGHNESS.

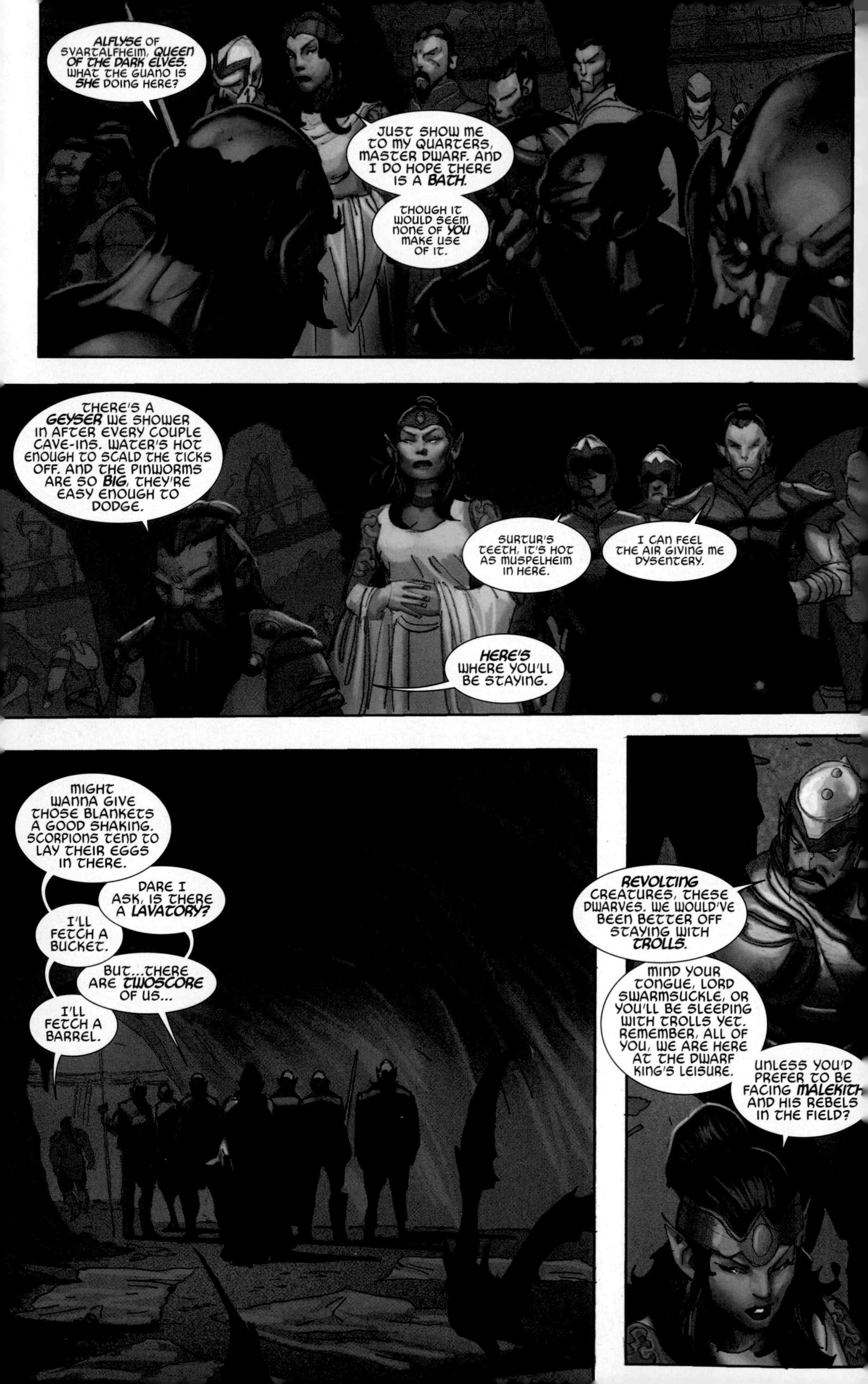

ALFLYSE OF SVARTALFHEIM, QUEEN OF THE DARK ELVES. WHAT THE GUANO IS SHE DOING HERE?
JUST SHOW ME TO MY QUARTERS, MASTER DWARF. AND I DO HOPE THERE IS A BATH.
THOUGH IT WOULD SEEM NONE OF YOU MAKE USE OF IT.
THERE'S A GEYSER WE SHOWER IN AFTER EVERY COUPLE CAVE-INS. WATER'S HOT ENOUGH TO SCALD THE TICKS OFF. AND THE PINWORMS ARE SO BIG, THEY'RE EASY ENOUGH TO DODGE.
SURTUR'S TEETH, IT'S HOT AS MUSPELHEIM IN HERE.
I CAN FEEL THE AIR GIVING ME DYSENTERY.
HERE'S WHERE YOU'LL BE STAYING.
MIGHT WANNA GIVE THOSE BLANKETS A GOOD SHAKING. SCORPIONS TEND TO LAY THEIR EGGS IN THERE.
DARE I ASK, IS THERE A LAVATORY?
I'LL FETCH A BUCKET.
BUT...THERE ARE TWOSCORE OF US...
I'LL FETCH A BARREL.
REVOLTING CREATURES, THESE DWARVES. WE WOULD'VE BEEN BETTER OFF STAYING WITH TROLLS.
MIND YOUR TONGUE, LORD SWARMSUCKLE, OR YOU'LL BE SLEEPING WITH TROLLS YET. REMEMBER, ALL OF YOU, WE ARE HERE AT THE DWARF KING'S LEISURE.
UNLESS YOU'D PREFER TO BE FACING MALEKITH AND HIS REBELS IN THE FIELD?

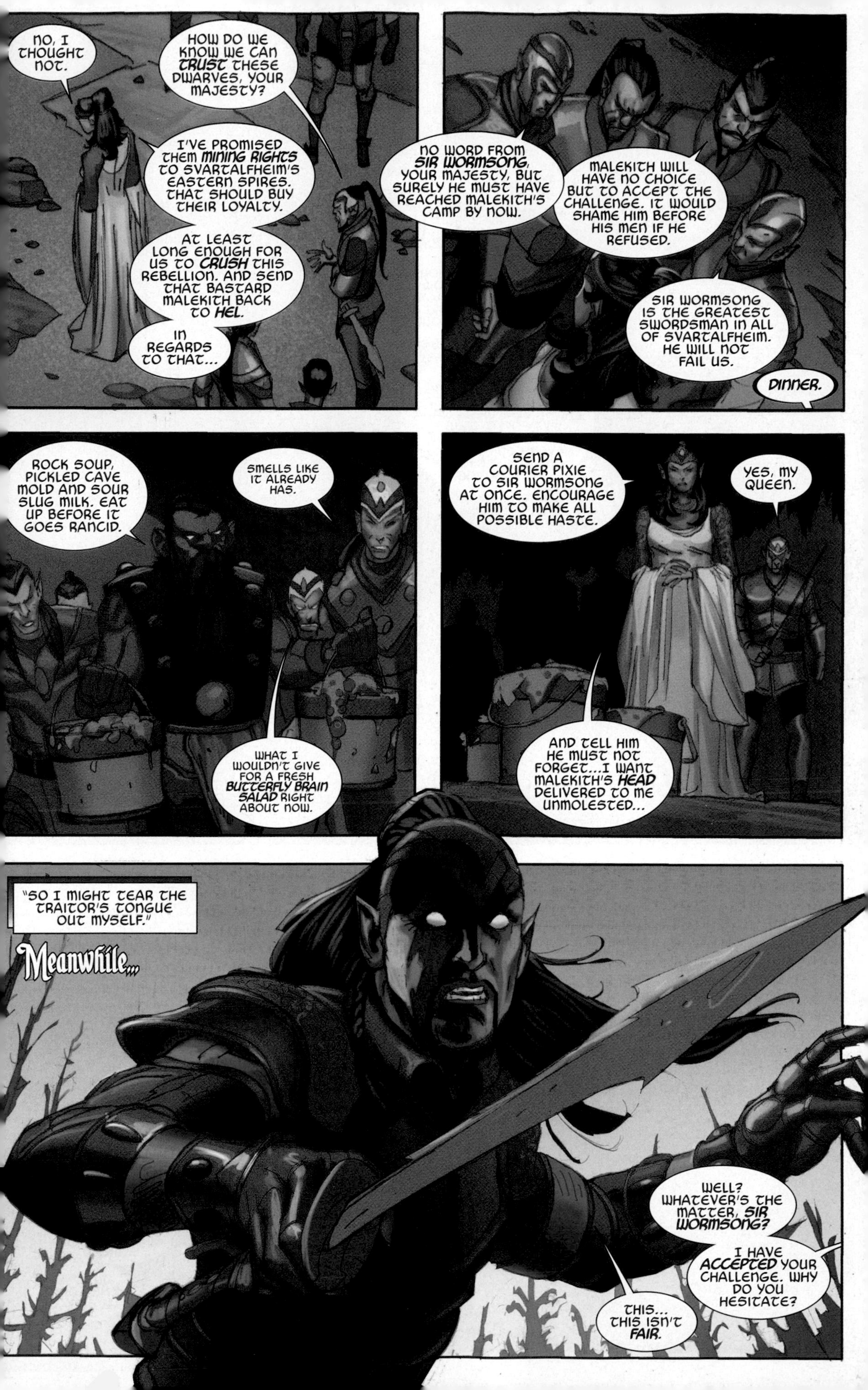
NO, I THOUGHT NOT.
HOW DO WE KNOW WE CAN TRUST THESE DWARVES, YOUR MAJESTY?
I'VE PROMISED THEM MINING RIGHTS TO SVARTALFHEIM'S EASTERN SPIRES. THAT SHOULD BUY THEIR LOYALTY.
AT LEAST LONG ENOUGH FOR US TO CRUSH THIS REBELLION. AND SEND THAT BASTARD MALEKITH BACK TO HEL.
IN REGARDS TO THAT...
NO WORD FROM SIR WORMSONG, YOUR MAJESTY, BUT SURELY HE MUST HAVE REACHED MALEKITH'S CAMP BY NOW.
MALEKITH WILL HAVE NO CHOICE BUT TO ACCEPT THE CHALLENGE. IT WOULD SHAME HIM BEFORE HIS MEN IF HE REFUSED.
SIR WORMSONG IS THE GREATEST SWORDSMAN IN ALL OF SVARTALFHEIM. HE WILL NOT FAIL US.
DINNER.
ROCK SOUP, PICKLED CAVE MOLD AND SOUR SLUG MILK. EAT UP BEFORE IT GOES RANCID.
SMELLS LIKE IT ALREADY HAS.
WHAT I WOULDN'T GIVE FOR A FRESH BUTTERFLY BRAIN SALAD RIGHT ABOUT NOW.
SEND A COURIER PIXIE TO SIR WORMSONG AT ONCE. ENCOURAGE HIM TO MAKE ALL POSSIBLE HASTE.
YES, MY QUEEN.
AND TELL HIM HE MUST NOT FORGET...I WANT MALEKITH'S HEAD DELIVERED TO ME UNMOLESTED...
"SO I MIGHT TEAR THE TRAITOR'S TONGUE OUT MYSELF."
Meanwhile...
WELL? WHATEVER'S THE MATTER, SIR WORMSONG?
I HAVE ACCEPTED YOUR CHALLENGE. WHY DO YOU HESITATE?
THIS... THIS ISN'T FAIR.

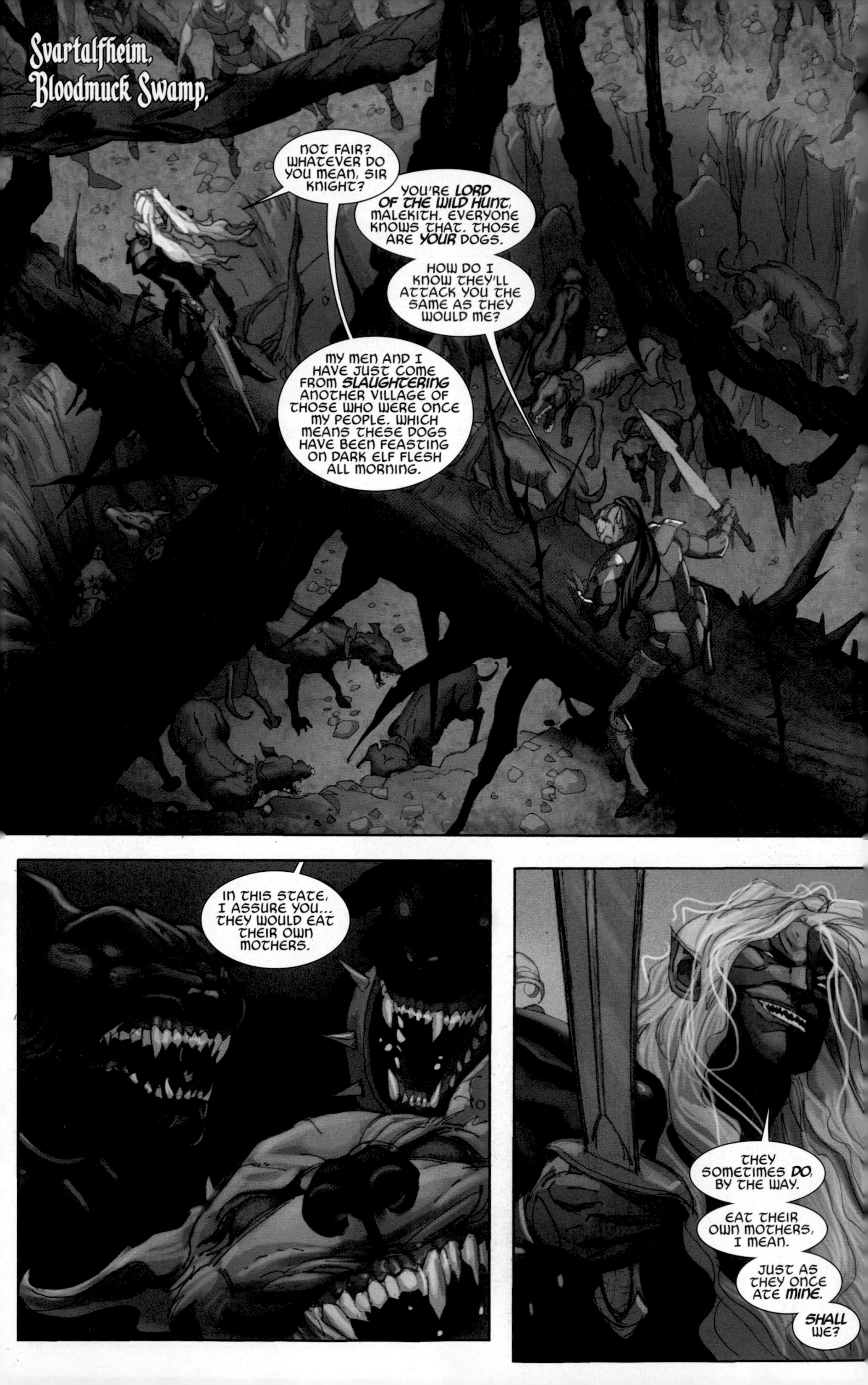
Svartalfheim, Bloodmuck Swamp.
NOT FAIR? WHATEVER DO YOU MEAN, SIR KNIGHT?
YOU'RE LORD OF THE WILD HUNT, MALEKITH. EVERYONE KNOWS THAT. THOSE ARE YOUR DOGS.
HOW DO I KNOW THEY'LL ATTACK YOU THE SAME AS THEY WOULD ME?
MY MEN AND I HAVE JUST COME FROM SLAUGHTERING ANOTHER VILLAGE OF THOSE WHO WERE ONCE MY PEOPLE. WHICH MEANS THESE DOGS HAVE BEEN FEASTING ON DARK ELF FLESH ALL MORNING.
IN THIS STATE, I ASSURE YOU... THEY WOULD EAT THEIR OWN MOTHERS.
THEY SOMETIMES DO, BY THE WAY.
EAT THEIR OWN MOTHERS, I MEAN.
JUST AS THEY ONCE ATE MINE.
SHALL WE?

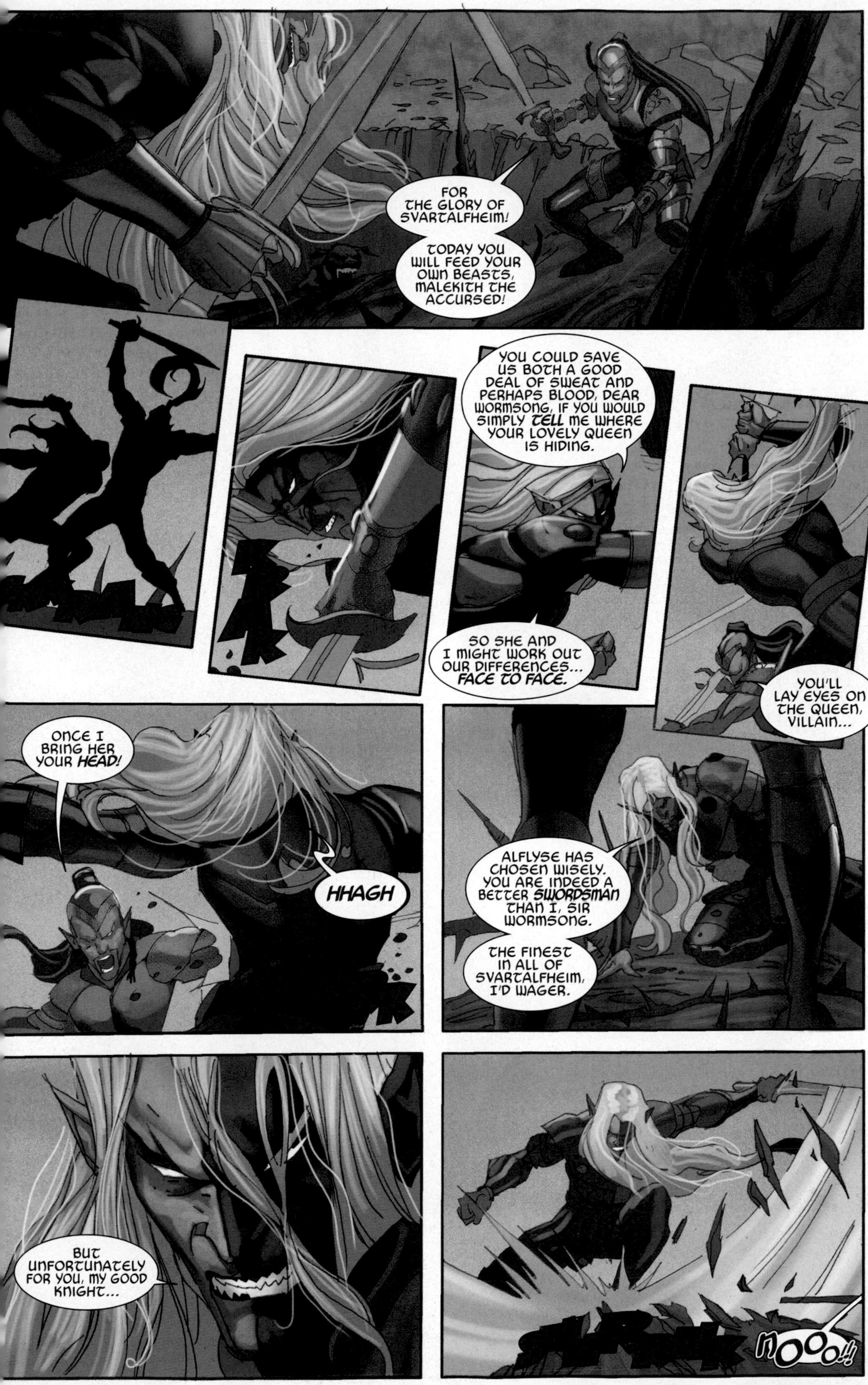
FOR THE GLORY OF SVARTALFHEIM!
TODAY YOU WILL FEED YOUR OWN BEASTS, MALEKITH THE ACCURSED!
YOU COULD SAVE US BOTH A GOOD DEAL OF SWEAT AND PERHAPS BLOOD, DEAR WORMSONG, IF YOU WOULD SIMPLY TELL ME WHERE YOUR LOVELY QUEEN IS HIDING.
SO SHE AND I MIGHT WORK OUT OUR DIFFERENCES... FACE TO FACE.
YOU'LL LAY EYES ON THE QUEEN, VILLAIN...
ONCE I BRING HER YOUR HEAD!
HHAGH
ALFLYSE HAS CHOSEN WISELY. YOU ARE INDEED A BETTER SWORDSMAN THAN I, SIR WORMSONG.
THE FINEST IN ALL OF SVARTALFHEIM, I'D WAGER.
BUT UNFORTUNATELY FOR YOU, MY GOOD KNIGHT...
NOOO!!

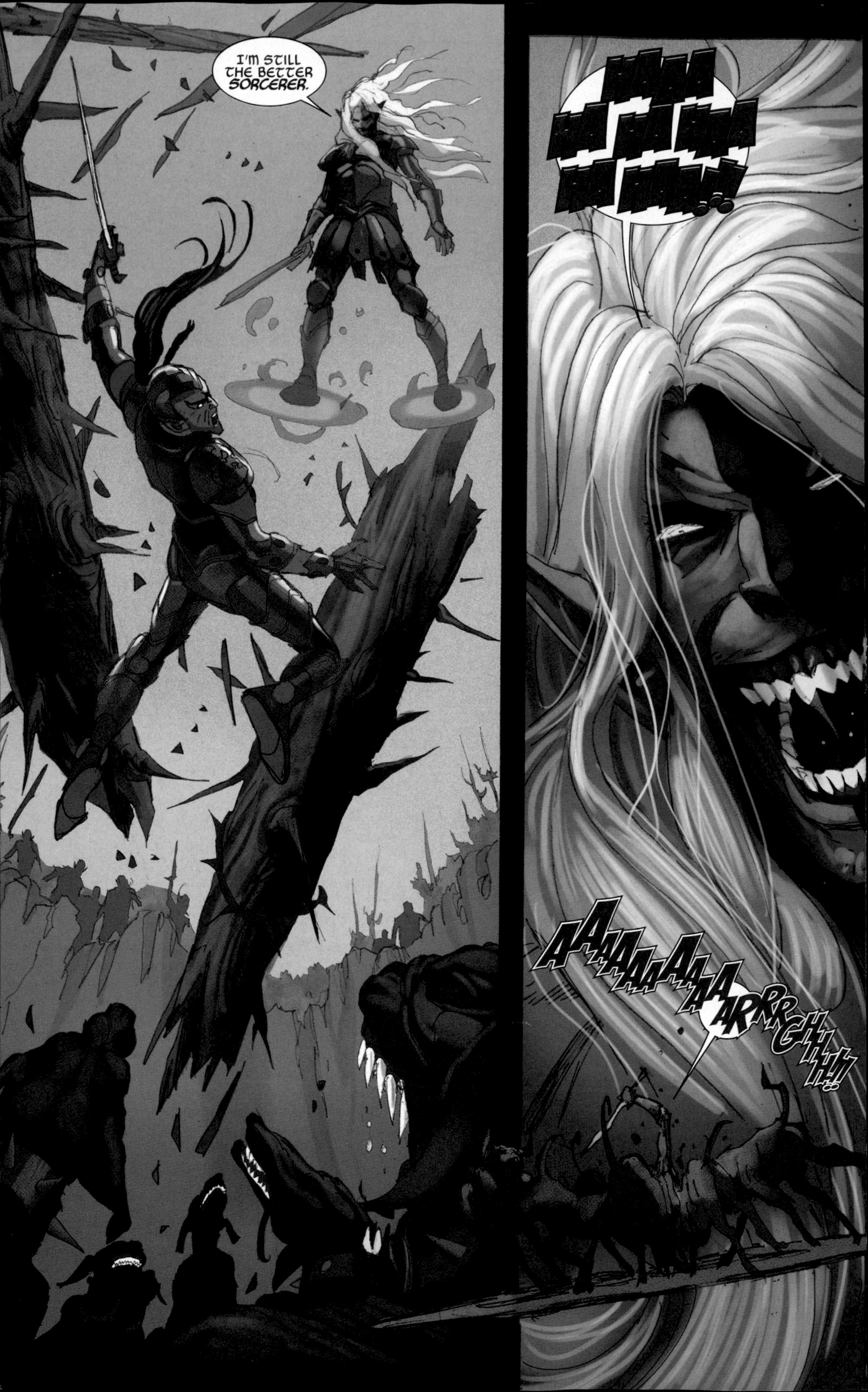
I'M STILL THE BETTER SORCERER.
AAAAAAAAAAARRRRGHHH!!

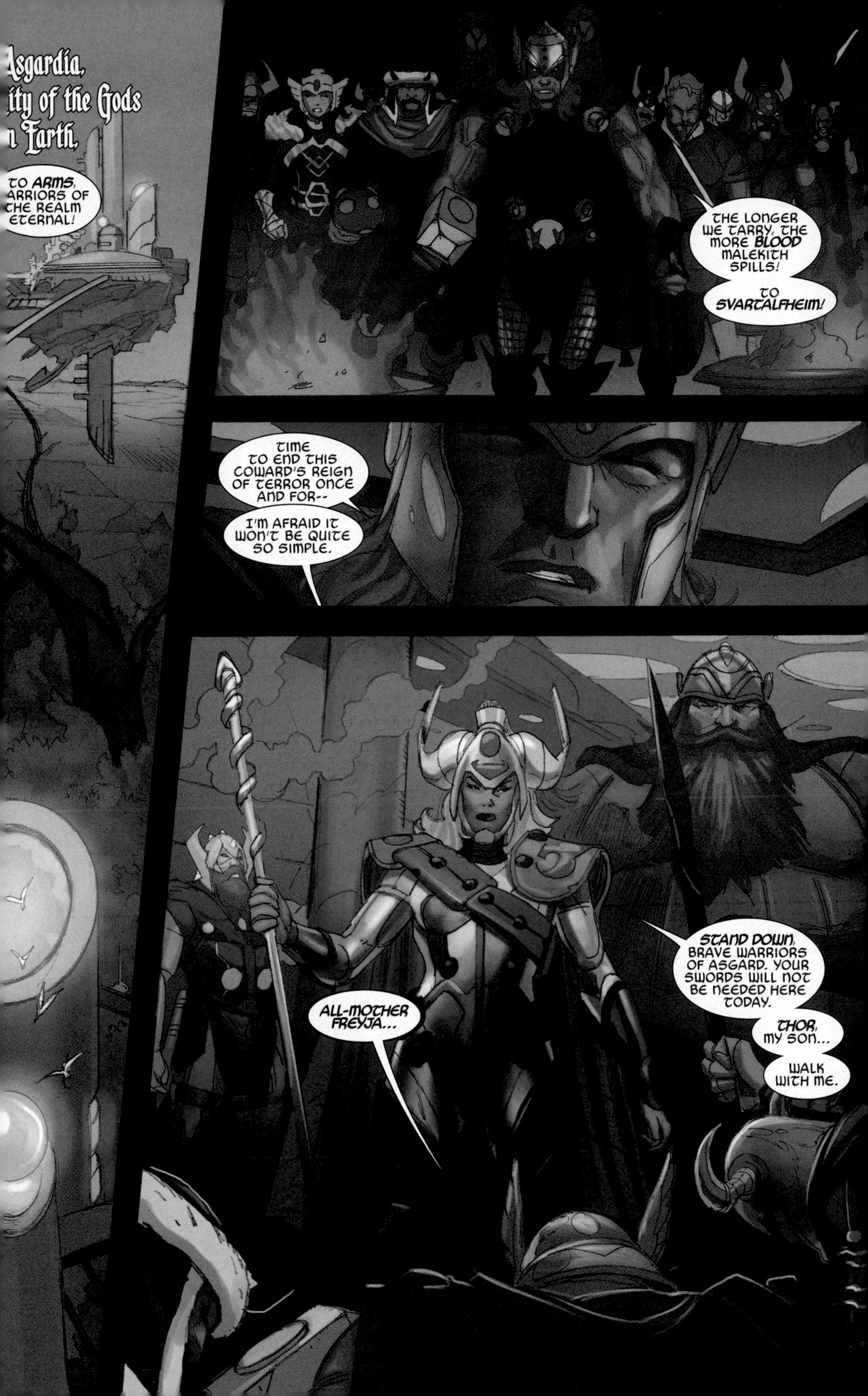
Asgardia,
ity of the Gods
n Earth,
TO ARMS, ARRIORS OF THE REALM ETERNAL!
THE LONGER WE TARRY, THE MORE BLOOD MALEKITH SPILLS!
TO SVARTALFHEIM!
TIME TO END THIS COWARD'S REIGN OF TERROR ONCE AND FOR--
I'M AFRAID IT WON'T BE QUITE SO SIMPLE.
STAND DOWN, BRAVE WARRIORS OF ASGARD. YOUR SWORDS WILL NOT BE NEEDED HERE TODAY.
ALL-MOTHER FREYJA...
THOR, MY SON...
WALK WITH ME.

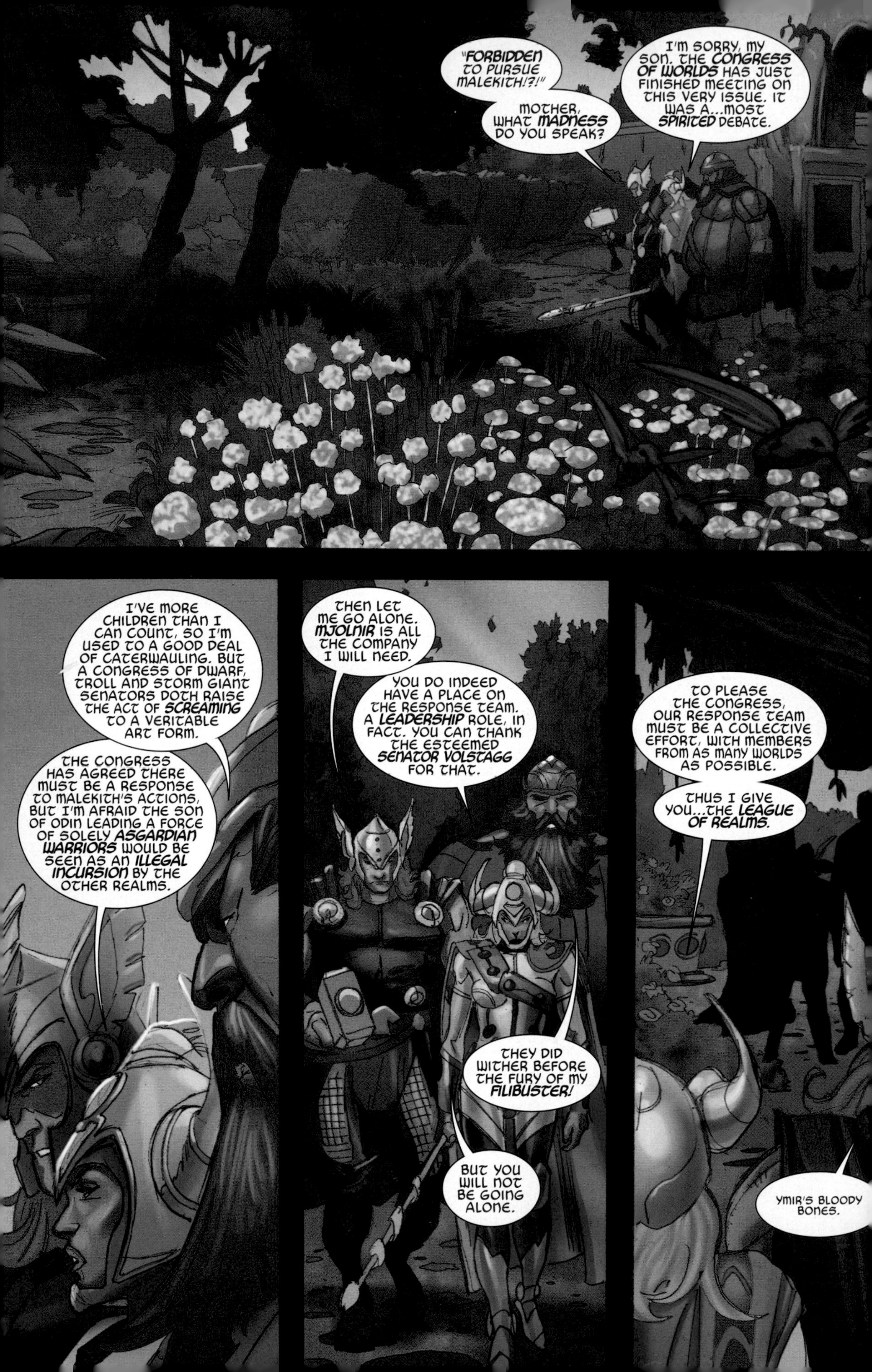
"FORBIDDEN TO PURSUE MALEKITH!?!"
MOTHER, WHAT MADNESS DO YOU SPEAK?
I'M SORRY, MY SON. THE CONGRESS OF WORLDS HAS JUST FINISHED MEETING ON THIS VERY ISSUE. IT WAS A...MOST SPIRITED DEBATE.
I'VE MORE CHILDREN THAN I CAN COUNT, SO I'M USED TO A GOOD DEAL OF CATERWAULING. BUT A CONGRESS OF DWARF, TROLL AND STORM GIANT SENATORS DOTH RAISE THE ACT OF SCREAMING TO A VERITABLE ART FORM.
THE CONGRESS HAS AGREED THERE MUST BE A RESPONSE TO MALEKITH'S ACTIONS, BUT I'M AFRAID THE SON OF ODIN LEADING A FORCE OF SOLELY ASGARDIAN WARRIORS WOULD BE SEEN AS AN ILLEGAL INCURSION BY THE OTHER REALMS.
THEN LET ME GO ALONE. MJOLNIR IS ALL THE COMPANY I WILL NEED.
YOU DO INDEED HAVE A PLACE ON THE RESPONSE TEAM. A LEADERSHIP ROLE, IN FACT. YOU CAN THANK THE ESTEEMED SENATOR VOLSTAGG FOR THAT.
THEY DID WITHER BEFORE THE FURY OF MY FILIBUSTER!
BUT YOU WILL NOT BE GOING ALONE.
TO PLEASE THE CONGRESS, OUR RESPONSE TEAM MUST BE A COLLECTIVE EFFORT, WITH MEMBERS FROM AS MANY WORLDS AS POSSIBLE.
THUS I GIVE YOU...THE LEAGUE OF REALMS.
YMIR'S BLOODY BONES.

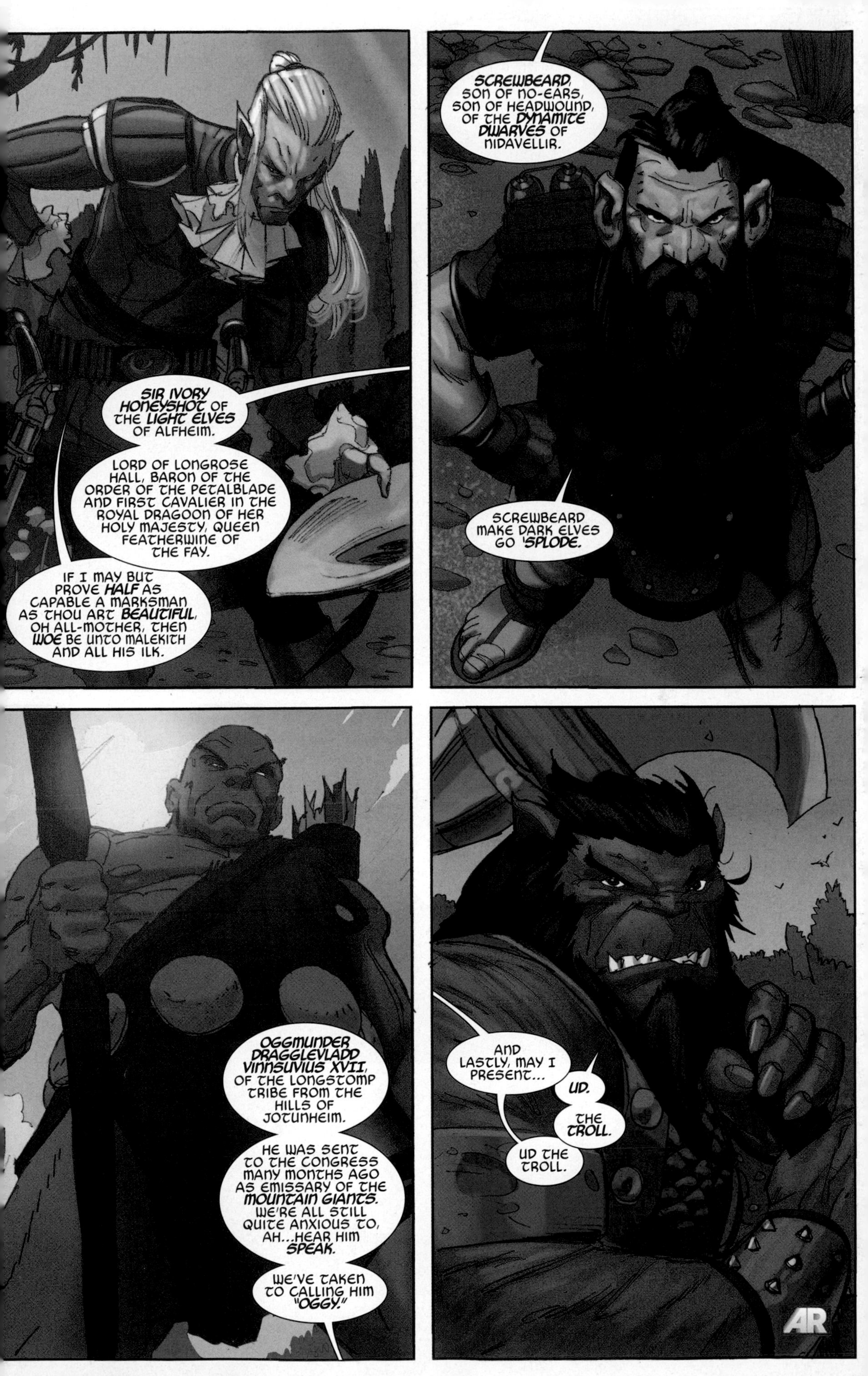
SIR IVORY HONEYSHOT OF THE LIGHT ELVES OF ALFHEIM.
LORD OF LONGROSE HALL, BARON OF THE ORDER OF THE PETALBLADE AND FIRST CAVALIER IN THE ROYAL DRAGOON OF HER HOLY MAJESTY, QUEEN FEATHERWINE OF THE FAY.
IF I MAY BUT PROVE HALF AS CAPABLE A MARKSMAN AS THOU ART BEAUTIFUL, OH ALL-MOTHER, THEN WOE BE UNTO MALEKITH AND ALL HIS ILK.
SCREWBEARD, SON OF NO-EARS, SON OF HEADWOUND, OF THE DYNAMITE DWARVES OF NIDAVELLIR.
SCREWBEARD MAKE DARK ELVES GO 'SPLODE.
OGGMUNDER DRAGGLEVLADD VINNSUVIUS XVII, OF THE LONGSTOMP TRIBE FROM THE HILLS OF JOTUNHEIM.
HE WAS SENT TO THE CONGRESS MANY MONTHS AGO AS EMISSARY OF THE MOUNTAIN GIANTS. WE'RE ALL STILL QUITE ANXIOUS TO, AH...HEAR HIM SPEAK.
WE'VE TAKEN TO CALLING HIM "OGGY."
AND LASTLY, MAY I PRESENT...
UD.
THE TROLL.
UD THE TROLL.

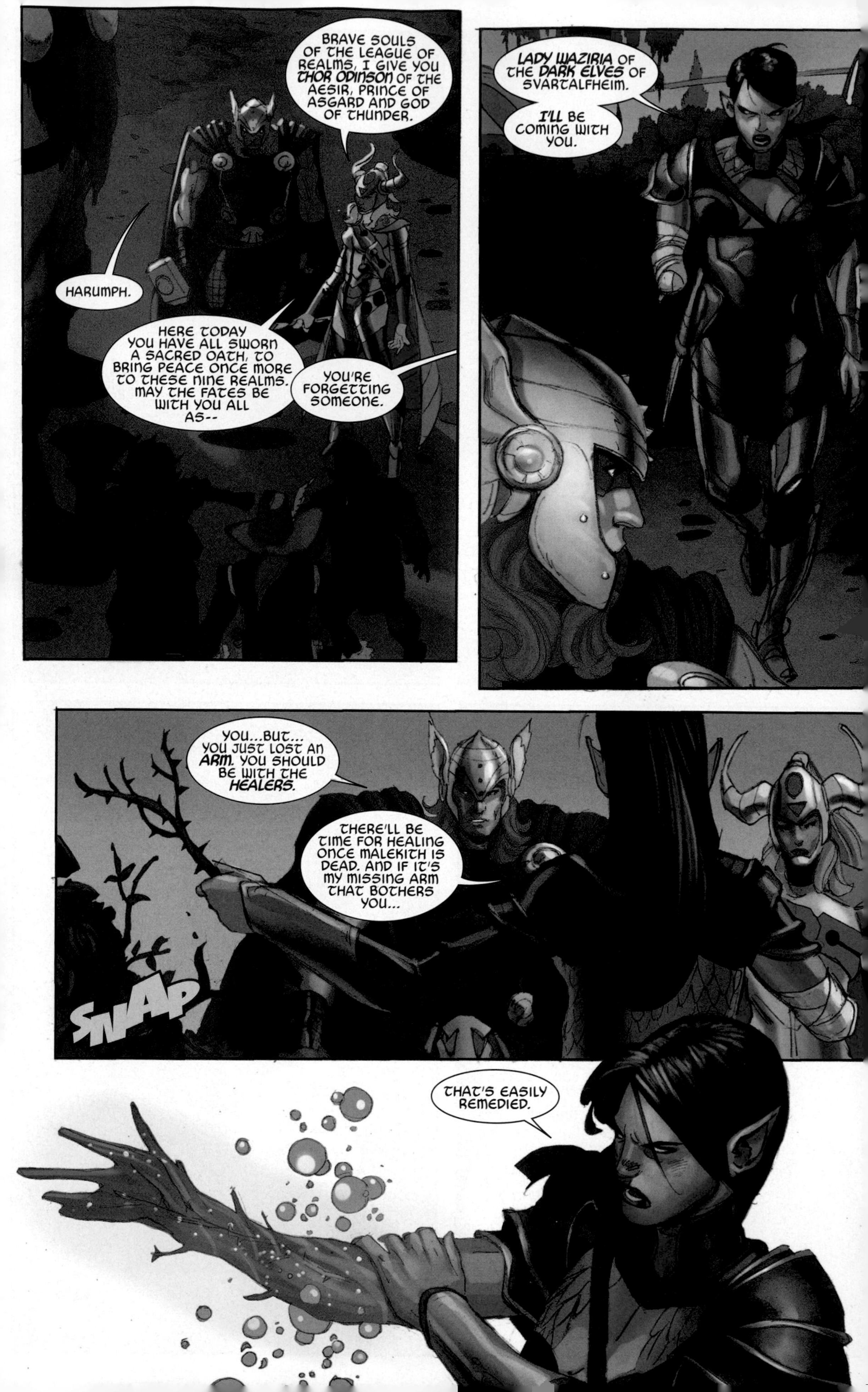
BRAVE SOULS OF THE LEAGUE OF REALMS, I GIVE YOU THOR ODINSON OF THE AESIR, PRINCE OF ASGARD AND GOD OF THUNDER.
HARUMPH.
HERE TODAY YOU HAVE ALL SWORN A SACRED OATH, TO BRING PEACE ONCE MORE TO THESE NINE REALMS. MAY THE FATES BE WITH YOU ALL AS--
YOU'RE FORGETTING SOMEONE.
LADY WAZIRIA OF THE DARK ELVES OF SVARTALFHEIM.
I'LL BE COMING WITH YOU.
YOU...BUT... YOU JUST LOST AN ARM. YOU SHOULD BE WITH THE HEALERS.
THERE'LL BE TIME FOR HEALING ONCE MALEKITH IS DEAD. AND IF IT'S MY MISSING ARM THAT BOTHERS YOU...
SNAP
THAT'S EASILY REMEDIED.

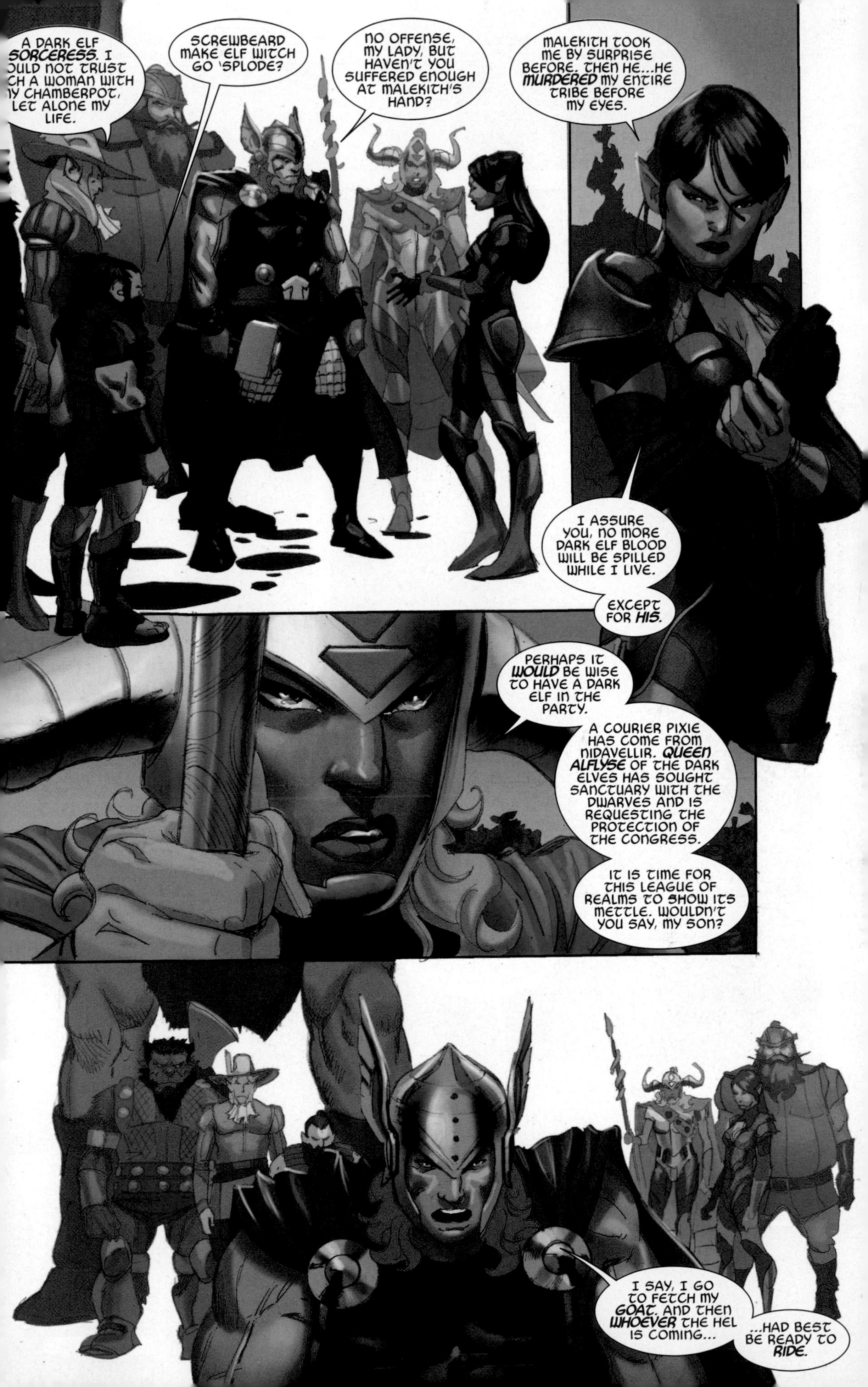
A DARK ELF SORCERESS. I OULD NOT TRUST CH A WOMAN WITH Y CHAMBERPOT, LET ALONE MY LIFE.
SCREWBEARD MAKE ELF WITCH GO 'SPLODE?
NO OFFENSE, MY LADY, BUT HAVEN'T YOU SUFFERED ENOUGH AT MALEKITH'S HAND?
MALEKITH TOOK ME BY SURPRISE BEFORE. THEN HE...HE MURDERED MY ENTIRE TRIBE BEFORE MY EYES.
I ASSURE YOU, NO MORE DARK ELF BLOOD WILL BE SPILLED WHILE I LIVE.
EXCEPT FOR HIS.
PERHAPS IT WOULD BE WISE TO HAVE A DARK ELF IN THE PARTY.
A COURIER PIXIE HAS COME FROM NIDAVELLIR. QUEEN ALFLYSE OF THE DARK ELVES HAS SOUGHT SANCTUARY WITH THE DWARVES AND IS REQUESTING THE PROTECTION OF THE CONGRESS.
IT IS TIME FOR THIS LEAGUE OF REALMS TO SHOW ITS METTLE. WOULDN'T YOU SAY, MY SON?
I SAY, I GO TO FETCH MY GOAT. AND THEN WHOEVER THE HEL IS COMING...
...HAD BEST BE READY TO RIDE.

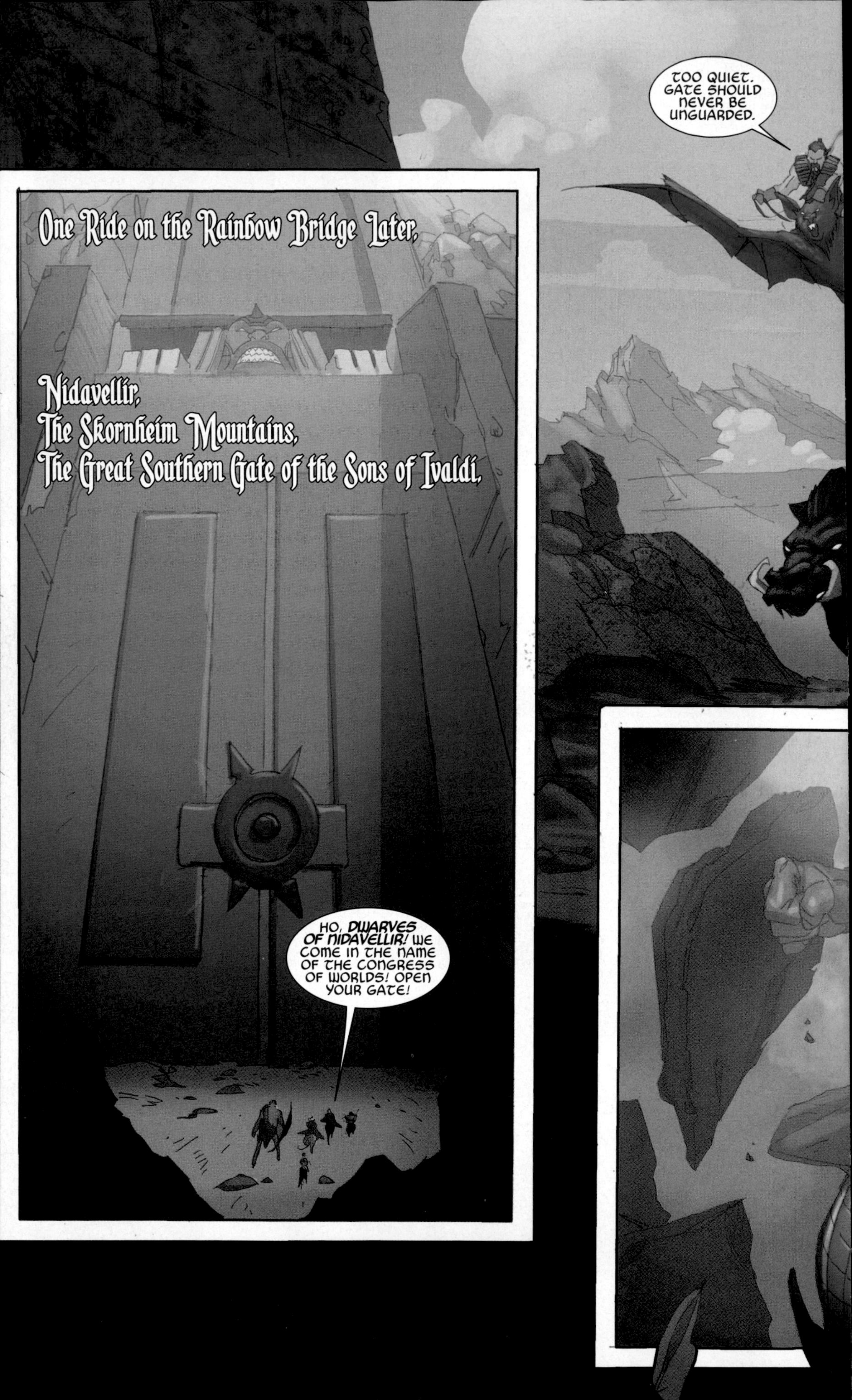
One Ride on the Rainbow Bridge Later,
Nidavellir,
The Skornheim Mountains,
The Great Southern Gate of the Sons of Ivaldi,
HO, DWARVES OF NIDAVELLIR! WE COME IN THE NAME OF THE CONGRESS OF WORLDS! OPEN YOUR GATE!
TOO QUIET. GATE SHOULD NEVER BE UNGUARDED.

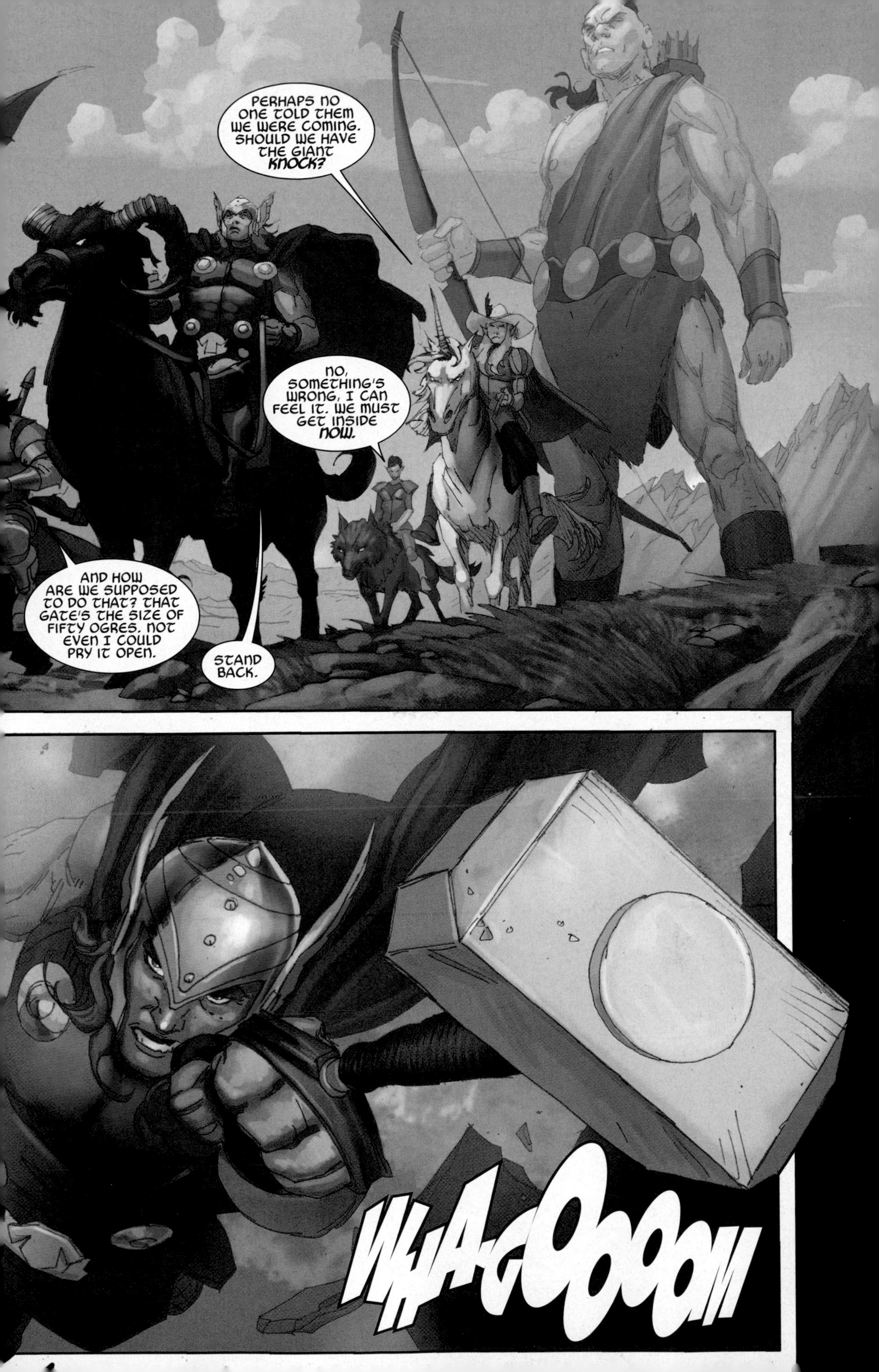
PERHAPS NO ONE TOLD THEM WE WERE COMING. SHOULD WE HAVE THE GIANT *KNOCK?*
NO, SOMETHING'S WRONG, I CAN FEEL IT. WE MUST GET INSIDE *NOW.*
AND HOW ARE WE SUPPOSED TO DO THAT? THAT GATE'S THE SIZE OF FIFTY OGRES. NOT EVEN I COULD PRY IT OPEN.
STAND BACK.
WHAGOOOOM

THE DARK ELVES ARE HERE!
SCUMTONGUE!
MURDERER, WHERE IS YOUR MASTER?!
EVEN IF OLE SCUMTONGUE COULD TALK, SOMETHING TELLS ME HIS ANSWER WOULD BE..."GO BURN IN SURTUR'S BOWELS, ASGARDIAN SWINE."
BURN.
YES, SOMEONE WILL BURN.
KRUUUNG
I SWEAR ON THE EYE OF ODIN, YOU ALL WILL BURN!
AAAAAAAAAARRGGGHHH!!!
HRGHH
AND I SWEAR BY THE TOE OF JORMUNGAND THAT YOU WILL BLEED, GOD OF BLUSTER.
SHUNK

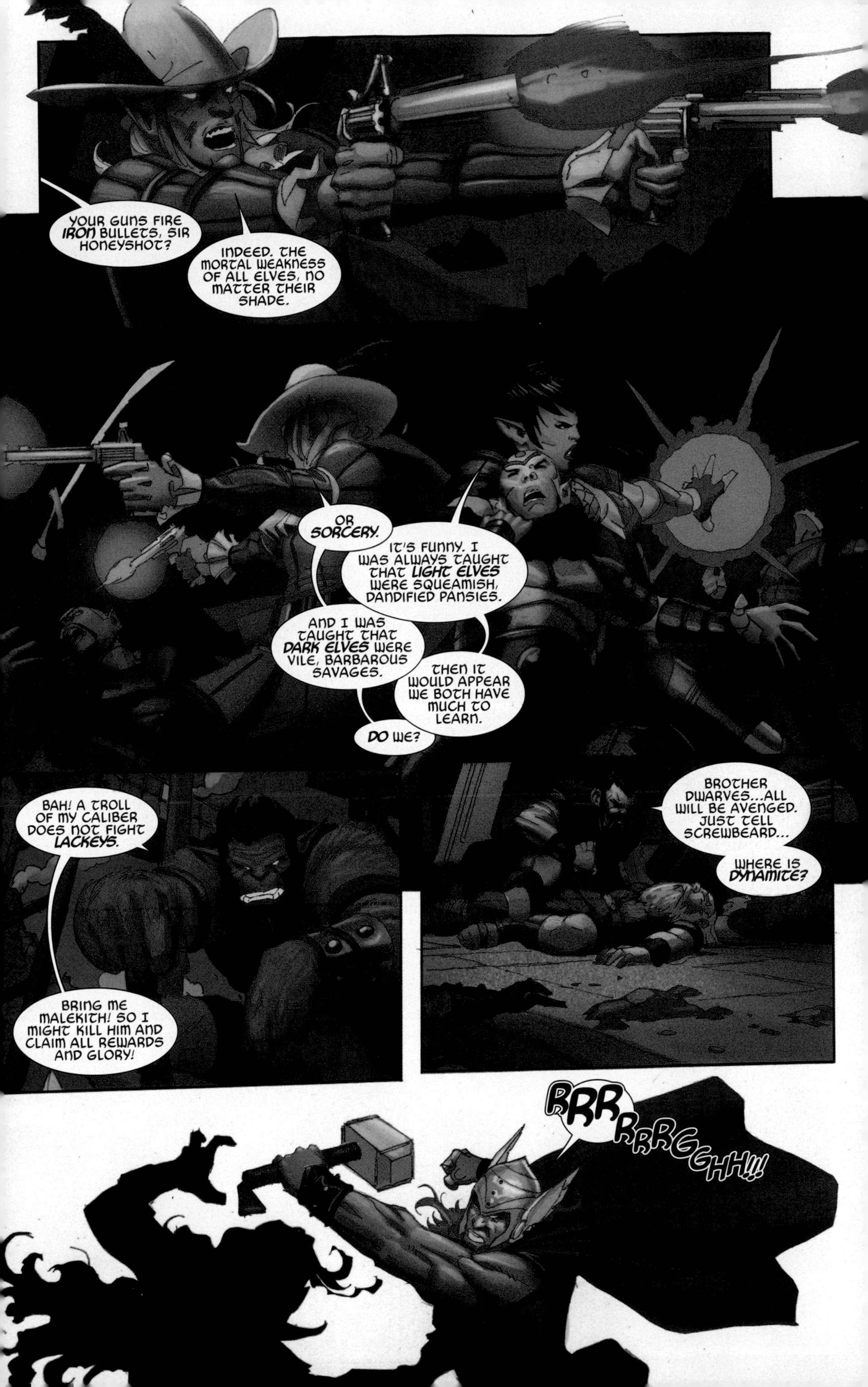
YOUR GUNS FIRE IRON BULLETS, SIR HONEYSHOT?
INDEED. THE MORTAL WEAKNESS OF ALL ELVES, NO MATTER THEIR SHADE.
OR SORCERY.
IT'S FUNNY. I WAS ALWAYS TAUGHT THAT LIGHT ELVES WERE SQUEAMISH, DANDIFIED PANSIES.
AND I WAS TAUGHT THAT DARK ELVES WERE VILE, BARBAROUS SAVAGES.
THEN IT WOULD APPEAR WE BOTH HAVE MUCH TO LEARN.
DO WE?
BAH! A TROLL OF MY CALIBER DOES NOT FIGHT LACKEYS.
BRING ME MALEKITH! SO I MIGHT KILL HIM AND CLAIM ALL REWARDS AND GLORY!
BROTHER DWARVES...ALL WILL BE AVENGED. JUST TELL SCREWBEARD...
WHERE IS DYNAMITE?
RRRRRRGGHH!!!

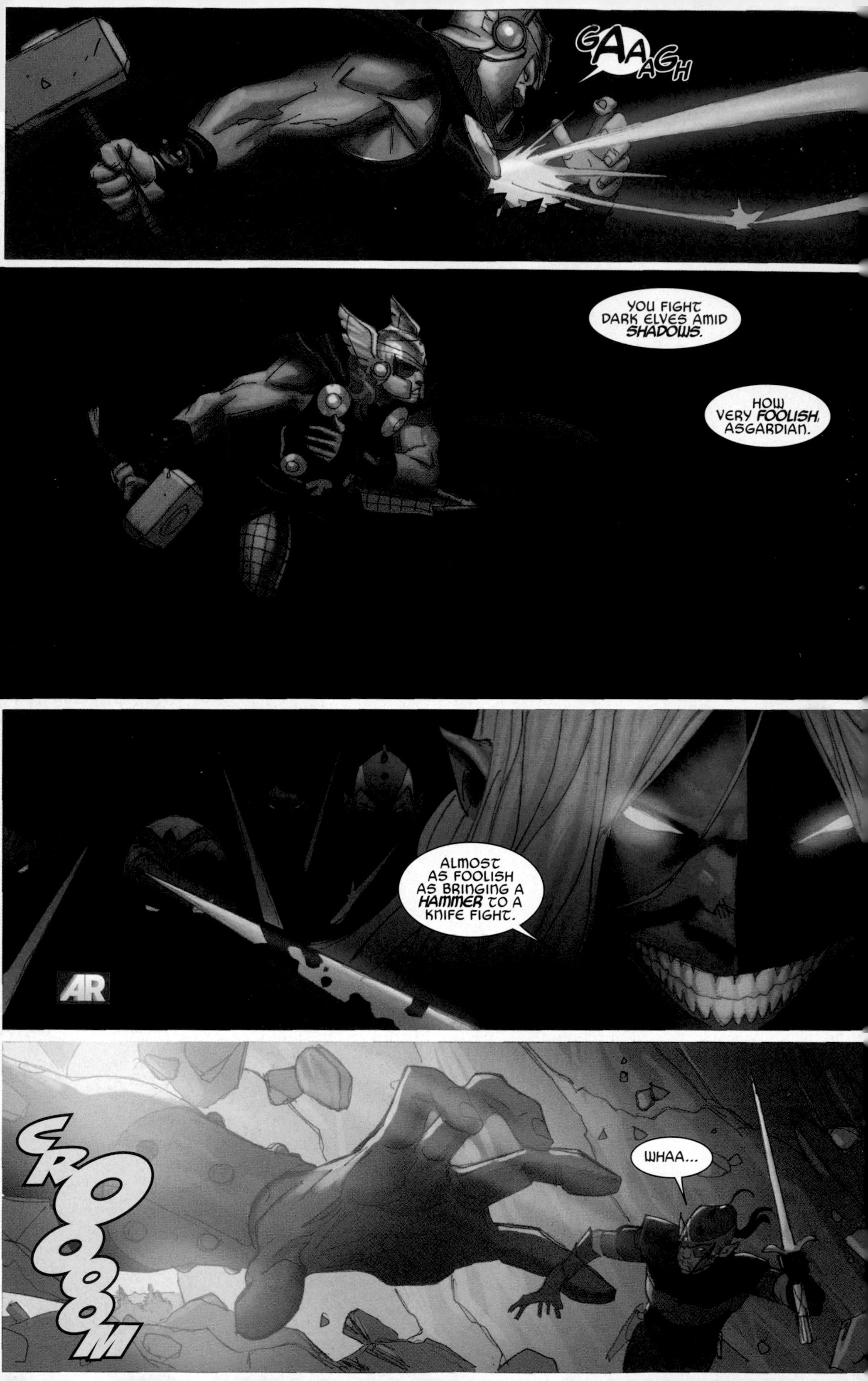
GAAAGH
YOU FIGHT DARK ELVES AMID SHADOWS.
HOW VERY FOOLISH, ASGARDIAN.
ALMOST AS FOOLISH AS BRINGING A HAMMER TO A KNIFE FIGHT.
AR
CROOOOOM
WHAA...

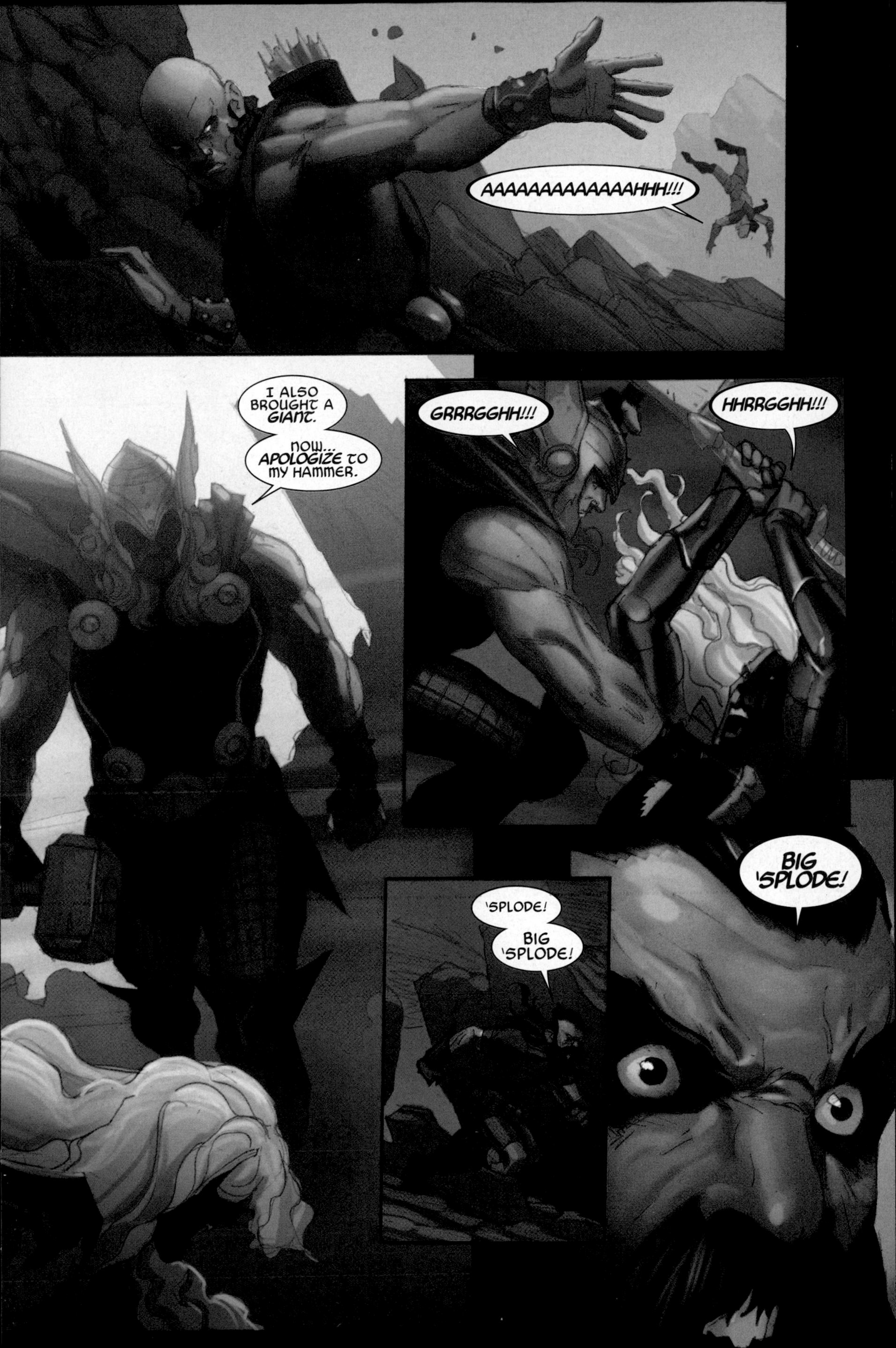
AAAAAAAAAAAAAAHHH!!!
I ALSO BROUGHT A GIANT.
NOW... APOLOGIZE TO MY HAMMER.
GRRRGGHH!!!
HHRRGGHH!!!
BIG 'SPLODE!
'SPLODE!
BIG 'SPLODE!

WHABOOOOOM!!
Moments Later,
I'M GOING TO MURDER THAT BLASTED DWARF! HE NEARLY BURIED US ALL!
SCREWBEARD KILL MANY ELVES.
KILL FEW MORE IF YOU NOT LIKE IT.
GRAAAGH, WHO DID THAT? I'LL GRIND THEIR BONES TO GOULASH!
THANK HEAVENS, THE TROLL SURVIVED.
WHERE'S MALEKITH? IS HE DEAD?
MALEKITH ESCAPED. AGAIN
ANY SIGN OF QUEEN ALFLYSE AND HER MEN?
PERHAPS. IT'S HARD TO TELL...

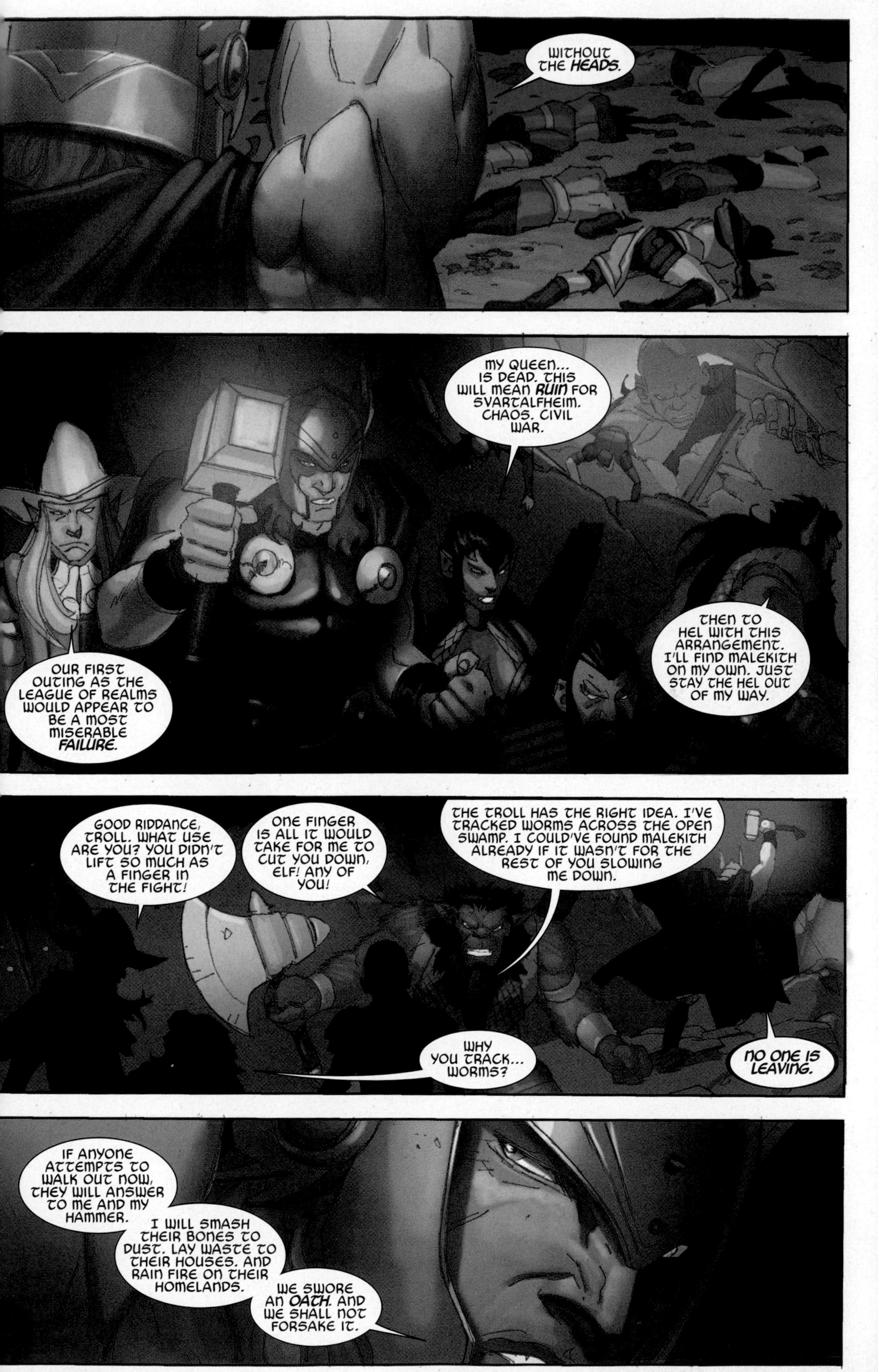
WITHOUT THE HEADS.
MY QUEEN... IS DEAD. THIS WILL MEAN RUIN FOR SVARTALFHEIM. CHAOS. CIVIL WAR.
OUR FIRST OUTING AS THE LEAGUE OF REALMS WOULD APPEAR TO BE A MOST MISERABLE FAILURE.
THEN TO HEL WITH THIS ARRANGEMENT. I'LL FIND MALEKITH ON MY OWN. JUST STAY THE HEL OUT OF MY WAY.
GOOD RIDDANCE, TROLL. WHAT USE ARE YOU? YOU DIDN'T LIFT SO MUCH AS A FINGER IN THE FIGHT!
ONE FINGER IS ALL IT WOULD TAKE FOR ME TO CUT YOU DOWN, ELF! ANY OF YOU!
THE TROLL HAS THE RIGHT IDEA. I'VE TRACKED WORMS ACROSS THE OPEN SWAMP. I COULD'VE FOUND MALEKITH ALREADY IF IT WASN'T FOR THE REST OF YOU SLOWING ME DOWN.
WHY YOU TRACK... WORMS?
NO ONE IS LEAVING.
IF ANYONE ATTEMPTS TO WALK OUT NOW, THEY WILL ANSWER TO ME AND MY HAMMER.
I WILL SMASH THEIR BONES TO DUST. LAY WASTE TO THEIR HOUSES. AND RAIN FIRE ON THEIR HOMELANDS.
WE SWORE AN OATH. AND WE SHALL NOT FORSAKE IT.

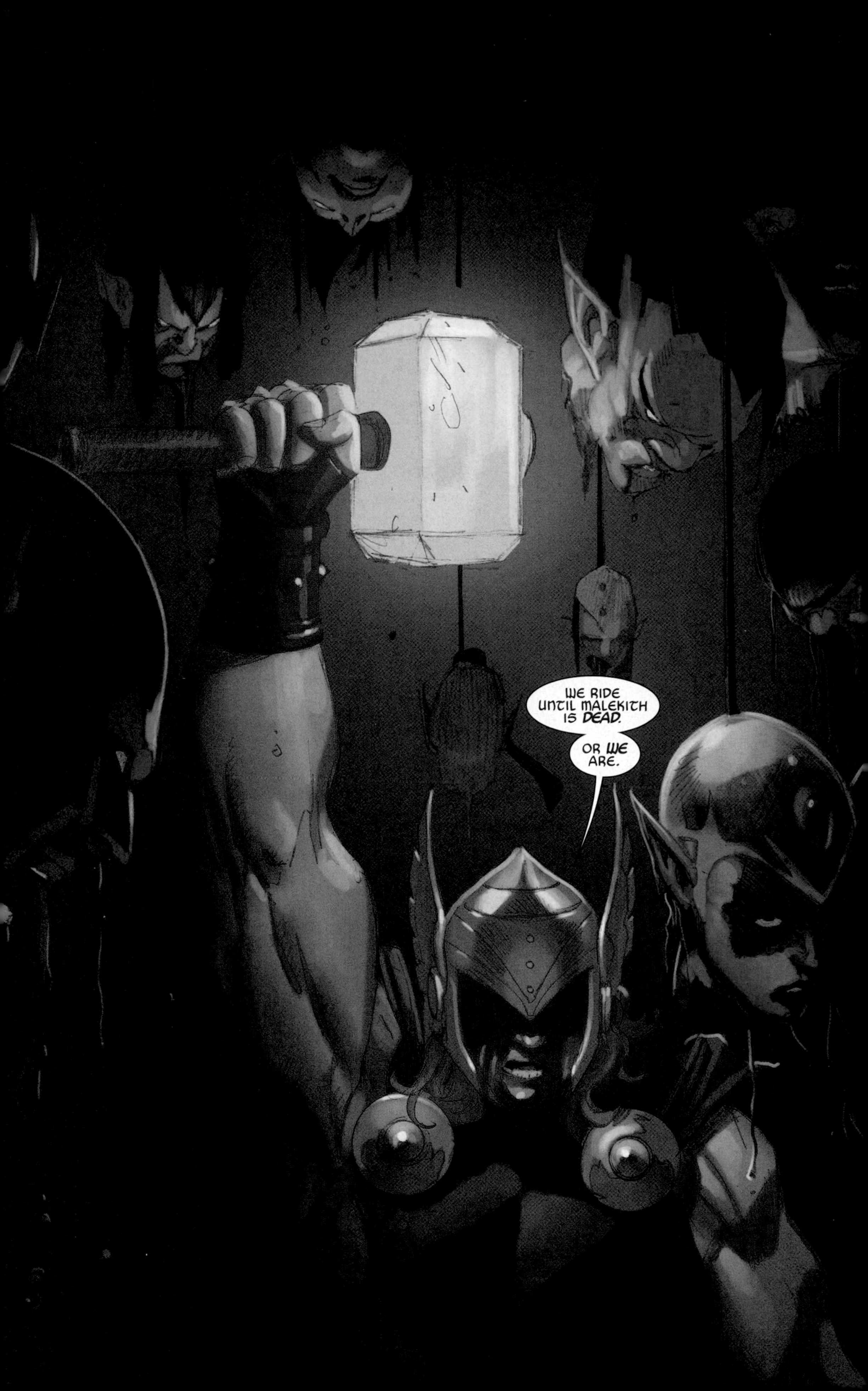
WE RIDE UNTIL MALEKITH IS **DEAD**.
OR **WE** ARE.

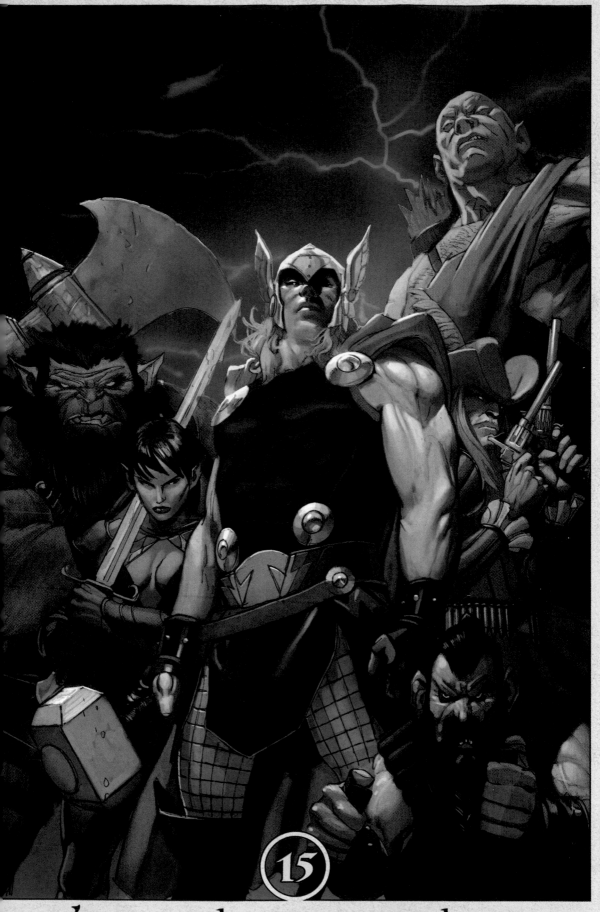

15

BURY MY HEART IN JOTUNHEIM

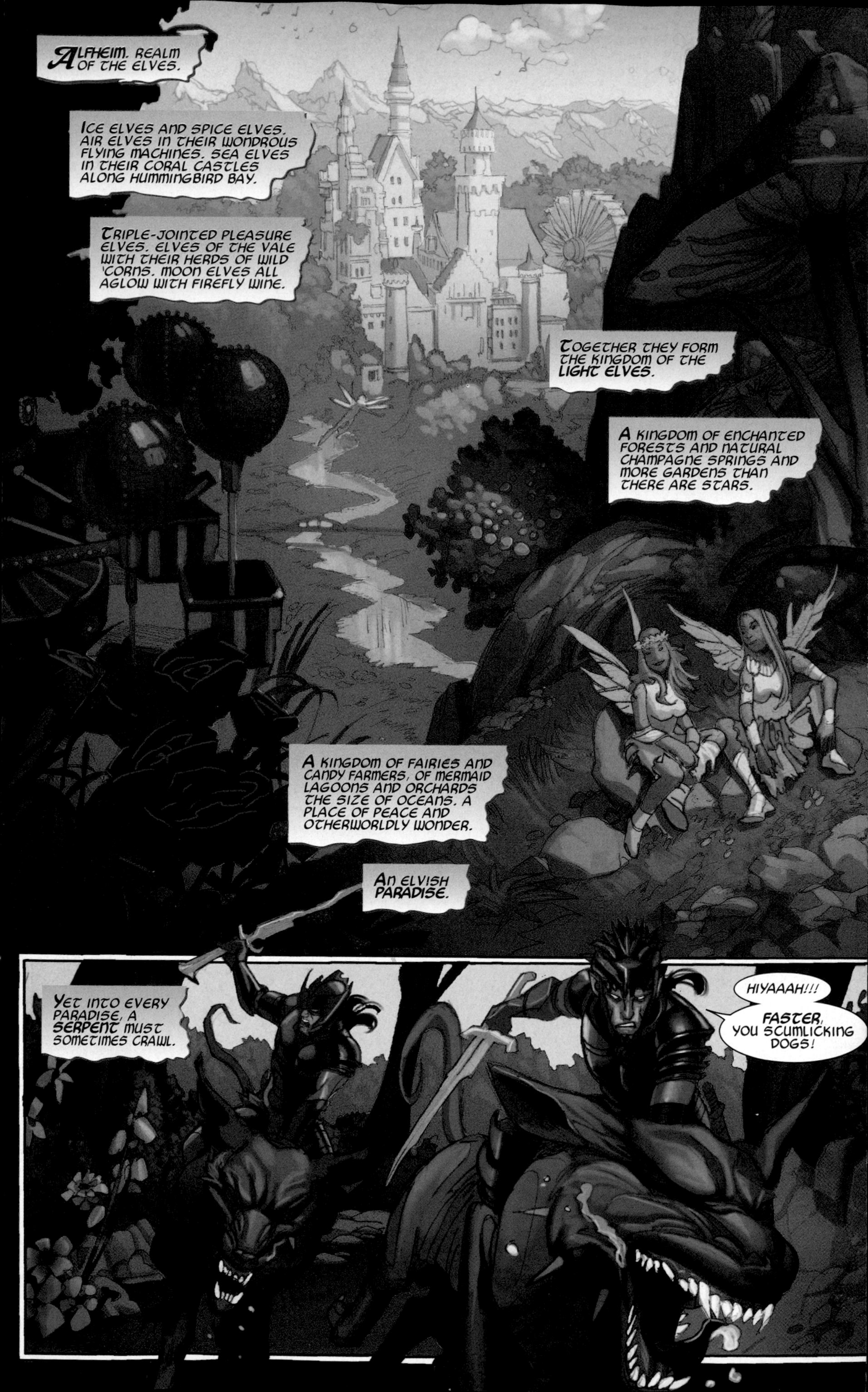

ALFHEIM. REALM OF THE ELVES.
ICE ELVES AND SPICE ELVES. AIR ELVES IN THEIR WONDROUS FLYING MACHINES. SEA ELVES IN THEIR CORAL CASTLES ALONG HUMMINGBIRD BAY.
TRIPLE-JOINTED PLEASURE ELVES. ELVES OF THE VALE WITH THEIR HERDS OF WILD 'CORNS. MOON ELVES ALL AGLOW WITH FIREFLY WINE.
TOGETHER THEY FORM THE KINGDOM OF THE LIGHT ELVES.
A KINGDOM OF ENCHANTED FORESTS AND NATURAL CHAMPAGNE SPRINGS AND MORE GARDENS THAN THERE ARE STARS.
A KINGDOM OF FAIRIES AND CANDY FARMERS, OF MERMAID LAGOONS AND ORCHARDS THE SIZE OF OCEANS. A PLACE OF PEACE AND OTHERWORLDLY WONDER.
AN ELVISH PARADISE.
YET INTO EVERY PARADISE, A SERPENT MUST SOMETIMES CRAWL.
HIYAAAH!!!
FASTER, YOU SCUMLICKING DOGS!

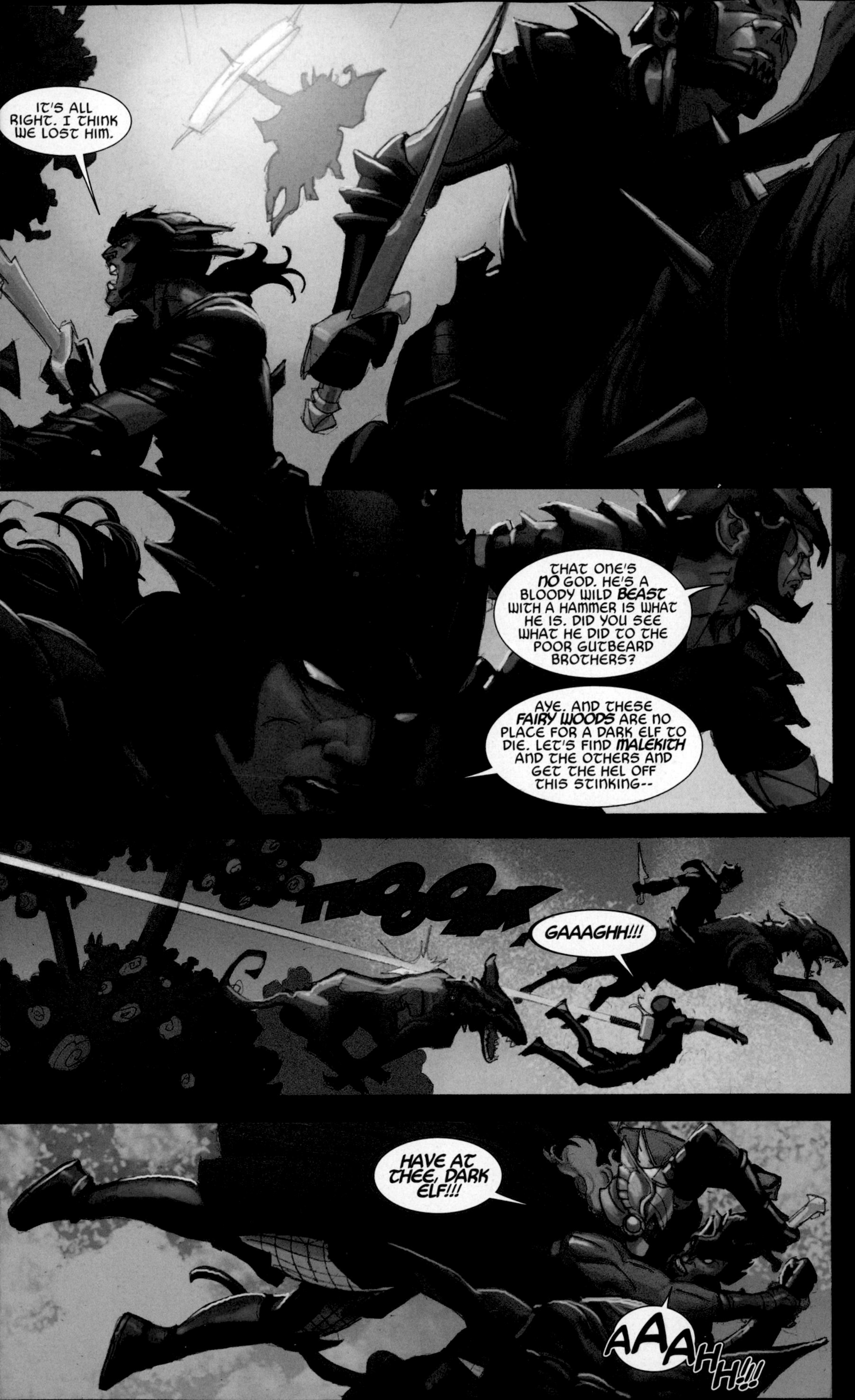
IT'S ALL RIGHT. I THINK WE LOST HIM.
THAT ONE'S NO GOD. HE'S A BLOODY WILD BEAST WITH A HAMMER IS WHAT HE IS. DID YOU SEE WHAT HE DID TO THE POOR GUTBEARD BROTHERS?
AYE. AND THESE FAIRY WOODS ARE NO PLACE FOR A DARK ELF TO DIE. LET'S FIND MALEKITH AND THE OTHERS AND GET THE HEL OFF THIS STINKING--
GAAAGHH!!!
HAVE AT THEE, DARK ELF!!!
AAAHHH!!!

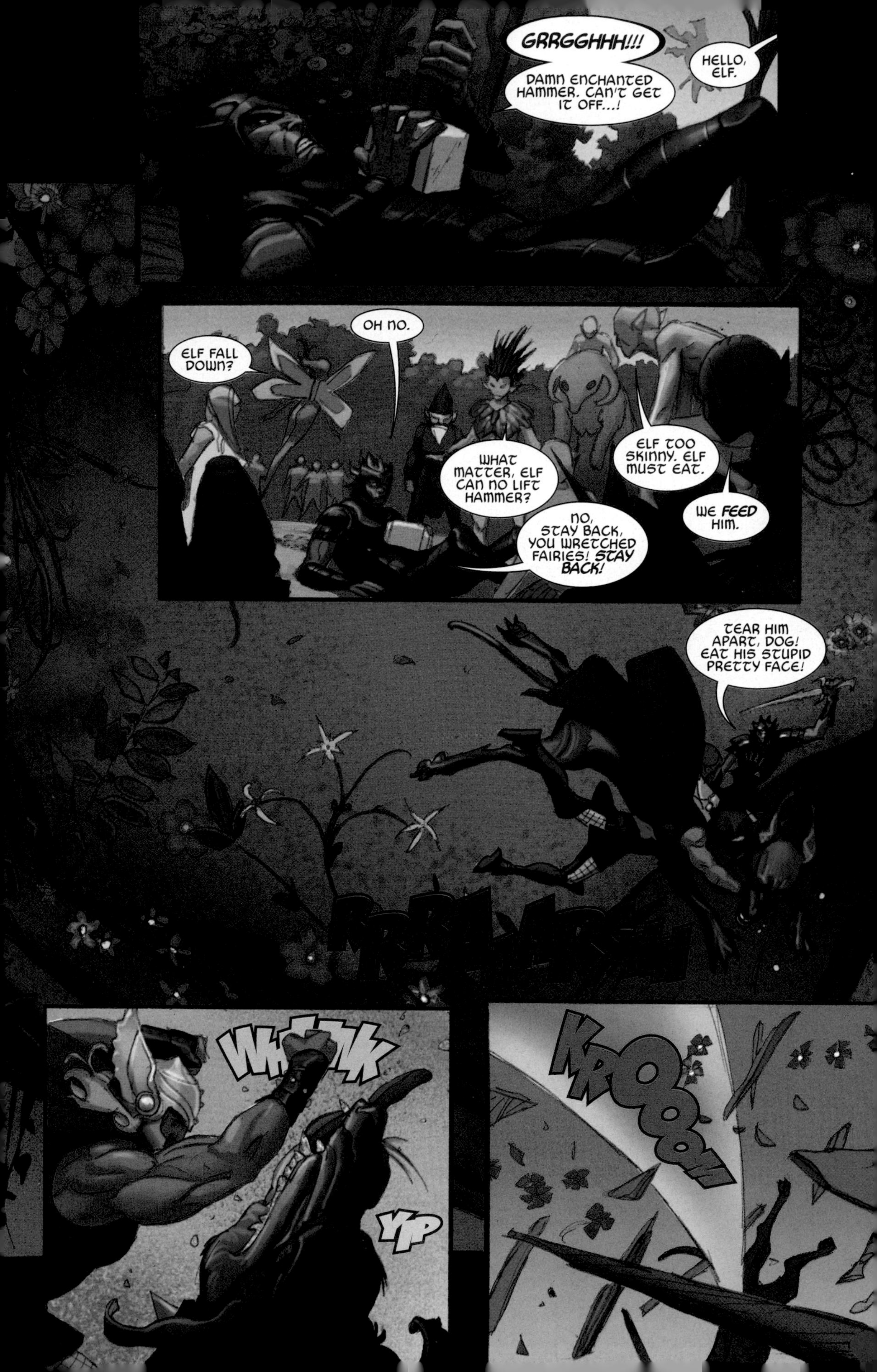
GRRGGHHH!!!
DAMN ENCHANTED HAMMER. CAN'T GET IT OFF...!
HELLO, ELF.
ELF FALL DOWN?
OH NO.
WHAT MATTER, ELF CAN NO LIFT HAMMER?
ELF TOO SKINNY. ELF MUST EAT.
WE FEED HIM.
NO, STAY BACK, YOU WRETCHED FAIRIES! STAY BACK!
TEAR HIM APART, DOG! EAT HIS STUPID PRETTY FACE!
WHTZK
YIP
KROOOOM

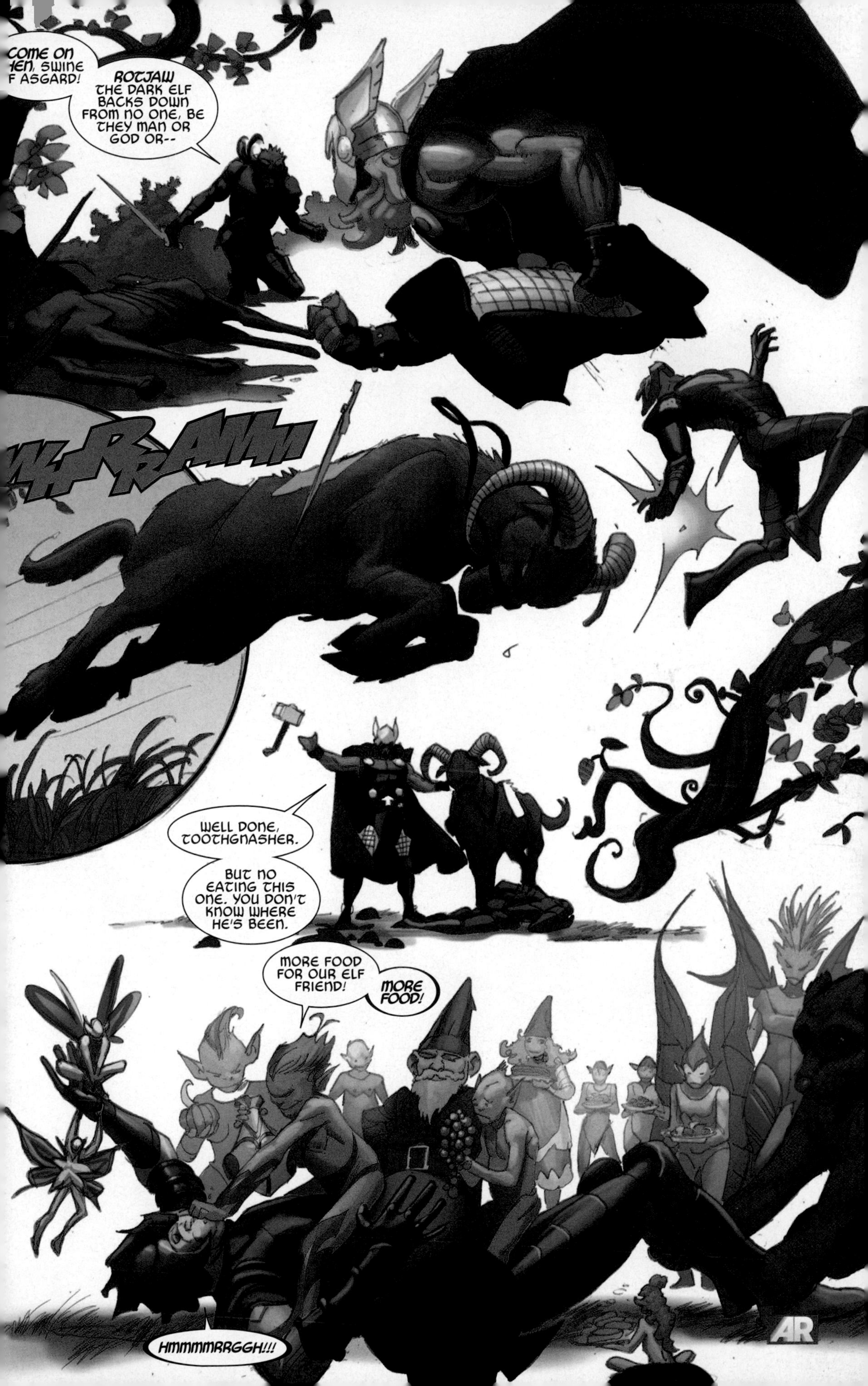
COME ON HEN, SWINE F ASGARD!
ROTJAW THE DARK ELF BACKS DOWN FROM NO ONE, BE THEY MAN OR GOD OR--
WHRRAMM
WELL DONE, TOOTHGNASHER.
BUT NO EATING THIS ONE. YOU DON'T KNOW WHERE HE'S BEEN.
MORE FOOD FOR OUR ELF FRIEND!
MORE FOOD!
HMMMMRRGGH!!!
AR

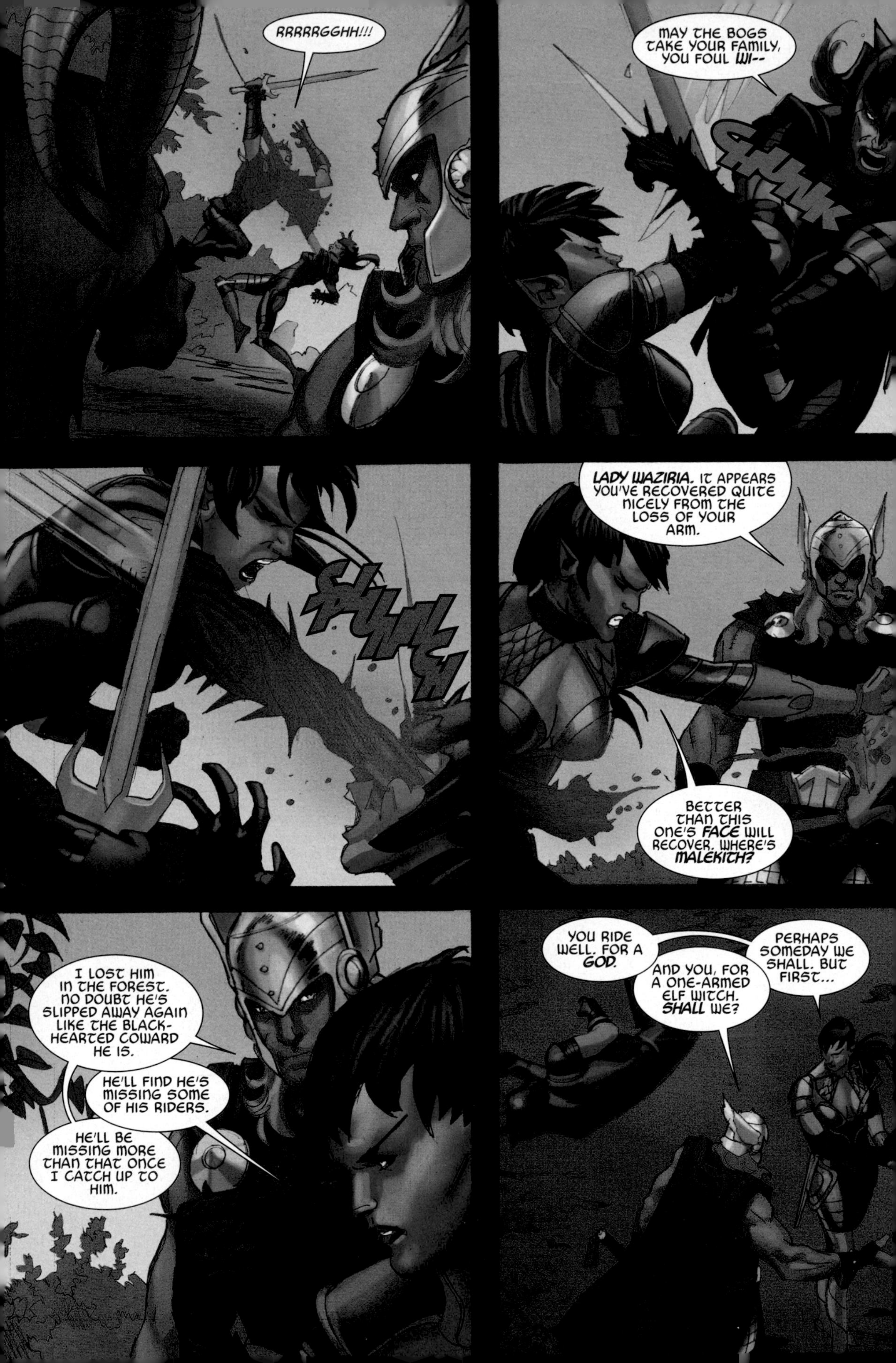
BRRRRGGHH!!!
MAY THE BOGS TAKE YOUR FAMILY, YOU FOUL WI--
CHUNK
SHLUNCH
LADY WAZIRIA. IT APPEARS YOU'VE RECOVERED QUITE NICELY FROM THE LOSS OF YOUR ARM.
BETTER THAN THIS ONE'S FACE WILL RECOVER. WHERE'S MALEKITH?
I LOST HIM IN THE FOREST. NO DOUBT HE'S SLIPPED AWAY AGAIN LIKE THE BLACK-HEARTED COWARD HE IS.
HE'LL FIND HE'S MISSING SOME OF HIS RIDERS.
HE'LL BE MISSING MORE THAN THAT ONCE I CATCH UP TO HIM.
YOU RIDE WELL. FOR A GOD.
AND YOU, FOR A ONE-ARMED ELF WITCH. SHALL WE?
PERHAPS SOMEDAY WE SHALL. BUT FIRST...

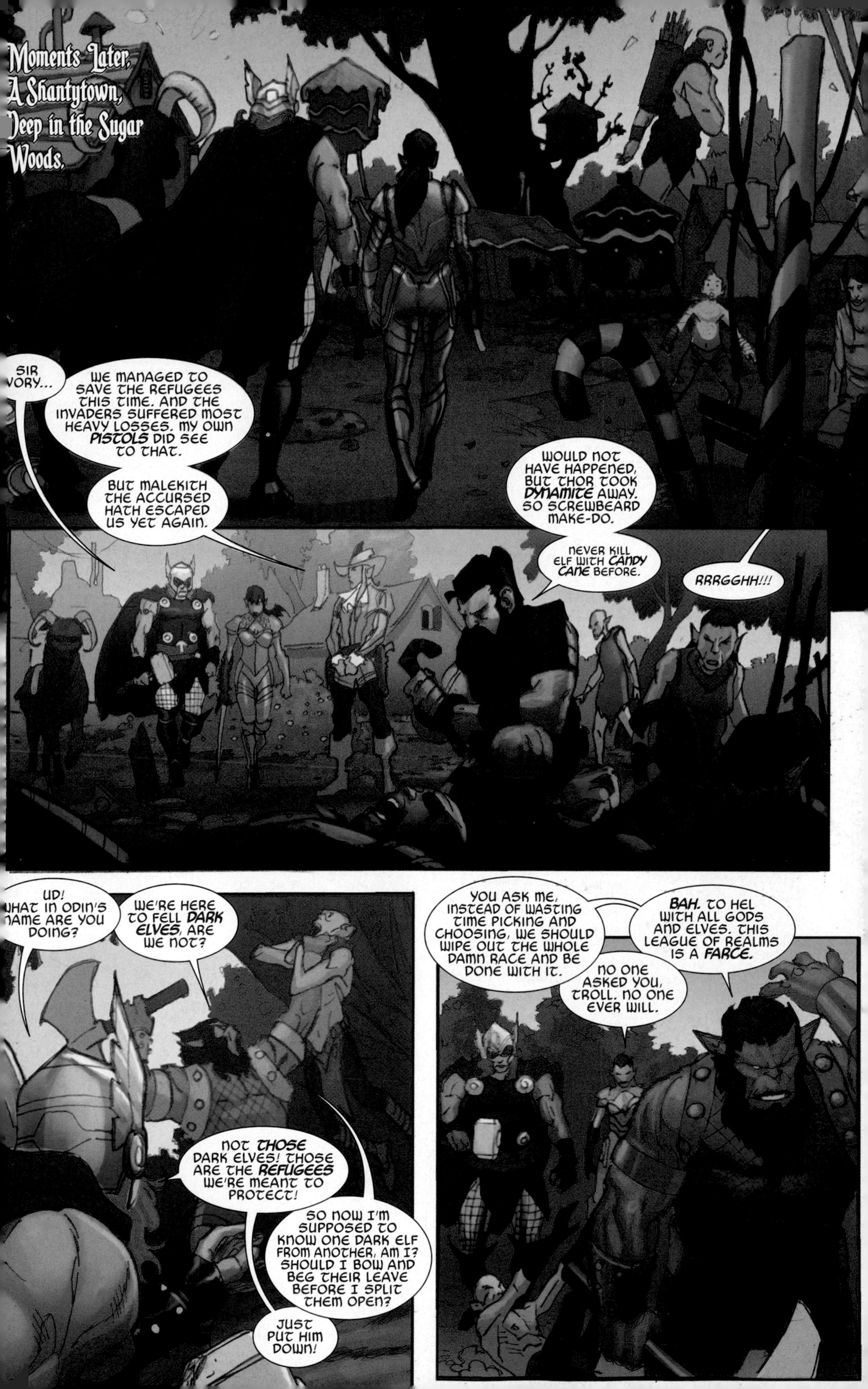
Moments Later, A Shantytown, Deep in the Sugar Woods.
SIR IVORY...
WE MANAGED TO SAVE THE REFUGEES THIS TIME. AND THE INVADERS SUFFERED MOST HEAVY LOSSES. MY OWN PISTOLS DID SEE TO THAT.
BUT MALEKITH THE ACCURSED HATH ESCAPED US YET AGAIN.
WOULD NOT HAVE HAPPENED, BUT THOR TOOK DYNAMITE AWAY. SO SCREWBEARD MAKE-DO.
NEVER KILL ELF WITH CANDY CANE BEFORE.
RRRGGHH!!!
UD! WHAT IN ODIN'S NAME ARE YOU DOING?
WE'RE HERE TO FELL DARK ELVES, ARE WE NOT?
NOT THOSE DARK ELVES! THOSE ARE THE REFUGEES WE'RE MEANT TO PROTECT!
SO NOW I'M SUPPOSED TO KNOW ONE DARK ELF FROM ANOTHER, AM I? SHOULD I BOW AND BEG THEIR LEAVE BEFORE I SPLIT THEM OPEN?
JUST PUT HIM DOWN!
YOU ASK ME, INSTEAD OF WASTING TIME PICKING AND CHOOSING, WE SHOULD WIPE OUT THE WHOLE DAMN RACE AND BE DONE WITH IT.
BAH. TO HEL WITH ALL GODS AND ELVES. THIS LEAGUE OF REALMS IS A FARCE.
NO ONE ASKED YOU, TROLL. NO ONE EVER WILL.

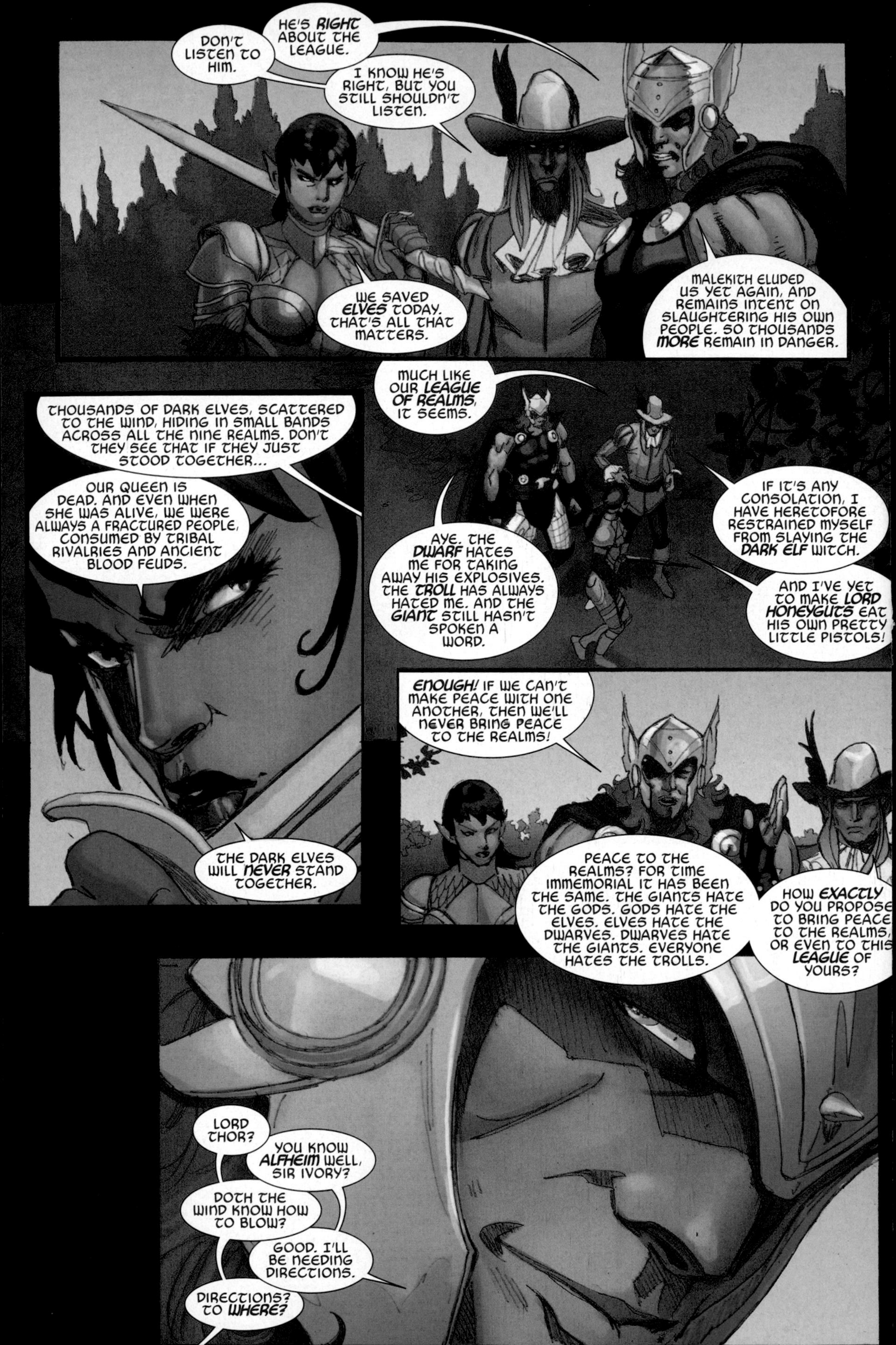
DON'T LISTEN TO HIM.
HE'S RIGHT ABOUT THE LEAGUE.
I KNOW HE'S RIGHT, BUT YOU STILL SHOULDN'T LISTEN.
WE SAVED ELVES TODAY. THAT'S ALL THAT MATTERS.
MALEKITH ELUDED US YET AGAIN, AND REMAINS INTENT ON SLAUGHTERING HIS OWN PEOPLE. SO THOUSANDS MORE REMAIN IN DANGER.
THOUSANDS OF DARK ELVES, SCATTERED TO THE WIND, HIDING IN SMALL BANDS ACROSS ALL THE NINE REALMS. DON'T THEY SEE THAT IF THEY JUST STOOD TOGETHER...
OUR QUEEN IS DEAD. AND EVEN WHEN SHE WAS ALIVE, WE WERE ALWAYS A FRACTURED PEOPLE, CONSUMED BY TRIBAL RIVALRIES AND ANCIENT BLOOD FEUDS.
THE DARK ELVES WILL NEVER STAND TOGETHER.
MUCH LIKE OUR LEAGUE OF REALMS, IT SEEMS.
AYE. THE DWARF HATES ME FOR TAKING AWAY HIS EXPLOSIVES. THE TROLL HAS ALWAYS HATED ME. AND THE GIANT STILL HASN'T SPOKEN A WORD.
IF IT'S ANY CONSOLATION, I HAVE HERETOFORE RESTRAINED MYSELF FROM SLAYING THE DARK ELF WITCH.
AND I'VE YET TO MAKE LORD HONEYGUTS EAT HIS OWN PRETTY LITTLE PISTOLS!
ENOUGH! IF WE CAN'T MAKE PEACE WITH ONE ANOTHER, THEN WE'LL NEVER BRING PEACE TO THE REALMS!
PEACE TO THE REALMS? FOR TIME IMMEMORIAL IT HAS BEEN THE SAME. THE GIANTS HATE THE GODS. GODS HATE THE ELVES. ELVES HATE THE DWARVES. DWARVES HATE THE GIANTS. EVERYONE HATES THE TROLLS.
HOW EXACTLY DO YOU PROPOSE TO BRING PEACE TO THE REALMS, OR EVEN TO THIS LEAGUE OF YOURS?
LORD THOR?
YOU KNOW ALFHEIM WELL, SIR IVORY?
DOTH THE WIND KNOW HOW TO BLOW?
GOOD. I'LL BE NEEDING DIRECTIONS.
DIRECTIONS? TO WHERE?

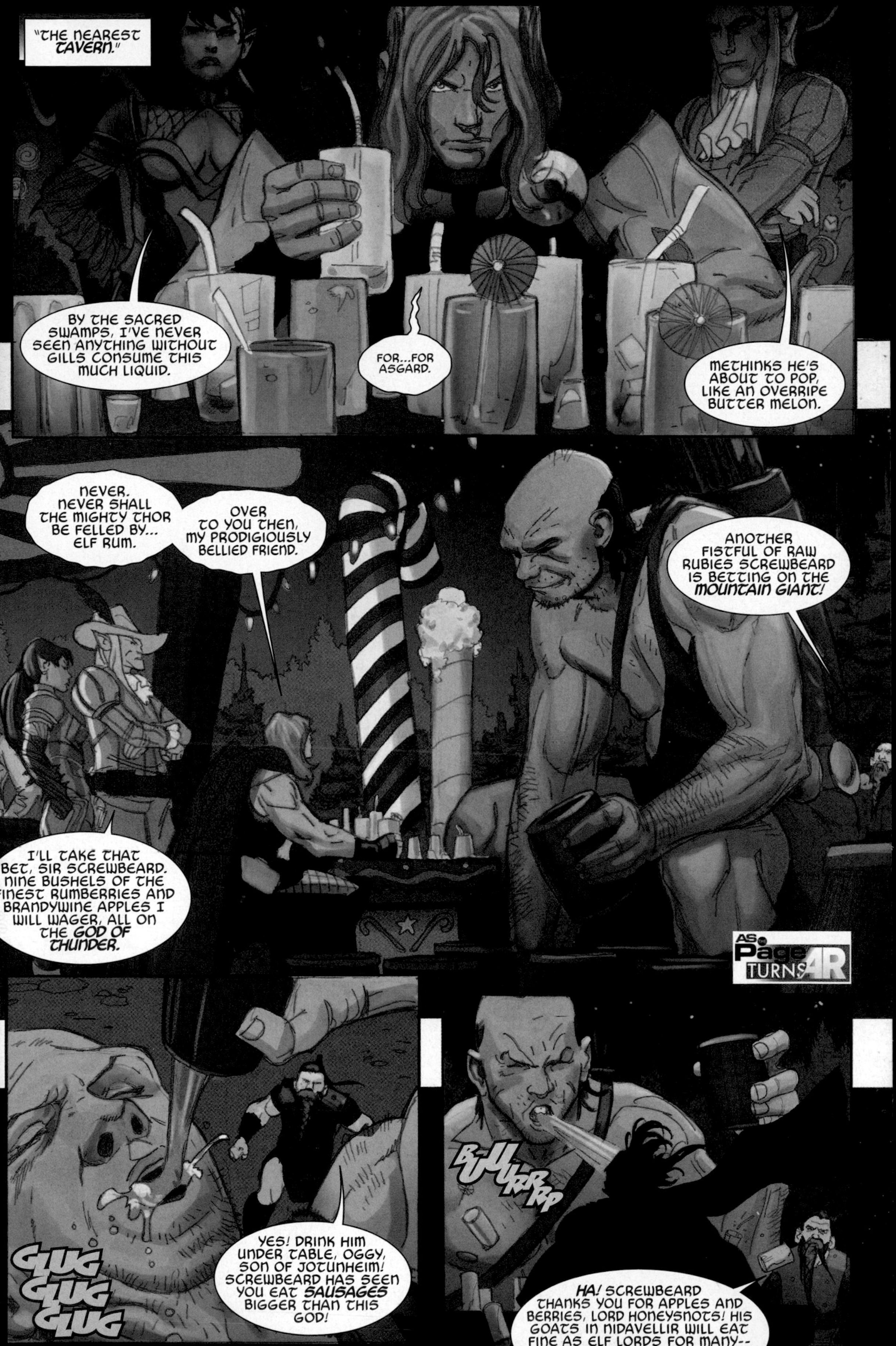
"THE NEAREST TAVERN."
BY THE SACRED SWAMPS, I'VE NEVER SEEN ANYTHING WITHOUT GILLS CONSUME THIS MUCH LIQUID.
FOR...FOR ASGARD.
METHINKS HE'S ABOUT TO POP, LIKE AN OVERRIPE BUTTER MELON.
NEVER. NEVER SHALL THE MIGHTY THOR BE FELLED BY... ELF RUM.
OVER TO YOU THEN, MY PRODIGIOUSLY BELLIED FRIEND.
ANOTHER FISTFUL OF RAW RUBIES SCREWBEARD IS BETTING ON THE MOUNTAIN GIANT!
I'LL TAKE THAT BET, SIR SCREWBEARD. NINE BUSHELS OF THE FINEST RUMBERRIES AND BRANDYWINE APPLES I WILL WAGER, ALL ON THE GOD OF THUNDER.
AS THE Page TURNS AR
GLUG GLUG GLUG
YES! DRINK HIM UNDER TABLE, OGGY, SON OF JOTUNHEIM! SCREWBEARD HAS SEEN YOU EAT SAUSAGES BIGGER THAN THIS GOD!
B-UURRRP
HA! SCREWBEARD THANKS YOU FOR APPLES AND BERRIES, LORD HONEYSNOTS! HIS GOATS IN NIDAVELLIR WILL EAT FINE AS ELF LORDS FOR MANY--

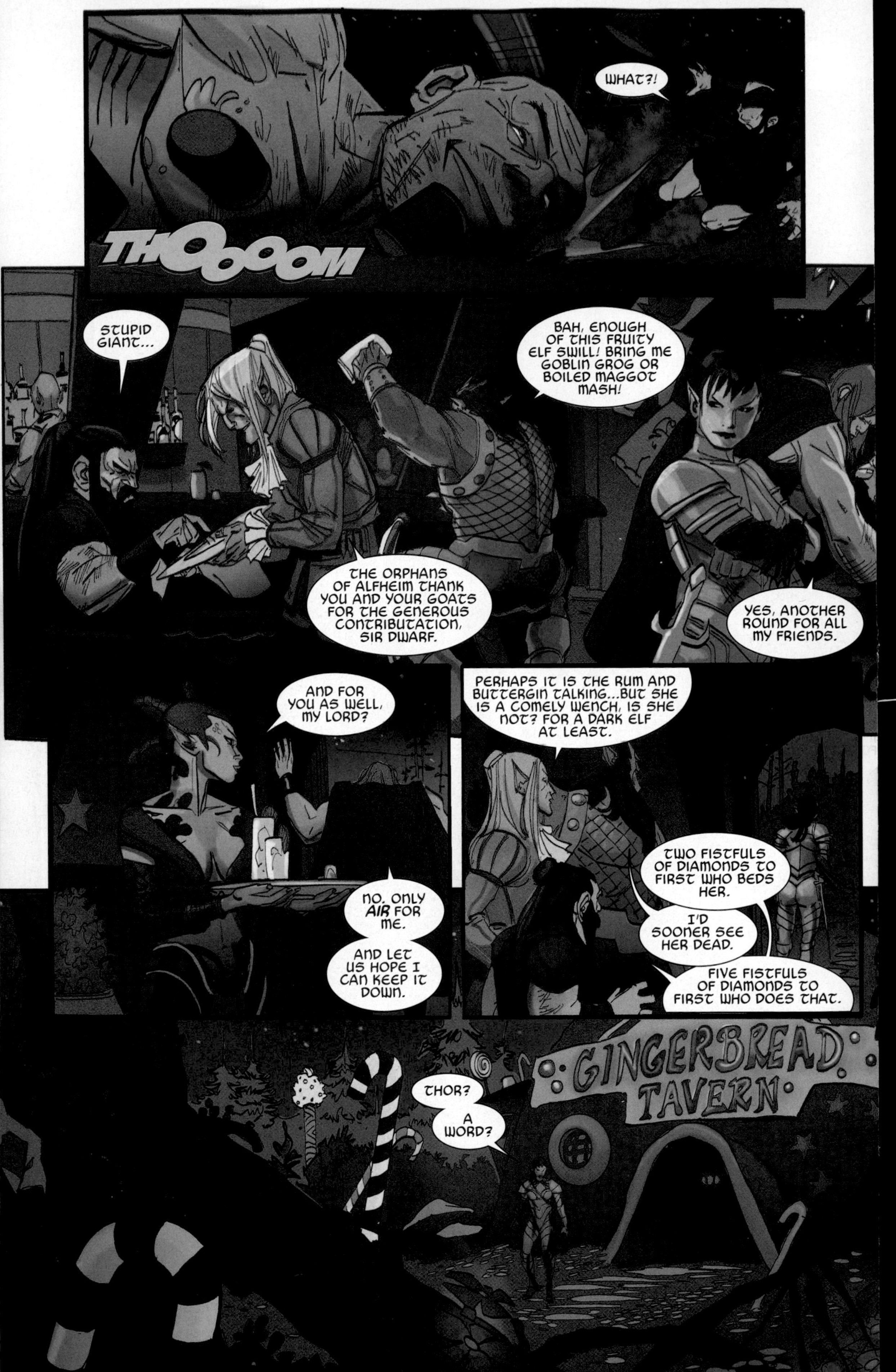
WHAT?!
THOOOOOM
STUPID GIANT...
BAH, ENOUGH OF THIS FRUITY ELF SWILL! BRING ME GOBLIN GROG OR BOILED MAGGOT MASH!
THE ORPHANS OF ALFHEIM THANK YOU AND YOUR GOATS FOR THE GENEROUS CONTRIBUTATION, SIR DWARF.
YES, ANOTHER ROUND FOR ALL MY FRIENDS.
AND FOR YOU AS WELL, MY LORD?
NO. ONLY AIR FOR ME.
AND LET US HOPE I CAN KEEP IT DOWN.
PERHAPS IT IS THE RUM AND BUTTERGIN TALKING...BUT SHE IS A COMELY WENCH, IS SHE NOT? FOR A DARK ELF AT LEAST.
TWO FISTFULS OF DIAMONDS TO FIRST WHO BEDS HER.
I'D SOONER SEE HER DEAD.
FIVE FISTFULS OF DIAMONDS TO FIRST WHO DOES THAT.
GINGERBREAD TAVERN
THOR?
A WORD?

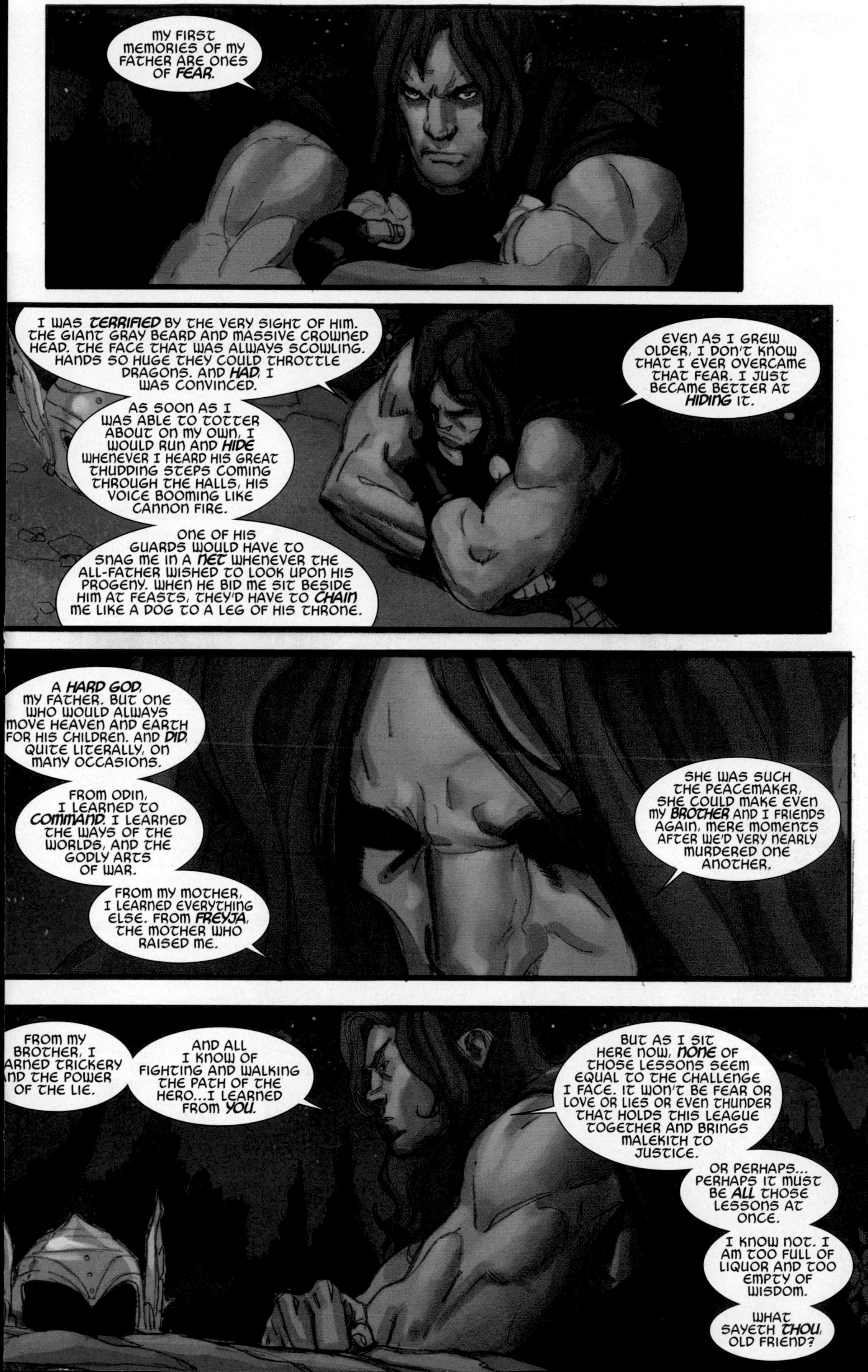
MY FIRST MEMORIES OF MY FATHER ARE ONES OF FEAR.
I WAS TERRIFIED BY THE VERY SIGHT OF HIM. THE GIANT GRAY BEARD AND MASSIVE CROWNED HEAD. THE FACE THAT WAS ALWAYS SCOWLING. HANDS SO HUGE THEY COULD THROTTLE DRAGONS. AND HAD, I WAS CONVINCED.
AS SOON AS I WAS ABLE TO TOTTER ABOUT ON MY OWN, I WOULD RUN AND HIDE WHENEVER I HEARD HIS GREAT THUDDING STEPS COMING THROUGH THE HALLS, HIS VOICE BOOMING LIKE CANNON FIRE.
ONE OF HIS GUARDS WOULD HAVE TO SNAG ME IN A NET WHENEVER THE ALL-FATHER WISHED TO LOOK UPON HIS PROGENY. WHEN HE BID ME SIT BESIDE HIM AT FEASTS, THEY'D HAVE TO CHAIN ME LIKE A DOG TO A LEG OF HIS THRONE.
EVEN AS I GREW OLDER, I DON'T KNOW THAT I EVER OVERCAME THAT FEAR. I JUST BECAME BETTER AT HIDING IT.
A HARD GOD, MY FATHER. BUT ONE WHO WOULD ALWAYS MOVE HEAVEN AND EARTH FOR HIS CHILDREN. AND DID, QUITE LITERALLY, ON MANY OCCASIONS.
FROM ODIN, I LEARNED TO COMMAND. I LEARNED THE WAYS OF THE WORLDS, AND THE GODLY ARTS OF WAR.
FROM MY MOTHER, I LEARNED EVERYTHING ELSE. FROM FREYJA, THE MOTHER WHO RAISED ME.
SHE WAS SUCH THE PEACEMAKER, SHE COULD MAKE EVEN MY BROTHER AND I FRIENDS AGAIN, MERE MOMENTS AFTER WE'D VERY NEARLY MURDERED ONE ANOTHER.
FROM MY BROTHER, I ARNED TRICKERY AND THE POWER OF THE LIE.
AND ALL I KNOW OF FIGHTING AND WALKING THE PATH OF THE HERO...I LEARNED FROM YOU.
BUT AS I SIT HERE NOW, NONE OF THOSE LESSONS SEEM EQUAL TO THE CHALLENGE I FACE. IT WON'T BE FEAR OR LOVE OR LIES OR EVEN THUNDER THAT HOLDS THIS LEAGUE TOGETHER AND BRINGS MALEKITH TO JUSTICE.
OR PERHAPS... PERHAPS IT MUST BE ALL THOSE LESSONS AT ONCE.
I KNOW NOT. I AM TOO FULL OF LIQUOR AND TOO EMPTY OF WISDOM.
WHAT SAYETH THOU, OLD FRIEND?

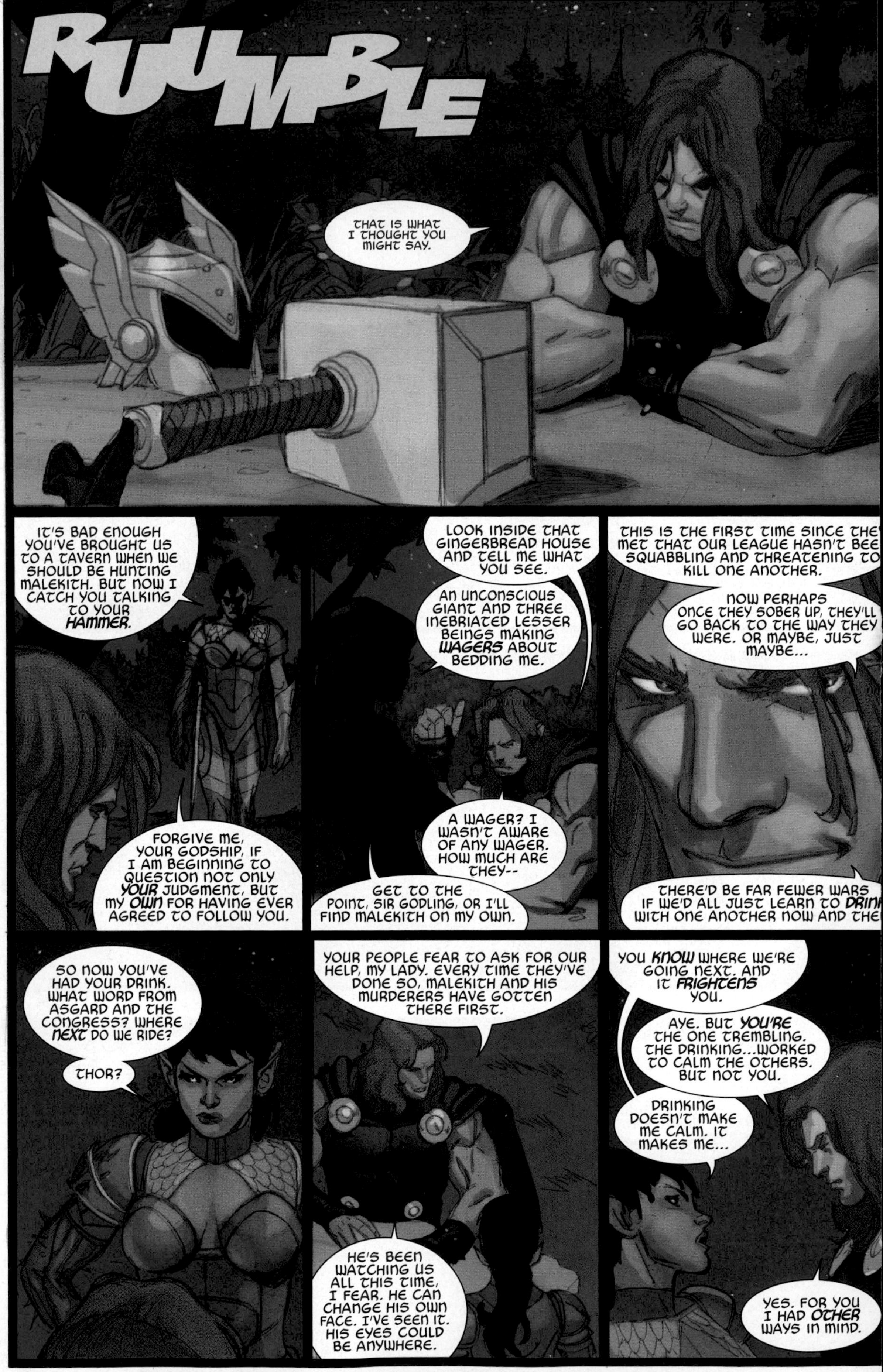
RUUMBLE
THAT IS WHAT I THOUGHT YOU MIGHT SAY.
IT'S BAD ENOUGH YOU'VE BROUGHT US TO A TAVERN WHEN WE SHOULD BE HUNTING MALEKITH. BUT NOW I CATCH YOU TALKING TO YOUR HAMMER.
FORGIVE ME, YOUR GODSHIP, IF I AM BEGINNING TO QUESTION NOT ONLY YOUR JUDGMENT, BUT MY OWN FOR HAVING EVER AGREED TO FOLLOW YOU.
LOOK INSIDE THAT GINGERBREAD HOUSE AND TELL ME WHAT YOU SEE.
AN UNCONSCIOUS GIANT AND THREE INEBRIATED LESSER BEINGS MAKING WAGERS ABOUT BEDDING ME.
A WAGER? I WASN'T AWARE OF ANY WAGER. HOW MUCH ARE THEY--
GET TO THE POINT, SIR GODLING, OR I'LL FIND MALEKITH ON MY OWN.
THIS IS THE FIRST TIME SINCE THE MET THAT OUR LEAGUE HASN'T BEE SQUABBLING AND THREATENING TO KILL ONE ANOTHER.
NOW PERHAPS ONCE THEY SOBER UP, THEY'LL GO BACK TO THE WAY THEY WERE. OR MAYBE, JUST MAYBE...
THERE'D BE FAR FEWER WARS IF WE'D ALL JUST LEARN TO DRIN WITH ONE ANOTHER NOW AND THE
SO NOW YOU'VE HAD YOUR DRINK. WHAT WORD FROM ASGARD AND THE CONGRESS? WHERE NEXT DO WE RIDE?
THOR?
YOUR PEOPLE FEAR TO ASK FOR OUR HELP, MY LADY. EVERY TIME THEY'VE DONE SO, MALEKITH AND HIS MURDERERS HAVE GOTTEN THERE FIRST.
HE'S BEEN WATCHING US ALL THIS TIME, I FEAR. HE CAN CHANGE HIS OWN FACE. I'VE SEEN IT. HIS EYES COULD BE ANYWHERE.
YOU KNOW WHERE WE'RE GOING NEXT. AND IT FRIGHTENS YOU.
AYE. BUT YOU'RE THE ONE TREMBLING. THE DRINKING...WORKED TO CALM THE OTHERS. BUT NOT YOU.
DRINKING DOESN'T MAKE ME CALM. IT MAKES ME...
YES. FOR YOU I HAD OTHER WAYS IN MIND.

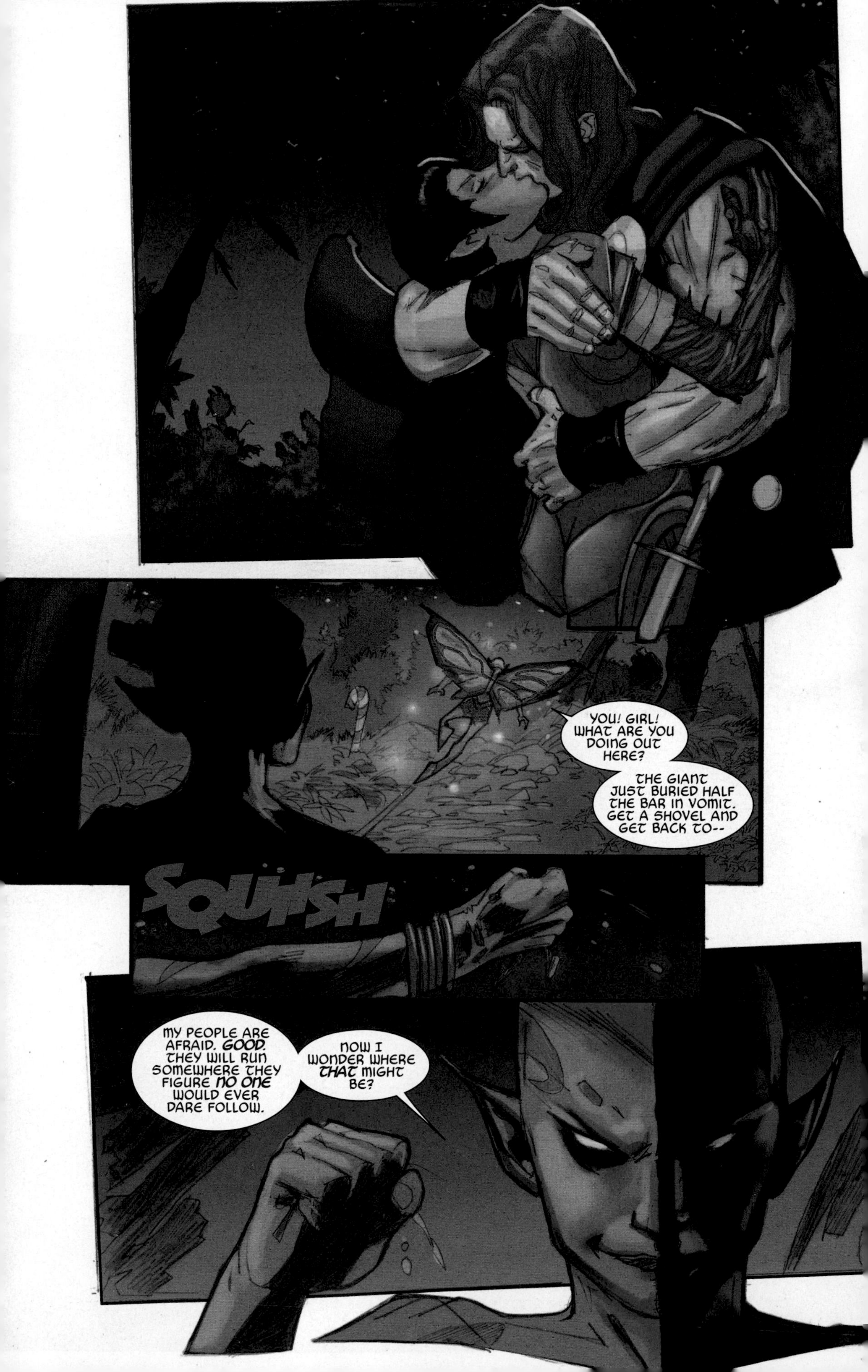
YOU! GIRL! WHAT ARE YOU DOING OUT HERE?
THE GIANT JUST BURIED HALF THE BAR IN VOMIT. GET A SHOVEL AND GET BACK TO--
SQUISH
MY PEOPLE ARE AFRAID. GOOD. THEY WILL RUN SOMEWHERE THEY FIGURE NO ONE WOULD EVER DARE FOLLOW.
NOW I WONDER WHERE THAT MIGHT BE?

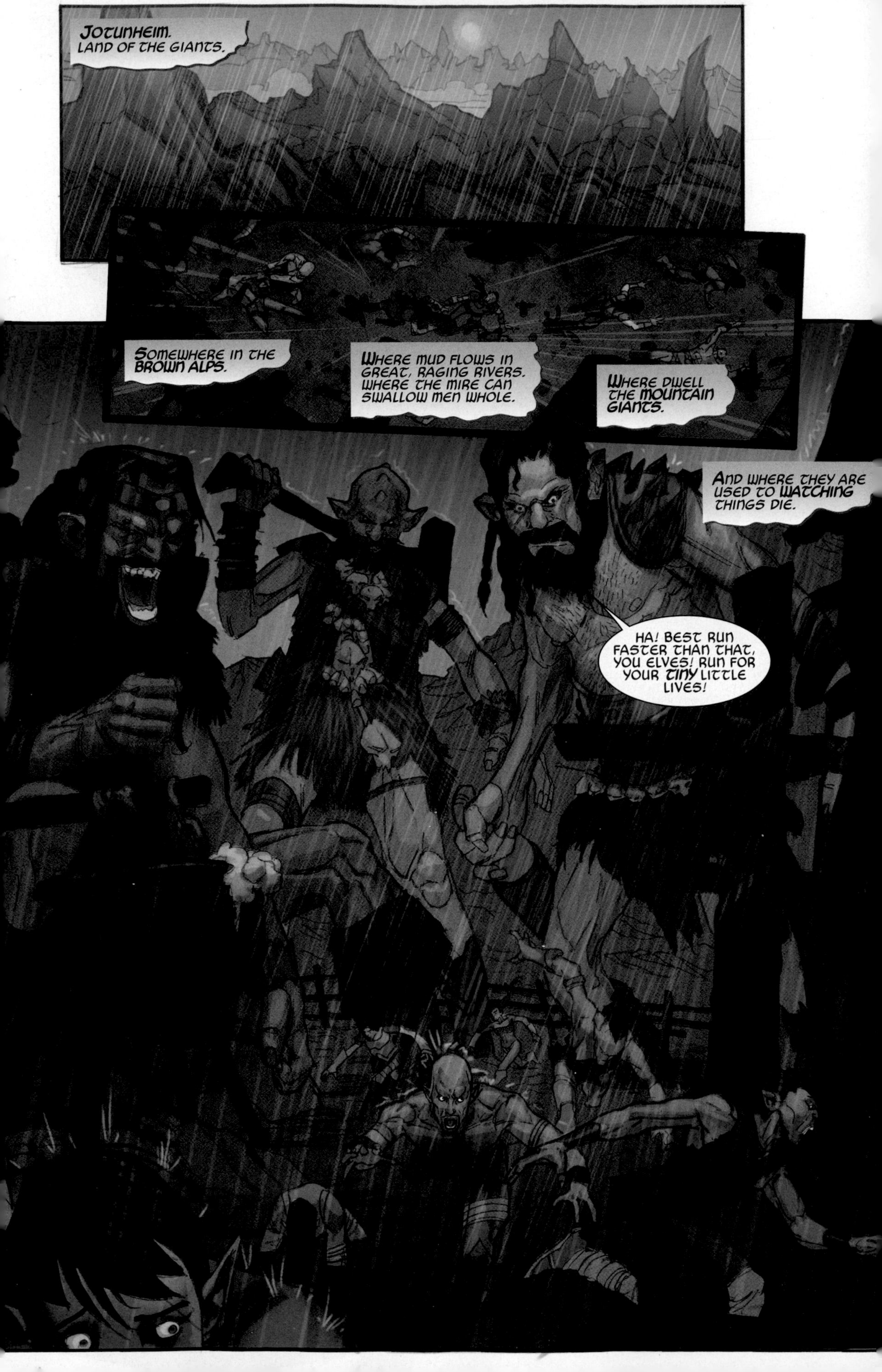
JOTUNHEIM.
LAND OF THE GIANTS.
SOMEWHERE IN THE BROWN ALPS.
WHERE MUD FLOWS IN GREAT, RAGING RIVERS. WHERE THE MIRE CAN SWALLOW MEN WHOLE.
WHERE DWELL THE MOUNTAIN GIANTS.
AND WHERE THEY ARE USED TO WATCHING THINGS DIE.
HA! BEST RUN FASTER THAN THAT, YOU ELVES! RUN FOR YOUR TINY LITTLE LIVES!

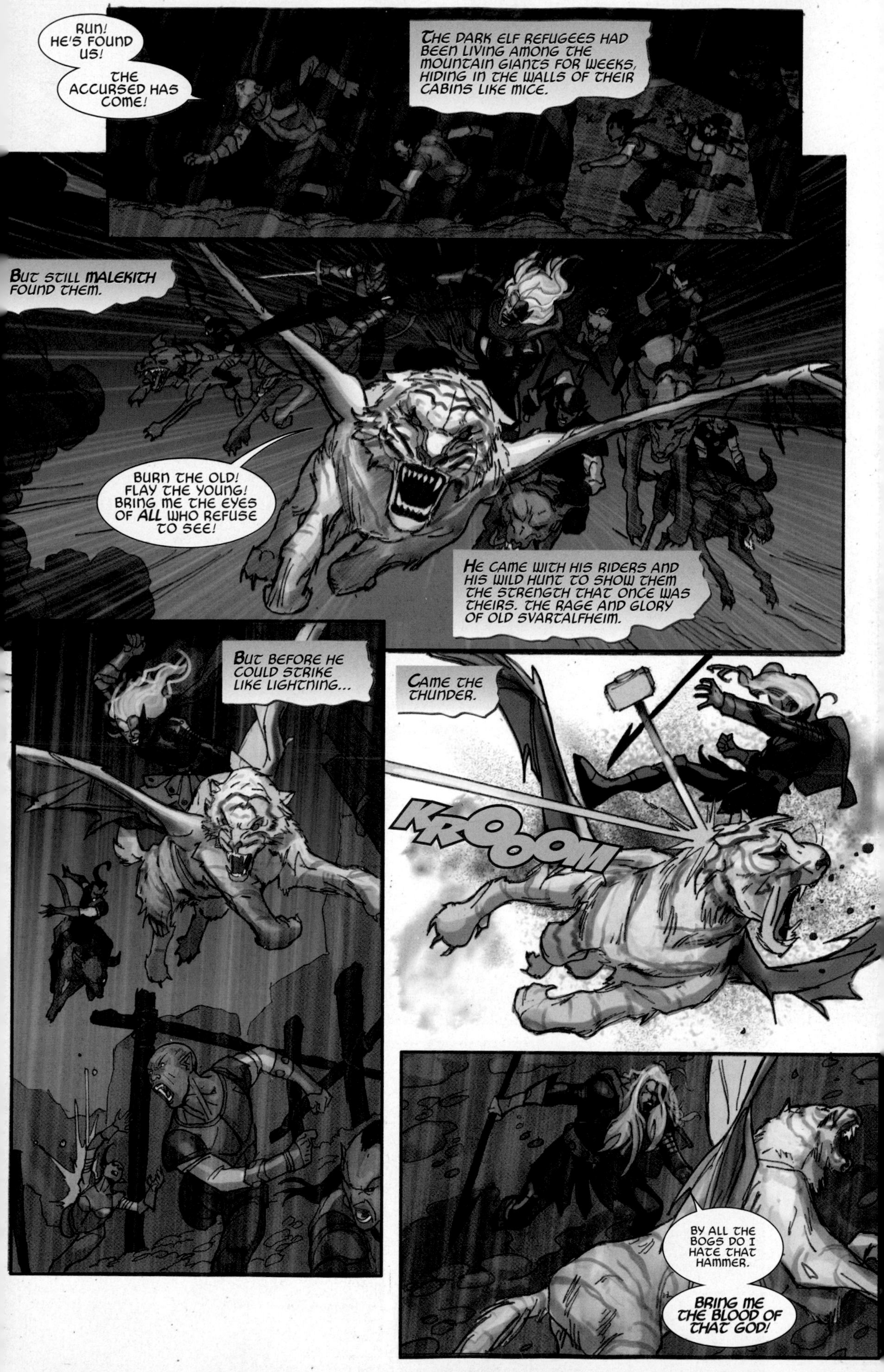
RUN! HE'S FOUND US!
THE ACCURSED HAS COME!
THE DARK ELF REFUGEES HAD BEEN LIVING AMONG THE MOUNTAIN GIANTS FOR WEEKS, HIDING IN THE WALLS OF THEIR CABINS LIKE MICE.
BUT STILL MALEKITH FOUND THEM.
BURN THE OLD! FLAY THE YOUNG! BRING ME THE EYES OF ALL WHO REFUSE TO SEE!
HE CAME WITH HIS RIDERS AND HIS WILD HUNT TO SHOW THEM THE STRENGTH THAT ONCE WAS THEIRS. THE RAGE AND GLORY OF OLD SVARTALFHEIM.
BUT BEFORE HE COULD STRIKE LIKE LIGHTNING...
CAME THE THUNDER.
KRROOOOM
BY ALL THE BOGS DO I HATE THAT HAMMER.
BRING ME THE BLOOD OF THAT GOD!

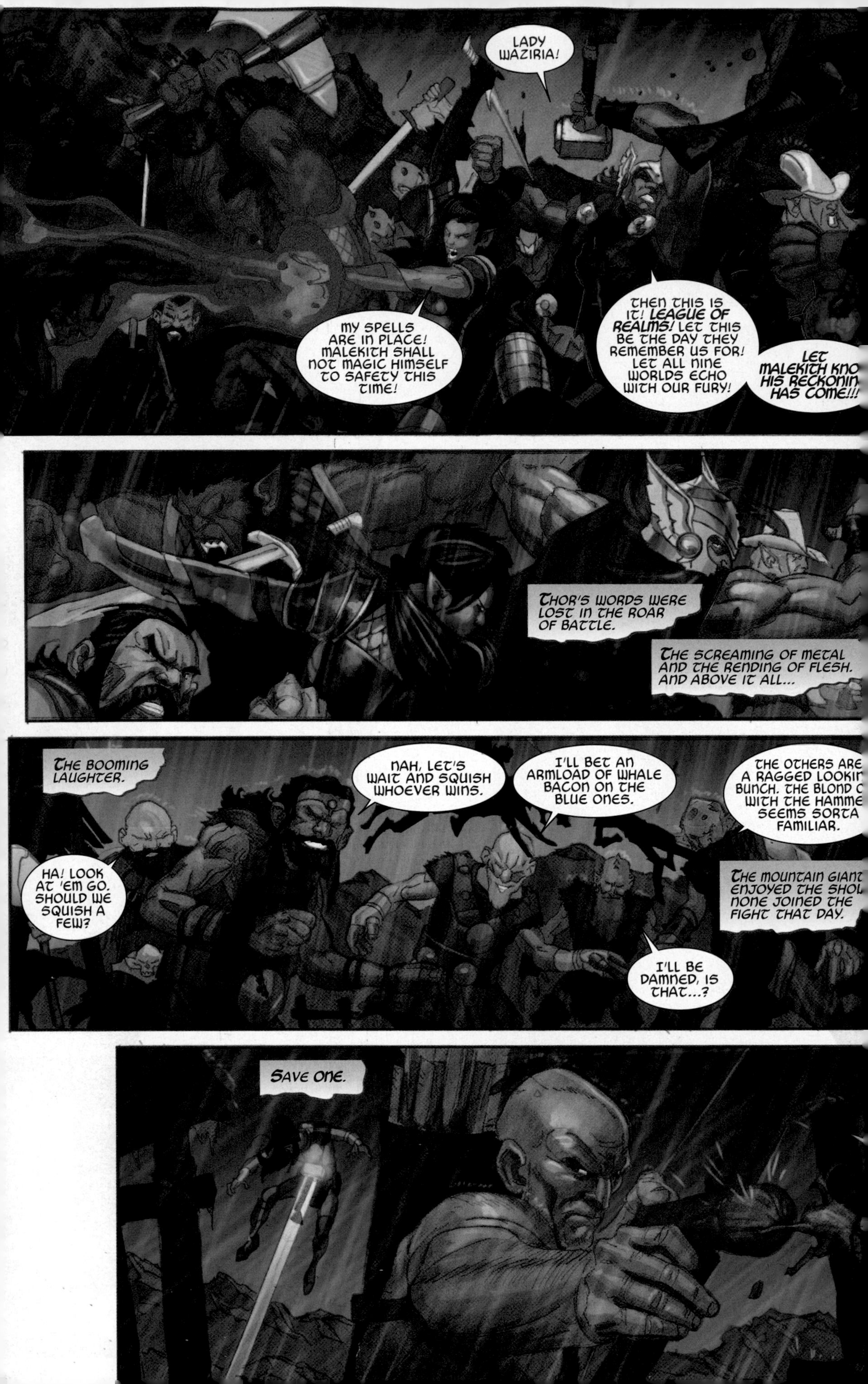
LADY WAZIRIA!
MY SPELLS ARE IN PLACE! MALEKITH SHALL NOT MAGIC HIMSELF TO SAFETY THIS TIME!
THEN THIS IS IT! LEAGUE OF REALMS! LET THIS BE THE DAY THEY REMEMBER US FOR! LET ALL NINE WORLDS ECHO WITH OUR FURY!
LET MALEKITH KNO HIS RECKONIN HAS COME!!!
THOR'S WORDS WERE LOST IN THE ROAR OF BATTLE.
THE SCREAMING OF METAL AND THE RENDING OF FLESH. AND ABOVE IT ALL...
THE BOOMING LAUGHTER.
HA! LOOK AT 'EM GO. SHOULD WE SQUISH A FEW?
NAH, LET'S WAIT AND SQUISH WHOEVER WINS.
I'LL BET AN ARMLOAD OF WHALE BACON ON THE BLUE ONES.
THE OTHERS ARE A RAGGED LOOKIN BUNCH. THE BLOND O WITH THE HAMME SEEMS SORTA FAMILIAR.
I'LL BE DAMNED, IS THAT...?
THE MOUNTAIN GIANT ENJOYED THE SHO NONE JOINED THE FIGHT THAT DAY.
SAVE ONE.

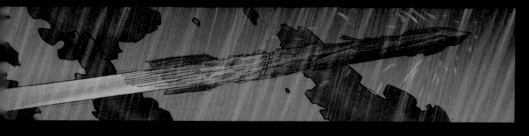

WHOOOOM

BY THE WINES OF GOSAMER, DID YOU SEE THAT?

HIS ARROWS FALL LIKE BOMBS.

SOMEONE SAY BOMBS?

OGGY! WAIT! STAY WITH US!

A VALIANT GIANT. WILL WONDERS NEVER CEASE.

WHAT NEXT? A WELL-DRESSED DWARF?

A TROLL WHO DRINKS IN MODERATION?

AN INTELLIGENT HUMAN?

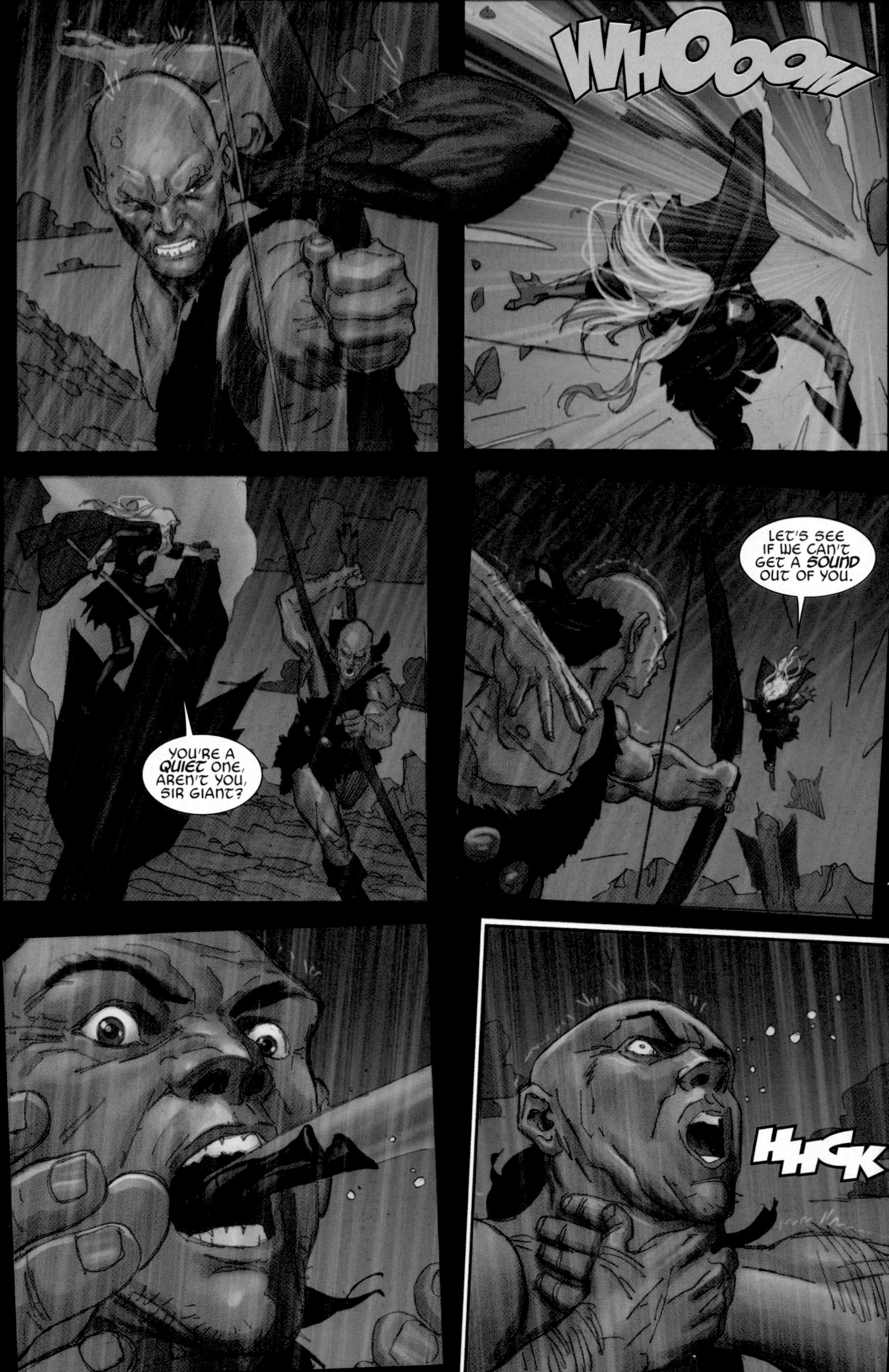
WHOOOOM
YOU'RE A QUIET ONE, AREN'T YOU, SIR GIANT?
LET'S SEE IF WE CAN'T GET A SOUND OUT OF YOU.
HHGK

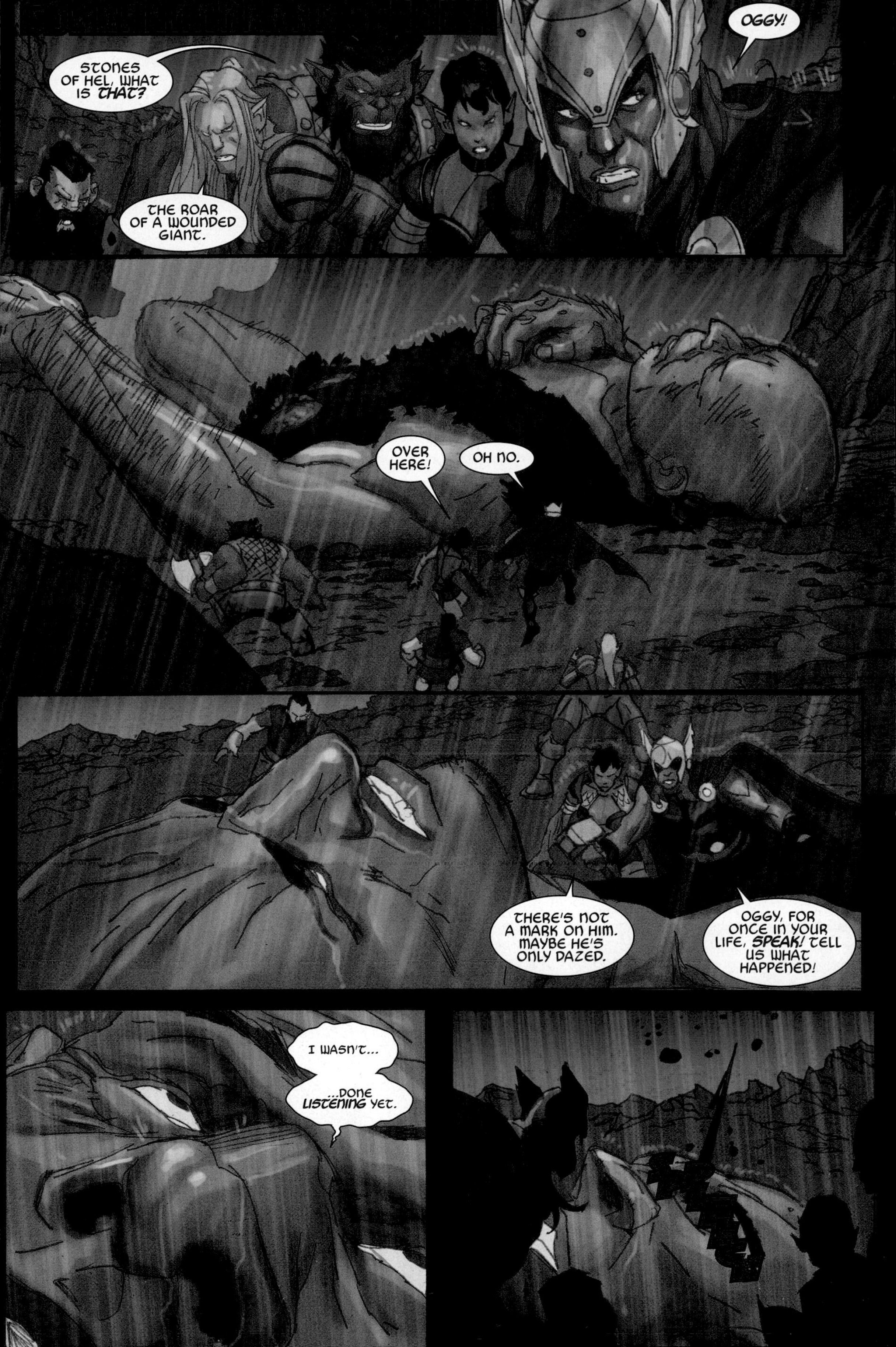
STONES OF HEL, WHAT IS THAT?
OGGY!
THE ROAR OF A WOUNDED GIANT.
OVER HERE!
OH NO.
THERE'S NOT A MARK ON HIM. MAYBE HE'S ONLY DAZED.
OGGY, FOR ONCE IN YOUR LIFE, SPEAK! TELL US WHAT HAPPENED!
I WASN'T...
...DONE LISTENING YET.

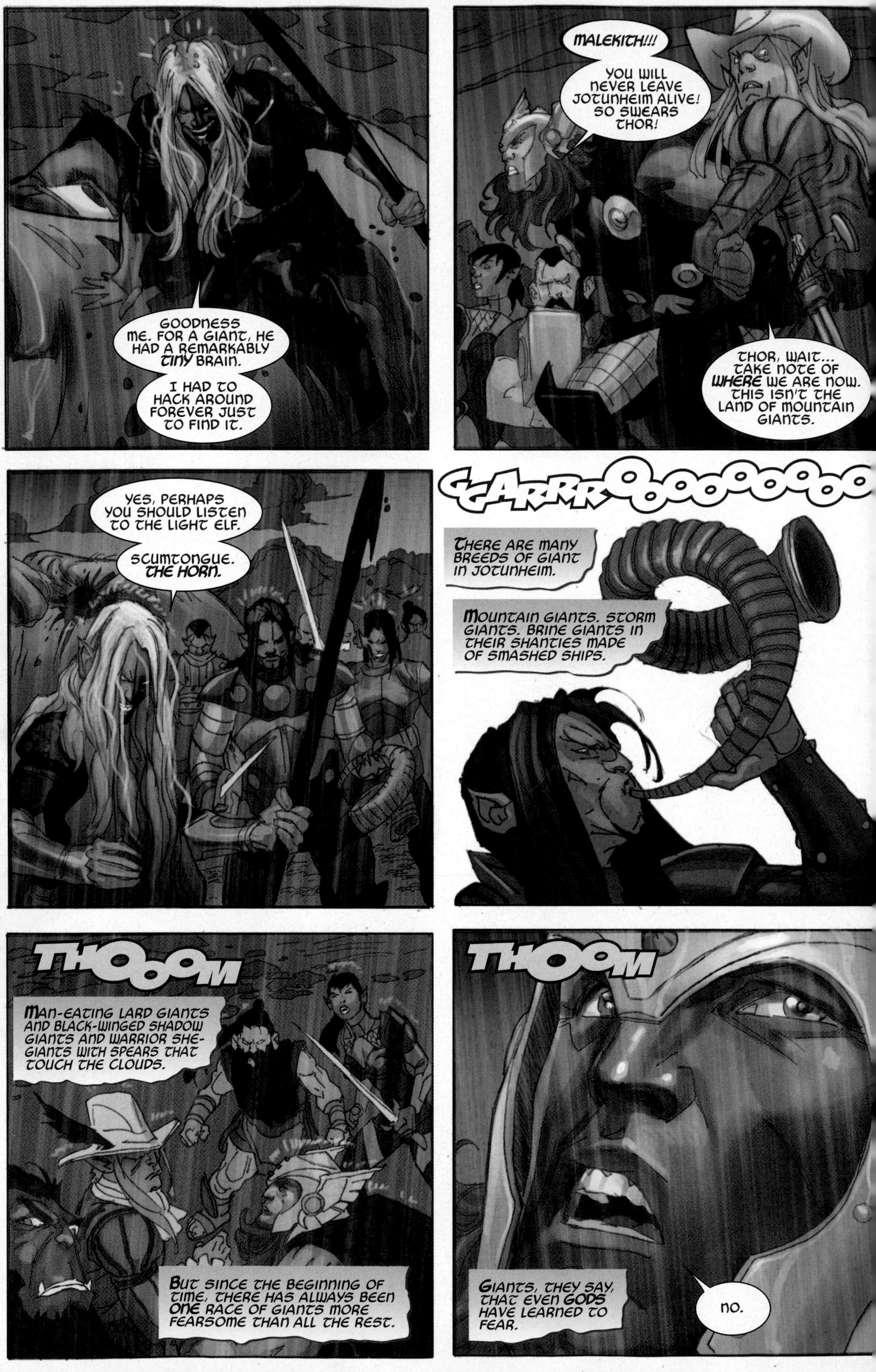
GOODNESS ME. FOR A GIANT, HE HAD A REMARKABLY TINY BRAIN.
I HAD TO HACK AROUND FOREVER JUST TO FIND IT.
MALEKITH!!!
YOU WILL NEVER LEAVE JOTUNHEIM ALIVE! SO SWEARS THOR!
THOR, WAIT... TAKE NOTE OF WHERE WE ARE NOW. THIS ISN'T THE LAND OF MOUNTAIN GIANTS.
YES, PERHAPS YOU SHOULD LISTEN TO THE LIGHT ELF.
SCUMTONGUE. THE HORN.
GARRROOOOOOOOO
THERE ARE MANY BREEDS OF GIANT IN JOTUNHEIM.
MOUNTAIN GIANTS. STORM GIANTS. BRINE GIANTS IN THEIR SHANTIES MADE OF SMASHED SHIPS.
THOOOM
MAN-EATING LARD GIANTS AND BLACK-WINGED SHADOW GIANTS AND WARRIOR SHE-GIANTS WITH SPEARS THAT TOUCH THE CLOUDS.
BUT SINCE THE BEGINNING OF TIME, THERE HAS ALWAYS BEEN ONE RACE OF GIANTS MORE FEARSOME THAN ALL THE REST.
THOOM
GIANTS, THEY SAY, THAT EVEN GODS HAVE LEARNED TO FEAR.
NO.

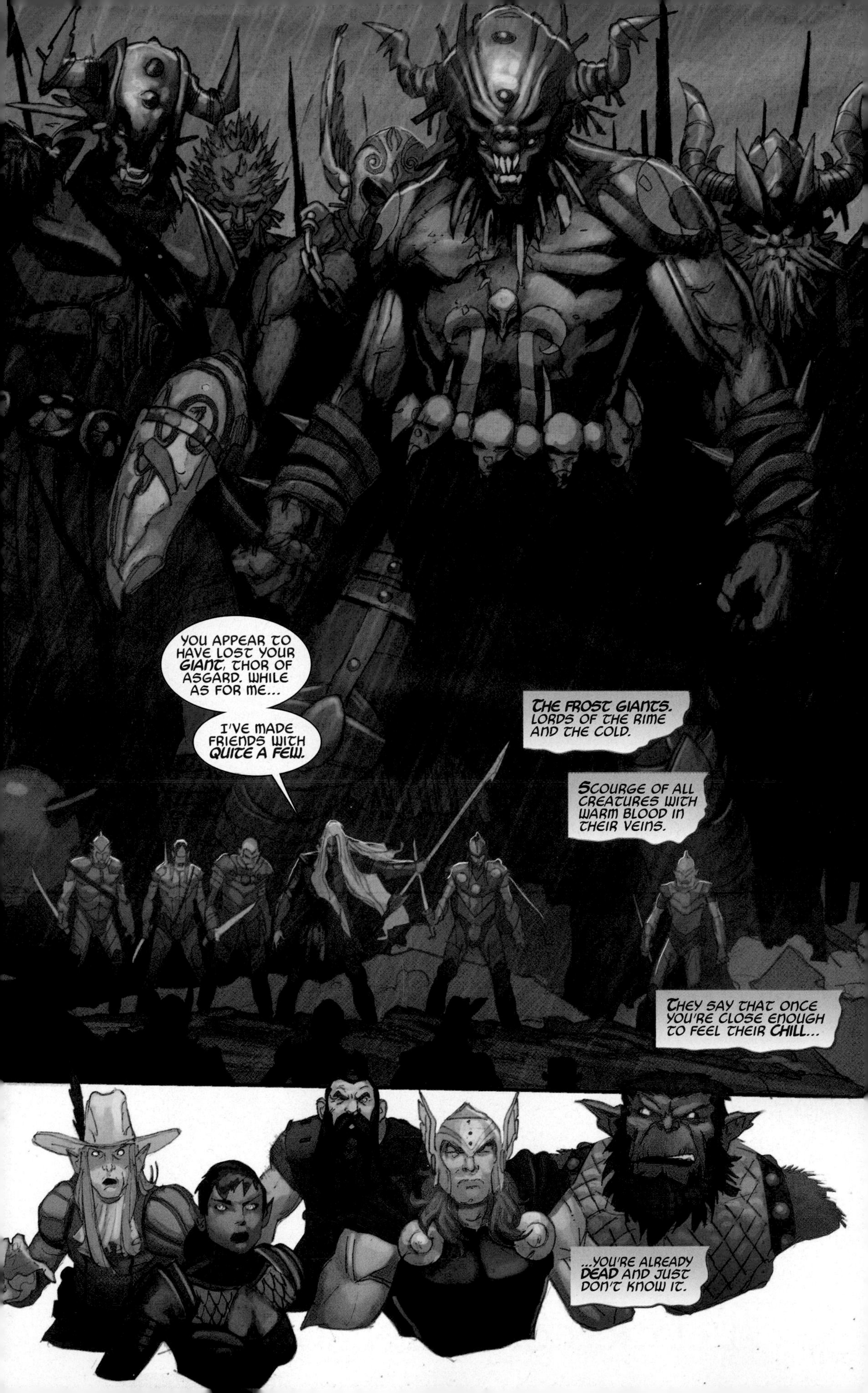

YOU APPEAR TO HAVE LOST YOUR GIANT, THOR OF ASGARD. WHILE AS FOR ME...
I'VE MADE FRIENDS WITH QUITE A FEW.
THE FROST GIANTS. LORDS OF THE RIME AND THE COLD.
SCOURGE OF ALL CREATURES WITH WARM BLOOD IN THEIR VEINS.
THEY SAY THAT ONCE YOU'RE CLOSE ENOUGH TO FEEL THEIR CHILL...
...YOU'RE ALREADY DEAD AND JUST DON'T KNOW IT.

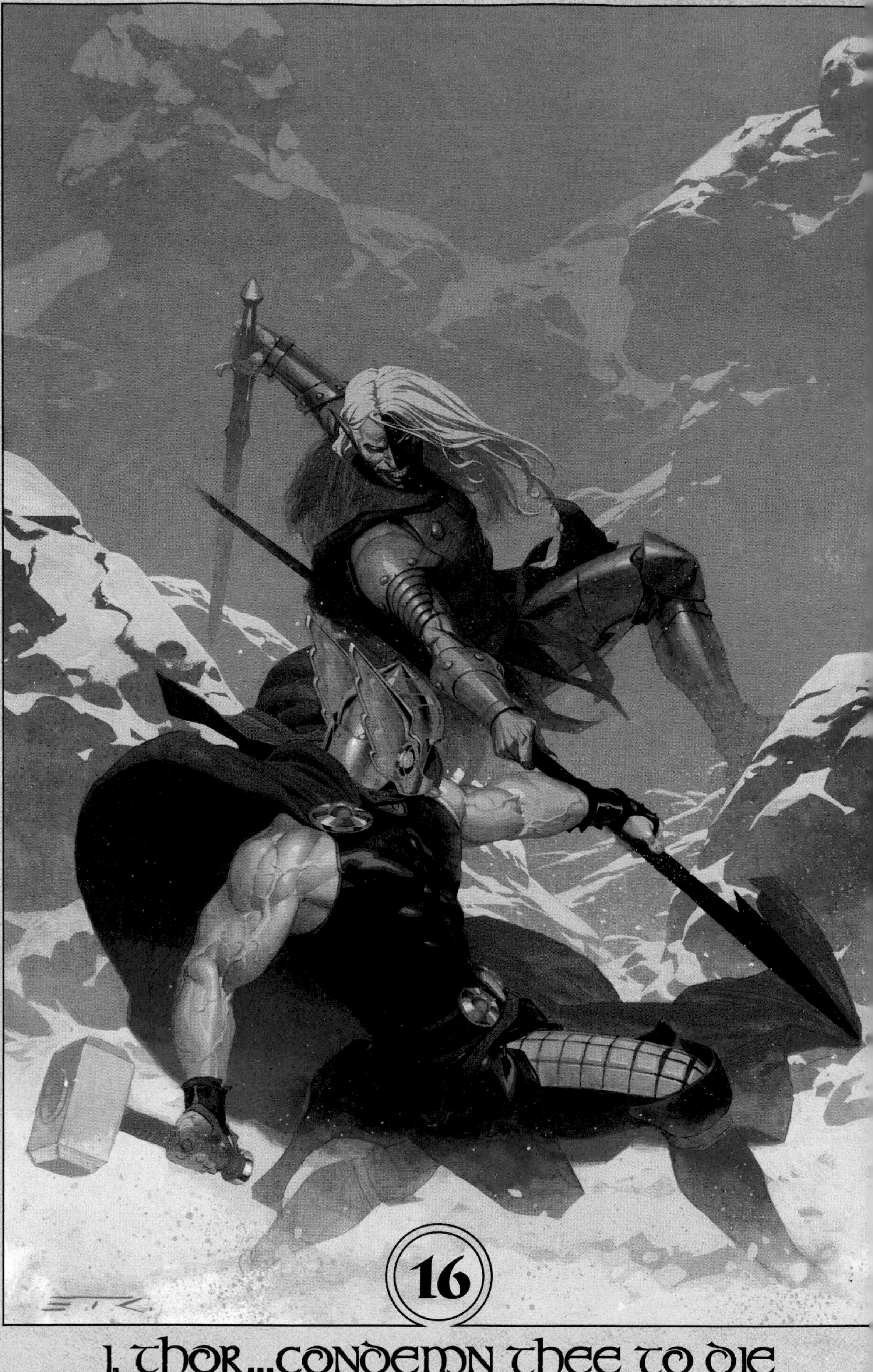
16

I, THOR...CONDEMN THEE TO DIE

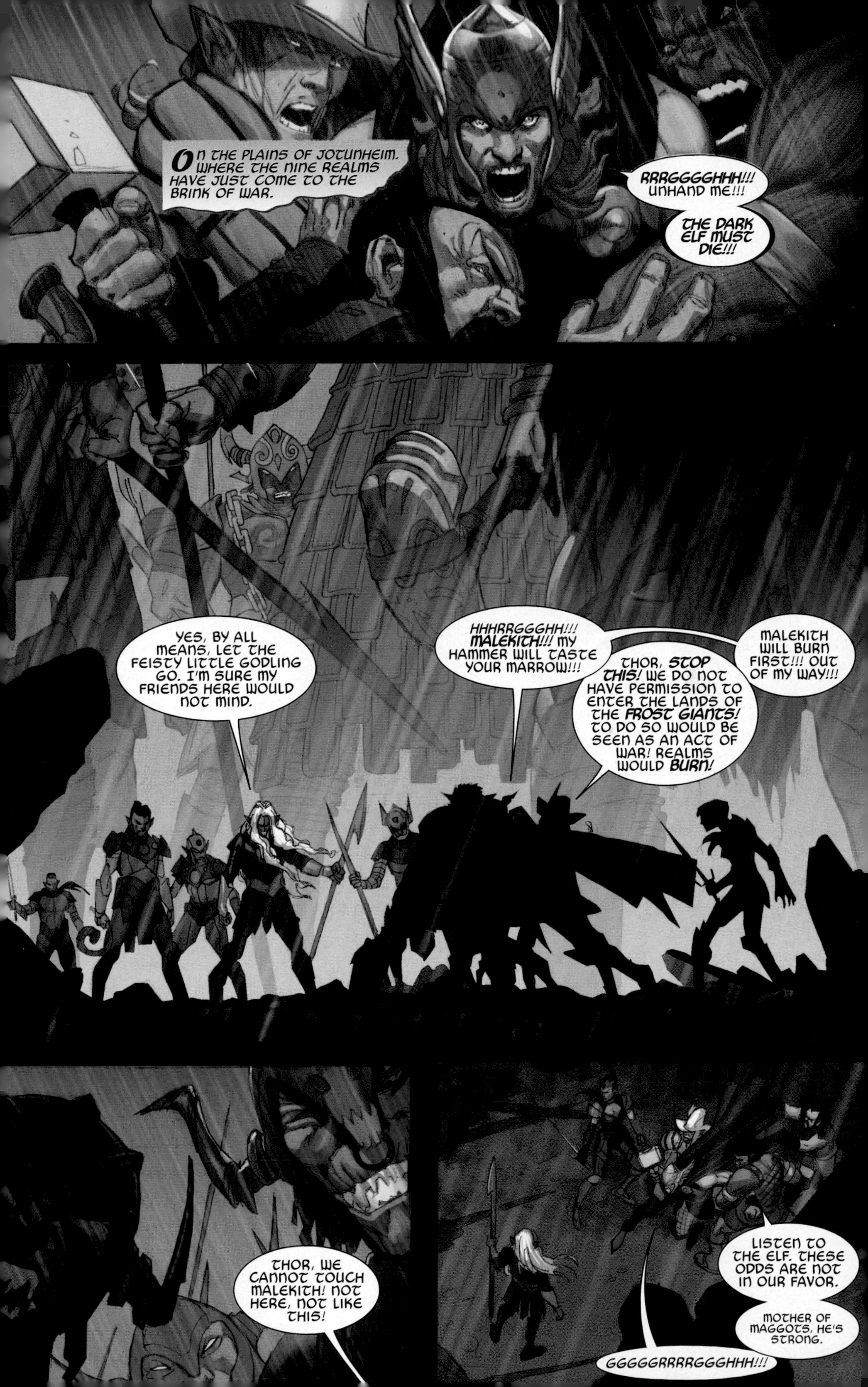

ON THE PLAINS OF JOTUNHEIM. WHERE THE NINE REALMS HAVE JUST COME TO THE BRINK OF WAR.
RRRGGGGHHH!!! UNHAND ME!!!
THE DARK ELF MUST DIE!!!
YES, BY ALL MEANS, LET THE FEISTY LITTLE GODLING GO. I'M SURE MY FRIENDS HERE WOULD NOT MIND.
HHHRRGGGHH!!! MALEKITH!!! MY HAMMER WILL TASTE YOUR MARROW!!!
THOR, STOP THIS! WE DO NOT HAVE PERMISSION TO ENTER THE LANDS OF THE FROST GIANTS! TO DO SO WOULD BE SEEN AS AN ACT OF WAR! REALMS WOULD BURN!
MALEKITH WILL BURN FIRST!!! OUT OF MY WAY!!!
THOR, WE CANNOT TOUCH MALEKITH! NOT HERE, NOT LIKE THIS!
LISTEN TO THE ELF. THESE ODDS ARE NOT IN OUR FAVOR.
MOTHER OF MAGGOTS, HE'S STRONG.
GGGGGRRRRGGGHHH!!!

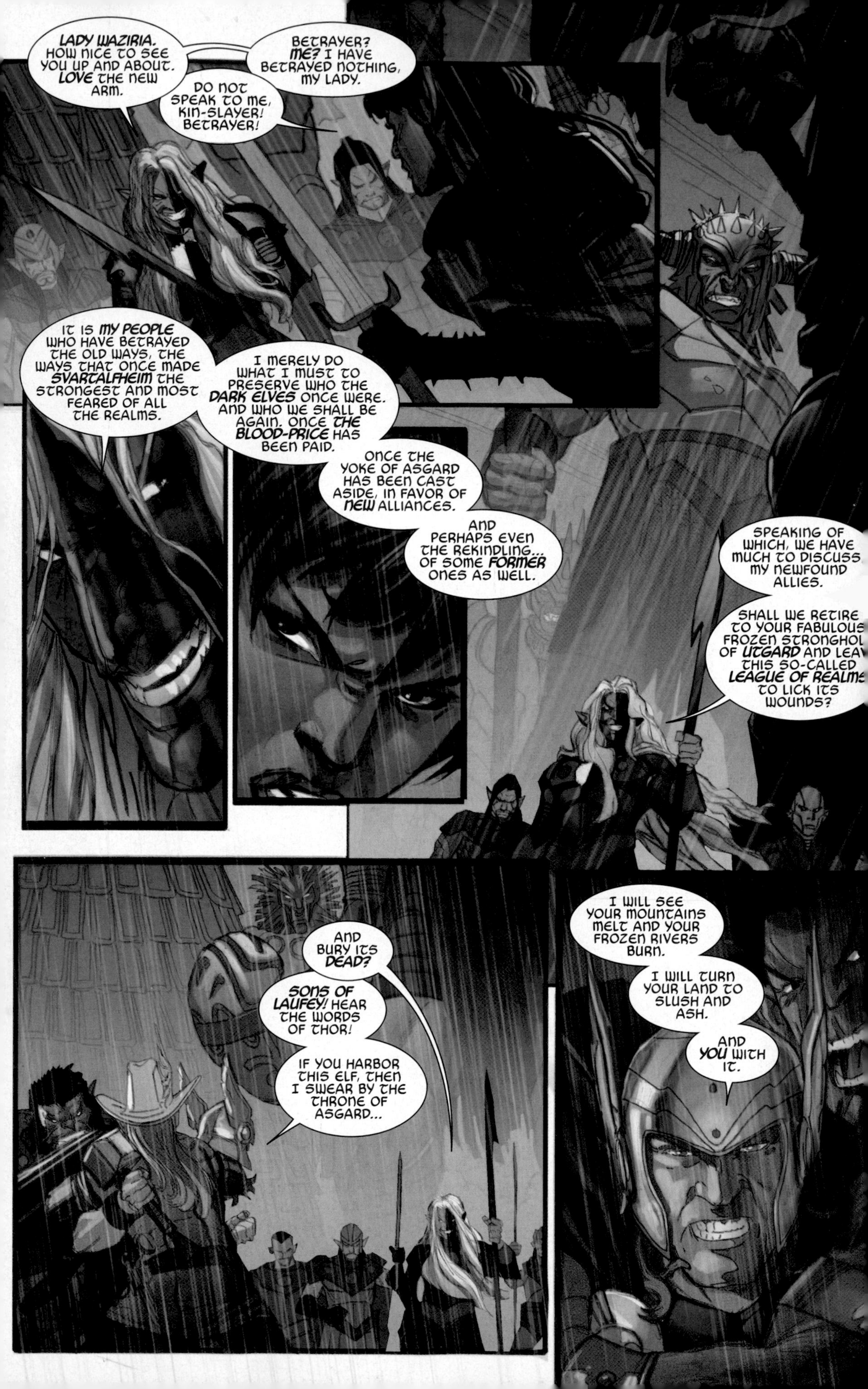
LADY WAZIRIA. HOW NICE TO SEE YOU UP AND ABOUT. LOVE THE NEW ARM.
DO NOT SPEAK TO ME, KIN-SLAYER! BETRAYER!
BETRAYER? ME? I HAVE BETRAYED NOTHING, MY LADY.
IT IS MY PEOPLE WHO HAVE BETRAYED THE OLD WAYS, THE WAYS THAT ONCE MADE SVARTALFHEIM THE STRONGEST AND MOST FEARED OF ALL THE REALMS.
I MERELY DO WHAT I MUST TO PRESERVE WHO THE DARK ELVES ONCE WERE. AND WHO WE SHALL BE AGAIN. ONCE THE BLOOD-PRICE HAS BEEN PAID.
ONCE THE YOKE OF ASGARD HAS BEEN CAST ASIDE, IN FAVOR OF NEW ALLIANCES.
AND PERHAPS EVEN THE REKINDLING... OF SOME FORMER ONES AS WELL.
SPEAKING OF WHICH, WE HAVE MUCH TO DISCUSS, MY NEWFOUND ALLIES.
SHALL WE RETIRE TO YOUR FABULOUS FROZEN STRONGHOL OF UTGARD AND LEA THIS SO-CALLED LEAGUE OF REALMS TO LICK ITS WOUNDS?
AND BURY ITS DEAD?
SONS OF LAUFEY! HEAR THE WORDS OF THOR!
IF YOU HARBOR THIS ELF, THEN I SWEAR BY THE THRONE OF ASGARD...
I WILL SEE YOUR MOUNTAINS MELT AND YOUR FROZEN RIVERS BURN.
I WILL TURN YOUR LAND TO SLUSH AND ASH.
AND YOU WITH IT.

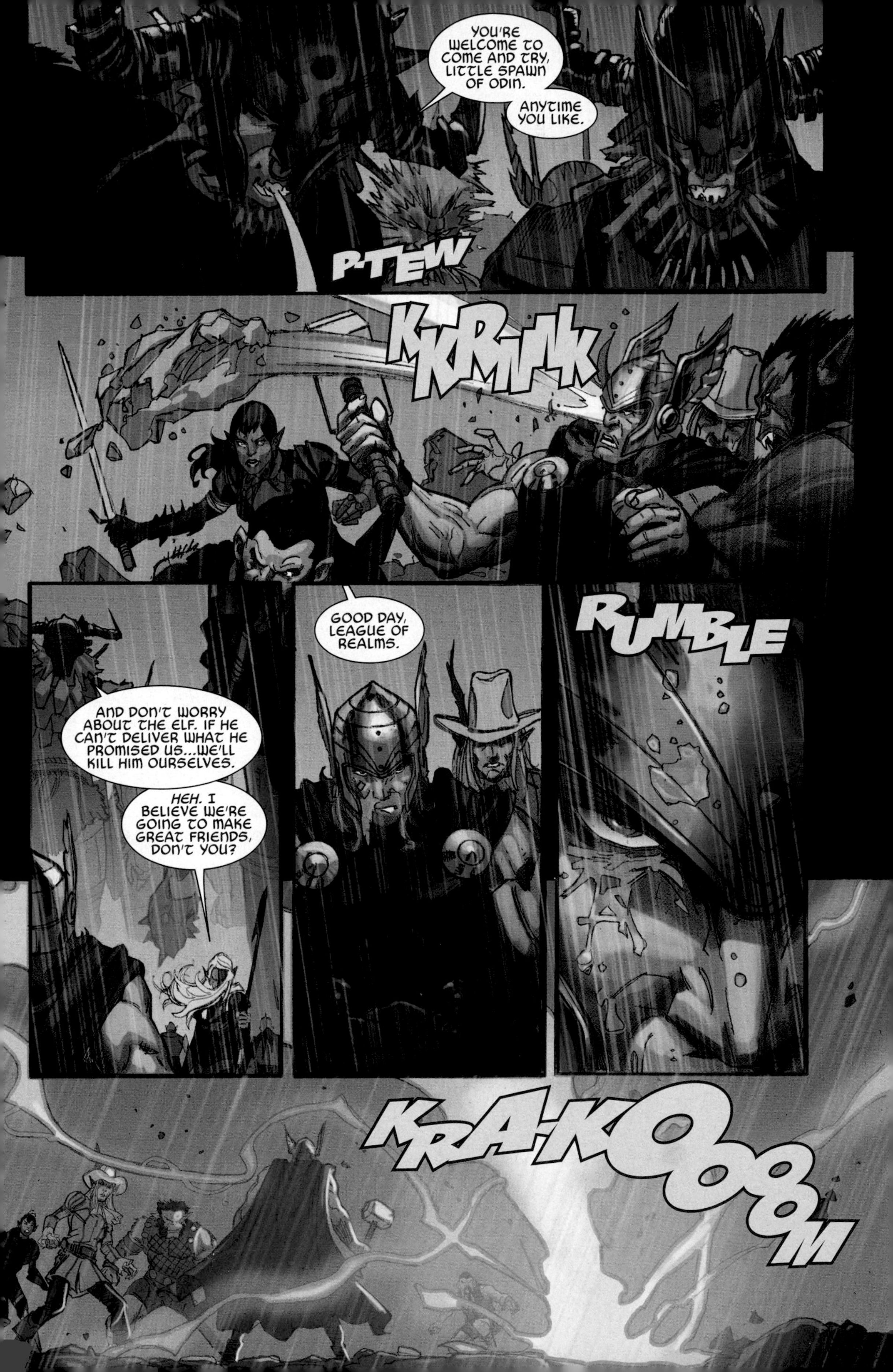
YOU'RE WELCOME TO COME AND TRY, LITTLE SPAWN OF ODIN.
ANYTIME YOU LIKE.
P-TEW
KKRMAK
AND DON'T WORRY ABOUT THE ELF. IF HE CAN'T DELIVER WHAT HE PROMISED US...WE'LL KILL HIM OURSELVES.
HEH. I BELIEVE WE'RE GOING TO MAKE GREAT FRIENDS, DON'T YOU?
GOOD DAY, LEAGUE OF REALMS.
RUMBLE
KRA-KOOOOOM

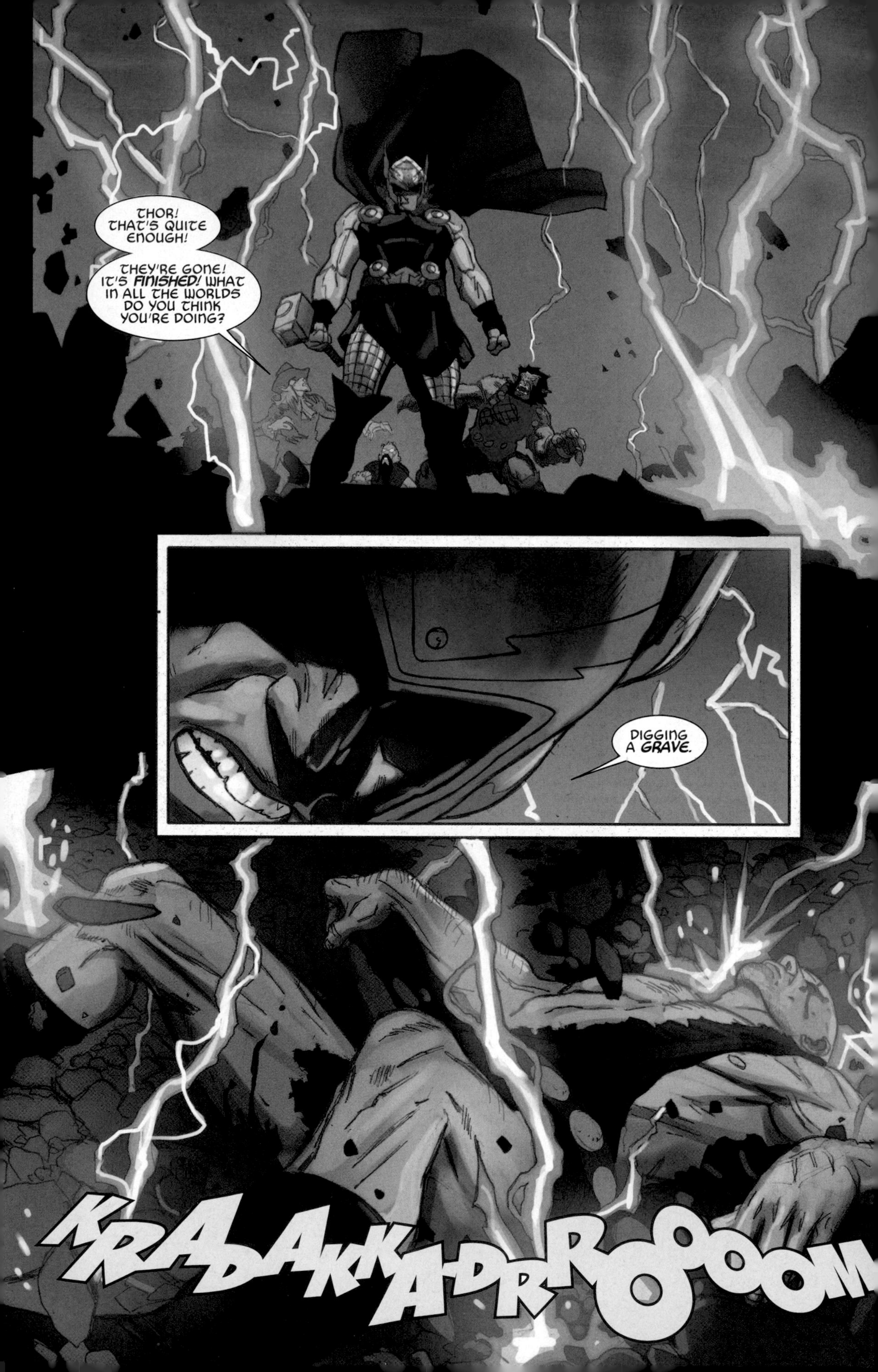
THOR! THAT'S QUITE ENOUGH!
THEY'RE GONE! IT'S FINISHED! WHAT IN ALL THE WORLDS DO YOU THINK YOU'RE DOING?
DIGGING A GRAVE.
KRADAKKA-DRRROOOOM

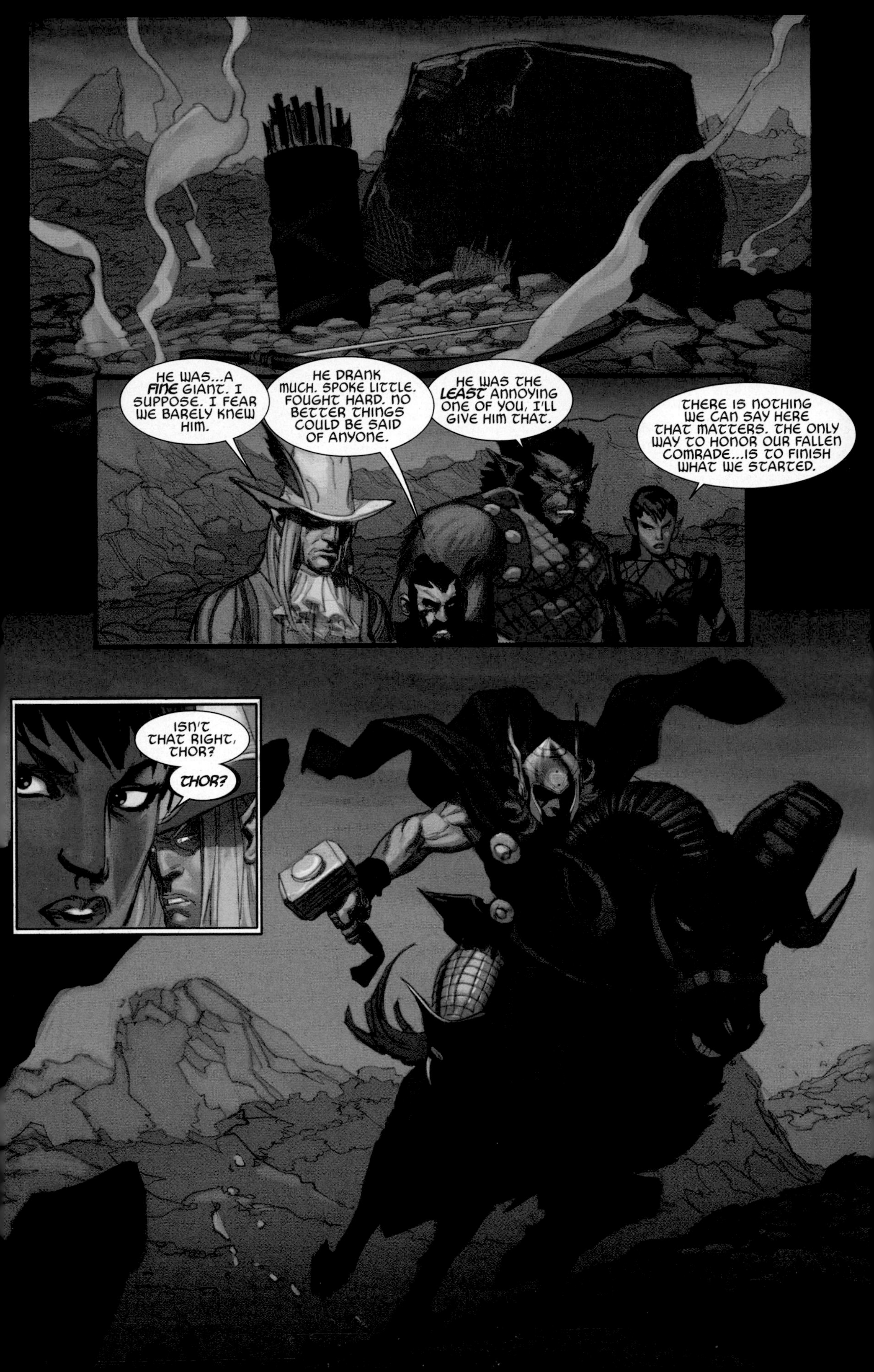

HE WAS...A FINE GIANT. I SUPPOSE. I FEAR WE BARELY KNEW HIM.
HE DRANK MUCH. SPOKE LITTLE. FOUGHT HARD. NO BETTER THINGS COULD BE SAID OF ANYONE.
HE WAS THE LEAST ANNOYING ONE OF YOU, I'LL GIVE HIM THAT.
THERE IS NOTHING WE CAN SAY HERE THAT MATTERS. THE ONLY WAY TO HONOR OUR FALLEN COMRADE...IS TO FINISH WHAT WE STARTED.
ISN'T THAT RIGHT, THOR?
THOR?

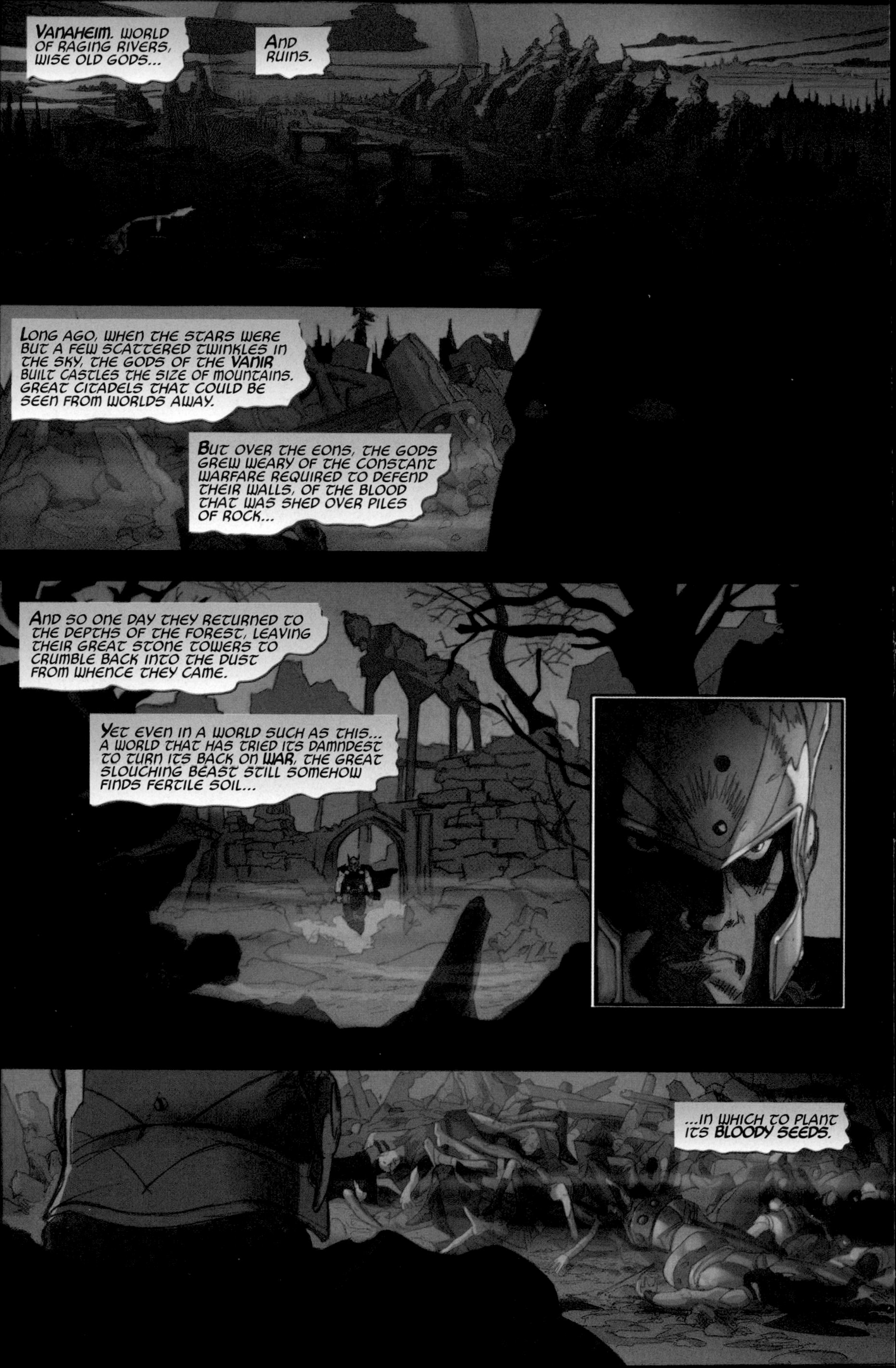
VANAHEIM. WORLD OF RAGING RIVERS, WISE OLD GODS...
AND RUINS.
LONG AGO, WHEN THE STARS WERE BUT A FEW SCATTERED TWINKLES IN THE SKY, THE GODS OF THE VANIR BUILT CASTLES THE SIZE OF MOUNTAINS. GREAT CITADELS THAT COULD BE SEEN FROM WORLDS AWAY.
BUT OVER THE EONS, THE GODS GREW WEARY OF THE CONSTANT WARFARE REQUIRED TO DEFEND THEIR WALLS, OF THE BLOOD THAT WAS SHED OVER PILES OF ROCK...
AND SO ONE DAY THEY RETURNED TO THE DEPTHS OF THE FOREST, LEAVING THEIR GREAT STONE TOWERS TO CRUMBLE BACK INTO THE DUST FROM WHENCE THEY CAME.
YET EVEN IN A WORLD SUCH AS THIS... A WORLD THAT HAS TRIED ITS DAMNDEST TO TURN ITS BACK ON WAR, THE GREAT SLOUCHING BEAST STILL SOMEHOW FINDS FERTILE SOIL...
...IN WHICH TO PLANT ITS BLOODY SEEDS.

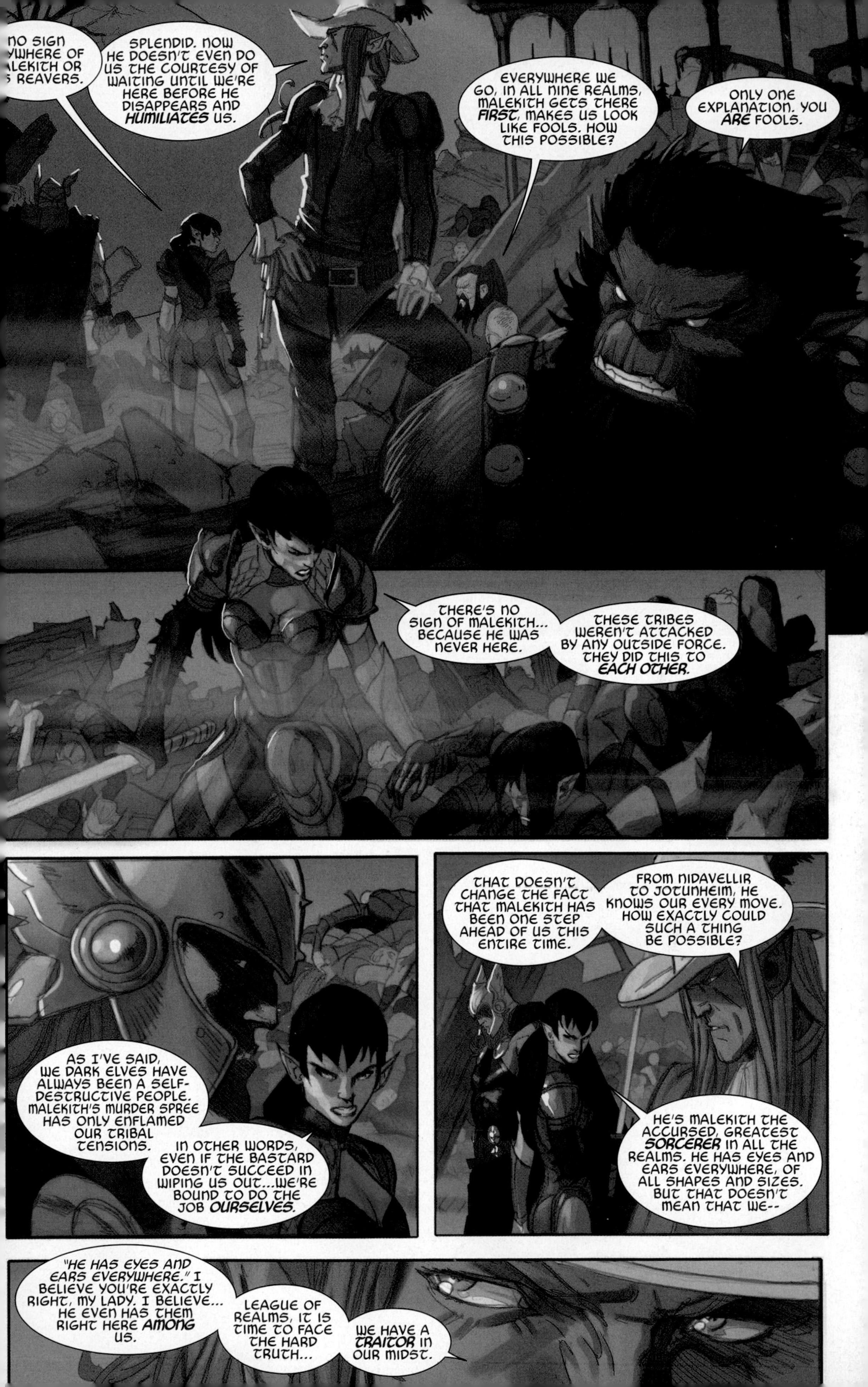

NO SIGN
YWHERE OF
MALEKITH OR
S REAVERS.
SPLENDID. NOW HE DOESN'T EVEN DO US THE COURTESY OF WAITING UNTIL WE'RE HERE BEFORE HE DISAPPEARS AND HUMILIATES US.
EVERYWHERE WE GO, IN ALL NINE REALMS, MALEKITH GETS THERE FIRST, MAKES US LOOK LIKE FOOLS. HOW THIS POSSIBLE?
ONLY ONE EXPLANATION. YOU ARE FOOLS.
THERE'S NO SIGN OF MALEKITH... BECAUSE HE WAS NEVER HERE.
THESE TRIBES WEREN'T ATTACKED BY ANY OUTSIDE FORCE. THEY DID THIS TO EACH OTHER.
AS I'VE SAID, WE DARK ELVES HAVE ALWAYS BEEN A SELF-DESTRUCTIVE PEOPLE. MALEKITH'S MURDER SPREE HAS ONLY ENFLAMED OUR TRIBAL TENSIONS.
IN OTHER WORDS, EVEN IF THE BASTARD DOESN'T SUCCEED IN WIPING US OUT...WE'RE BOUND TO DO THE JOB OURSELVES.
THAT DOESN'T CHANGE THE FACT THAT MALEKITH HAS BEEN ONE STEP AHEAD OF US THIS ENTIRE TIME.
FROM NIDAVELLIR TO JOTUNHEIM, HE KNOWS OUR EVERY MOVE. HOW EXACTLY COULD SUCH A THING BE POSSIBLE?
HE'S MALEKITH THE ACCURSED, GREATEST SORCERER IN ALL THE REALMS. HE HAS EYES AND EARS EVERYWHERE, OF ALL SHAPES AND SIZES. BUT THAT DOESN'T MEAN THAT WE--
"HE HAS EYES AND EARS EVERYWHERE." I BELIEVE YOU'RE EXACTLY RIGHT, MY LADY. I BELIEVE... HE EVEN HAS THEM RIGHT HERE AMONG US.
LEAGUE OF REALMS, IT IS TIME TO FACE THE HARD TRUTH...
WE HAVE A TRAITOR IN OUR MIDST.

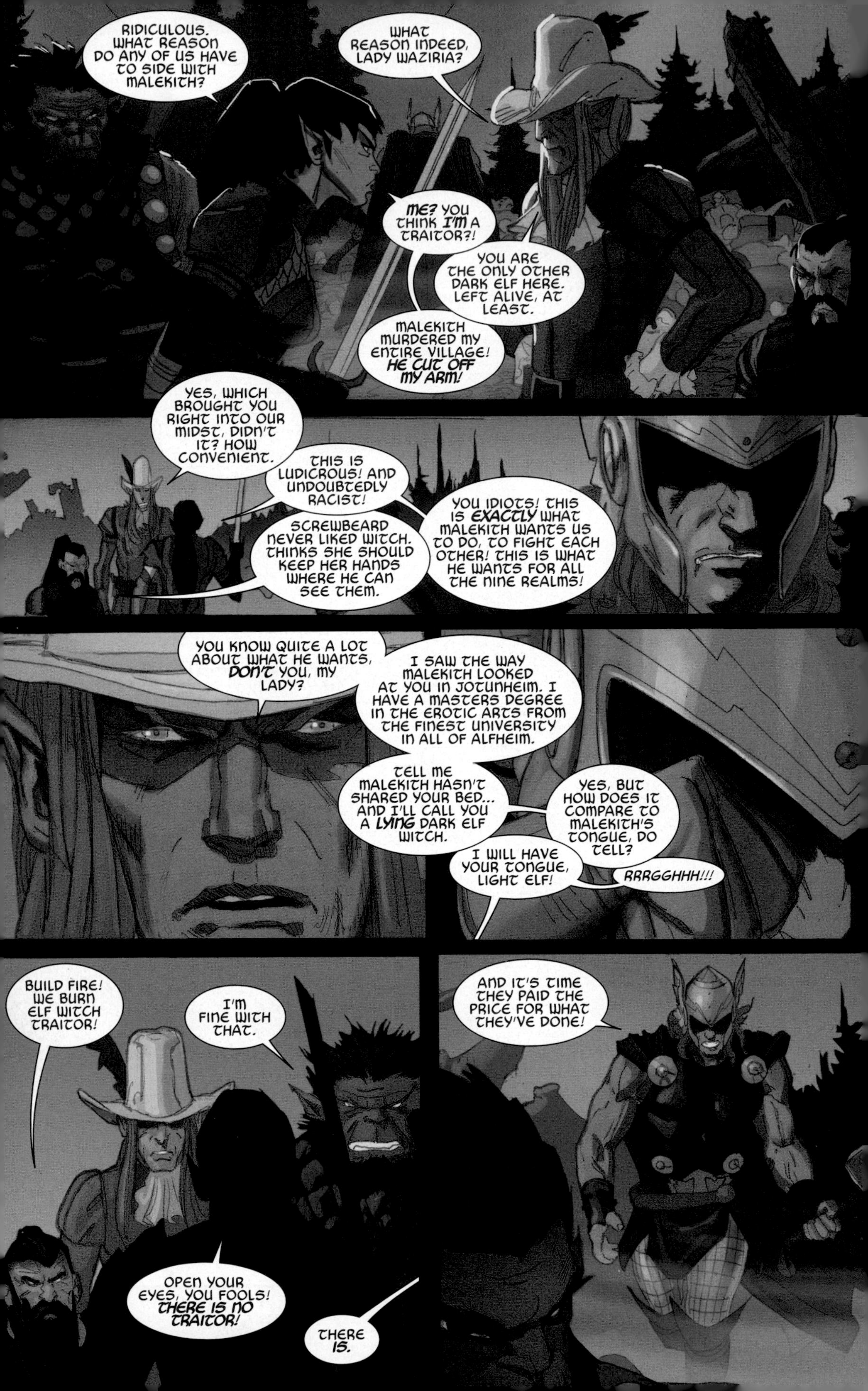
RIDICULOUS. WHAT REASON DO ANY OF US HAVE TO SIDE WITH MALEKITH?
WHAT REASON INDEED, LADY WAZIRIA?
ME? YOU THINK I'M A TRAITOR?!
YOU ARE THE ONLY OTHER DARK ELF HERE. LEFT ALIVE, AT LEAST.
MALEKITH MURDERED MY ENTIRE VILLAGE! HE CUT OFF MY ARM!
YES, WHICH BROUGHT YOU RIGHT INTO OUR MIDST, DIDN'T IT? HOW CONVENIENT.
THIS IS LUDICROUS! AND UNDOUBTEDLY RACIST!
SCREWBEARD NEVER LIKED WITCH. THINKS SHE SHOULD KEEP HER HANDS WHERE HE CAN SEE THEM.
YOU IDIOTS! THIS IS EXACTLY WHAT MALEKITH WANTS US TO DO, TO FIGHT EACH OTHER! THIS IS WHAT HE WANTS FOR ALL THE NINE REALMS!
YOU KNOW QUITE A LOT ABOUT WHAT HE WANTS, DON'T YOU, MY LADY?
I SAW THE WAY MALEKITH LOOKED AT YOU IN JOTUNHEIM. I HAVE A MASTERS DEGREE IN THE EROTIC ARTS FROM THE FINEST UNIVERSITY IN ALL OF ALFHEIM.
TELL ME MALEKITH HASN'T SHARED YOUR BED... AND I'LL CALL YOU A LYING DARK ELF WITCH.
YES, BUT HOW DOES IT COMPARE TO MALEKITH'S TONGUE, DO TELL?
I WILL HAVE YOUR TONGUE, LIGHT ELF!
RRRGGHHH!!!
BUILD FIRE! WE BURN ELF WITCH TRAITOR!
I'M FINE WITH THAT.
OPEN YOUR EYES, YOU FOOLS! THERE IS NO TRAITOR!
THERE IS.
AND IT'S TIME THEY PAID THE PRICE FOR WHAT THEY'VE DONE!

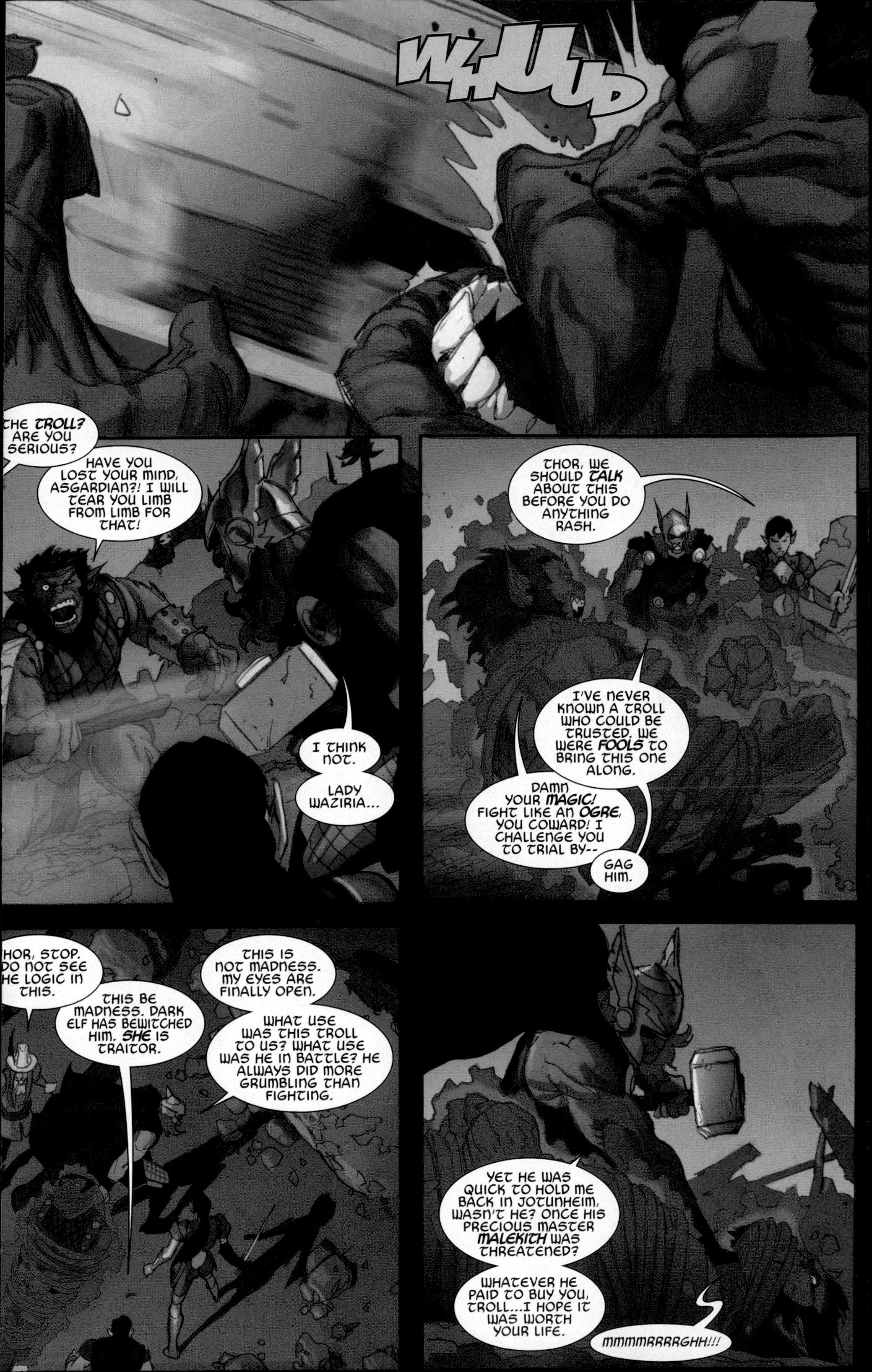
WHUUD
THE TROLL? ARE YOU SERIOUS?
HAVE YOU LOST YOUR MIND, ASGARDIAN?! I WILL TEAR YOU LIMB FROM LIMB FOR THAT!
I THINK NOT.
LADY WAZIRIA...
THOR, WE SHOULD TALK ABOUT THIS BEFORE YOU DO ANYTHING RASH.
I'VE NEVER KNOWN A TROLL WHO COULD BE TRUSTED. WE WERE FOOLS TO BRING THIS ONE ALONG.
DAMN YOUR MAGIC! FIGHT LIKE AN OGRE, YOU COWARD! I CHALLENGE YOU TO TRIAL BY--
GAG HIM.
HOR, STOP. DO NOT SEE HE LOGIC IN THIS.
THIS BE MADNESS. DARK ELF HAS BEWITCHED HIM. SHE IS TRAITOR.
THIS IS NOT MADNESS. MY EYES ARE FINALLY OPEN.
WHAT USE WAS THIS TROLL TO US? WHAT USE WAS HE IN BATTLE? HE ALWAYS DID MORE GRUMBLING THAN FIGHTING.
YET HE WAS QUICK TO HOLD ME BACK IN JOTUNHEIM, WASN'T HE? ONCE HIS PRECIOUS MASTER MALEKITH WAS THREATENED?
WHATEVER HE PAID TO BUY YOU, TROLL...I HOPE IT WAS WORTH YOUR LIFE.
MMMMRRRRGHH!!!

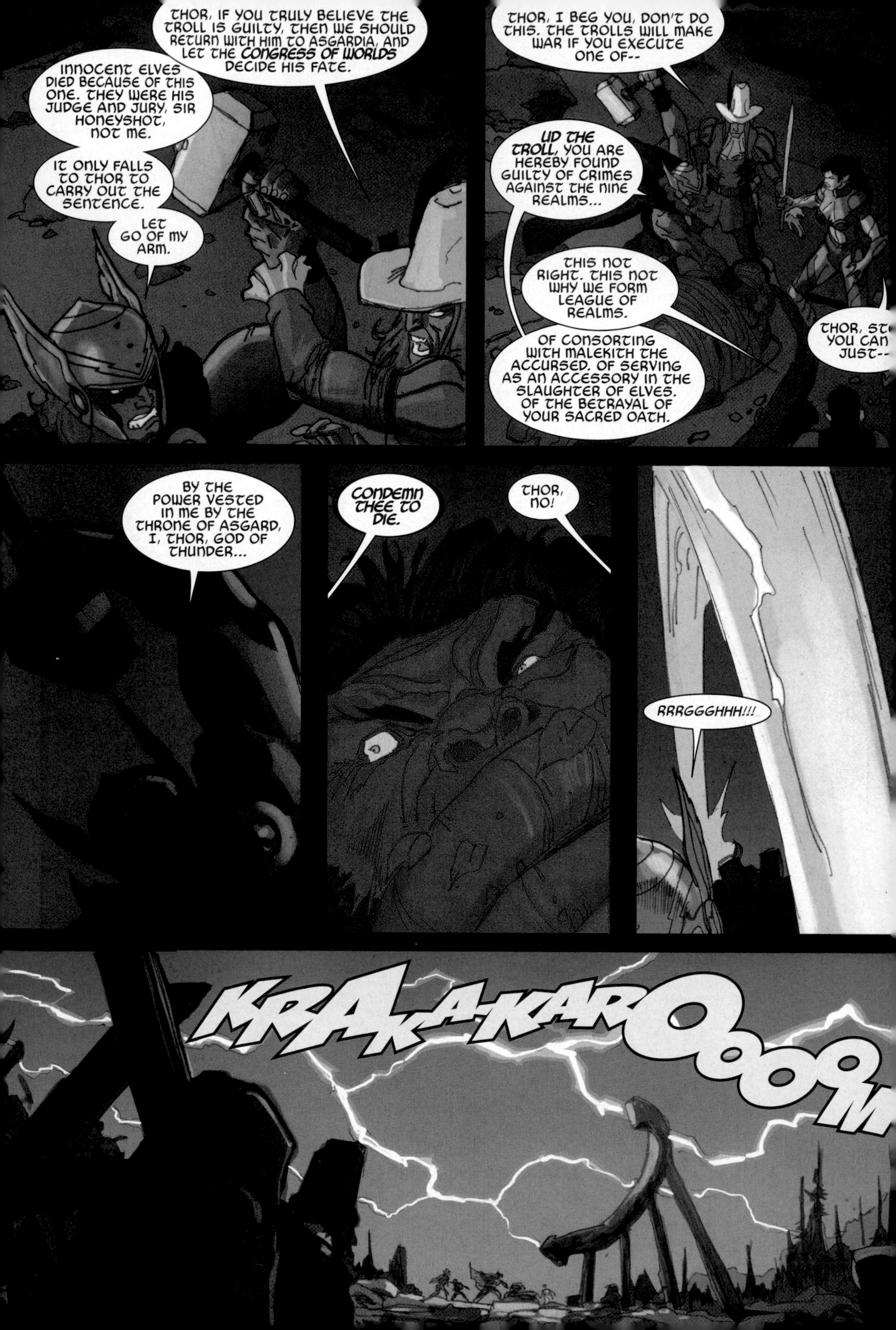
THOR, IF YOU TRULY BELIEVE THE TROLL IS GUILTY, THEN WE SHOULD RETURN WITH HIM TO ASGARDIA, AND LET THE CONGRESS OF WORLDS DECIDE HIS FATE.
INNOCENT ELVES DIED BECAUSE OF THIS ONE. THEY WERE HIS JUDGE AND JURY, SIR HONEYSHOT, NOT ME.
IT ONLY FALLS TO THOR TO CARRY OUT THE SENTENCE.
LET GO OF MY ARM.
THOR, I BEG YOU, DON'T DO THIS. THE TROLLS WILL MAKE WAR IF YOU EXECUTE ONE OF--
UD THE TROLL, YOU ARE HEREBY FOUND GUILTY OF CRIMES AGAINST THE NINE REALMS...
THIS NOT RIGHT. THIS NOT WHY WE FORM LEAGUE OF REALMS.
OF CONSORTING WITH MALEKITH THE ACCURSED. OF SERVING AS AN ACCESSORY IN THE SLAUGHTER OF ELVES. OF THE BETRAYAL OF YOUR SACRED OATH.
THOR, ST YOU CAN JUST--
BY THE POWER VESTED IN ME BY THE THRONE OF ASGARD, I, THOR, GOD OF THUNDER...
CONDEMN THEE TO DIE.
THOR, NO!
RRRGGGHHH!!!
KRAKA-KAROOOOOM

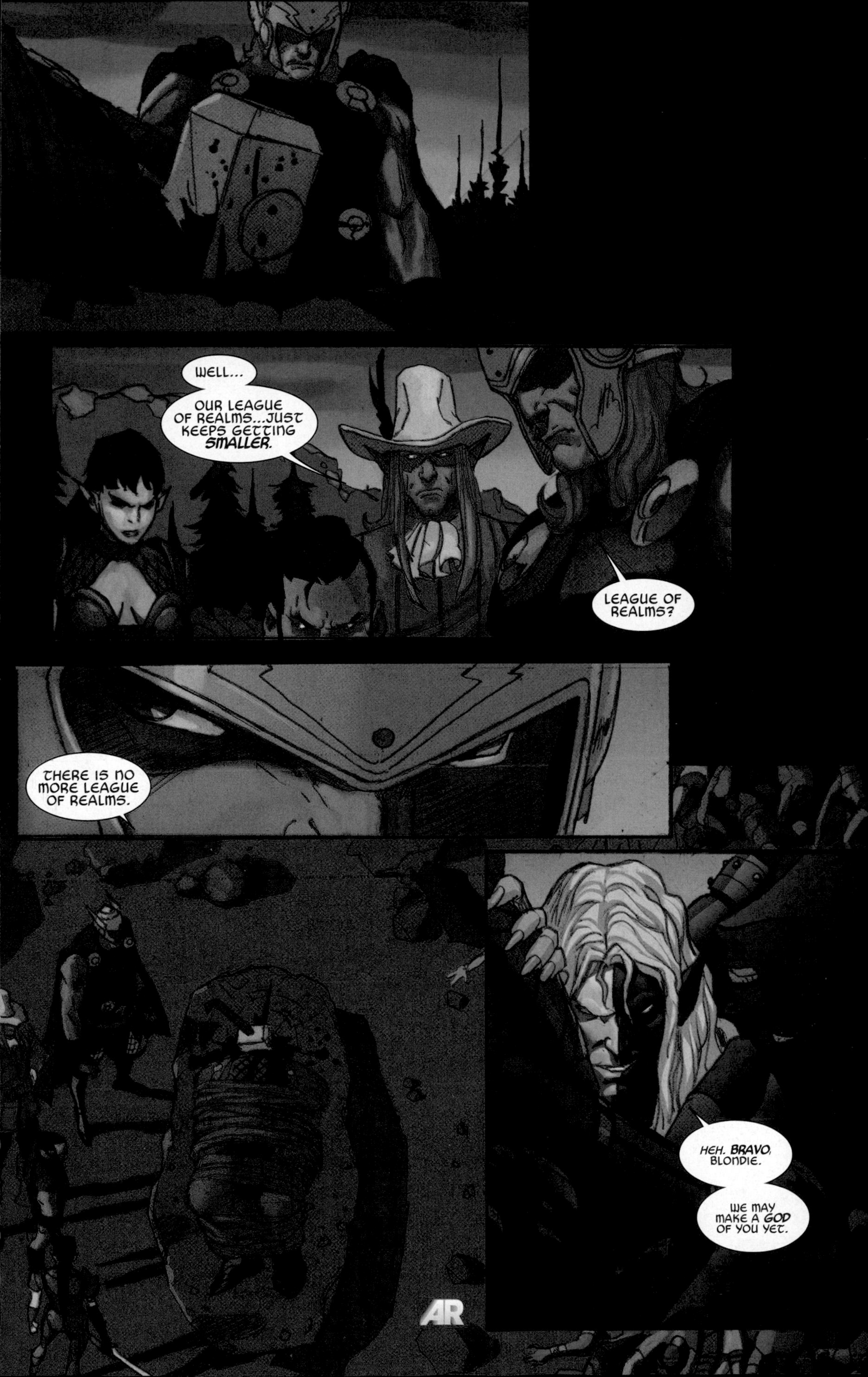
WELL...
OUR LEAGUE OF REALMS...JUST KEEPS GETTING SMALLER.
LEAGUE OF REALMS?
THERE IS NO MORE LEAGUE OF REALMS.
HEH. BRAVO, BLONDIE.
WE MAY MAKE A GOD OF YOU YET.
AR

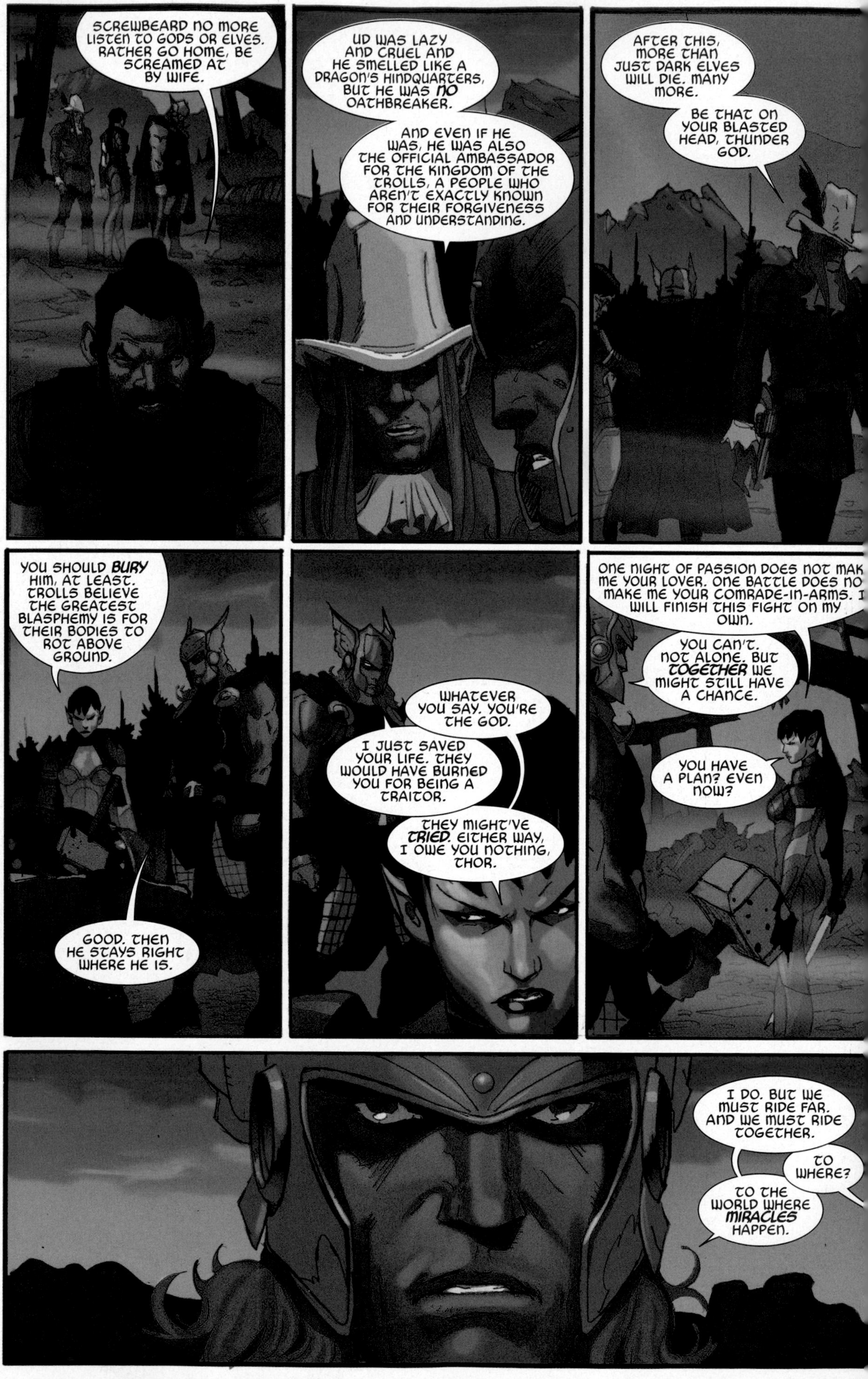
SCREWBEARD NO MORE LISTEN TO GODS OR ELVES. RATHER GO HOME, BE SCREAMED AT BY WIFE.
UD WAS LAZY AND CRUEL AND HE SMELLED LIKE A DRAGON'S HINDQUARTERS, BUT HE WAS NO OATHBREAKER.
AND EVEN IF HE WAS, HE WAS ALSO THE OFFICIAL AMBASSADOR FOR THE KINGDOM OF THE TROLLS, A PEOPLE WHO AREN'T EXACTLY KNOWN FOR THEIR FORGIVENESS AND UNDERSTANDING.
AFTER THIS, MORE THAN JUST DARK ELVES WILL DIE. MANY MORE.
BE THAT ON YOUR BLASTED HEAD, THUNDER GOD.
YOU SHOULD BURY HIM, AT LEAST. TROLLS BELIEVE THE GREATEST BLASPHEMY IS FOR THEIR BODIES TO ROT ABOVE GROUND.
GOOD. THEN HE STAYS RIGHT WHERE HE IS.
WHATEVER YOU SAY. YOU'RE THE GOD.
I JUST SAVED YOUR LIFE. THEY WOULD HAVE BURNED YOU FOR BEING A TRAITOR.
THEY MIGHT'VE TRIED. EITHER WAY, I OWE YOU NOTHING, THOR.
ONE NIGHT OF PASSION DOES NOT MAK ME YOUR LOVER. ONE BATTLE DOES NO MAKE ME YOUR COMRADE-IN-ARMS. I WILL FINISH THIS FIGHT ON MY OWN.
YOU CAN'T. NOT ALONE. BUT TOGETHER WE MIGHT STILL HAVE A CHANCE.
YOU HAVE A PLAN? EVEN NOW?
I DO. BUT WE MUST RIDE FAR. AND WE MUST RIDE TOGETHER.
TO WHERE?
TO THE WORLD WHERE MIRACLES HAPPEN.

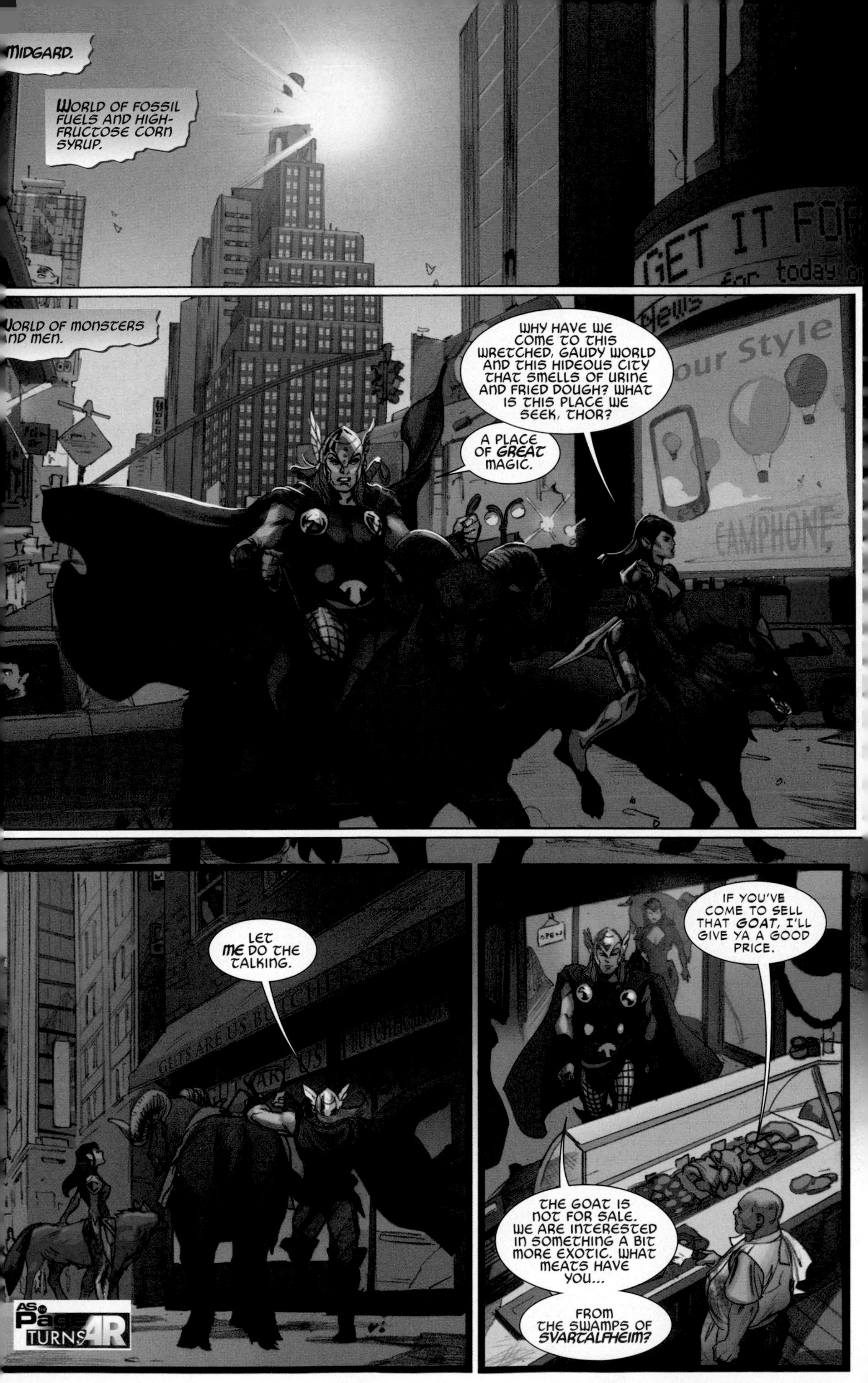
MIDGARD.
WORLD OF FOSSIL FUELS AND HIGH-FRUCTOSE CORN SYRUP.
GET IT FO
for today
WORLD OF MONSTERS AND MEN.
WHY HAVE WE COME TO THIS WRETCHED, GAUDY WORLD AND THIS HIDEOUS CITY THAT SMELLS OF URINE AND FRIED DOUGH? WHAT IS THIS PLACE WE SEEK, THOR?
A PLACE OF GREAT MAGIC.
our Style
CAMPHONE
LET ME DO THE TALKING.
GUTS ARE US BUTCHER SHOP
OPEN
IF YOU'VE COME TO SELL THAT GOAT, I'LL GIVE YA A GOOD PRICE.
THE GOAT IS NOT FOR SALE. WE ARE INTERESTED IN SOMETHING A BIT MORE EXOTIC. WHAT MEATS HAVE YOU...
FROM THE SWAMPS OF SVARTALFHEIM?
AS Page TURNS AR

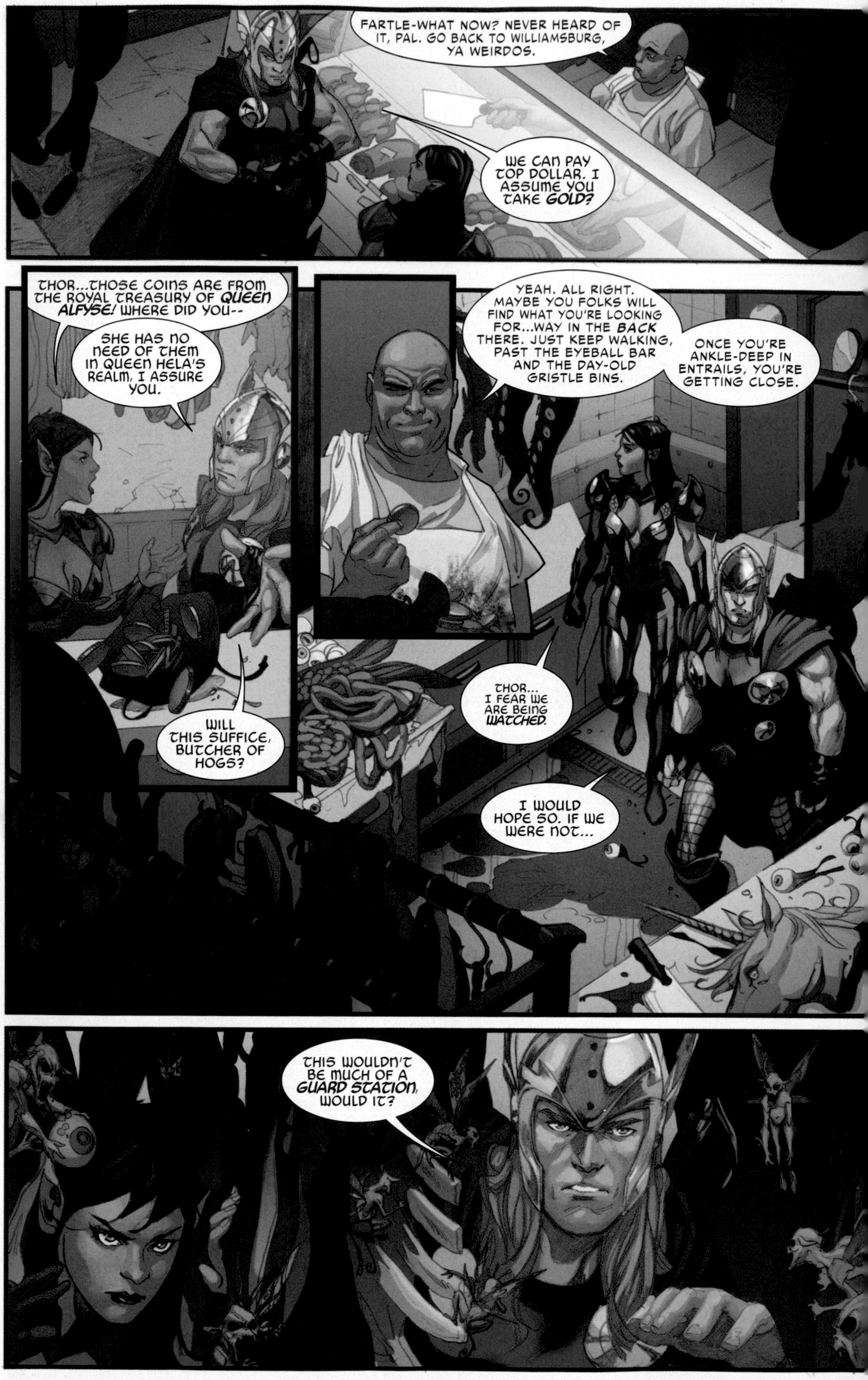
FARTLE-WHAT NOW? NEVER HEARD OF IT, PAL. GO BACK TO WILLIAMSBURG, YA WEIRDOS.
WE CAN PAY TOP DOLLAR. I ASSUME YOU TAKE GOLD?
THOR...THOSE COINS ARE FROM THE ROYAL TREASURY OF QUEEN ALFYSE! WHERE DID YOU--
SHE HAS NO NEED OF THEM IN QUEEN HELA'S REALM, I ASSURE YOU.
WILL THIS SUFFICE, BUTCHER OF HOGS?
YEAH. ALL RIGHT. MAYBE YOU FOLKS WILL FIND WHAT YOU'RE LOOKING FOR...WAY IN THE BACK THERE. JUST KEEP WALKING, PAST THE EYEBALL BAR AND THE DAY-OLD GRISTLE BINS.
ONCE YOU'RE ANKLE-DEEP IN ENTRAILS, YOU'RE GETTING CLOSE.
THOR... I FEAR WE ARE BEING WATCHED.
I WOULD HOPE SO. IF WE WERE NOT...
THIS WOULDN'T BE MUCH OF A GUARD STATION, WOULD IT?

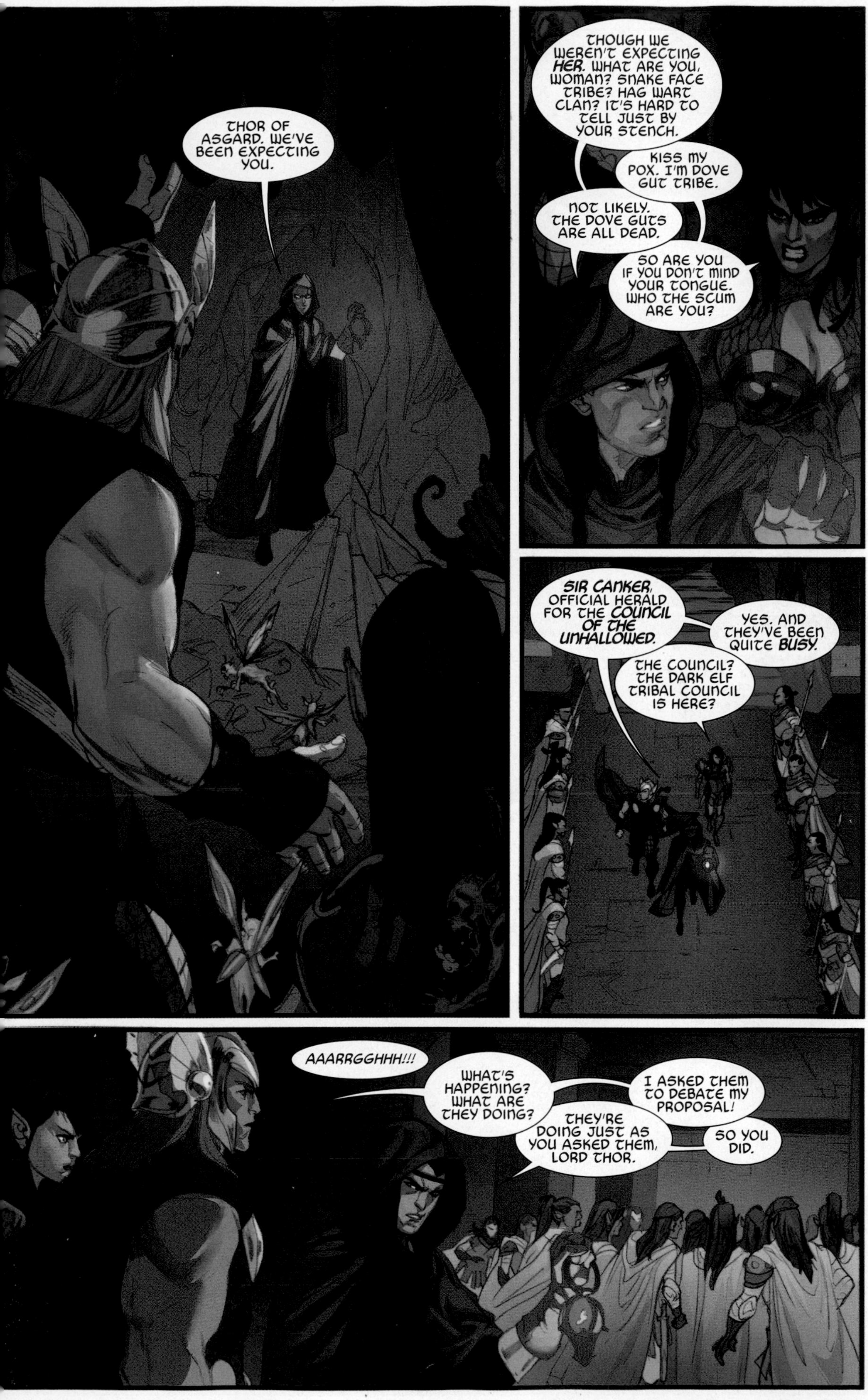
THOR OF ASGARD. WE'VE BEEN EXPECTING YOU.
THOUGH WE WEREN'T EXPECTING HER. WHAT ARE YOU, WOMAN? SNAKE FACE TRIBE? HAG WART CLAN? IT'S HARD TO TELL JUST BY YOUR STENCH.
KISS MY POX. I'M DOVE GUT TRIBE.
NOT LIKELY. THE DOVE GUTS ARE ALL DEAD.
SO ARE YOU IF YOU DON'T MIND YOUR TONGUE. WHO THE SCUM ARE YOU?
SIR CANKER, OFFICIAL HERALD FOR THE COUNCIL OF THE UNHALLOWED.
YES. AND THEY'VE BEEN QUITE BUSY.
THE COUNCIL? THE DARK ELF TRIBAL COUNCIL IS HERE?
AAARRGGHHH!!!
WHAT'S HAPPENING? WHAT ARE THEY DOING?
I ASKED THEM TO DEBATE MY PROPOSAL!
THEY'RE DOING JUST AS YOU ASKED THEM, LORD THOR.
SO YOU DID.

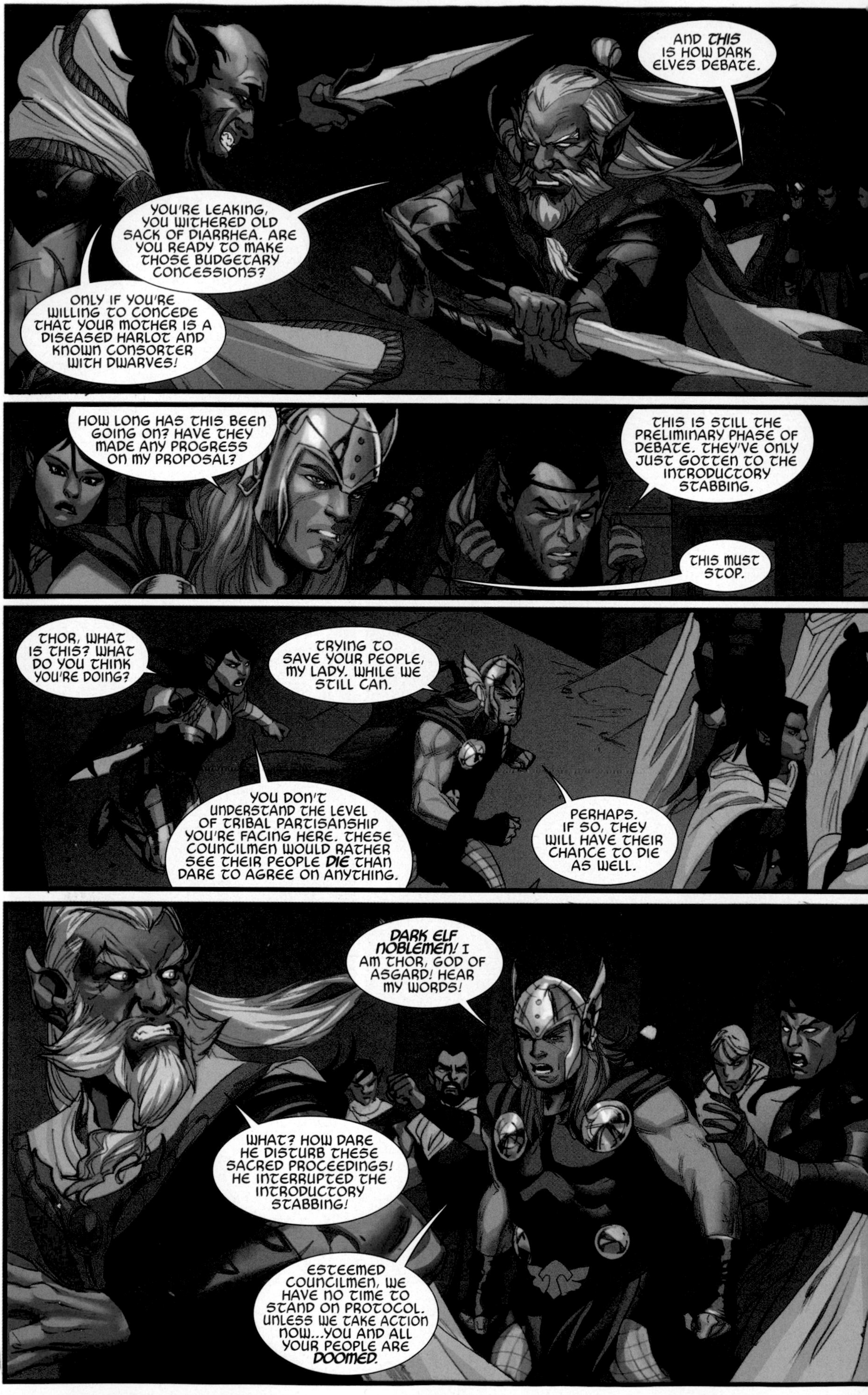
AND THIS IS HOW DARK ELVES DEBATE.
YOU'RE LEAKING, YOU WITHERED OLD SACK OF DIARRHEA. ARE YOU READY TO MAKE THOSE BUDGETARY CONCESSIONS?
ONLY IF YOU'RE WILLING TO CONCEDE THAT YOUR MOTHER IS A DISEASED HARLOT AND KNOWN CONSORTER WITH DWARVES!
HOW LONG HAS THIS BEEN GOING ON? HAVE THEY MADE ANY PROGRESS ON MY PROPOSAL?
THIS IS STILL THE PRELIMINARY PHASE OF DEBATE. THEY'VE ONLY JUST GOTTEN TO THE INTRODUCTORY STABBING.
THIS MUST STOP.
THOR, WHAT IS THIS? WHAT DO YOU THINK YOU'RE DOING?
TRYING TO SAVE YOUR PEOPLE, MY LADY. WHILE WE STILL CAN.
YOU DON'T UNDERSTAND THE LEVEL OF TRIBAL PARTISANSHIP YOU'RE FACING HERE. THESE COUNCILMEN WOULD RATHER SEE THEIR PEOPLE DIE THAN DARE TO AGREE ON ANYTHING.
PERHAPS. IF SO, THEY WILL HAVE THEIR CHANCE TO DIE AS WELL.
DARK ELF NOBLEMEN! I AM THOR, GOD OF ASGARD! HEAR MY WORDS!
WHAT? HOW DARE HE DISTURB THESE SACRED PROCEEDINGS! HE INTERRUPTED THE INTRODUCTORY STABBING!
ESTEEMED COUNCILMEN, WE HAVE NO TIME TO STAND ON PROTOCOL. UNLESS WE TAKE ACTION NOW...YOU AND ALL YOUR PEOPLE ARE DOOMED.

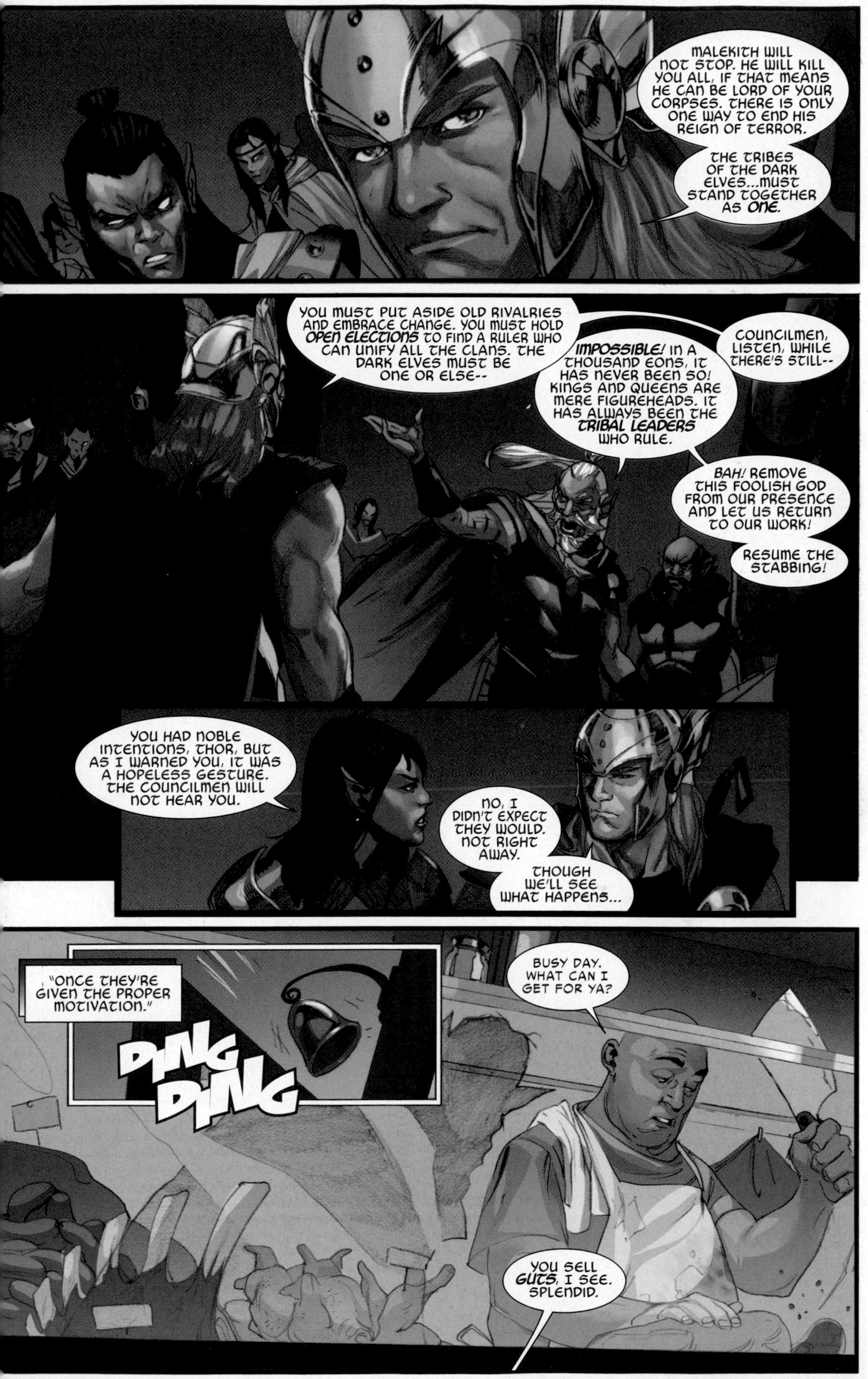
MALEKITH WILL NOT STOP. HE WILL KILL YOU ALL, IF THAT MEANS HE CAN BE LORD OF YOUR CORPSES. THERE IS ONLY ONE WAY TO END HIS REIGN OF TERROR.
THE TRIBES OF THE DARK ELVES...MUST STAND TOGETHER AS ONE.
YOU MUST PUT ASIDE OLD RIVALRIES AND EMBRACE CHANGE. YOU MUST HOLD OPEN ELECTIONS TO FIND A RULER WHO CAN UNIFY ALL THE CLANS. THE DARK ELVES MUST BE ONE OR ELSE--
IMPOSSIBLE! IN A THOUSAND EONS, IT HAS NEVER BEEN SO! KINGS AND QUEENS ARE MERE FIGUREHEADS. IT HAS ALWAYS BEEN THE TRIBAL LEADERS WHO RULE.
COUNCILMEN, LISTEN, WHILE THERE'S STILL--
BAH! REMOVE THIS FOOLISH GOD FROM OUR PRESENCE AND LET US RETURN TO OUR WORK!
RESUME THE STABBING!
YOU HAD NOBLE INTENTIONS, THOR, BUT AS I WARNED YOU, IT WAS A HOPELESS GESTURE. THE COUNCILMEN WILL NOT HEAR YOU.
NO, I DIDN'T EXPECT THEY WOULD. NOT RIGHT AWAY.
THOUGH WE'LL SEE WHAT HAPPENS...
"ONCE THEY'RE GIVEN THE PROPER MOTIVATION."
DING DING
BUSY DAY. WHAT CAN I GET FOR YA?
YOU SELL GUTS, I SEE. SPLENDID.

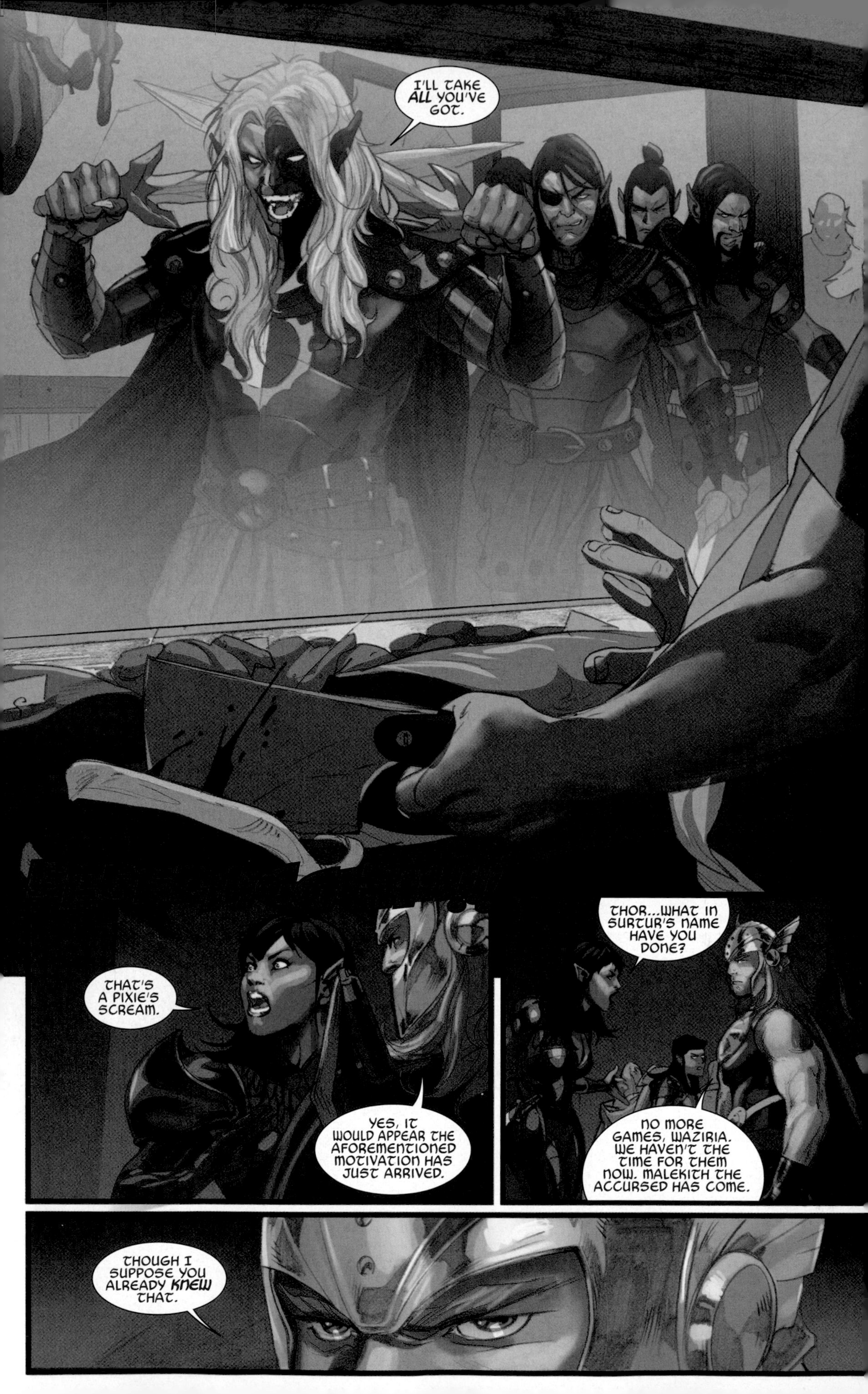
I'LL TAKE ALL YOU'VE GOT.
THAT'S A PIXIE'S SCREAM.
YES, IT WOULD APPEAR THE AFOREMENTIONED MOTIVATION HAS JUST ARRIVED.
THOR...WHAT IN SURTUR'S NAME HAVE YOU DONE?
NO MORE GAMES, WAZIRIA. WE HAVEN'T THE TIME FOR THEM NOW. MALEKITH THE ACCURSED HAS COME.
THOUGH I SUPPOSE YOU ALREADY KNEW THAT.

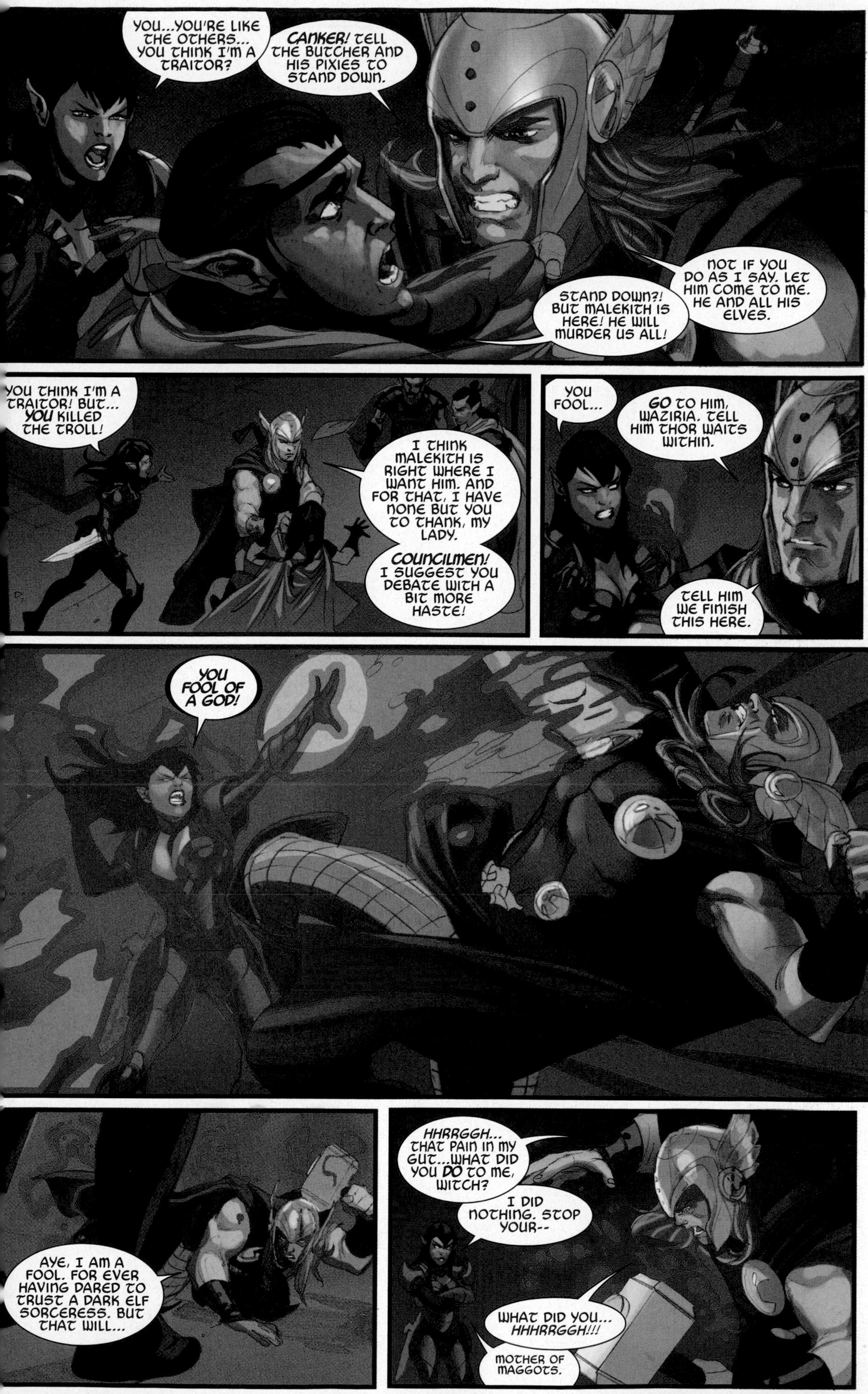
YOU...YOU'RE LIKE THE OTHERS... YOU THINK I'M A TRAITOR?
CANKER! TELL THE BUTCHER AND HIS PIXIES TO STAND DOWN.
STAND DOWN?! BUT MALEKITH IS HERE! HE WILL MURDER US ALL!
NOT IF YOU DO AS I SAY. LET HIM COME TO ME. HE AND ALL HIS ELVES.
YOU THINK I'M A TRAITOR! BUT... YOU KILLED THE TROLL!
I THINK MALEKITH IS RIGHT WHERE I WANT HIM. AND FOR THAT, I HAVE NONE BUT YOU TO THANK, MY LADY.
COUNCILMEN! I SUGGEST YOU DEBATE WITH A BIT MORE HASTE!
YOU FOOL...
GO TO HIM, WAZIRIA. TELL HIM THOR WAITS WITHIN.
TELL HIM WE FINISH THIS HERE.
YOU FOOL OF A GOD!
AYE, I AM A FOOL. FOR EVER HAVING DARED TO TRUST A DARK ELF SORCERESS. BUT THAT WILL...
HHRRGGH... THAT PAIN IN MY GUT...WHAT DID YOU DO TO ME, WITCH?
I DID NOTHING. STOP YOUR--
WHAT DID YOU... HHHRRGGH!!!
MOTHER OF MAGGOTS.

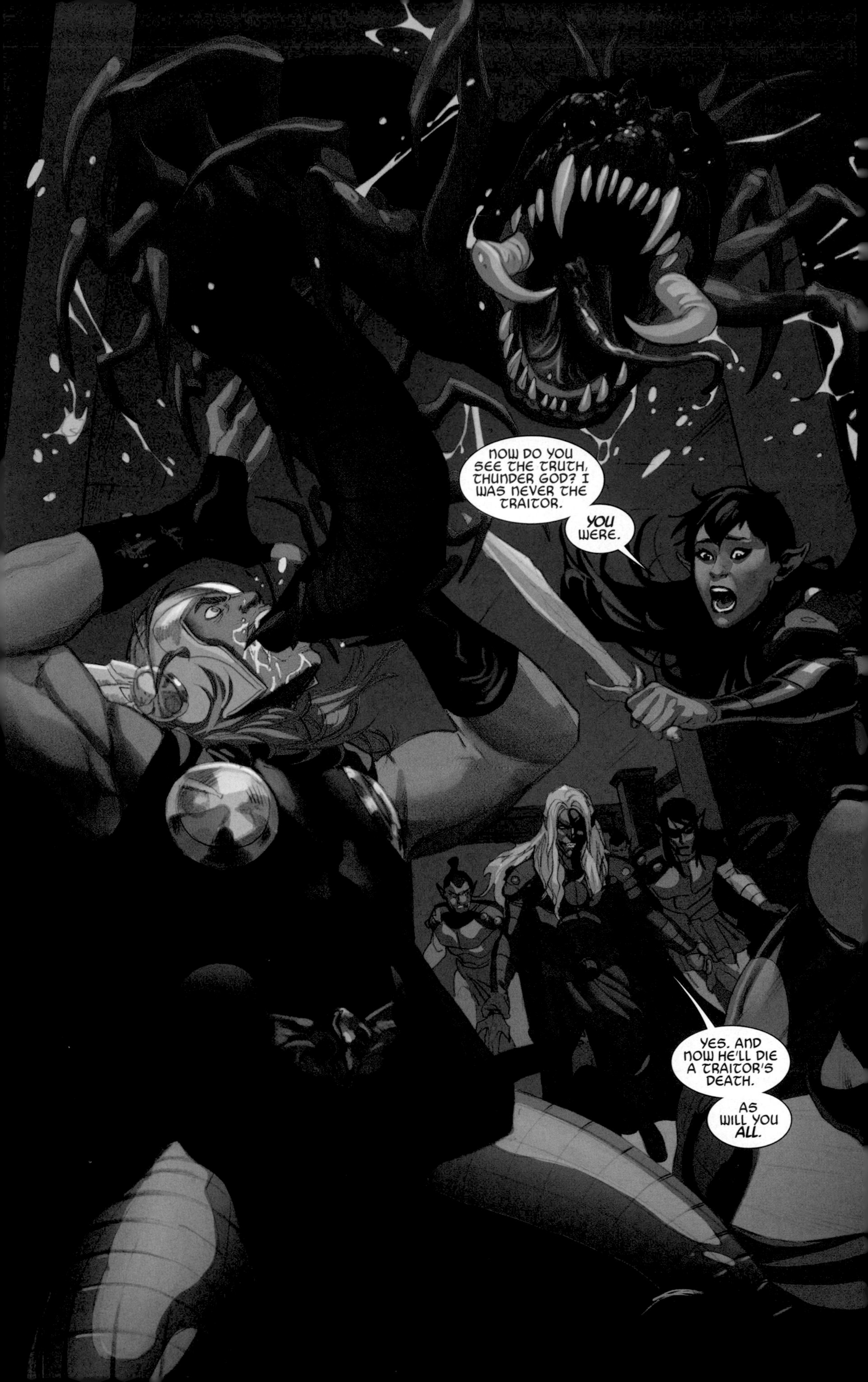
NOW DO YOU SEE THE TRUTH, THUNDER GOD? I WAS NEVER THE TRAITOR.
YOU WERE.
YES. AND NOW HE'LL DIE A TRAITOR'S DEATH.
AS WILL YOU ALL.

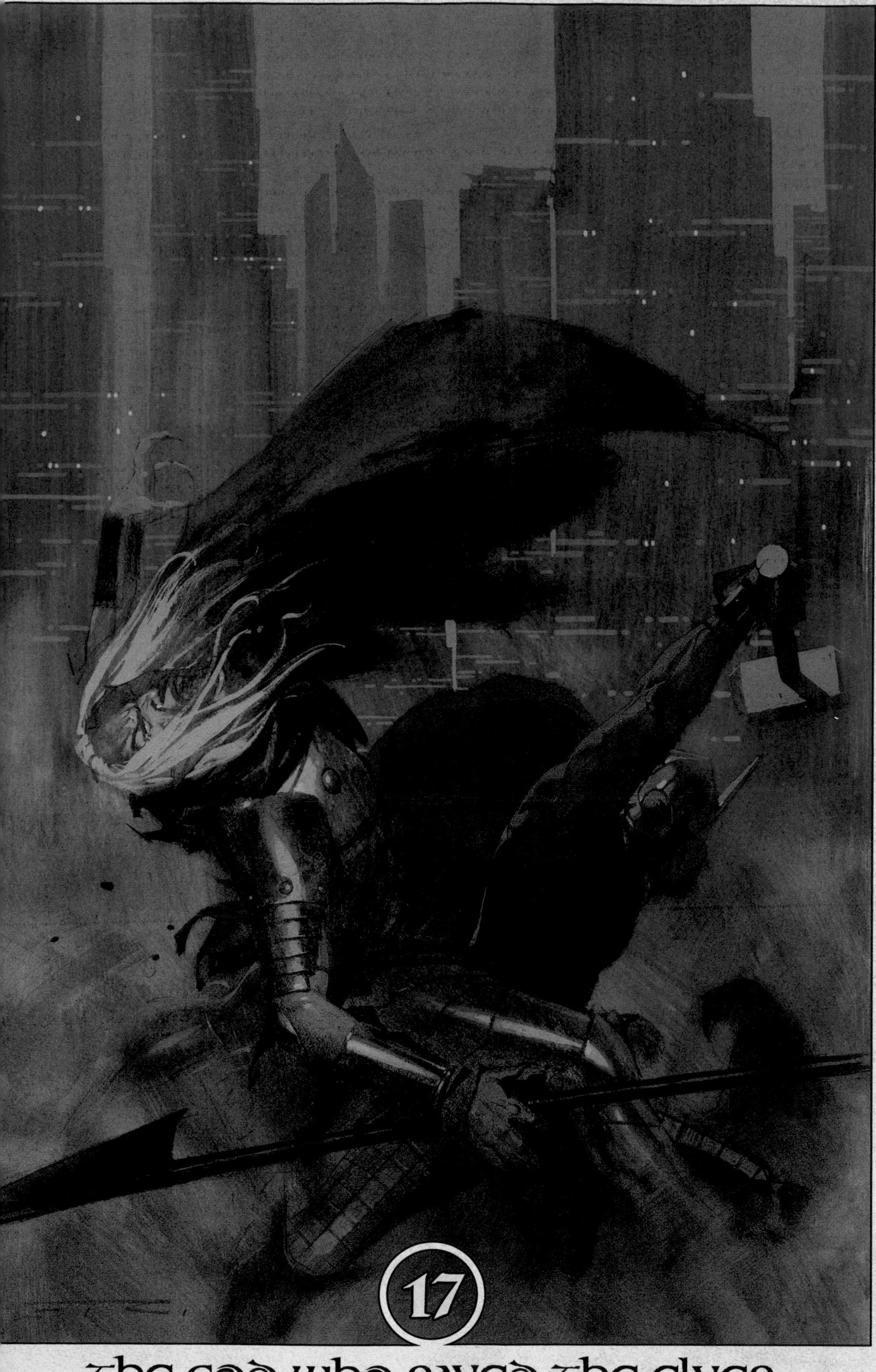

17

The God Who Saved the Elves

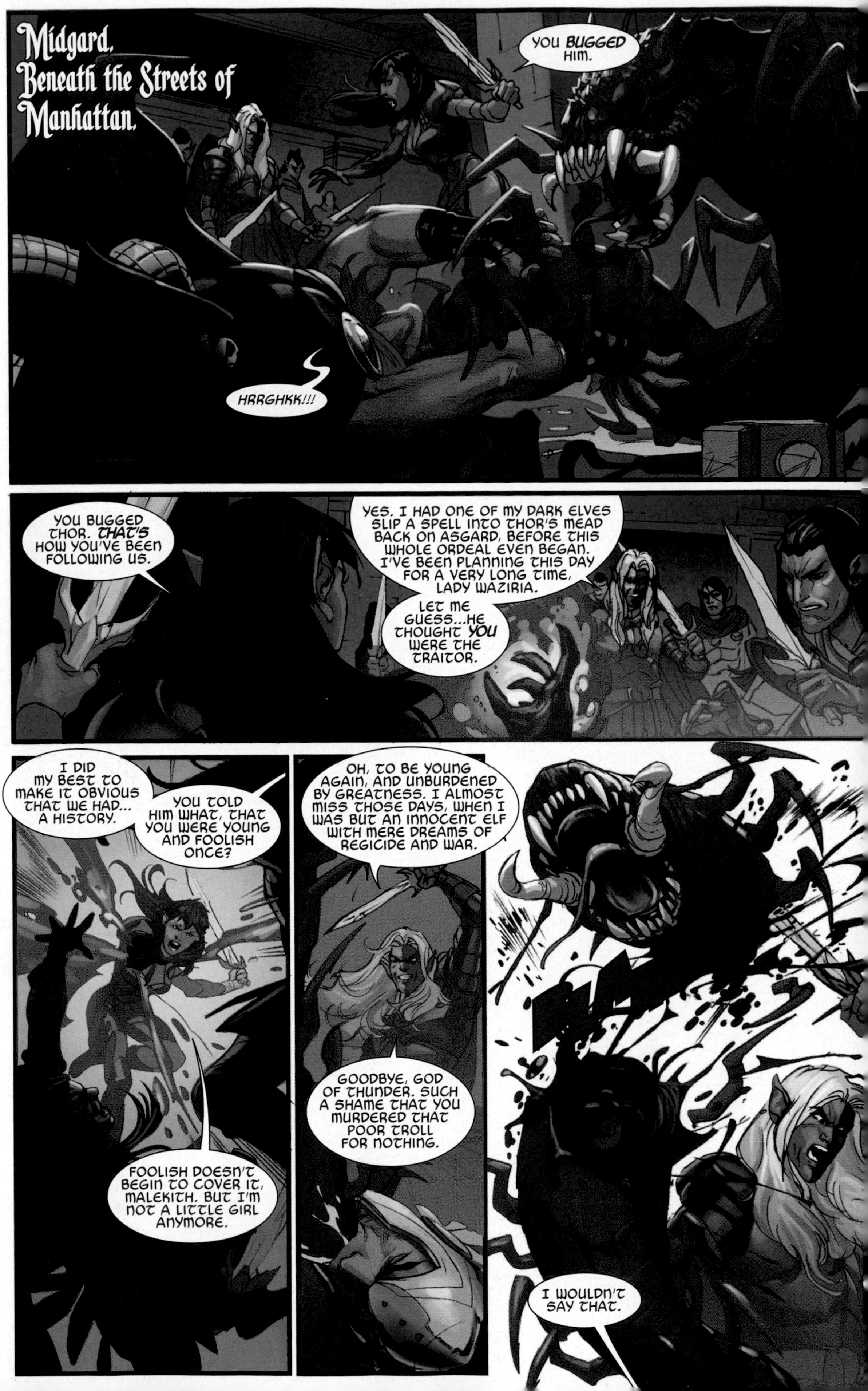
Midgard, Beneath the Streets of Manhattan.
YOU BUGGED HIM.
HRRGHKK!!!
YOU BUGGED THOR. THAT'S HOW YOU'VE BEEN FOLLOWING US.
YES. I HAD ONE OF MY DARK ELVES SLIP A SPELL INTO THOR'S MEAD BACK ON ASGARD, BEFORE THIS WHOLE ORDEAL EVEN BEGAN. I'VE BEEN PLANNING THIS DAY FOR A VERY LONG TIME, LADY WAZIRIA.
LET ME GUESS...HE THOUGHT YOU WERE THE TRAITOR.
I DID MY BEST TO MAKE IT OBVIOUS THAT WE HAD... A HISTORY.
YOU TOLD HIM WHAT, THAT YOU WERE YOUNG AND FOOLISH ONCE?
FOOLISH DOESN'T BEGIN TO COVER IT, MALEKITH. BUT I'M NOT A LITTLE GIRL ANYMORE.
OH, TO BE YOUNG AGAIN, AND UNBURDENED BY GREATNESS. I ALMOST MISS THOSE DAYS, WHEN I WAS BUT AN INNOCENT ELF WITH MERE DREAMS OF REGICIDE AND WAR.
GOODBYE, GOD OF THUNDER. SUCH A SHAME THAT YOU MURDERED THAT POOR TROLL FOR NOTHING.
I WOULDN'T SAY THAT.

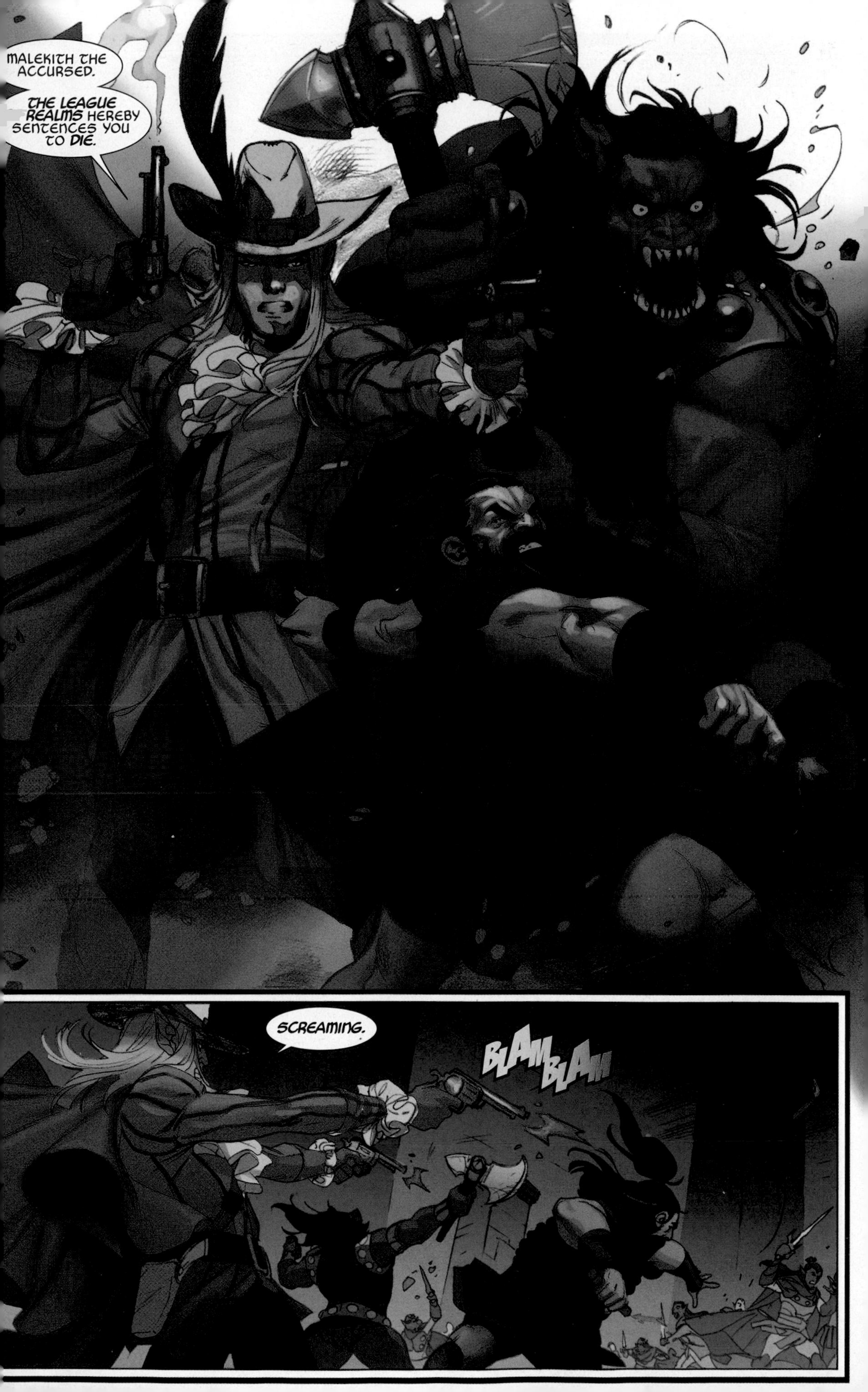
MALEKITH THE ACCURSED.
THE LEAGUE REALMS HEREBY SENTENCES YOU TO DIE.
SCREAMING.
BLAM BLAM

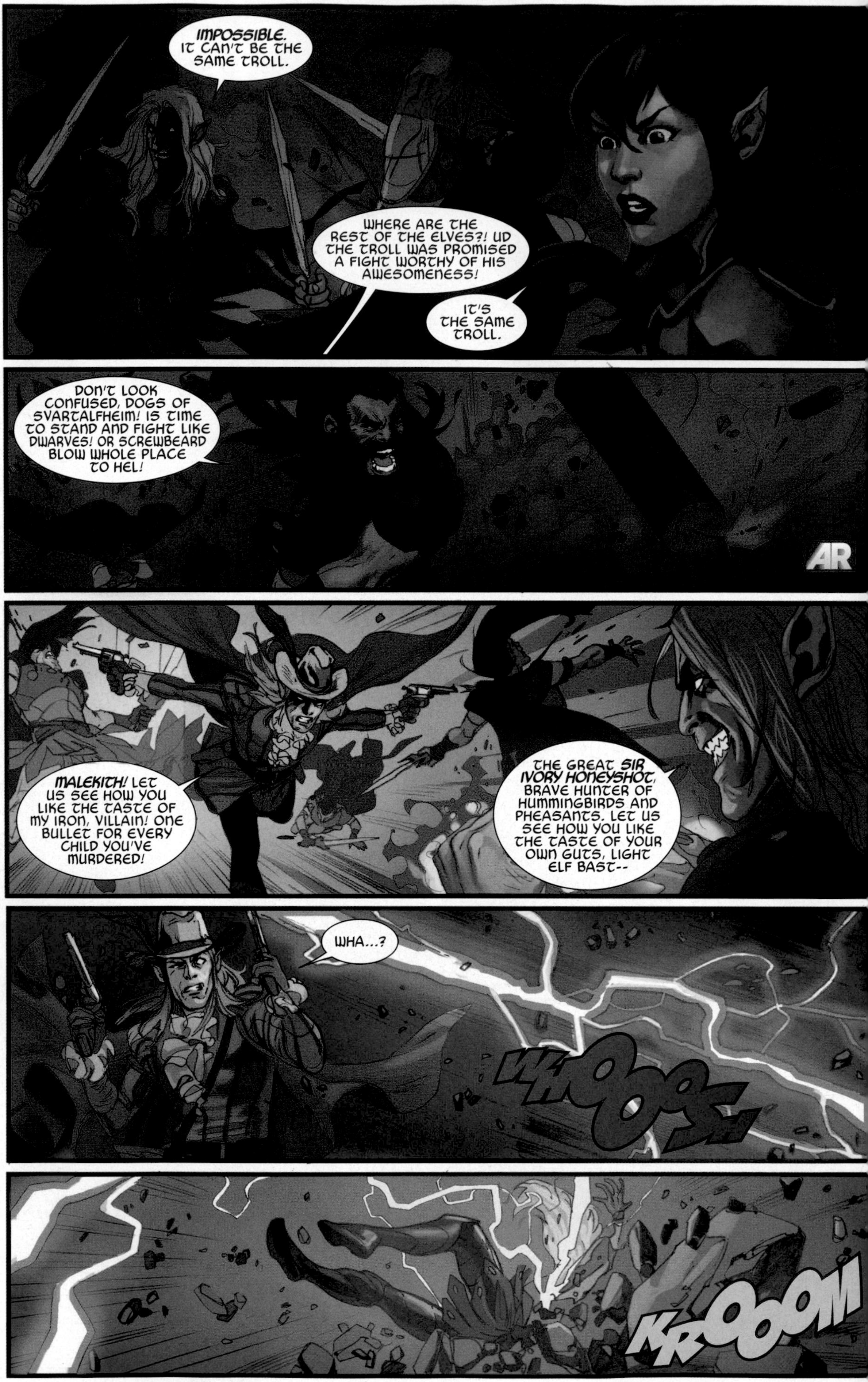
IMPOSSIBLE. IT CAN'T BE THE SAME TROLL.
WHERE ARE THE REST OF THE ELVES?! UD THE TROLL WAS PROMISED A FIGHT WORTHY OF HIS AWESOMENESS!
IT'S THE SAME TROLL.
DON'T LOOK CONFUSED, DOGS OF SVARTALFHEIM! IS TIME TO STAND AND FIGHT LIKE DWARVES! OR SCREWBEARD BLOW WHOLE PLACE TO HEL!
AR
MALEKITH! LET US SEE HOW YOU LIKE THE TASTE OF MY IRON, VILLAIN! ONE BULLET FOR EVERY CHILD YOU'VE MURDERED!
THE GREAT SIR IVORY HONEYSHOT, BRAVE HUNTER OF HUMMINGBIRDS AND PHEASANTS. LET US SEE HOW YOU LIKE THE TASTE OF YOUR OWN GUTS, LIGHT ELF BAST--
WHA...?
WHOOOSH
KROOOOM

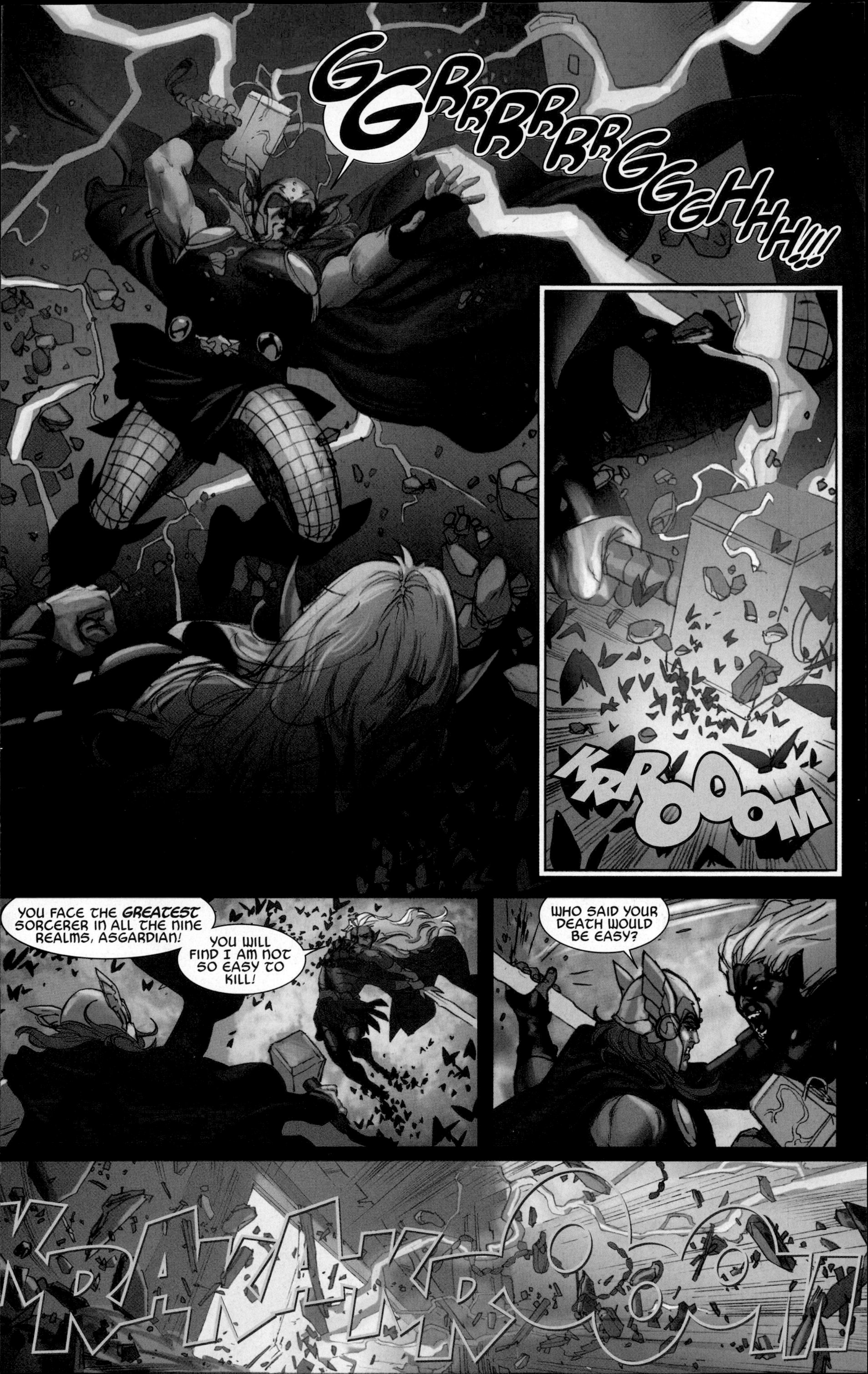
GGRRRRRRRGGGHHH!!!
KRROOOM
YOU FACE THE GREATEST SORCERER IN ALL THE NINE REALMS, ASGARDIAN!
YOU WILL FIND I AM NOT SO EASY TO KILL!
WHO SAID YOUR DEATH WOULD BE EASY?

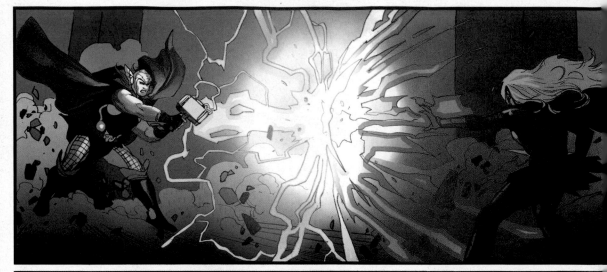

HEH. I SUPPOSE YOU KNOW A LITTLE SOMETHING ABOUT SORCERY YOURSELF, DON'T YOU?

THAT WAS QUITE THE LITTLE PANTOMIME YOU PUT TOGETHER BACK IN VANAHEIM, WHEN YOU CONVINCED ME YOU'D SLAIN THE TROLL. WHERE EXACTLY DID YOU PICK UP THAT SPELL?

YOU DON'T GROW UP THE BROTHER OF LOKI... WITHOUT LEARNING A FEW OF HIS TRICKS.

WOOOM

WELL THEN...

ALLOW ME TO SHOW YOU A FEW OF MINE.

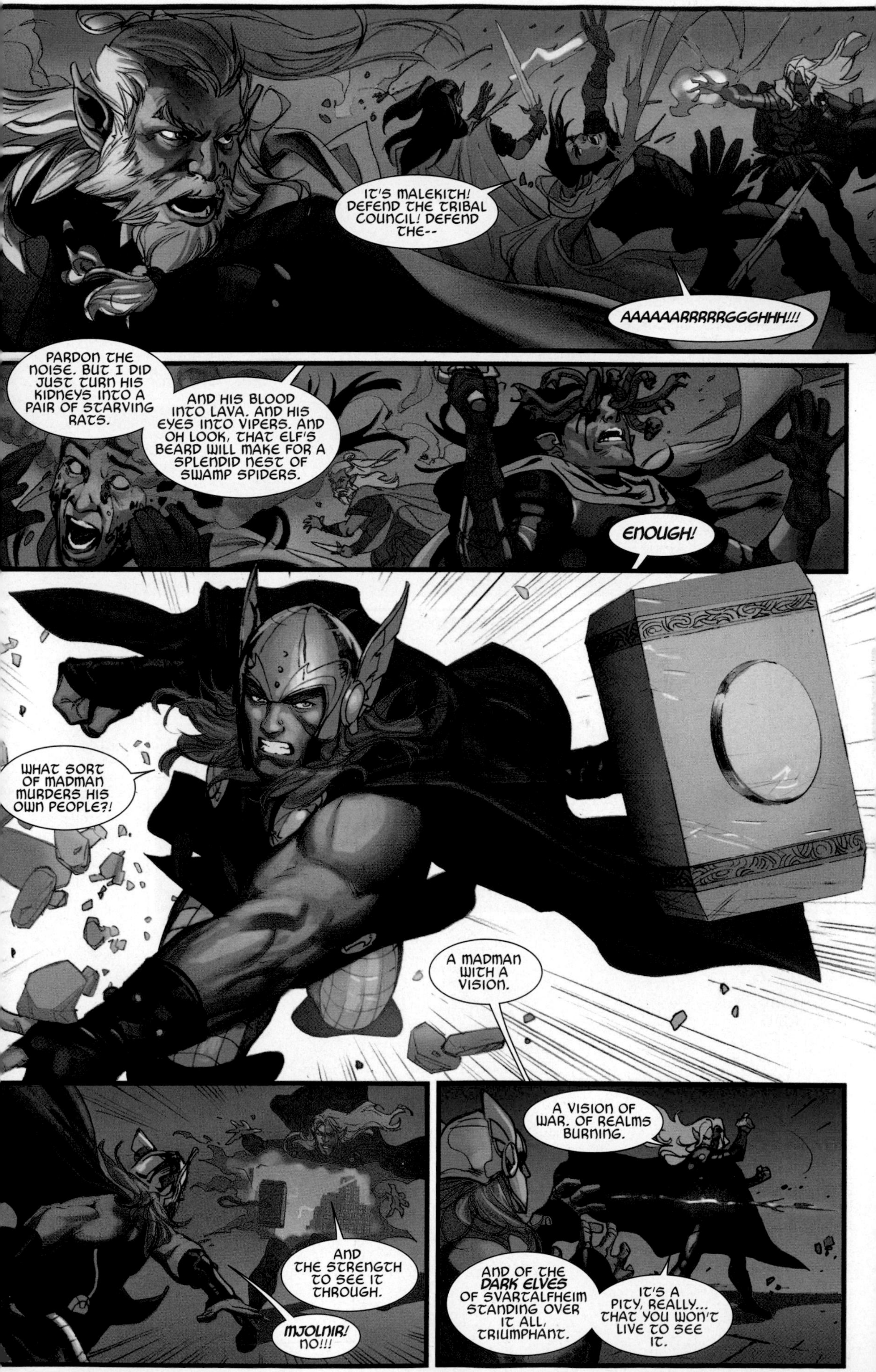
IT'S MALEKITH! DEFEND THE TRIBAL COUNCIL! DEFEND THE--
AAAAAARRRRRGGGHHH!!!
PARDON THE NOISE. BUT I DID JUST TURN HIS KIDNEYS INTO A PAIR OF STARVING RATS.
AND HIS BLOOD INTO LAVA. AND HIS EYES INTO VIPERS. AND OH LOOK, THAT ELF'S BEARD WILL MAKE FOR A SPLENDID NEST OF SWAMP SPIDERS.
ENOUGH!
WHAT SORT OF MADMAN MURDERS HIS OWN PEOPLE?!
A MADMAN WITH A VISION.
AND THE STRENGTH TO SEE IT THROUGH.
MJOLNIR! NO!!!
A VISION OF WAR. OF REALMS BURNING.
AND OF THE DARK ELVES OF SVARTALFHEIM STANDING OVER IT ALL, TRIUMPHANT.
IT'S A PITY, REALLY... THAT YOU WON'T LIVE TO SEE IT.

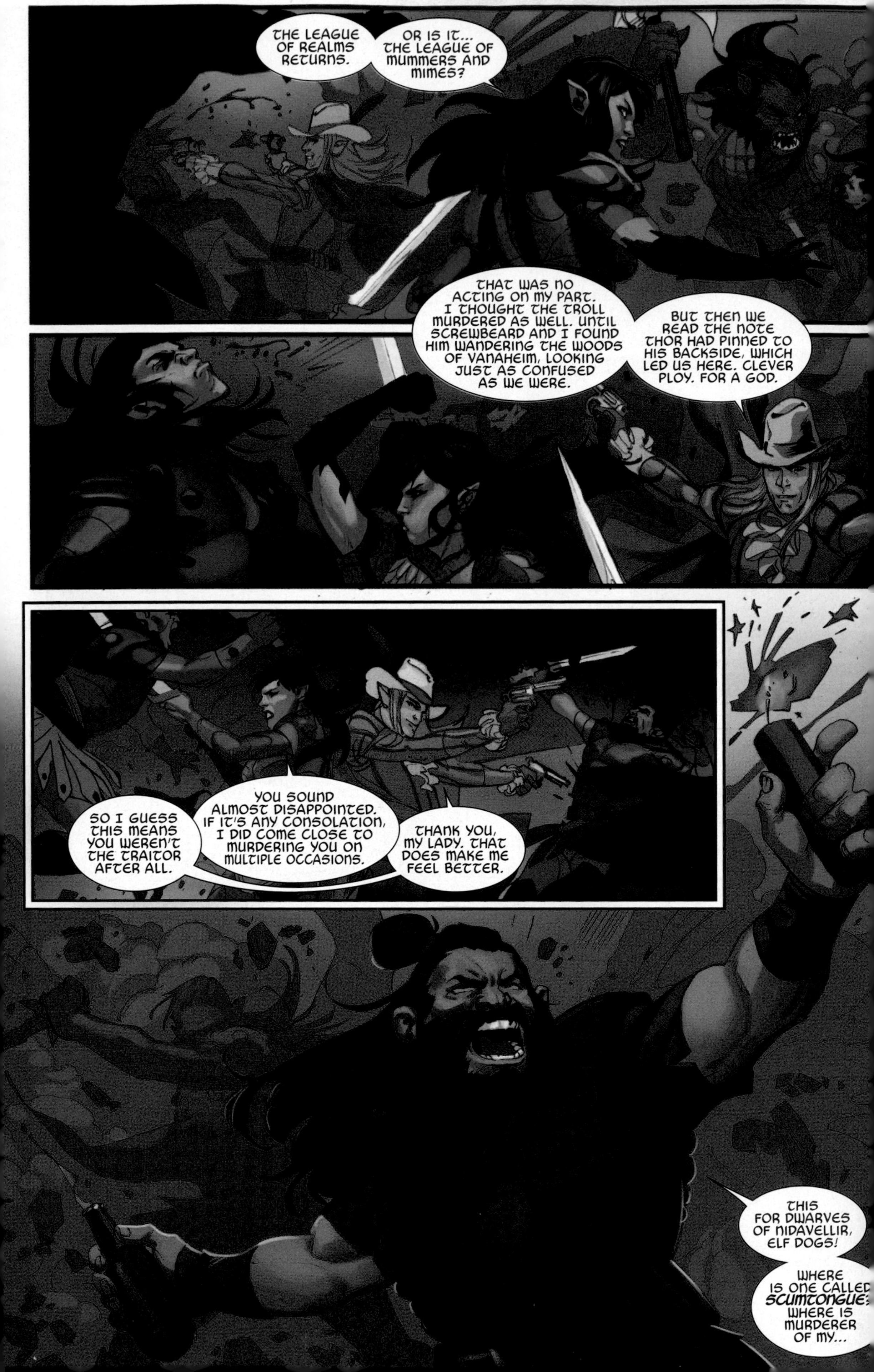
THE LEAGUE OF REALMS RETURNS.
OR IS IT... THE LEAGUE OF MUMMERS AND MIMES?
THAT WAS NO ACTING ON MY PART. I THOUGHT THE TROLL MURDERED AS WELL. UNTIL SCREWBEARD AND I FOUND HIM WANDERING THE WOODS OF VANAHEIM, LOOKING JUST AS CONFUSED AS WE WERE.
BUT THEN WE READ THE NOTE THOR HAD PINNED TO HIS BACKSIDE, WHICH LED US HERE. CLEVER PLOY. FOR A GOD.
SO I GUESS THIS MEANS YOU WEREN'T THE TRAITOR AFTER ALL.
YOU SOUND ALMOST DISAPPOINTED. IF IT'S ANY CONSOLATION, I DID COME CLOSE TO MURDERING YOU ON MULTIPLE OCCASIONS.
THANK YOU, MY LADY. THAT DOES MAKE ME FEEL BETTER.
THIS FOR DWARVES OF NIDAVELLIR, ELF DOGS!
WHERE IS ONE CALLED *SCUMTONGUE*? WHERE IS MURDERER OF MY...

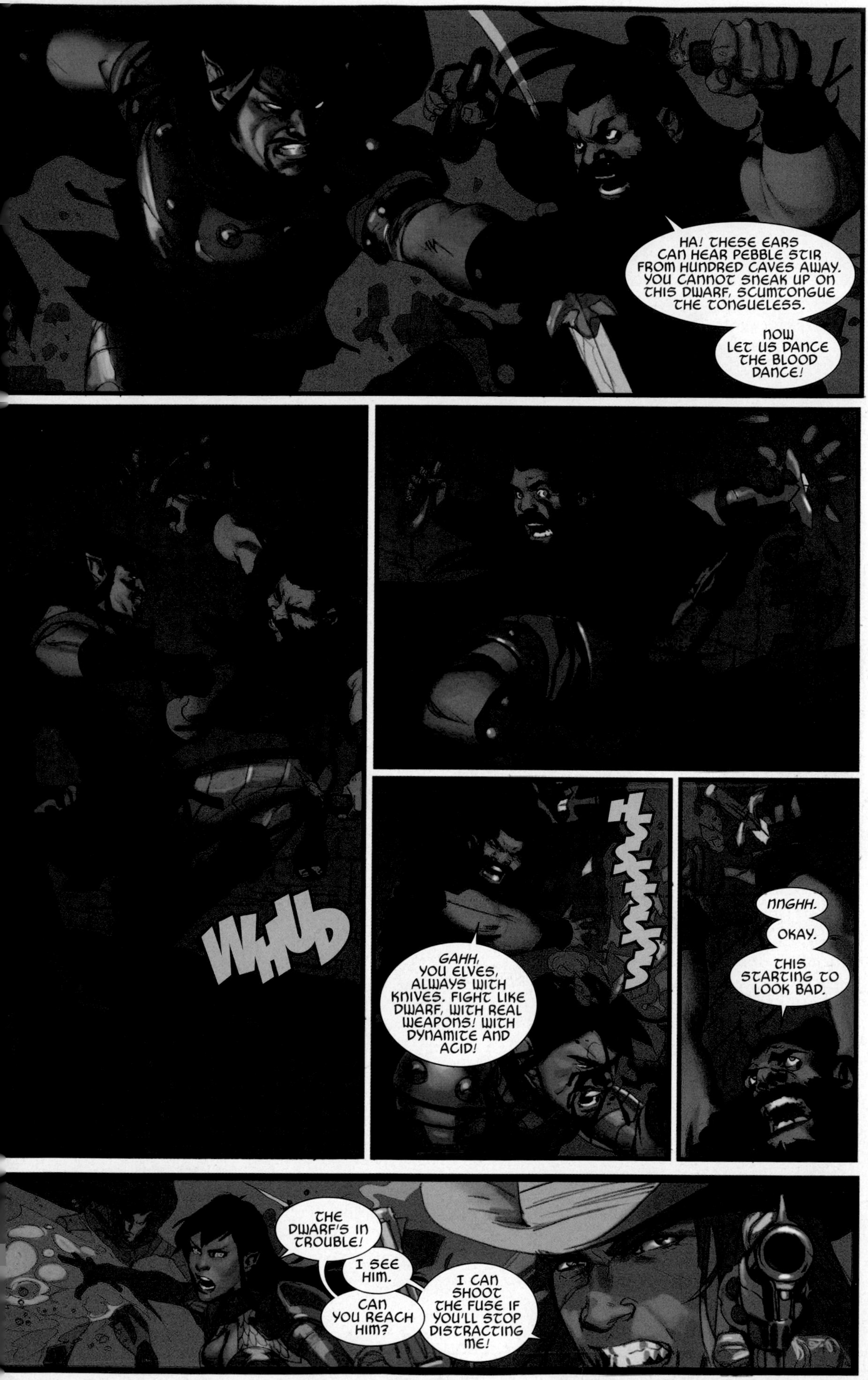

HA! THESE EARS CAN HEAR PEBBLE STIR FROM HUNDRED CAVES AWAY. YOU CANNOT SNEAK UP ON THIS DWARF, SCUMTONGUE THE TONGUELESS.
NOW LET US DANCE THE BLOOD DANCE!
WHUD
GAHH, YOU ELVES, ALWAYS WITH KNIVES. FIGHT LIKE DWARF, WITH REAL WEAPONS! WITH DYNAMITE AND ACID!
NNGHH.
OKAY.
THIS STARTING TO LOOK BAD.
THE DWARF'S IN TROUBLE!
I SEE HIM.
CAN YOU REACH HIM?
I CAN SHOOT THE FUSE IF YOU'LL STOP DISTRACTING ME!

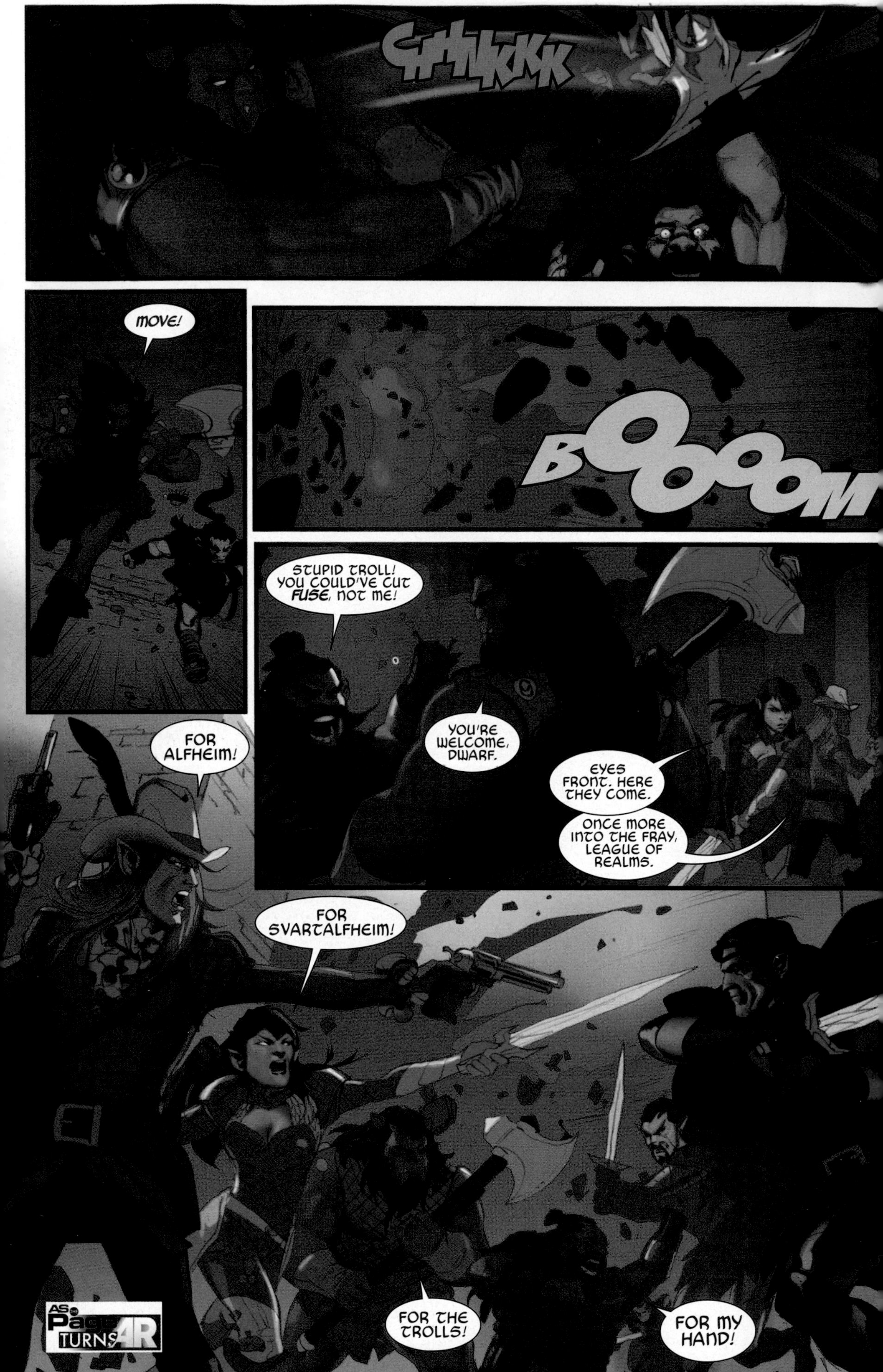
CHHKKK
MOVE!
BOOOOOM
STUPID TROLL! YOU COULD'VE CUT FUSE, NOT ME!
YOU'RE WELCOME, DWARF.
EYES FRONT. HERE THEY COME.
ONCE MORE INTO THE FRAY, LEAGUE OF REALMS.
FOR ALFHEIM!
FOR SVARTALFHEIM!
FOR THE TROLLS!
FOR MY HAND!
AS THE Page TURNS AR

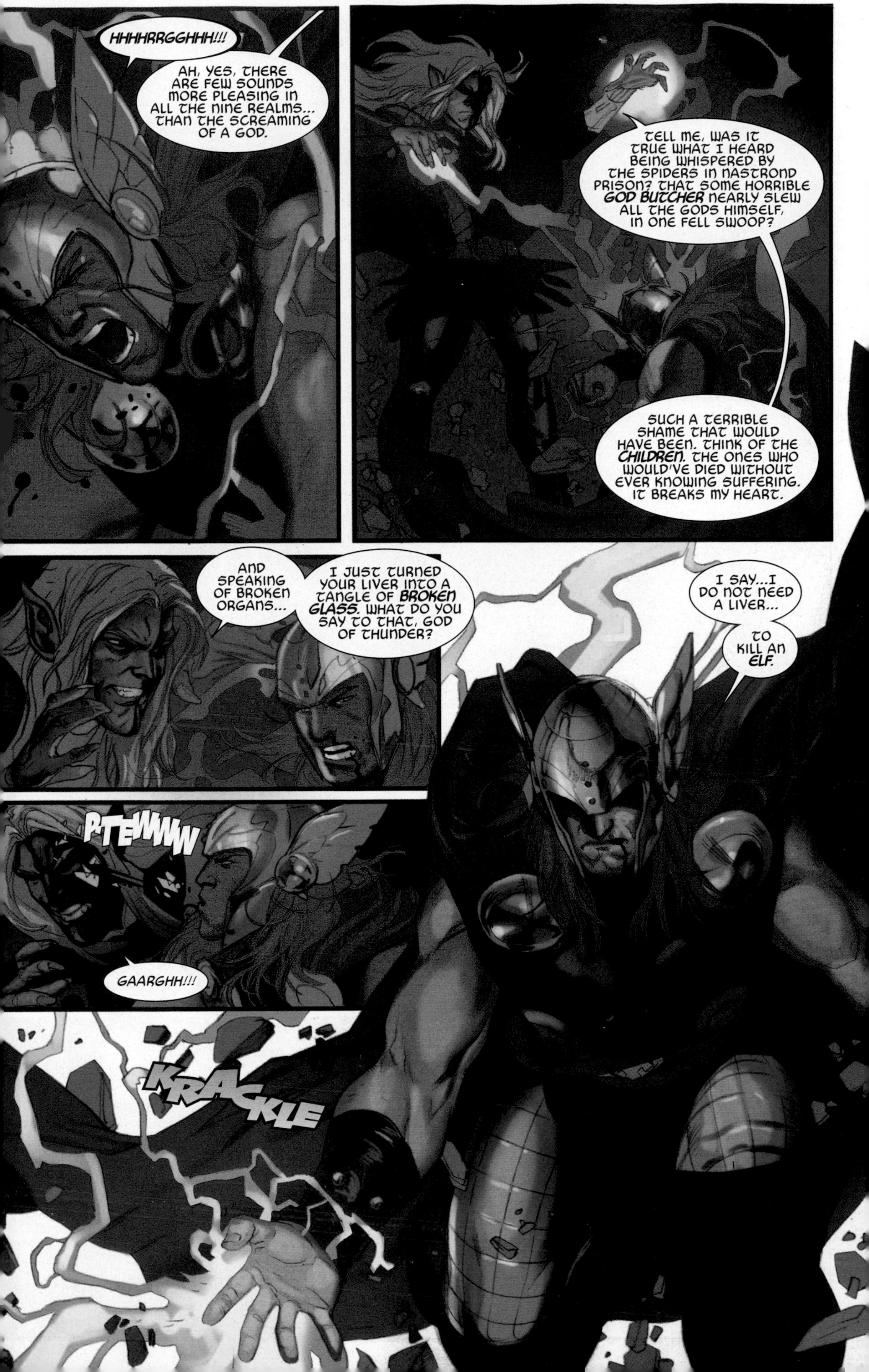
HHHHRRGGHHH!!!
AH, YES, THERE ARE FEW SOUNDS MORE PLEASING IN ALL THE NINE REALMS... THAN THE SCREAMING OF A GOD.
TELL ME, WAS IT TRUE WHAT I HEARD BEING WHISPERED BY THE SPIDERS IN NASTROND PRISON? THAT SOME HORRIBLE GOD BUTCHER NEARLY SLEW ALL THE GODS HIMSELF, IN ONE FELL SWOOP?
SUCH A TERRIBLE SHAME THAT WOULD HAVE BEEN. THINK OF THE CHILDREN. THE ONES WHO WOULD'VE DIED WITHOUT EVER KNOWING SUFFERING. IT BREAKS MY HEART.
AND SPEAKING OF BROKEN ORGANS...
I JUST TURNED YOUR LIVER INTO A TANGLE OF BROKEN GLASS. WHAT DO YOU SAY TO THAT, GOD OF THUNDER?
I SAY...I DO NOT NEED A LIVER...
TO KILL AN ELF.
PTEWWW
GAARGHH!!!
KRACKLE

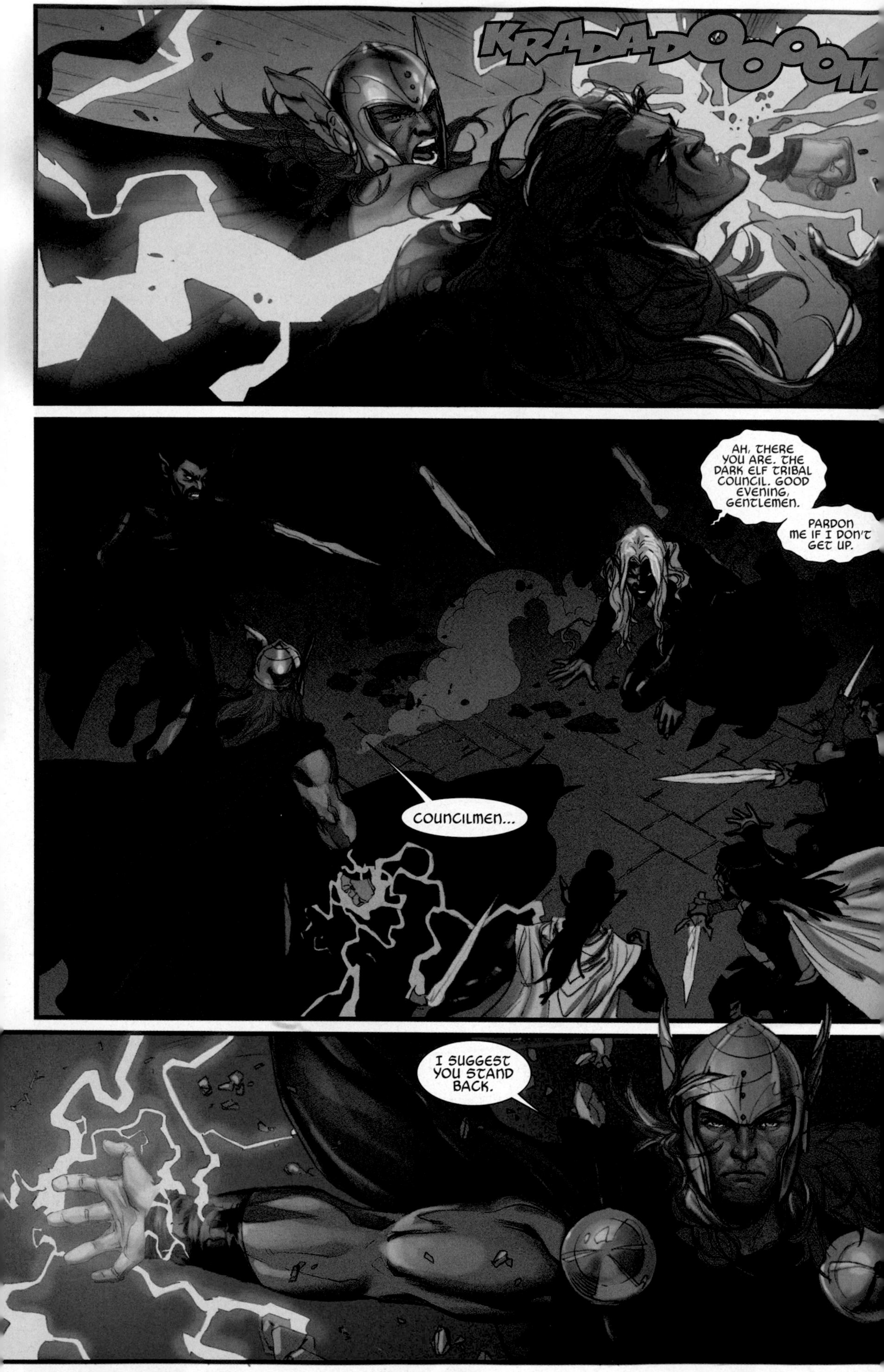
KRADADOOOOOOM
AH, THERE YOU ARE. THE DARK ELF TRIBAL COUNCIL. GOOD EVENING, GENTLEMEN.
PARDON ME IF I DON'T GET UP.
COUNCILMEN...
I SUGGEST YOU STAND BACK.

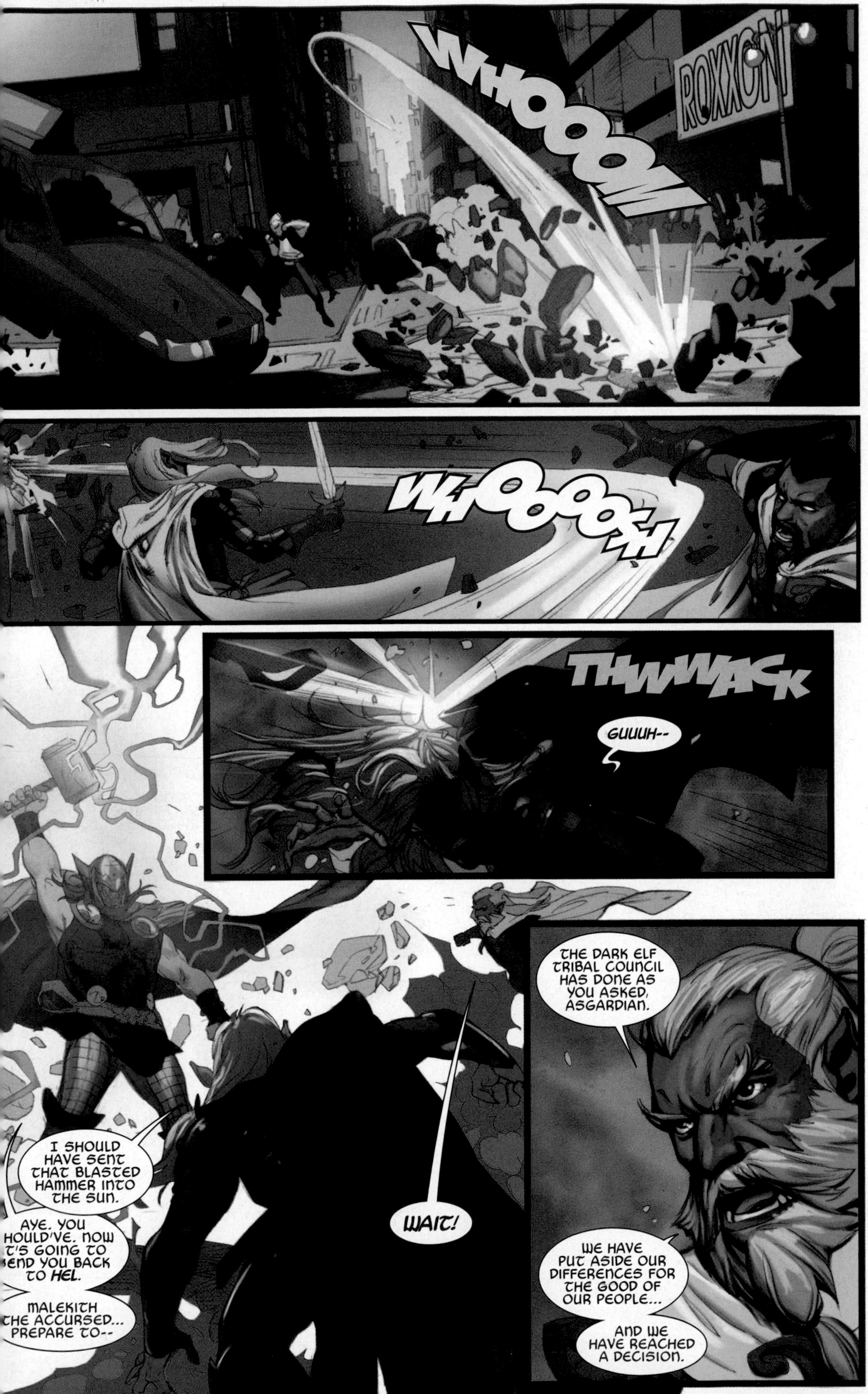

WHOOOOM
ROXXON
WHOOOOOSH
THWWACK
GUUUH--
I SHOULD HAVE SENT THAT BLASTED HAMMER INTO THE SUN.
AYE. YOU HOULD'VE. NOW T'S GOING TO END YOU BACK TO HEL.
MALEKITH THE ACCURSED... PREPARE TO--
WAIT!
THE DARK ELF TRIBAL COUNCIL HAS DONE AS YOU ASKED, ASGARDIAN.
WE HAVE PUT ASIDE OUR DIFFERENCES FOR THE GOOD OF OUR PEOPLE...
AND WE HAVE REACHED A DECISION.

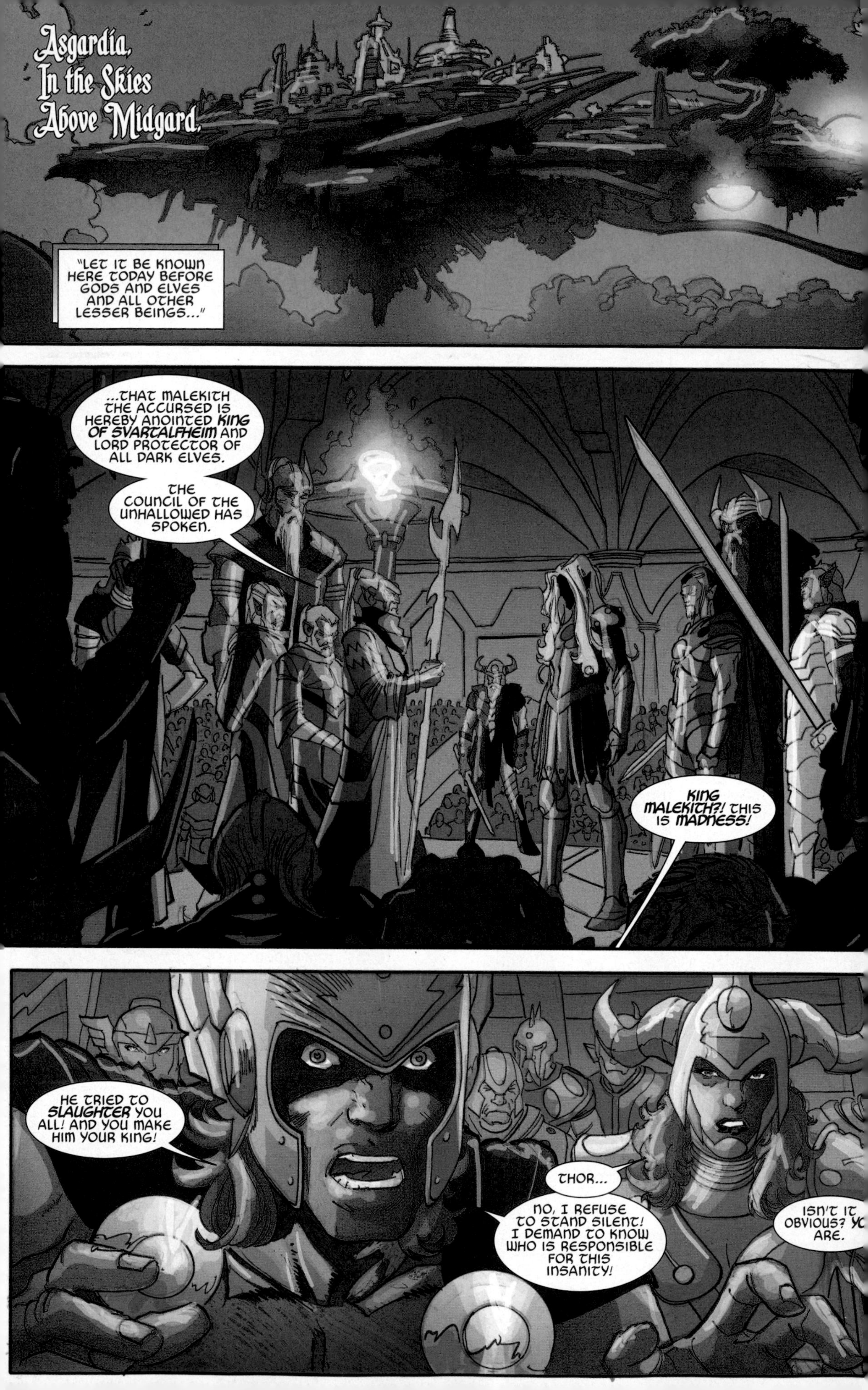
Asgardia, In the Skies Above Midgard.
"LET IT BE KNOWN HERE TODAY BEFORE GODS AND ELVES AND ALL OTHER LESSER BEINGS..."
...THAT MALEKITH THE ACCURSED IS HEREBY ANOINTED KING OF SVARTALFHEIM AND LORD PROTECTOR OF ALL DARK ELVES.
THE COUNCIL OF THE UNHALLOWED HAS SPOKEN.
KING MALEKITH?! THIS IS MADNESS!
HE TRIED TO SLAUGHTER YOU ALL! AND YOU MAKE HIM YOUR KING!
THOR...
NO, I REFUSE TO STAND SILENT! I DEMAND TO KNOW WHO IS RESPONSIBLE FOR THIS INSANITY!
ISN'T IT OBVIOUS? YC ARE.

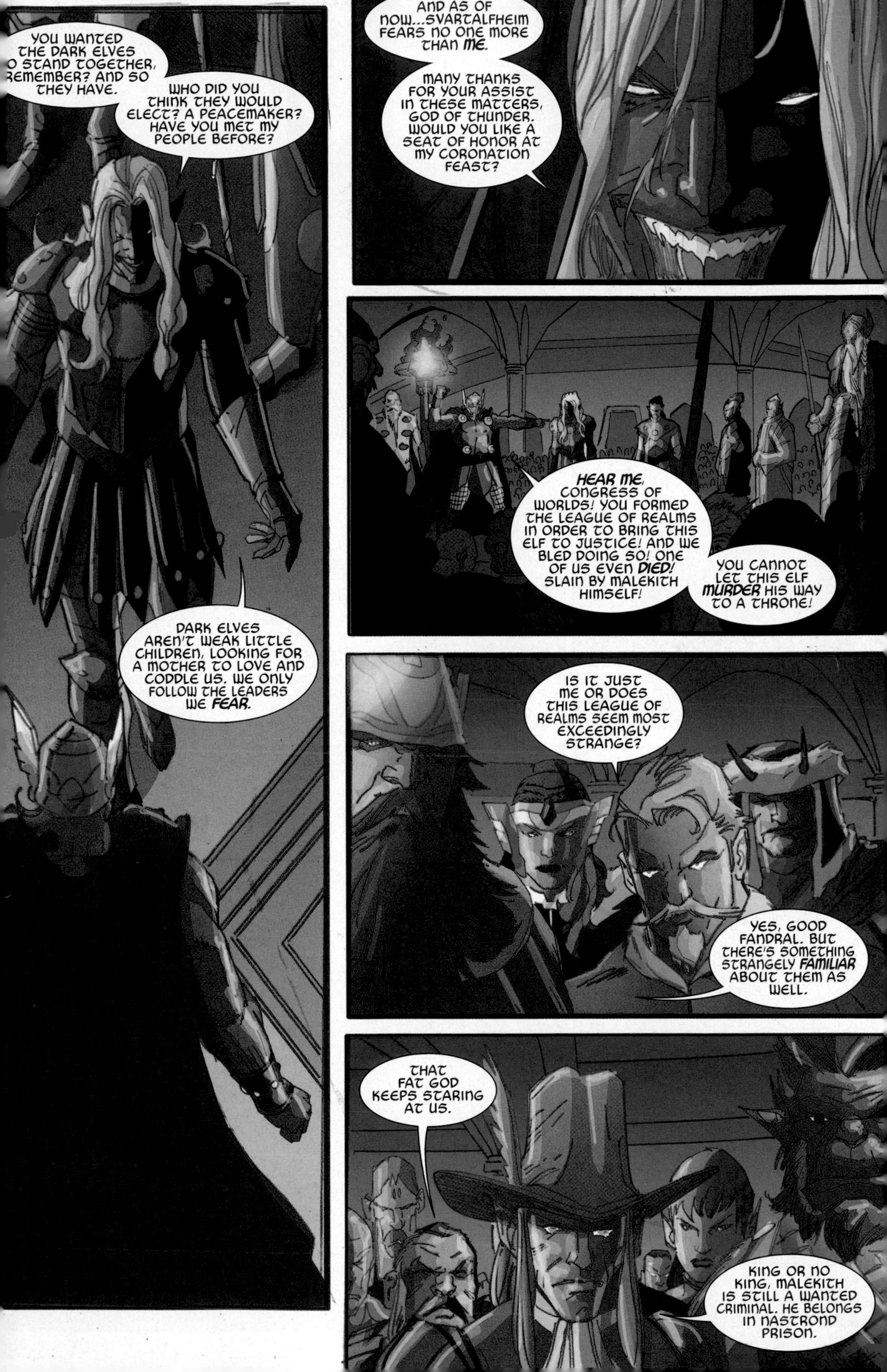
YOU WANTED THE DARK ELVES TO STAND TOGETHER, REMEMBER? AND SO THEY HAVE.
WHO DID YOU THINK THEY WOULD ELECT? A PEACEMAKER? HAVE YOU MET MY PEOPLE BEFORE?
DARK ELVES AREN'T WEAK LITTLE CHILDREN, LOOKING FOR A MOTHER TO LOVE AND CODDLE US. WE ONLY FOLLOW THE LEADERS WE FEAR.
AND AS OF NOW...SVARTALFHEIM FEARS NO ONE MORE THAN ME.
MANY THANKS FOR YOUR ASSIST IN THESE MATTERS, GOD OF THUNDER. WOULD YOU LIKE A SEAT OF HONOR AT MY CORONATION FEAST?
HEAR ME, CONGRESS OF WORLDS! YOU FORMED THE LEAGUE OF REALMS IN ORDER TO BRING THIS ELF TO JUSTICE! AND WE BLED DOING SO! ONE OF US EVEN DIED! SLAIN BY MALEKITH HIMSELF!
YOU CANNOT LET THIS ELF MURDER HIS WAY TO A THRONE!
IS IT JUST ME OR DOES THIS LEAGUE OF REALMS SEEM MOST EXCEEDINGLY STRANGE?
YES, GOOD FANDRAL. BUT THERE'S SOMETHING STRANGELY FAMILIAR ABOUT THEM AS WELL.
THAT FAT GOD KEEPS STARING AT US.
KING OR NO KING, MALEKITH IS STILL A WANTED CRIMINAL. HE BELONGS IN NASTROND PRISON.

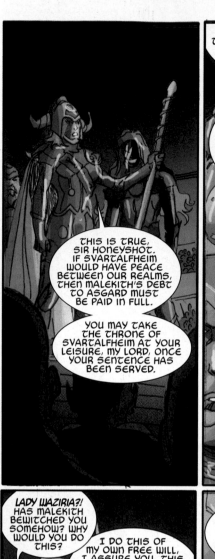

THIS IS TRUE, SIR HONEYSHOT. IF SVARTALFHEIM WOULD HAVE PEACE BETWEEN OUR REALMS, THEN MALEKITH'S DEBT TO ASGARD MUST BE PAID IN FULL.

YOU MAY TAKE THE THRONE OF SVARTALFHEIM AT YOUR LEISURE, MY LORD, ONCE YOUR SENTENCE HAS BEEN SERVED.

WHAT DID YOU HAVE LEFT TO GO? A MERE THOUSAND YEARS OR SO? I'M SURE YOUR PEOPLE WILL WAIT FOR YOU.

I INVOKE THE ROYAL RIGHT TO CALL A PROXY.

A PROXY? WHY YES, OF COURSE. IF YOU CAN FIND A VOLUNTEER WILLING TO TAKE YOUR PLACE IN THE SNAKE PITS OF NIFFLEHEIM, THEN BY ALL MEANS--

I WILL.

I WILL BE HIS PROXY.

LADY WAZIRIA?! HAS MALEKITH BEWITCHED YOU SOMEHOW? WHY WOULD YOU DO THIS?

I DO THIS OF MY OWN FREE WILL, I ASSURE YOU. THIS IS THE WAY IT MUST BE. THIS WILL END THE BLOODSHED. MY PEOPLE WILL BE SAFE ONCE MORE.

BUT BEWARE, THOR... AS YOURS WILL NOT.

I AM SORRY, MY LADY...FOR EVER DOUBTING YOU. FOR EVERYTHING THAT--

NEVER APOLOGIZE, ASGARDIAN, FOR ANYTHING THAT YOU ARE. YOU FIGHT LIKE A TROLL. DRINK LIKE A GIANT. MAKE LOVE LIKE AN ELF. WOULD THAT ALL GODS WERE MORE LIKE THOR.

NOW...GIVE ME ONE LAST MEMORY...TO KEEP ME WARM IN THE LAND OF THE DEAD.

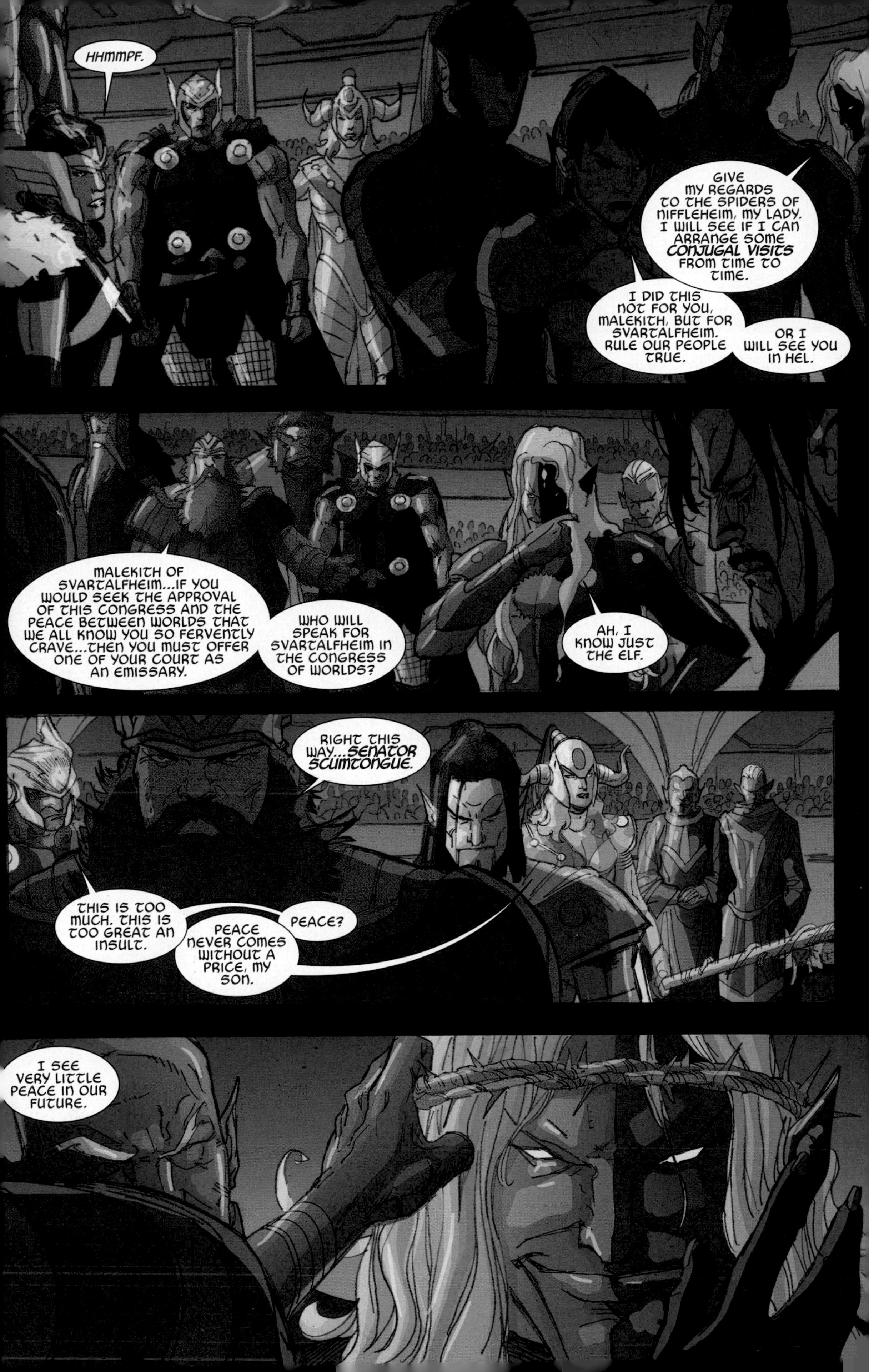
HHMMPF.
GIVE MY REGARDS TO THE SPIDERS OF NIFFLEHEIM, MY LADY. I WILL SEE IF I CAN ARRANGE SOME CONJUGAL VISITS FROM TIME TO TIME.
I DID THIS NOT FOR YOU, MALEKITH, BUT FOR SVARTALFHEIM. RULE OUR PEOPLE TRUE.
OR I WILL SEE YOU IN HEL.
MALEKITH OF SVARTALFHEIM...IF YOU WOULD SEEK THE APPROVAL OF THIS CONGRESS AND THE PEACE BETWEEN WORLDS THAT WE ALL KNOW YOU SO FERVENTLY CRAVE...THEN YOU MUST OFFER ONE OF YOUR COURT AS AN EMISSARY.
WHO WILL SPEAK FOR SVARTALFHEIM IN THE CONGRESS OF WORLDS?
AH, I KNOW JUST THE ELF.
RIGHT THIS WAY...SENATOR SCUMTONGUE.
THIS IS TOO MUCH. THIS IS TOO GREAT AN INSULT.
PEACE?
PEACE NEVER COMES WITHOUT A PRICE, MY SON.
I SEE VERY LITTLE PEACE IN OUR FUTURE.

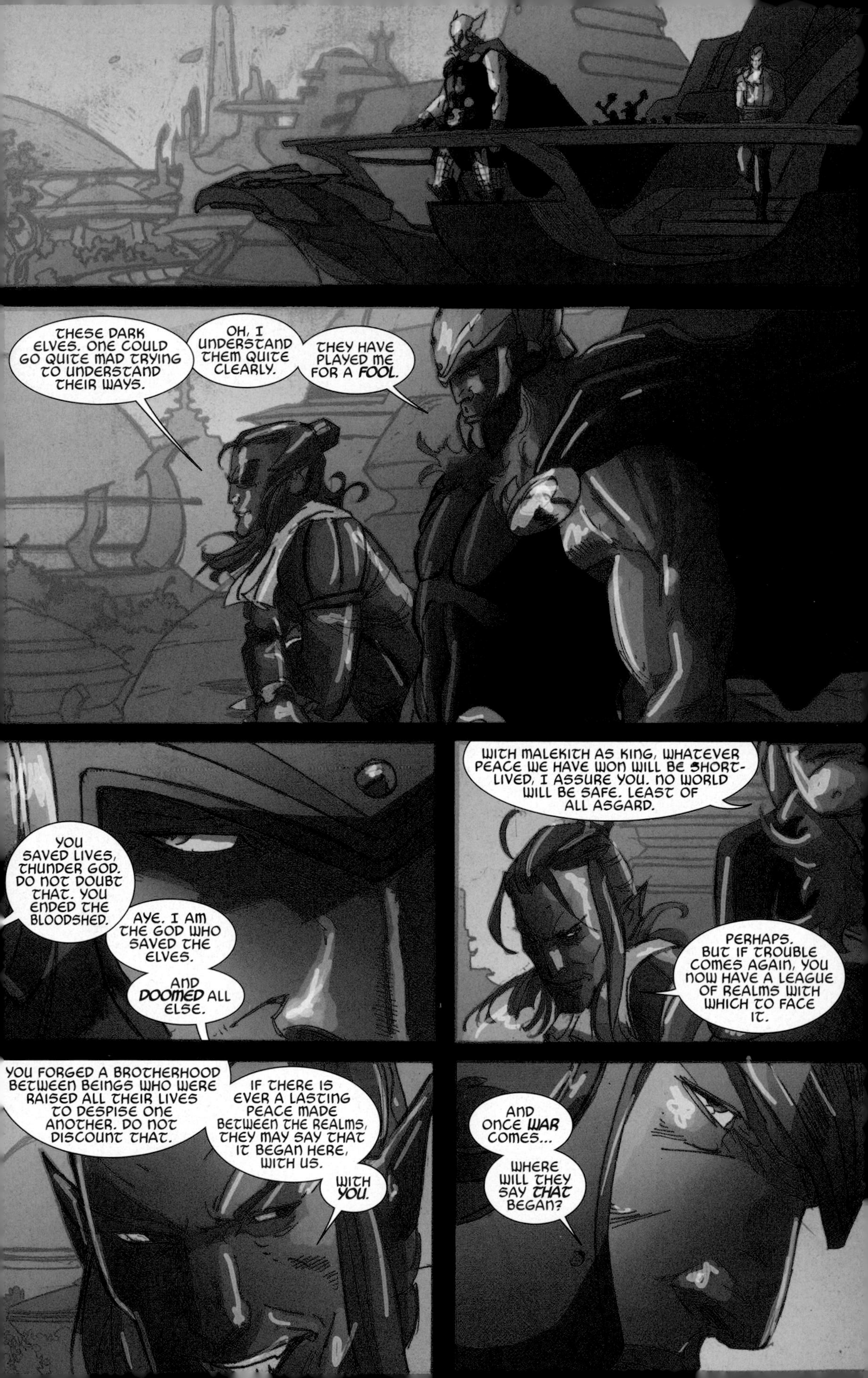

THESE DARK ELVES. ONE COULD GO QUITE MAD TRYING TO UNDERSTAND THEIR WAYS.
OH, I UNDERSTAND THEM QUITE CLEARLY.
THEY HAVE PLAYED ME FOR A FOOL.
YOU SAVED LIVES, THUNDER GOD. DO NOT DOUBT THAT. YOU ENDED THE BLOODSHED.
AYE. I AM THE GOD WHO SAVED THE ELVES.
AND DOOMED ALL ELSE.
WITH MALEKITH AS KING, WHATEVER PEACE WE HAVE WON WILL BE SHORT-LIVED, I ASSURE YOU. NO WORLD WILL BE SAFE. LEAST OF ALL ASGARD.
PERHAPS. BUT IF TROUBLE COMES AGAIN, YOU NOW HAVE A LEAGUE OF REALMS WITH WHICH TO FACE IT.
YOU FORGED A BROTHERHOOD BETWEEN BEINGS WHO WERE RAISED ALL THEIR LIVES TO DESPISE ONE ANOTHER. DO NOT DISCOUNT THAT.
IF THERE IS EVER A LASTING PEACE MADE BETWEEN THE REALMS, THEY MAY SAY THAT IT BEGAN HERE, WITH US.
WITH YOU.
AND ONCE WAR COMES...
WHERE WILL THEY SAY THAT BEGAN?

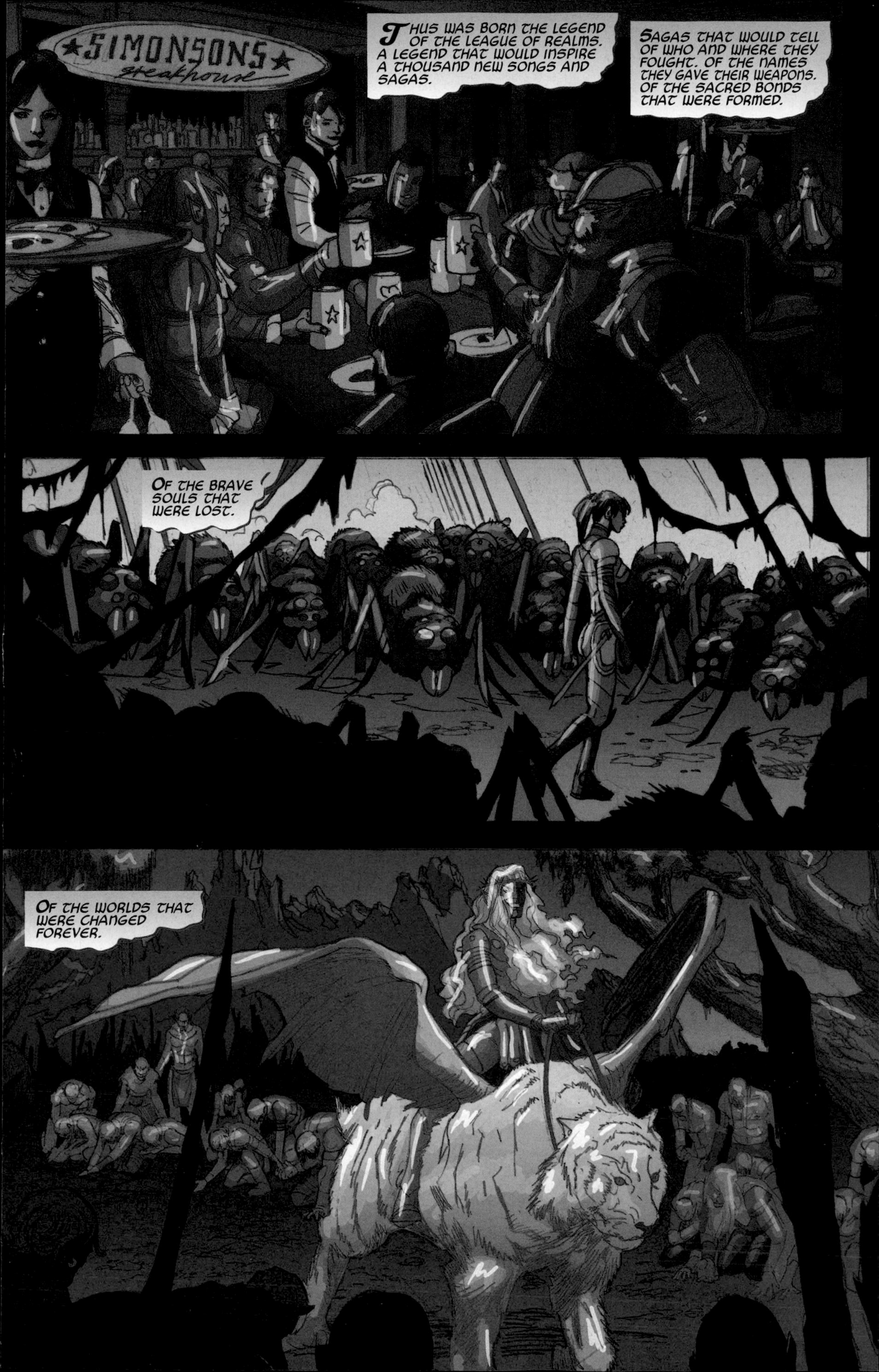
SIMONSONS
steakhouse
THUS WAS BORN THE LEGEND OF THE LEAGUE OF REALMS. A LEGEND THAT WOULD INSPIRE A THOUSAND NEW SONGS AND SAGAS.
SAGAS THAT WOULD TELL OF WHO AND WHERE THEY FOUGHT. OF THE NAMES THEY GAVE THEIR WEAPONS. OF THE SACRED BONDS THAT WERE FORMED.
OF THE BRAVE SOULS THAT WERE LOST.
OF THE WORLDS THAT WERE CHANGED FOREVER.

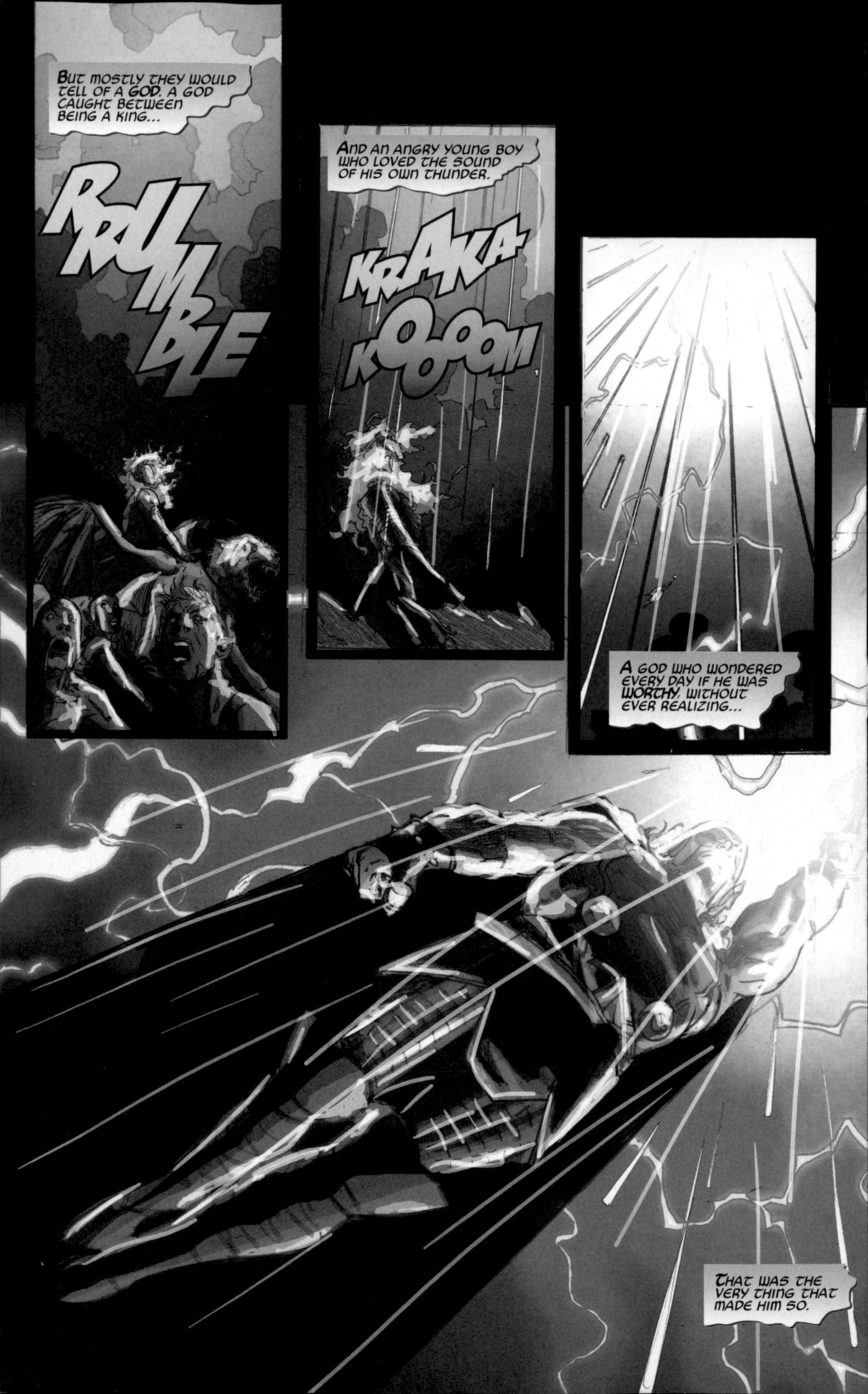
But mostly they would tell of a GOD. A god caught between being a king...
RRUMBLE
And an angry young boy who loved the sound of his own thunder.
KRAKA KOOOOM
A god who wondered every day if he was WORTHY, without ever realizing...
That was the very thing that made him so.

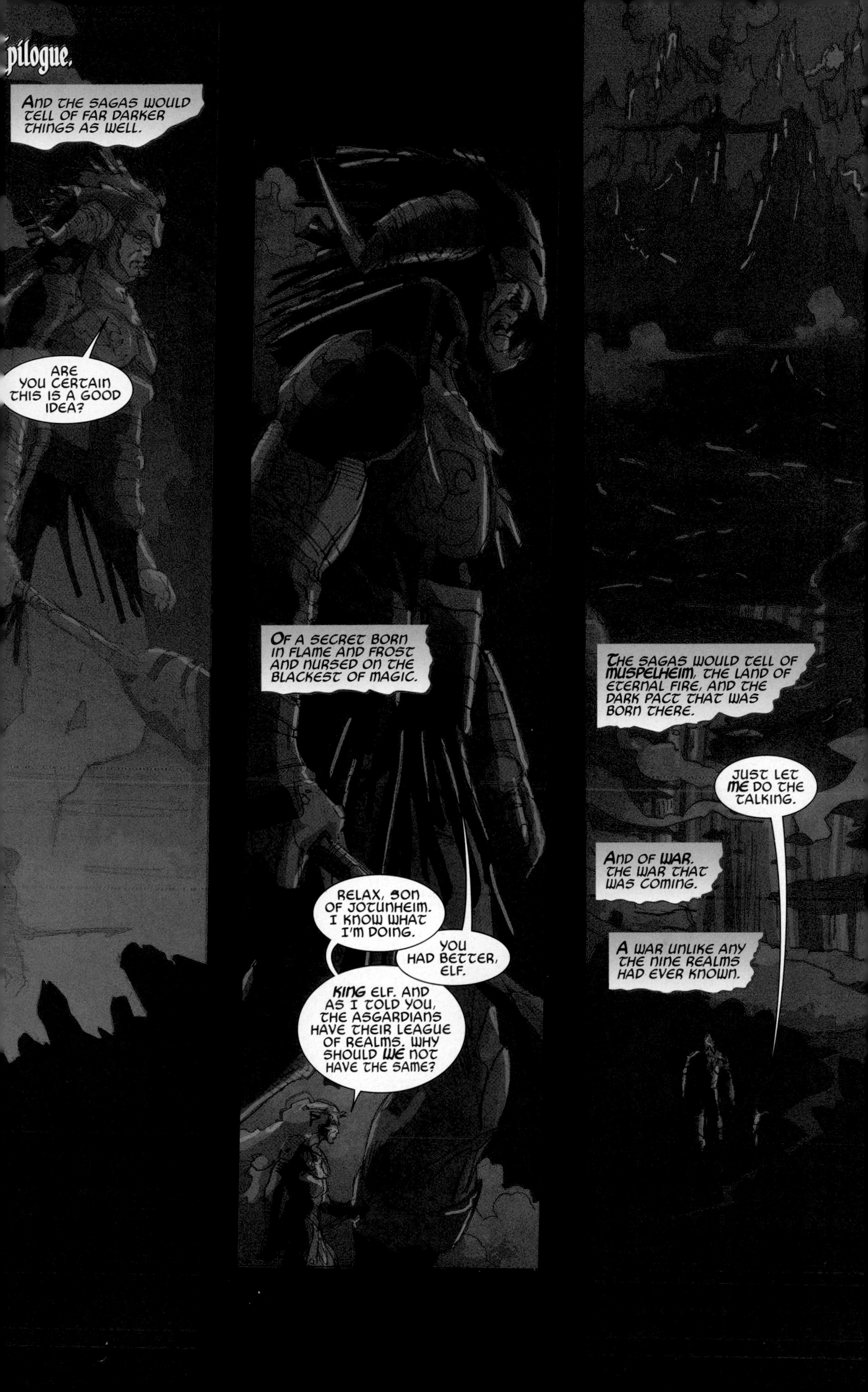
Epilogue.
And the sagas would tell of far darker things as well.
Are you certain this is a good idea?
Of a secret born in flame and frost and nursed on the blackest of magic.
Relax, son of Jotunheim. I know what I'm doing.
You had better, elf.
King elf. And as I told you, the Asgardians have their League of Realms. Why should we not have the same?
The sagas would tell of Muspelheim, the land of eternal fire, and the dark pact that was born there.
Just let me do the talking.
And of war. The war that was coming.
A war unlike any the nine realms had ever known.

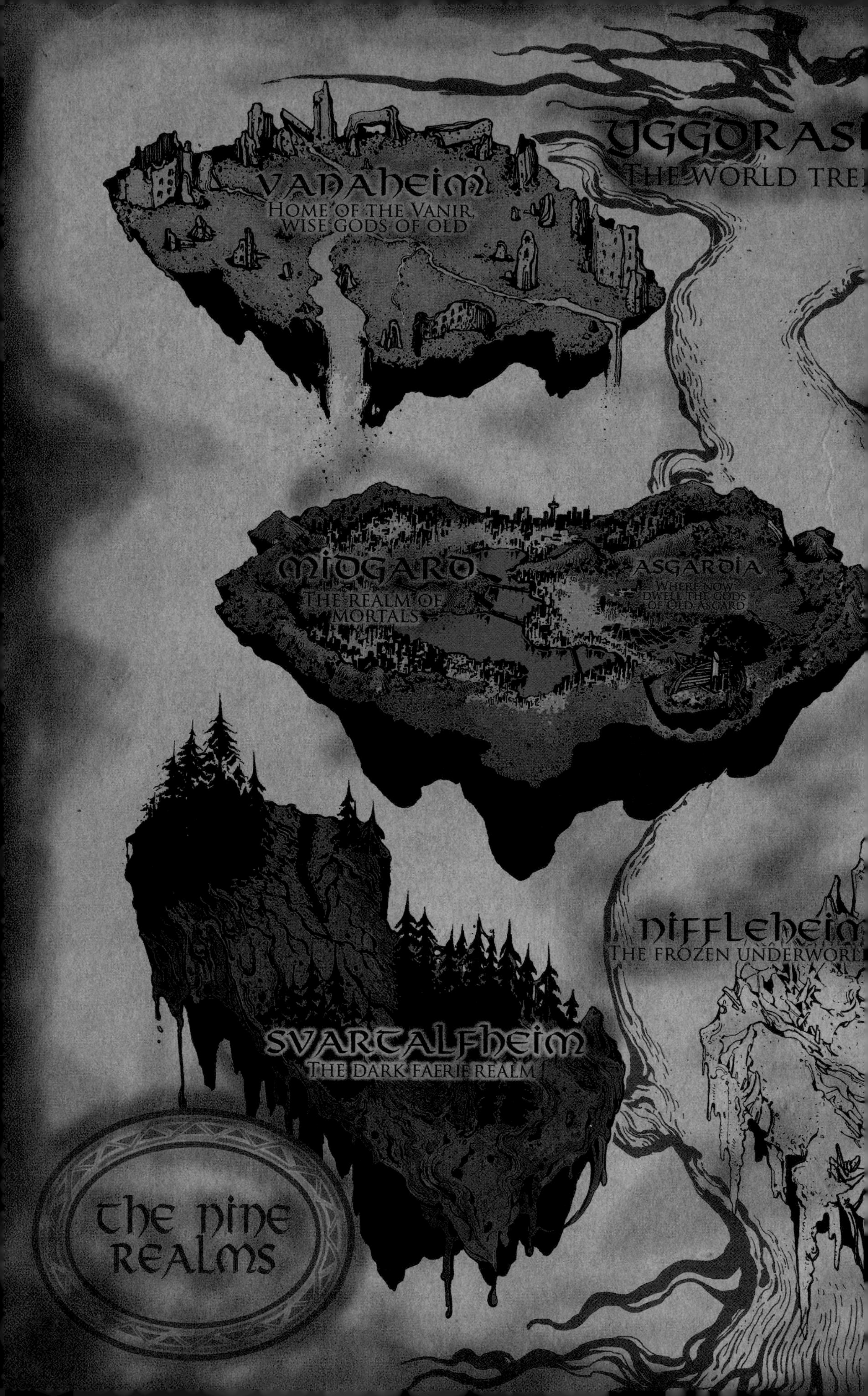
YGGDRASI
THE WORLD TRE
VANAHEIM
HOME OF THE VANIR, WISE GODS OF OLD
MIDGARD
THE REALM OF MORTALS
ASGARDIA
WHERE NOW DWELL THE GODS OF OLD ASGARD
NIFFLEHEIM
THE FROZEN UNDERWORL
SVARTALFHEIM
THE DARK FAERIE REALM
THE NINE REALMS

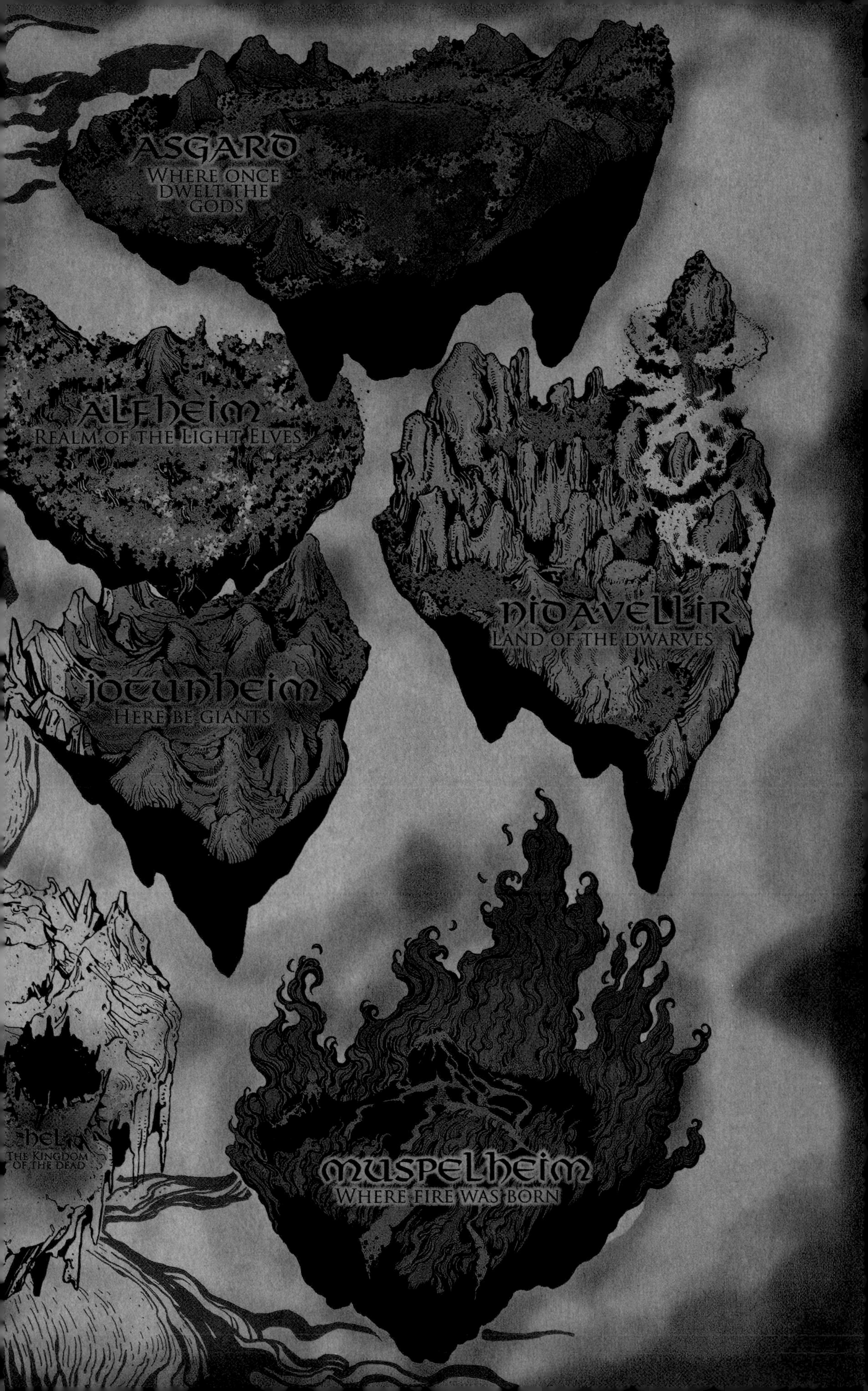
ASGARD
Where once dwelt the gods
ALFHEIM
Realm of the Light Elves
NIDAVELLIR
Land of the dwarves
JOTUNHEIM
Here be giants
HEL
The Kingdom of the dead
MUSPELHEIM
Where fire was born

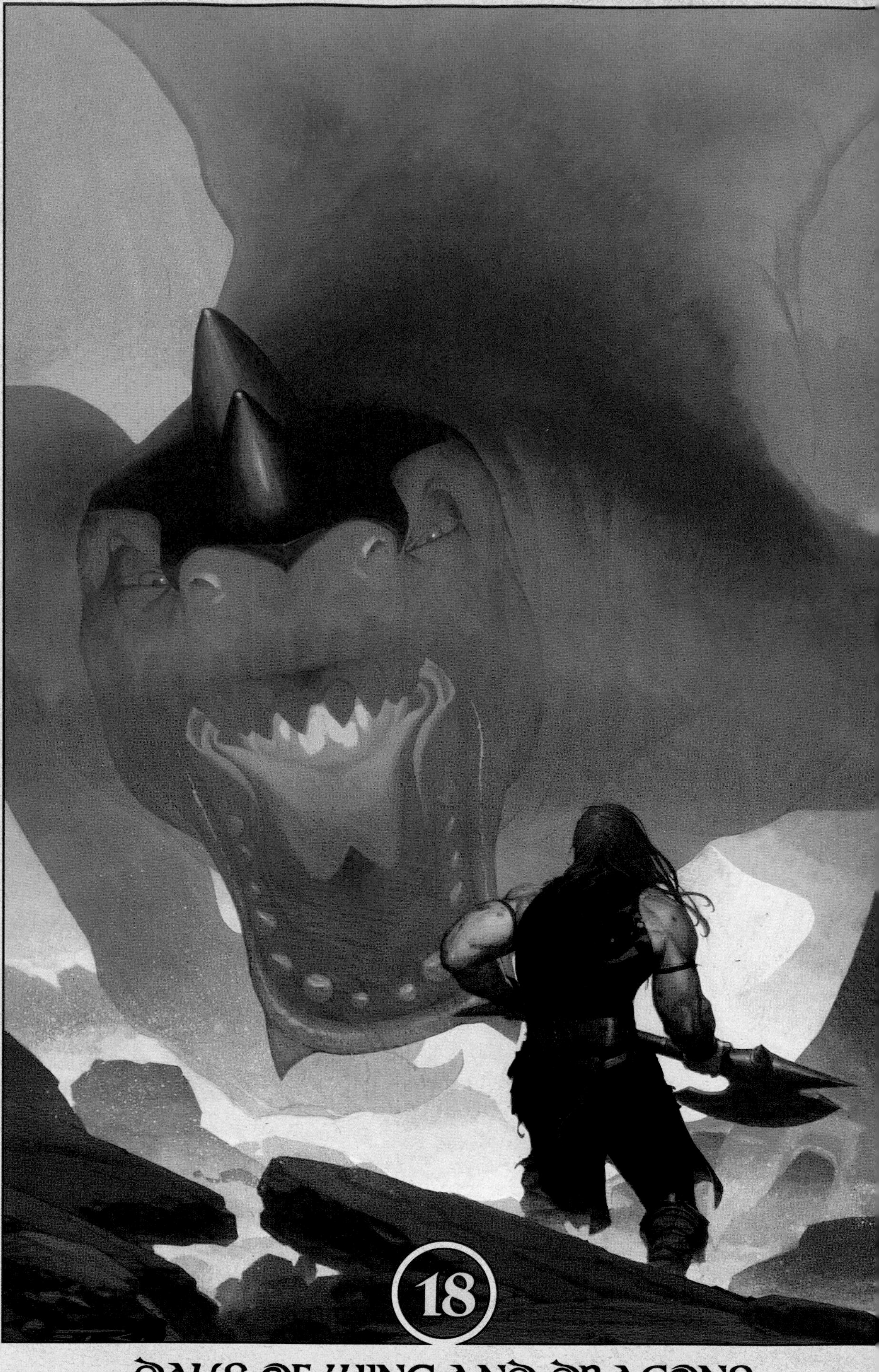
18

DAYS OF WINE AND DRAGONS

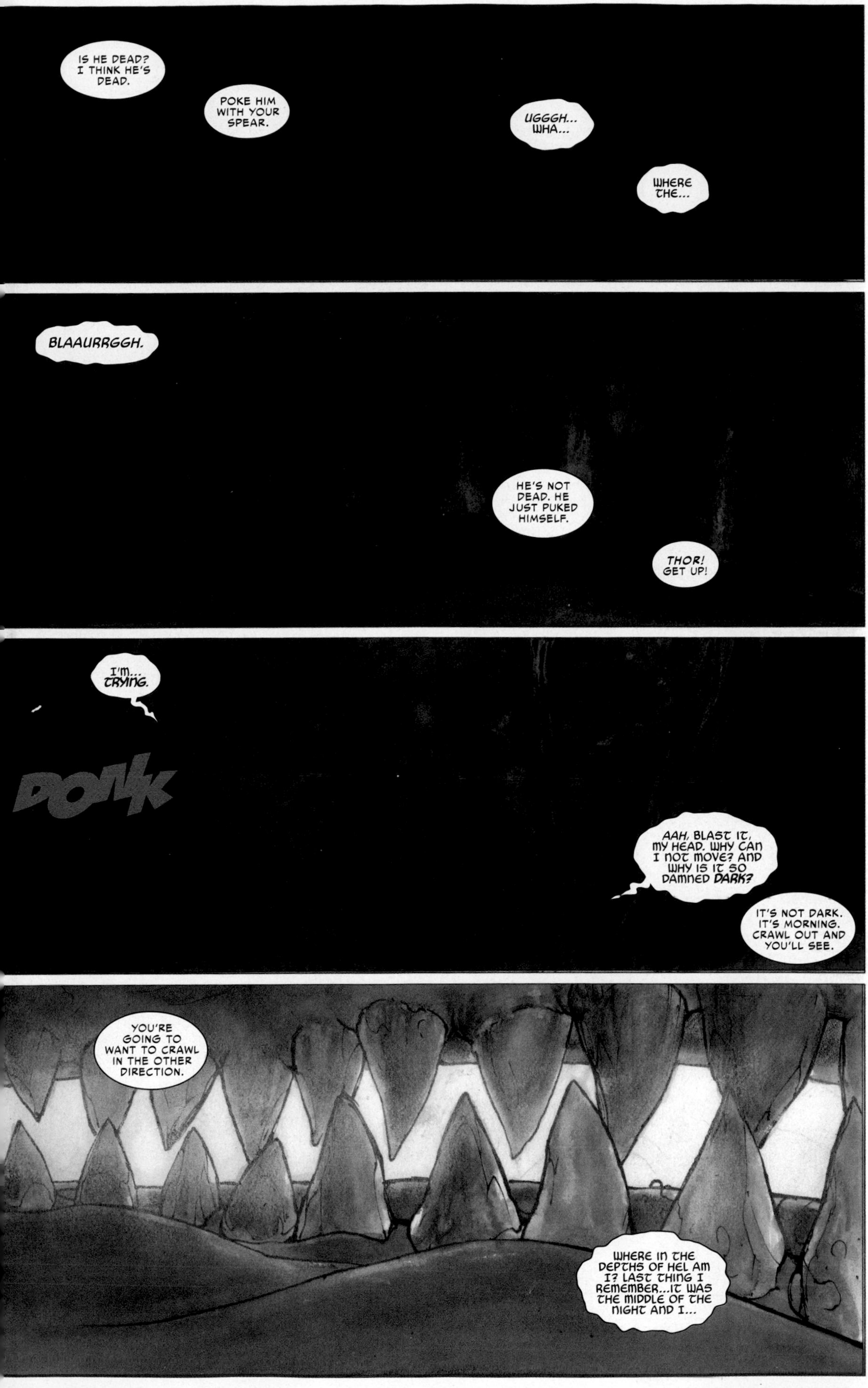
IS HE DEAD? I THINK HE'S DEAD.
POKE HIM WITH YOUR SPEAR.
UGGGH... WHA...
WHERE THE...
BLAAURRGGH.
HE'S NOT DEAD. HE JUST PUKED HIMSELF.
THOR! GET UP!
I'M... TRYING.
DONK
AAH, BLAST IT, MY HEAD. WHY CAN I NOT MOVE? AND WHY IS IT SO DAMNED DARK?
IT'S NOT DARK. IT'S MORNING. CRAWL OUT AND YOU'LL SEE.
YOU'RE GOING TO WANT TO CRAWL IN THE OTHER DIRECTION.
WHERE IN THE DEPTHS OF HEL AM I? LAST THING I REMEMBER...IT WAS THE MIDDLE OF THE NIGHT AND I...

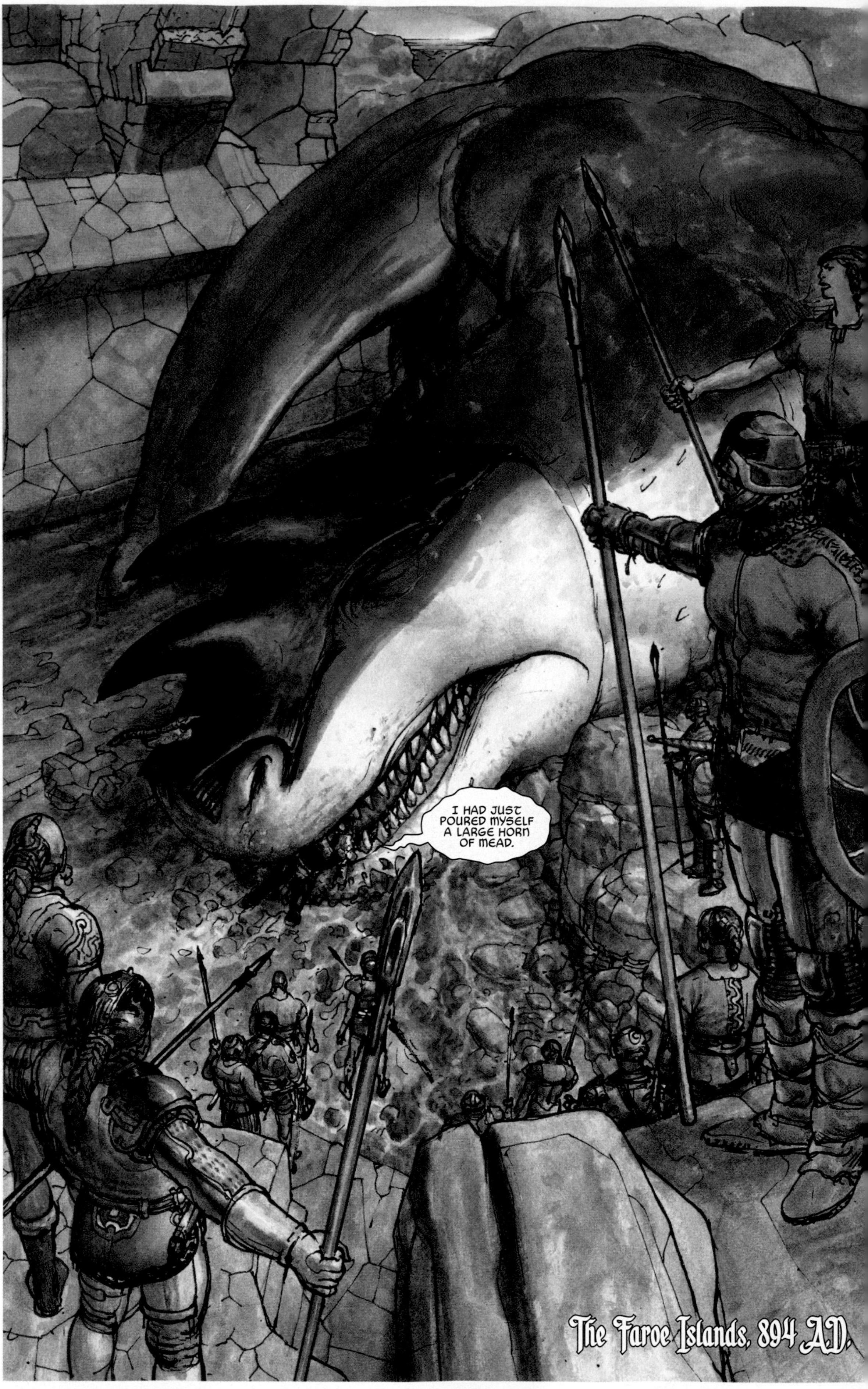
I HAD JUST POURED MYSELF A LARGE HORN OF MEAD.
The Faroe Islands, 894 A.D.

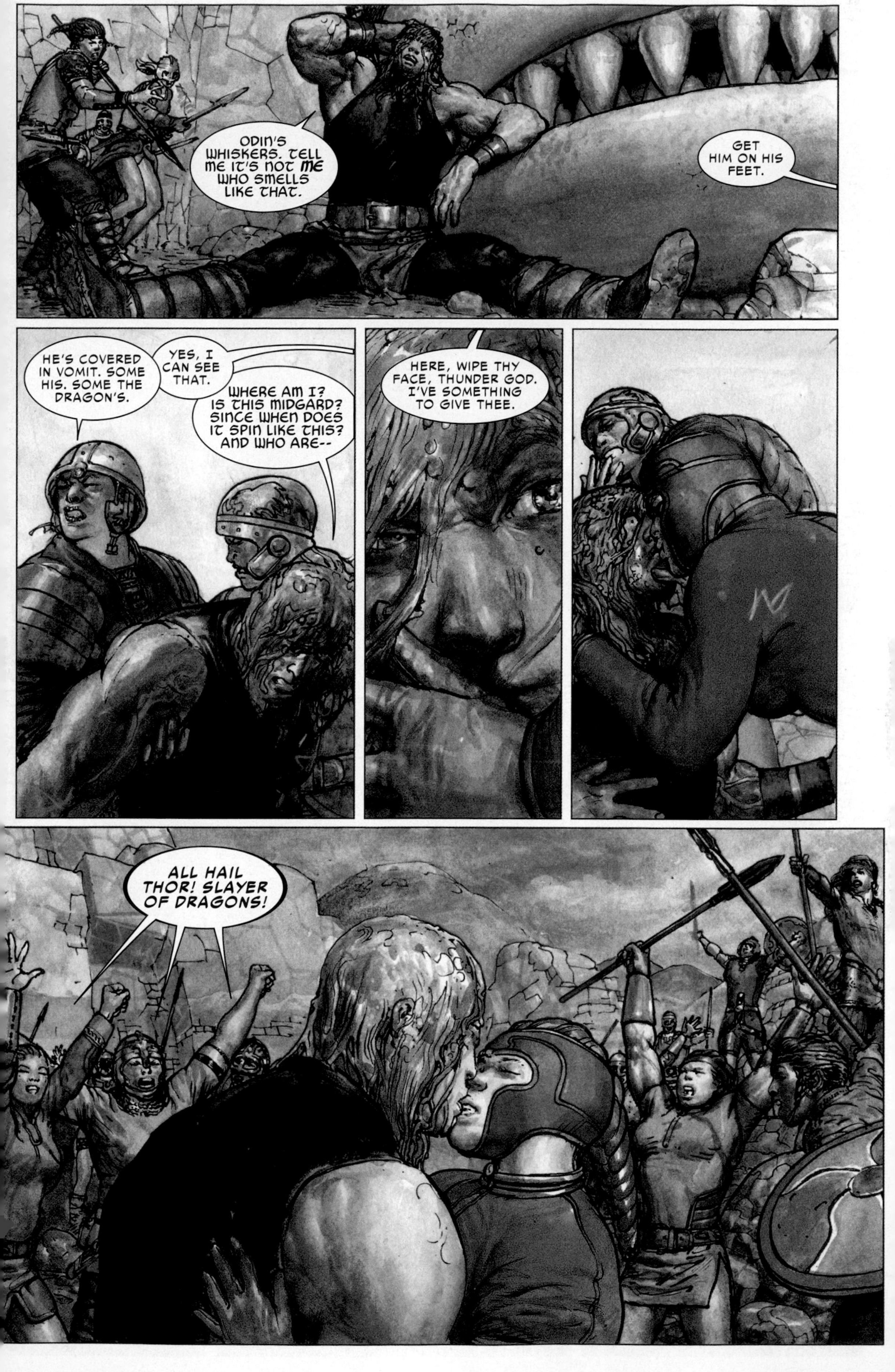
ODIN'S WHISKERS. TELL ME IT'S NOT ME WHO SMELLS LIKE THAT.
GET HIM ON HIS FEET.
HE'S COVERED IN VOMIT. SOME HIS. SOME THE DRAGON'S.
YES, I CAN SEE THAT.
WHERE AM I? IS THIS MIDGARD? SINCE WHEN DOES IT SPIN LIKE THIS? AND WHO ARE--
HERE, WIPE THY FACE, THUNDER GOD. I'VE SOMETHING TO GIVE THEE.
ALL HAIL THOR! SLAYER OF DRAGONS!

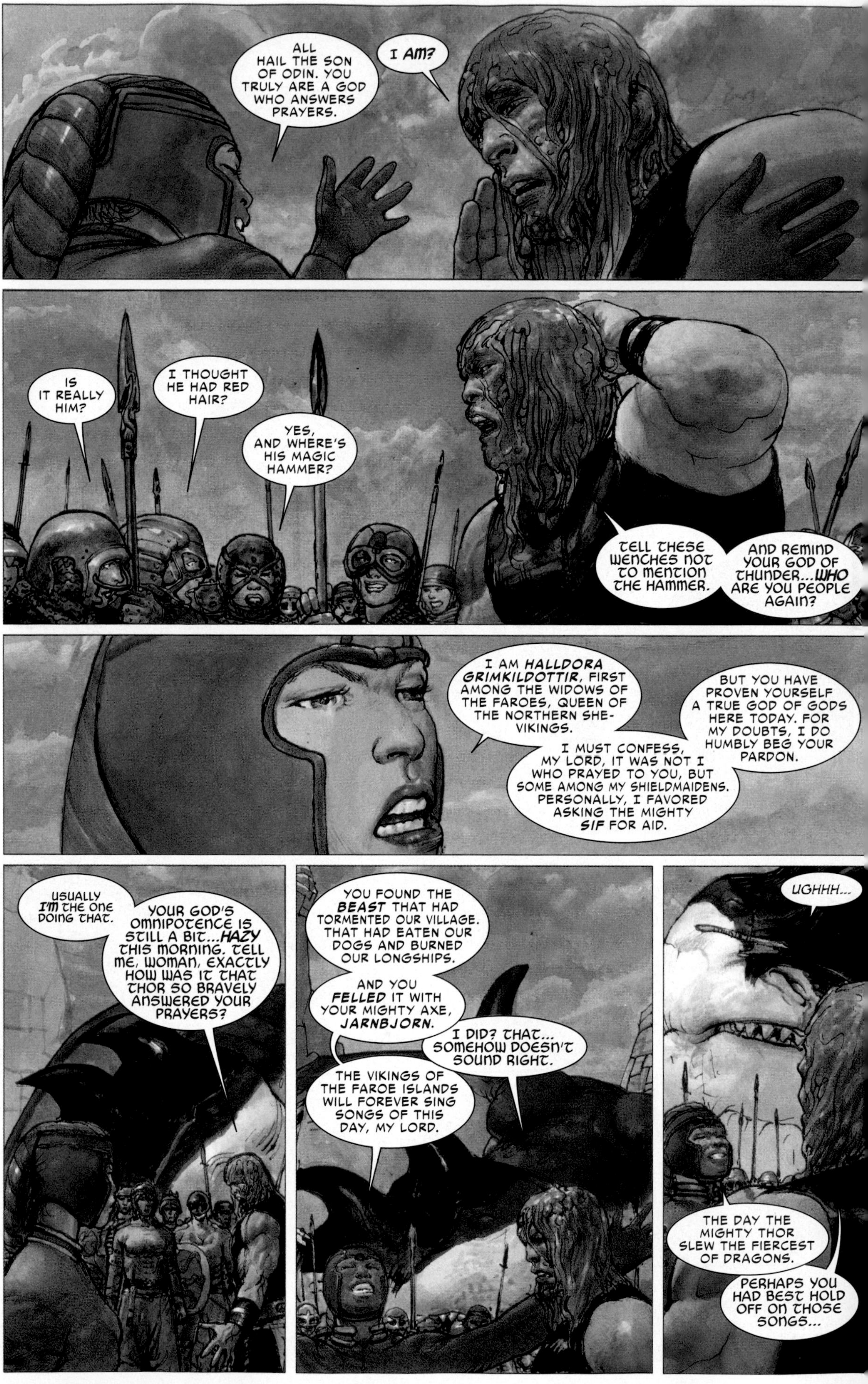
ALL HAIL THE SON OF ODIN. YOU TRULY ARE A GOD WHO ANSWERS PRAYERS.
I *AM*?
IS IT REALLY HIM?
I THOUGHT HE HAD RED HAIR?
YES, AND WHERE'S HIS MAGIC HAMMER?
TELL THESE WENCHES NOT TO MENTION THE HAMMER.
AND REMIND YOUR GOD OF THUNDER... *WHO* ARE YOU PEOPLE AGAIN?
I AM *HALLDORA GRIMKILDOTTIR*, FIRST AMONG THE WIDOWS OF THE FAROES, QUEEN OF THE NORTHERN SHE-VIKINGS.
I MUST CONFESS, MY LORD, IT WAS NOT I WHO PRAYED TO YOU, BUT SOME AMONG MY SHIELDMAIDENS. PERSONALLY, I FAVORED ASKING THE MIGHTY *SIF* FOR AID.
BUT YOU HAVE PROVEN YOURSELF A TRUE GOD OF GODS HERE TODAY. FOR MY DOUBTS, I DO HUMBLY BEG YOUR PARDON.
USUALLY *I'M* THE ONE DOING THAT.
YOUR GOD'S OMNIPOTENCE IS STILL A BIT... *HAZY* THIS MORNING. TELL ME, WOMAN, EXACTLY HOW WAS IT THAT THOR SO BRAVELY ANSWERED YOUR PRAYERS?
YOU FOUND THE *BEAST* THAT HAD TORMENTED OUR VILLAGE. THAT HAD EATEN OUR DOGS AND BURNED OUR LONGSHIPS.
AND YOU *FELLED* IT WITH YOUR MIGHTY AXE, *JARNBJORN*.
I DID? THAT... SOMEHOW DOESN'T SOUND RIGHT.
THE VIKINGS OF THE FAROE ISLANDS WILL FOREVER SING SONGS OF THIS DAY, MY LORD.
UGHHH...
THE DAY THE MIGHTY THOR SLEW THE FIERCEST OF DRAGONS.
PERHAPS YOU HAD BEST HOLD OFF ON THOSE SONGS...

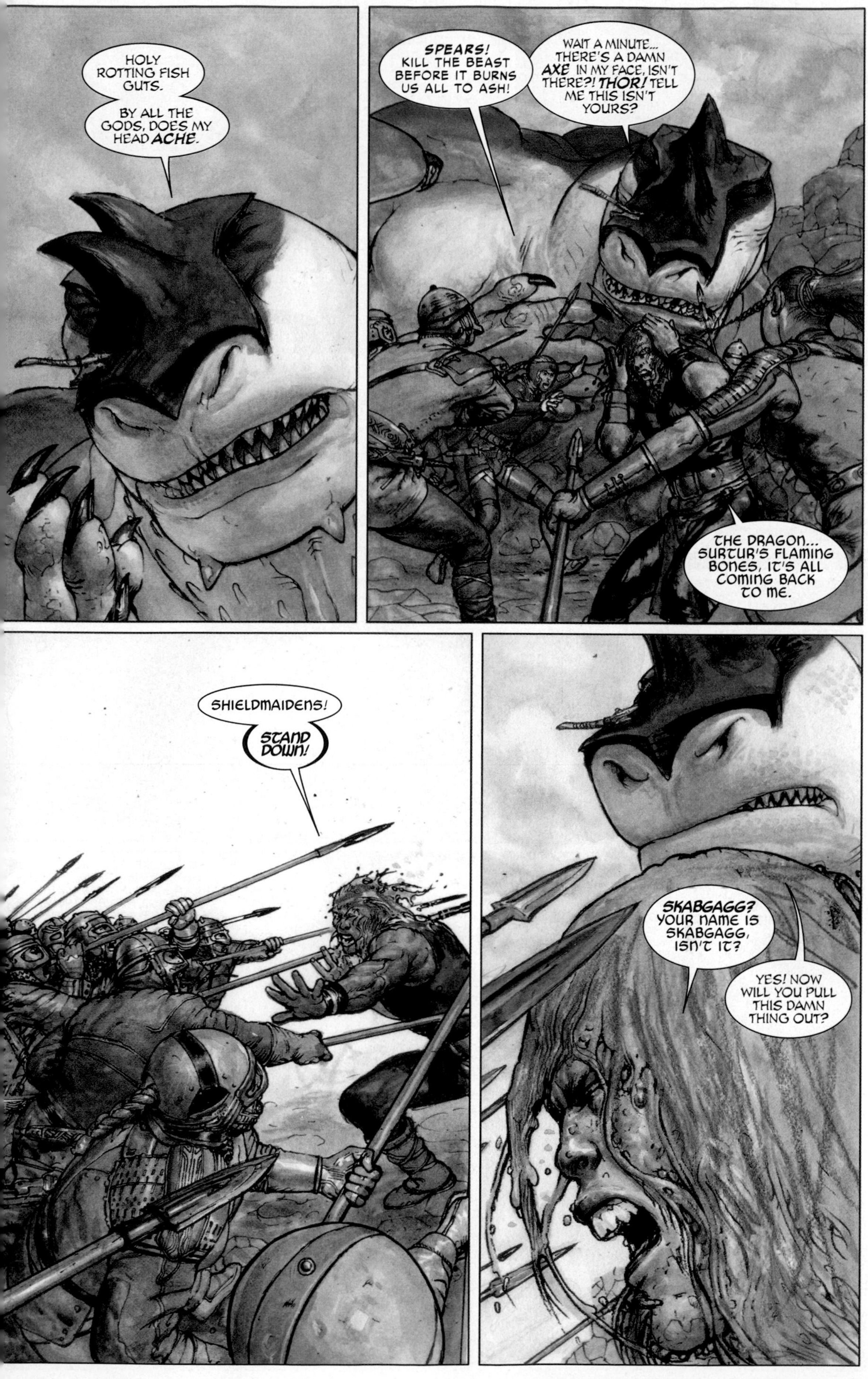

HOLY ROTTING FISH GUTS.
BY ALL THE GODS, DOES MY HEAD ACHE.
SPEARS! KILL THE BEAST BEFORE IT BURNS US ALL TO ASH!
WAIT A MINUTE... THERE'S A DAMN AXE IN MY FACE, ISN'T THERE?! THOR! TELL ME THIS ISN'T YOURS?
THE DRAGON... SURTUR'S FLAMING BONES, IT'S ALL COMING BACK TO ME.
SHIELDMAIDENS!
STAND DOWN!
SKABGAGG? YOUR NAME IS SKABGAGG, ISN'T IT?
YES! NOW WILL YOU PULL THIS DAMN THING OUT?

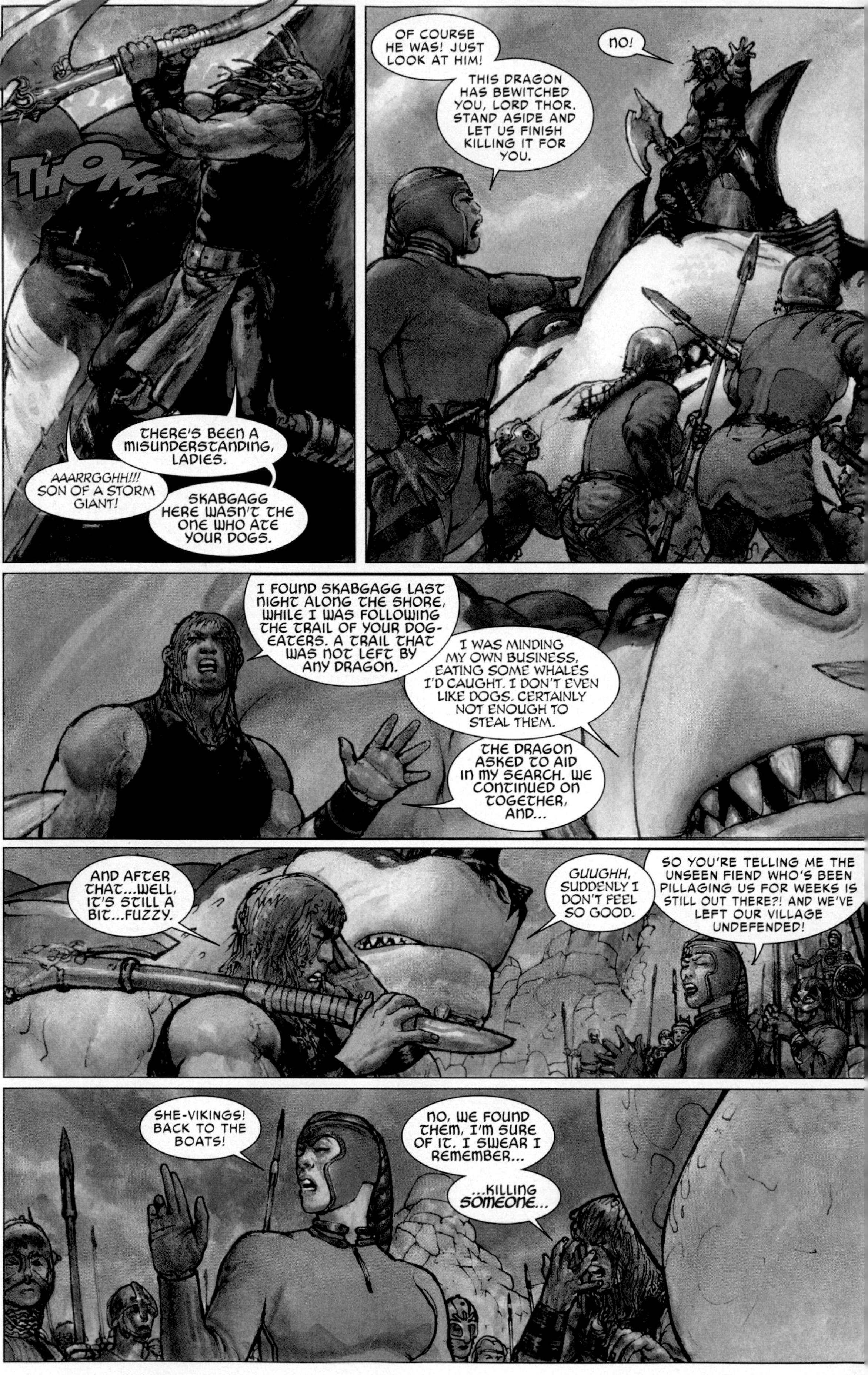
THOKK
THERE'S BEEN A MISUNDERSTANDING, LADIES.
AAARRGGHH!!! SON OF A STORM GIANT!
SKABGAGG HERE WASN'T THE ONE WHO ATE YOUR DOGS.
OF COURSE HE WAS! JUST LOOK AT HIM!
THIS DRAGON HAS BEWITCHED YOU, LORD THOR. STAND ASIDE AND LET US FINISH KILLING IT FOR YOU.
NO!
I FOUND SKABGAGG LAST NIGHT ALONG THE SHORE, WHILE I WAS FOLLOWING THE TRAIL OF YOUR DOG-EATERS. A TRAIL THAT WAS NOT LEFT BY ANY DRAGON.
I WAS MINDING MY OWN BUSINESS, EATING SOME WHALES I'D CAUGHT. I DON'T EVEN LIKE DOGS. CERTAINLY NOT ENOUGH TO STEAL THEM.
THE DRAGON ASKED TO AID IN MY SEARCH. WE CONTINUED ON TOGETHER, AND...
AND AFTER THAT...WELL, IT'S STILL A BIT...FUZZY.
GUUGHH, SUDDENLY I DON'T FEEL SO GOOD.
SO YOU'RE TELLING ME THE UNSEEN FIEND WHO'S BEEN PILLAGING US FOR WEEKS IS STILL OUT THERE?! AND WE'VE LEFT OUR VILLAGE UNDEFENDED!
SHE-VIKINGS! BACK TO THE BOATS!
NO, WE FOUND THEM, I'M SURE OF IT. I SWEAR I REMEMBER...
...KILLING SOMEONE...

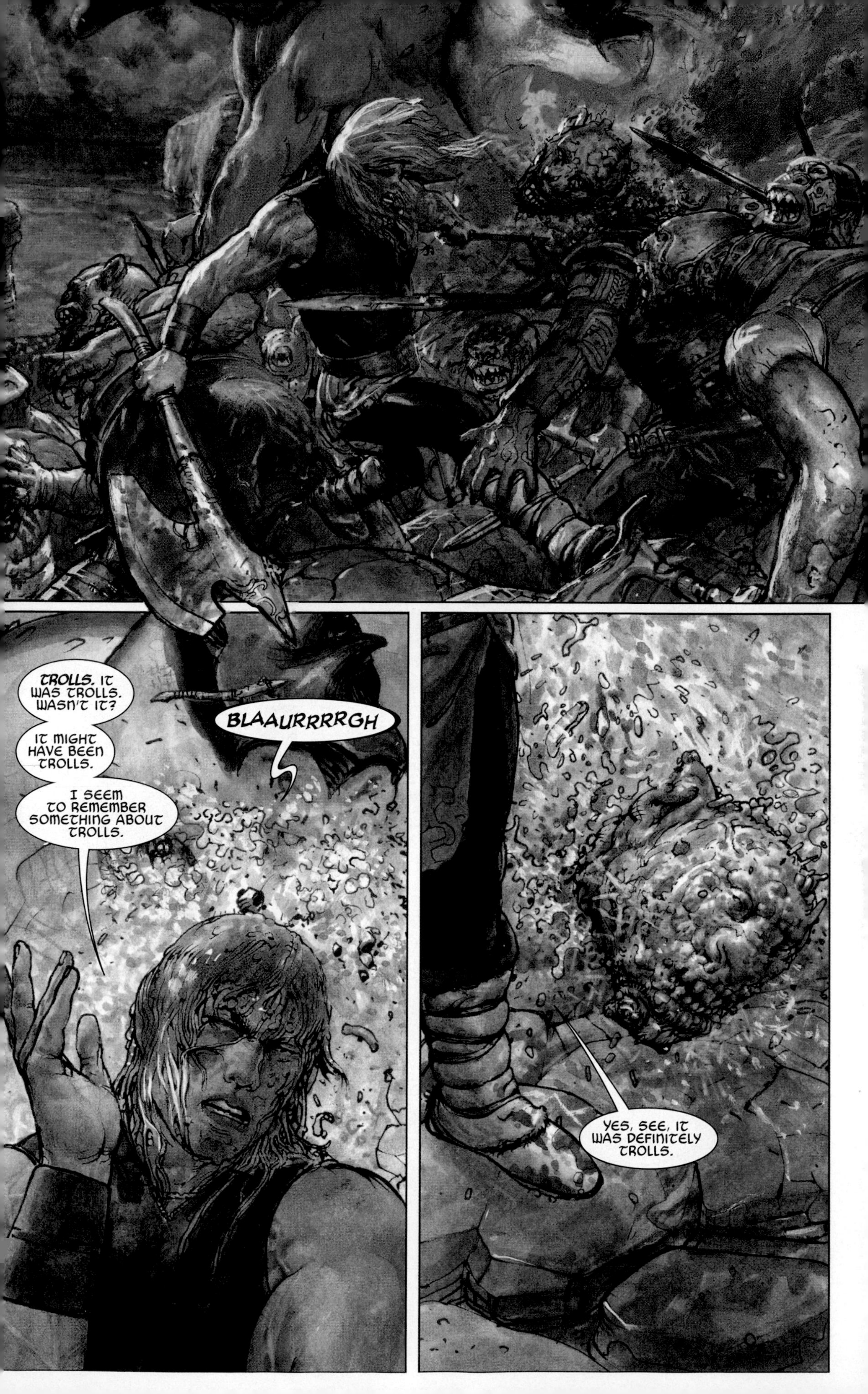
TROLLS. IT WAS TROLLS. WASN'T IT?
IT MIGHT HAVE BEEN TROLLS.
I SEEM TO REMEMBER SOMETHING ABOUT TROLLS.
BLAAURRRRGH
YES, SEE, IT WAS DEFINITELY TROLLS.

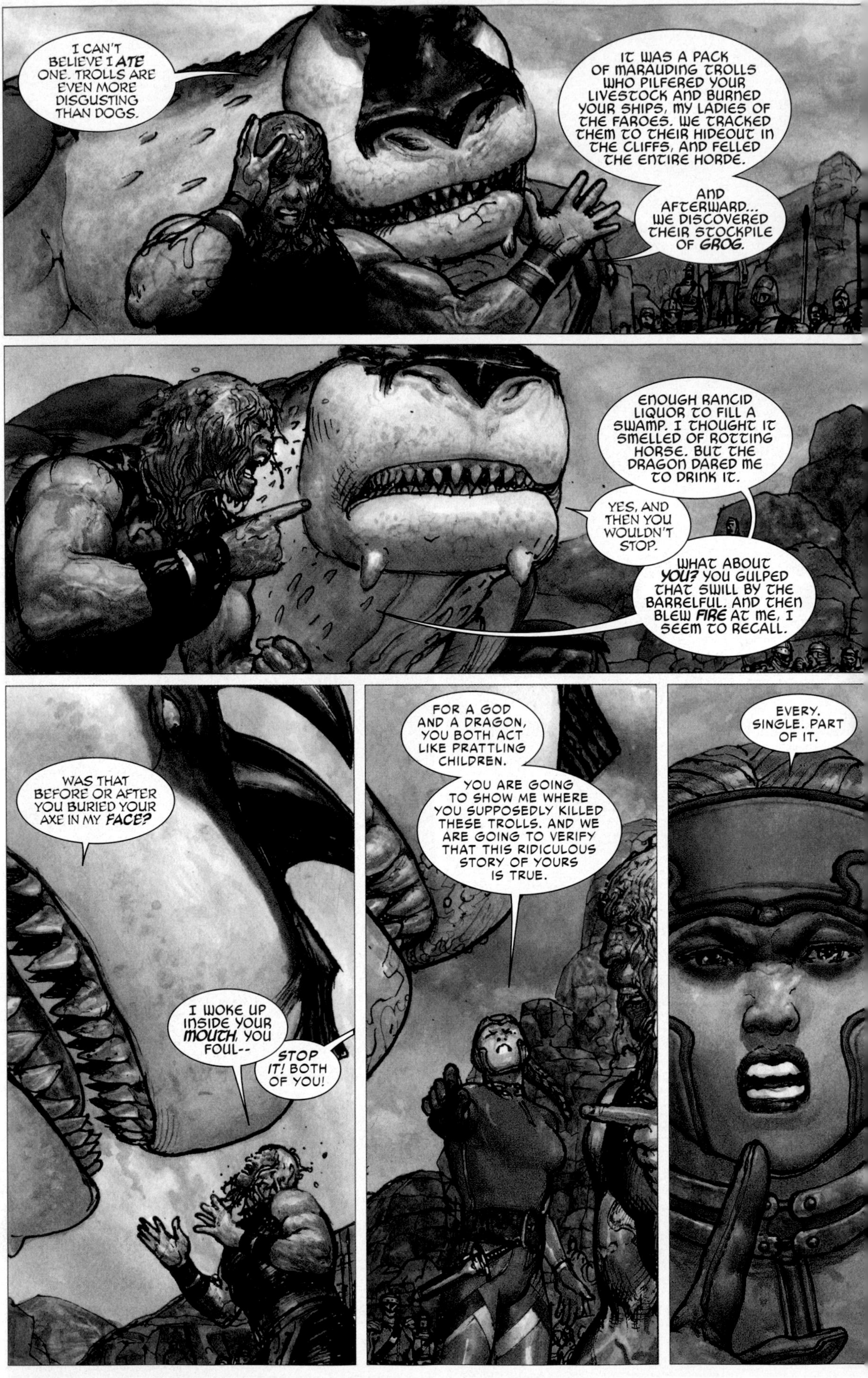
I CAN'T BELIEVE I ATE ONE. TROLLS ARE EVEN MORE DISGUSTING THAN DOGS.
IT WAS A PACK OF MARAUDING TROLLS WHO PILFERED YOUR LIVESTOCK AND BURNED YOUR SHIPS, MY LADIES OF THE FAROES. WE TRACKED THEM TO THEIR HIDEOUT IN THE CLIFFS, AND FELLED THE ENTIRE HORDE.
AND AFTERWARD... WE DISCOVERED THEIR STOCKPILE OF GROG.
ENOUGH RANCID LIQUOR TO FILL A SWAMP. I THOUGHT IT SMELLED OF ROTTING HORSE. BUT THE DRAGON DARED ME TO DRINK IT.
YES, AND THEN YOU WOULDN'T STOP.
WHAT ABOUT YOU? YOU GULPED THAT SWILL BY THE BARRELFUL. AND THEN BLEW FIRE AT ME, I SEEM TO RECALL.
WAS THAT BEFORE OR AFTER YOU BURIED YOUR AXE IN MY FACE?
I WOKE UP INSIDE YOUR MOUTH, YOU FOUL--
STOP IT! BOTH OF YOU!
FOR A GOD AND A DRAGON, YOU BOTH ACT LIKE PRATTLING CHILDREN.
YOU ARE GOING TO SHOW ME WHERE YOU SUPPOSEDLY KILLED THESE TROLLS. AND WE ARE GOING TO VERIFY THAT THIS RIDICULOUS STORY OF YOURS IS TRUE.
EVERY. SINGLE. PART OF IT.

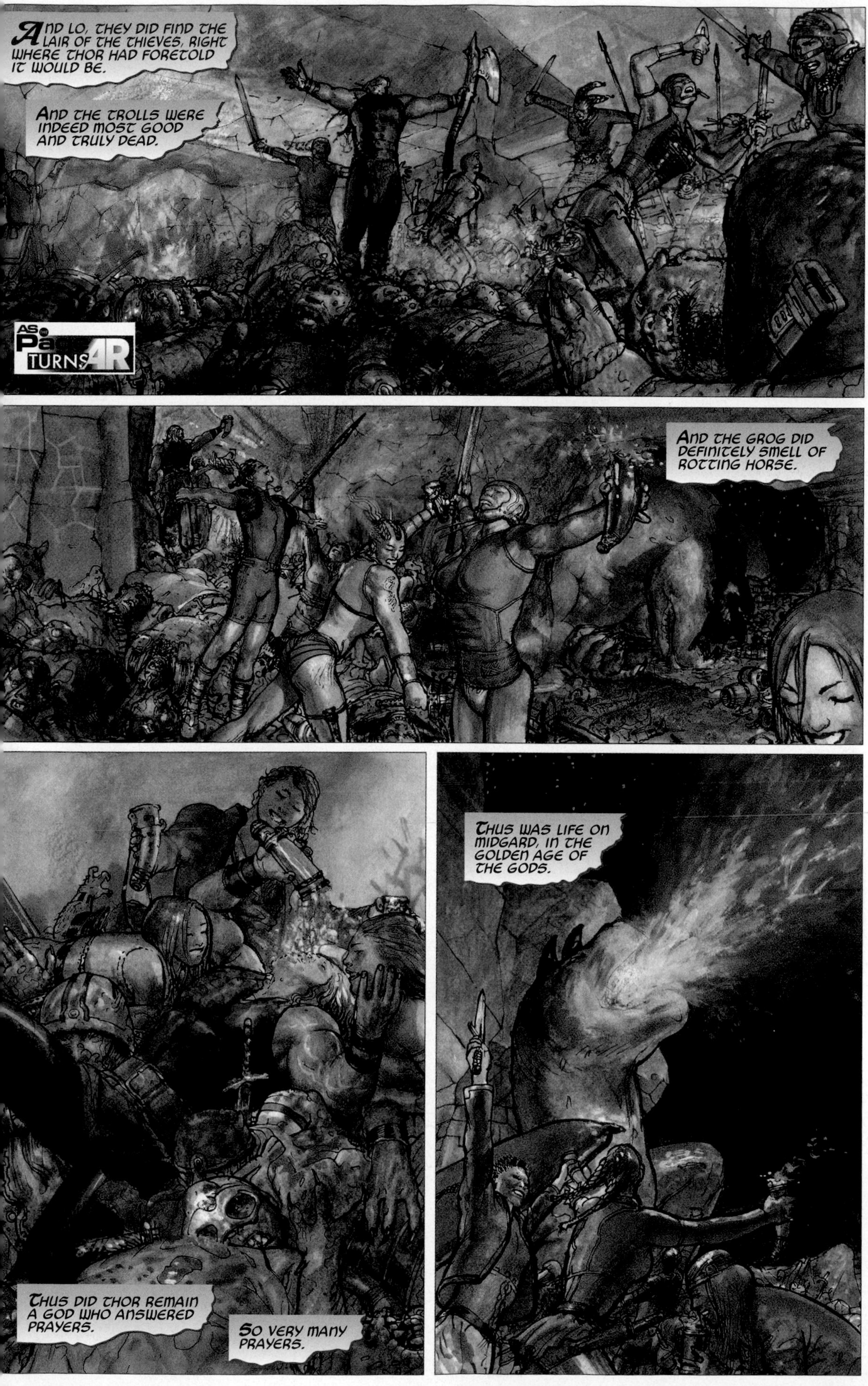
AND LO, THEY DID FIND THE LAIR OF THE THIEVES, RIGHT WHERE THOR HAD FORETOLD IT WOULD BE.
AND THE TROLLS WERE INDEED MOST GOOD AND TRULY DEAD.
AS THE Page TURNS AR
AND THE GROG DID DEFINITELY SMELL OF ROTTING HORSE.
THUS DID THOR REMAIN A GOD WHO ANSWERED PRAYERS.
SO VERY MANY PRAYERS.
THUS WAS LIFE ON MIDGARD, IN THE GOLDEN AGE OF THE GODS.

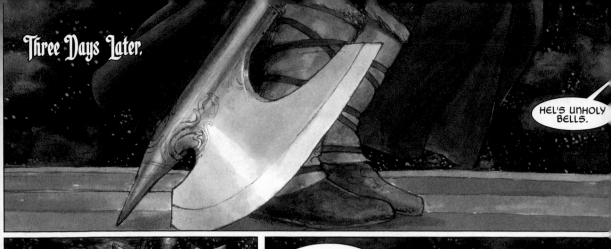

HEL'S UNHOLY BELLS.

GET THEE TO A *BATH*, SON OF ODIN. THOU ART BEFOULING THE RAINBOW BRIDGE WITH THY STENCH OF...OF DRAGON BILE AND TROLL INEBRIANTS.

BEHOLD, THE VAUNTED NOSE OF *HEIMDALL* THE EVER-VIGILANT!

REMEMBER THY PLACE, THOR. THOU ART THE GOD OF THUNDER, NOT THE GOD OF DEBAUCHERY.

AND THOU ART NOT THE GOD OF MEDDLING IN MY AFFAIRS, GATEKEEPER! *STAND ASIDE!*

THY ROYAL FATHER HAS BEEN LOOKING FOR THEE FOR MANY DAYS.

MY FATHER IS OMNIPOTENT! HE MUST NOT HAVE LOOKED VERY HARD!

YOU SHOULD GO TO HIM AND BEG HIS MERCY.

YES, OF COURSE. I WILL DO SO FORTHWITH, GOOD HEIMDALL! WITH ALL THE SPEED I CAN MUSTER!

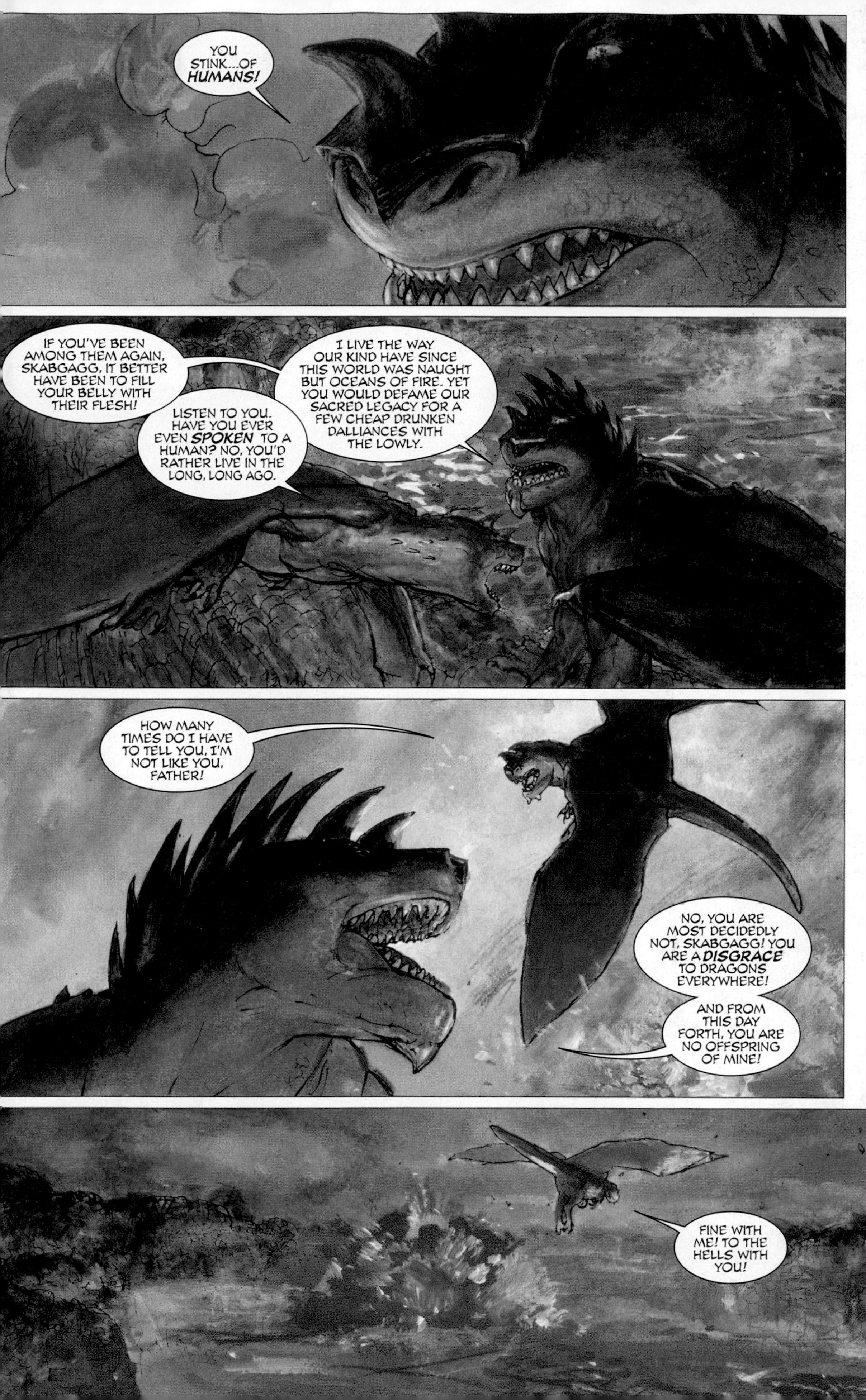
YOU STINK...OF HUMANS!
IF YOU'VE BEEN AMONG THEM AGAIN, SKABGAGG, IT BETTER HAVE BEEN TO FILL YOUR BELLY WITH THEIR FLESH!
LISTEN TO YOU. HAVE YOU EVER EVEN SPOKEN TO A HUMAN? NO, YOU'D RATHER LIVE IN THE LONG, LONG AGO.
I LIVE THE WAY OUR KIND HAVE SINCE THIS WORLD WAS NAUGHT BUT OCEANS OF FIRE. YET YOU WOULD DEFAME OUR SACRED LEGACY FOR A FEW CHEAP DRUNKEN DALLIANCES WITH THE LOWLY.
HOW MANY TIMES DO I HAVE TO TELL YOU, I'M NOT LIKE YOU, FATHER!
NO, YOU ARE MOST DECIDEDLY NOT, SKABGAGG! YOU ARE A DISGRACE TO DRAGONS EVERYWHERE!
AND FROM THIS DAY FORTH, YOU ARE NO OFFSPRING OF MINE!
FINE WITH ME! TO THE HELLS WITH YOU!

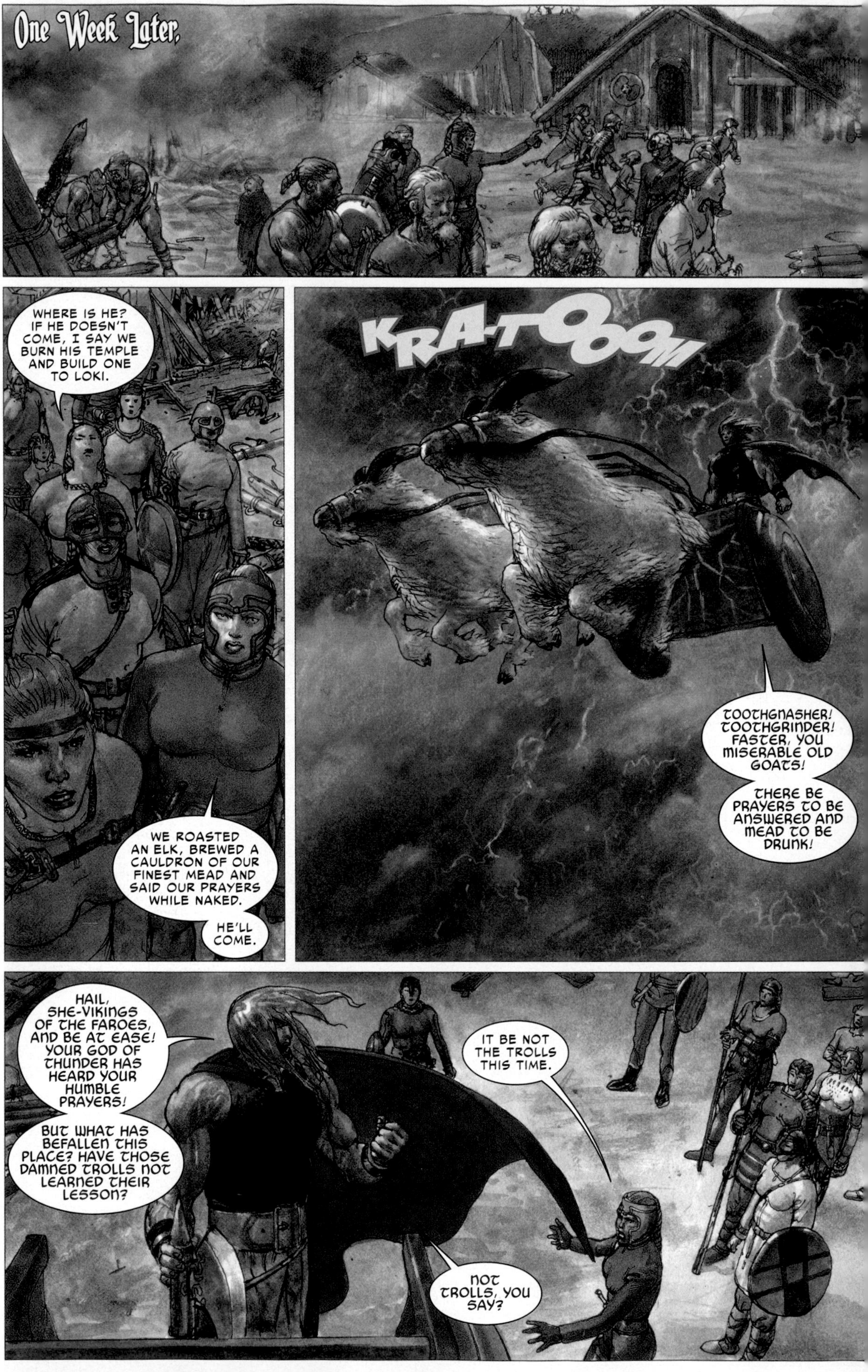
One Week Later.
WHERE IS HE? IF HE DOESN'T COME, I SAY WE BURN HIS TEMPLE AND BUILD ONE TO LOKI.
WE ROASTED AN ELK, BREWED A CAULDRON OF OUR FINEST MEAD AND SAID OUR PRAYERS WHILE NAKED.
HE'LL COME.
KRA-TOOOOM
TOOTHGNASHER! TOOTHGRINDER! FASTER, YOU MISERABLE OLD GOATS!
THERE BE PRAYERS TO BE ANSWERED AND MEAD TO BE DRUNK!
HAIL, SHE-VIKINGS OF THE FAROES, AND BE AT EASE! YOUR GOD OF THUNDER HAS HEARD YOUR HUMBLE PRAYERS!
BUT WHAT HAS BEFALLEN THIS PLACE? HAVE THOSE DAMNED TROLLS NOT LEARNED THEIR LESSON?
IT BE NOT THE TROLLS THIS TIME.
NOT TROLLS, YOU SAY?

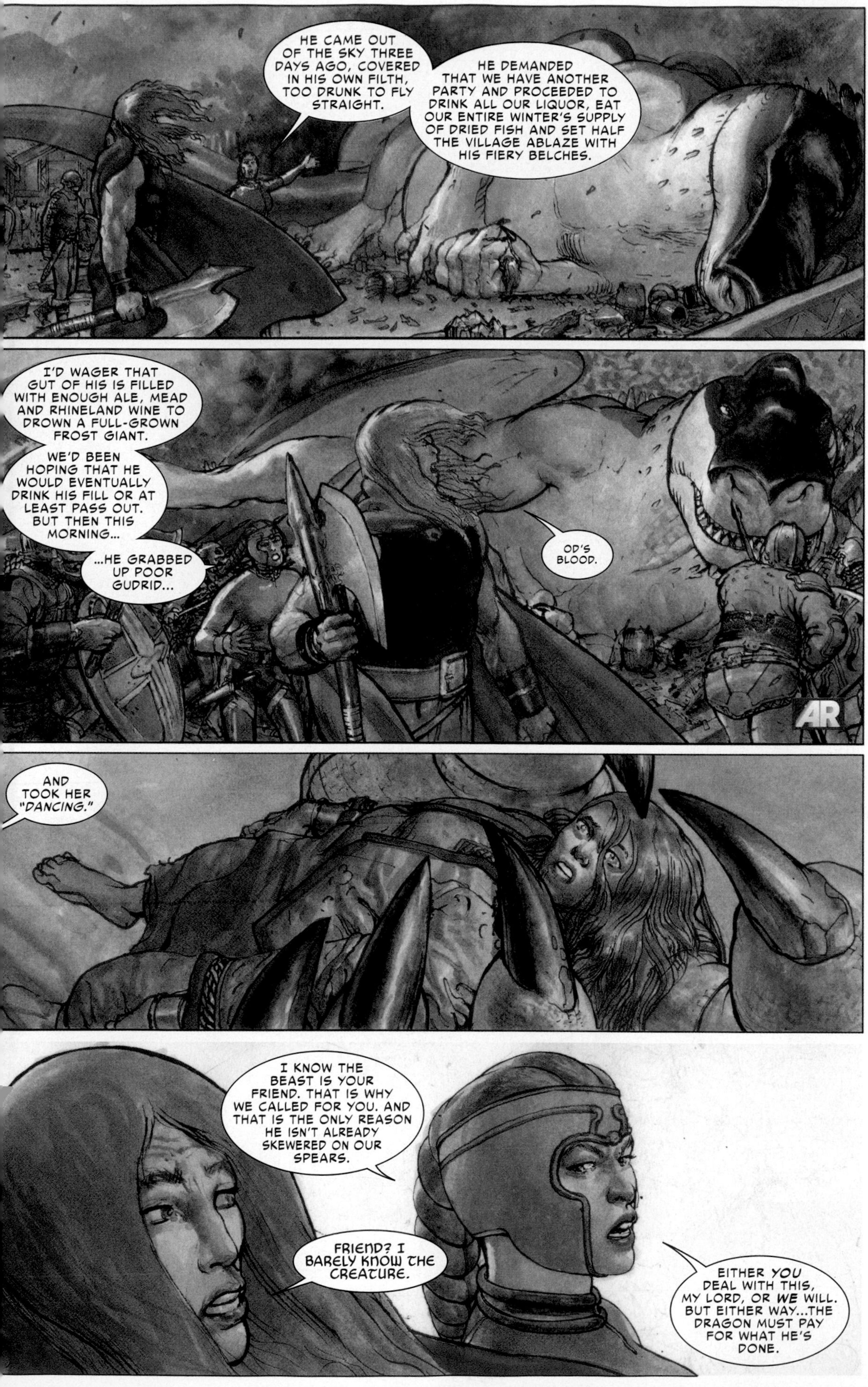
HE CAME OUT OF THE SKY THREE DAYS AGO, COVERED IN HIS OWN FILTH, TOO DRUNK TO FLY STRAIGHT.
HE DEMANDED THAT WE HAVE ANOTHER PARTY AND PROCEEDED TO DRINK ALL OUR LIQUOR, EAT OUR ENTIRE WINTER'S SUPPLY OF DRIED FISH AND SET HALF THE VILLAGE ABLAZE WITH HIS FIERY BELCHES.
I'D WAGER THAT GUT OF HIS IS FILLED WITH ENOUGH ALE, MEAD AND RHINELAND WINE TO DROWN A FULL-GROWN FROST GIANT.
WE'D BEEN HOPING THAT HE WOULD EVENTUALLY DRINK HIS FILL OR AT LEAST PASS OUT. BUT THEN THIS MORNING...
...HE GRABBED UP POOR GUDRID...
OD'S BLOOD.
AND TOOK HER "DANCING."
I KNOW THE BEAST IS YOUR FRIEND. THAT IS WHY WE CALLED FOR YOU. AND THAT IS THE ONLY REASON HE ISN'T ALREADY SKEWERED ON OUR SPEARS.
FRIEND? I BARELY KNOW THE CREATURE.
EITHER YOU DEAL WITH THIS, MY LORD, OR WE WILL. BUT EITHER WAY...THE DRAGON MUST PAY FOR WHAT HE'S DONE.

SKABGAGG!
THOR!
THOR, MY FRIEND! FINALLY, YOU'VE ARRIVED! NOW THE REVELING CAN TRULY BEGIN!
THOUGH IT SEEMS SOMEONE HAS DRANK ALL THE MEAD.
THIS ENDS NOW, SKABGAGG. SURRENDER YOURSELF. I DO NOT WISH TO HARM YOU.
HARM ME? NO ONE'S GETTING HARMED, OLD FRIEND, WE'RE JUST...HAVING FUN IS ALL. JUST AS WE DID BEFORE.
RIGHT, GUDRID? GUDRID, WAKE UP!
I KEEP SHAKING HER, BUT SHE WON'T WAKE UP.
LAST WARNING, DRAGON. PUT THE WOMAN DOWN.
YOU...SMELL SO STRANGE, GUDRID.
YOU MAKE ME FEEL AS IF...AS IF I HADN'T EATEN ANYTHING IN...SO VERY LONG...

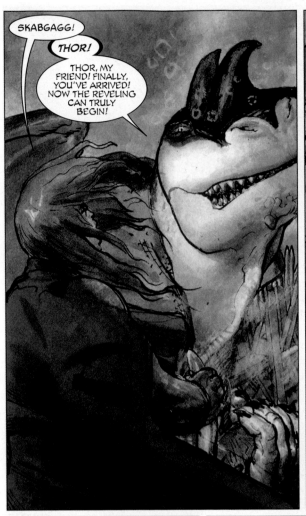

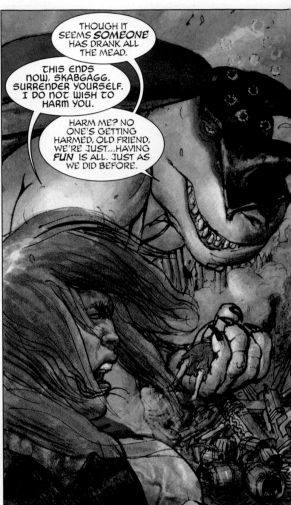

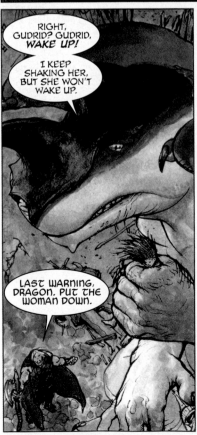

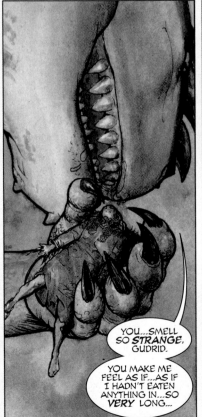

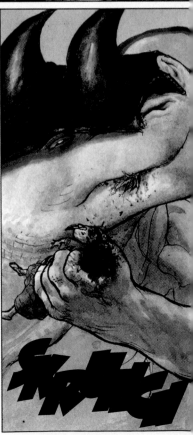

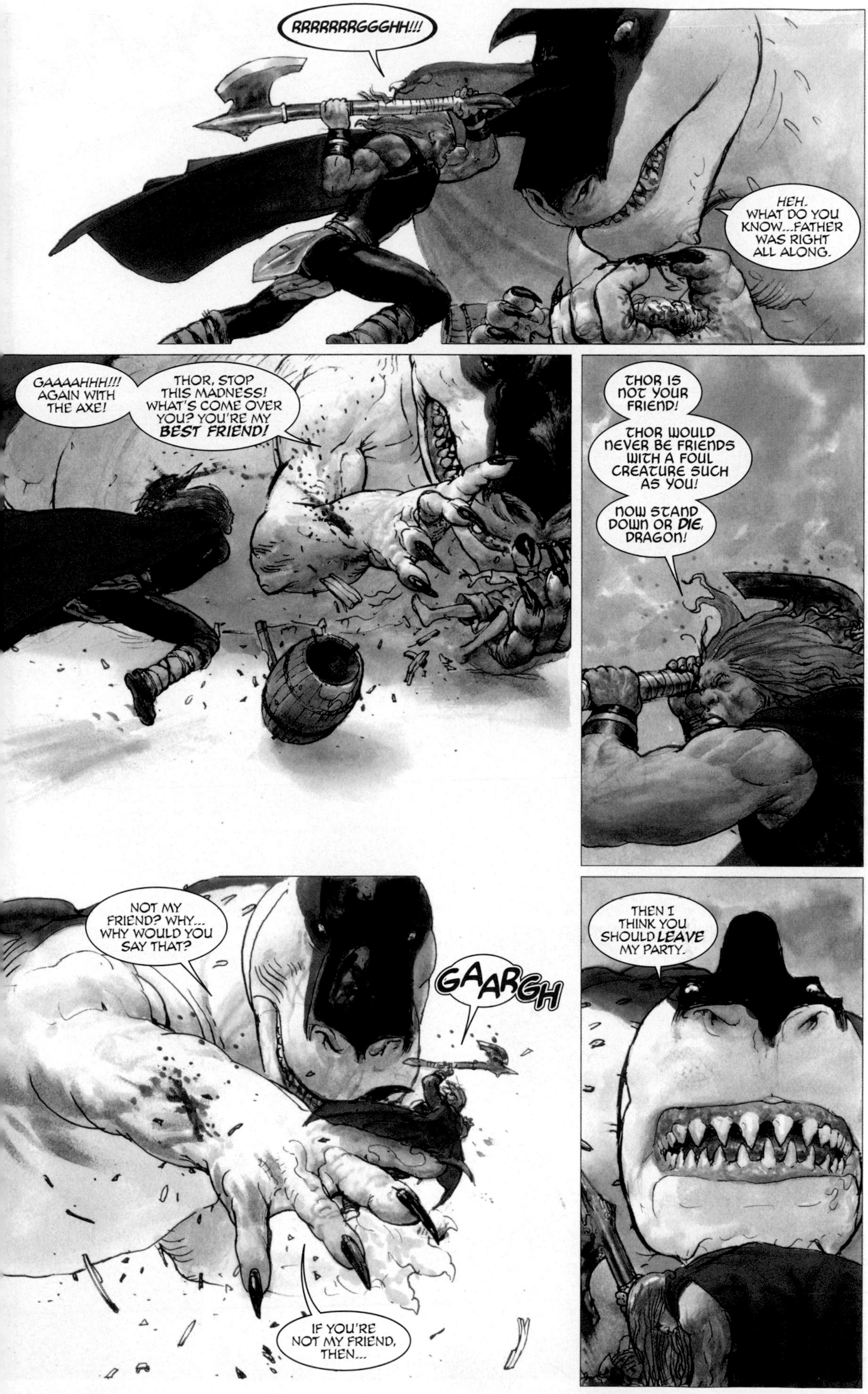
RRRRRRRGGGHH!!!
HEH. WHAT DO YOU KNOW...FATHER WAS RIGHT ALL ALONG.
GAAAAHHH!!! AGAIN WITH THE AXE!
THOR, STOP THIS MADNESS! WHAT'S COME OVER YOU? YOU'RE MY BEST FRIEND!
THOR IS NOT YOUR FRIEND!
THOR WOULD NEVER BE FRIENDS WITH A FOUL CREATURE SUCH AS YOU!
NOW STAND DOWN OR DIE, DRAGON!
NOT MY FRIEND? WHY... WHY WOULD YOU SAY THAT?
GAARGH
IF YOU'RE NOT MY FRIEND, THEN...
THEN I THINK YOU SHOULD LEAVE MY PARTY.

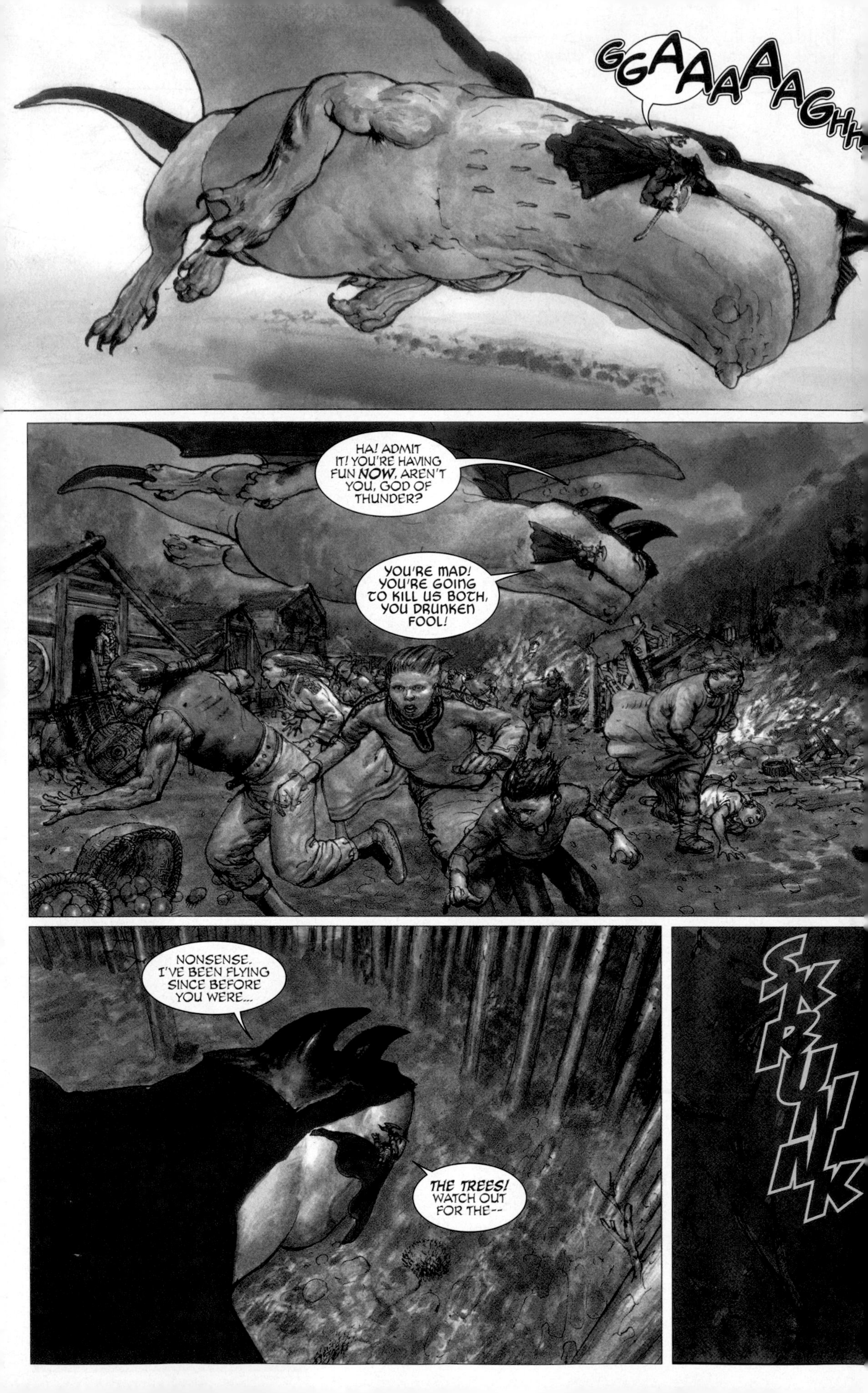
GGAAAAAAGHH
HA! ADMIT IT! YOU'RE HAVING FUN NOW, AREN'T YOU, GOD OF THUNDER?
YOU'RE MAD! YOU'RE GOING TO KILL US BOTH, YOU DRUNKEN FOOL!
NONSENSE. I'VE BEEN FLYING SINCE BEFORE YOU WERE...
THE TREES! WATCH OUT FOR THE--
SKRUNK

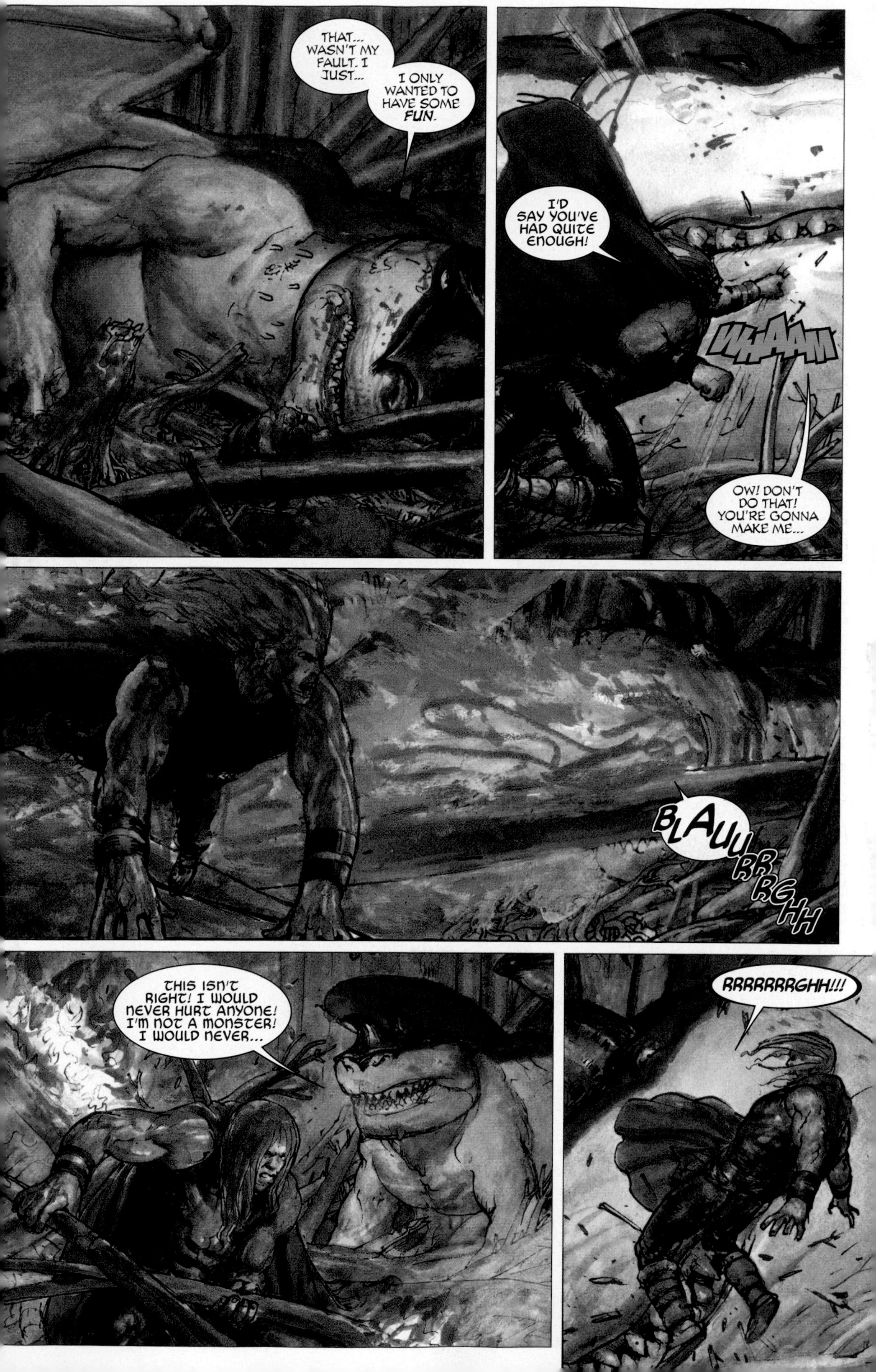
THAT... WASN'T MY FAULT. I JUST...
I ONLY WANTED TO HAVE SOME FUN.
I'D SAY YOU'VE HAD QUITE ENOUGH!
WHAAAM
OW! DON'T DO THAT! YOU'RE GONNA MAKE ME...
BLAUURRRGHH
THIS ISN'T RIGHT! I WOULD NEVER HURT ANYONE! I'M NOT A MONSTER! I WOULD NEVER...
RRRRRRRGHH!!!

SKABGAGG, LISTEN TO ME...

I MISSPOKE BEFORE, OUT OF ANGER. I *AM* YOUR FRIEND. AND AS YOUR FRIEND, I BEG OF YOU, ONE LAST TIME...

STOP THIS. BEFORE SOMEONE ELSE GETS HURT.

MOST LIKELY *YOU.*

I KNOW WHAT YOU'RE DOING. YOU'RE *JUDGING* ME, AREN'T YOU? YOU GODS, ALWAYS SO JUDGMENTAL...

SKABGAGG, FOR THE LOVE OF--!

YES. I AM SKABGAGG.

I AM SKABGAGG THE *DRAGON!* SON OF THE WINGED VIPERS FROM THE MOUNTAINS OF FIRE, WHO ATE THE FLESH OF THE FIRST MAN! WHO WERE ANCIENT WHEN THIS WORLD WAS NAUGHT BUT OCEANS OF FIRE!

I AM BROTHER TO NIDHOGG, THE EATER OF THE TREE, AND JORMUNGAND, THE MIDGARD SERPENT, WHO IS DESTINED TO BE YOUR DOOM COME THE DAY OF RAGNAROK!

I REFUSE TO BE JUDGED BY THE LIKES OF YOU, LITTLE ASGARDIAN!

BY YOU OR ANY OTHER DAMN GOD!

SO BE IT, DRAGON.

HAVE AT ME THEN.

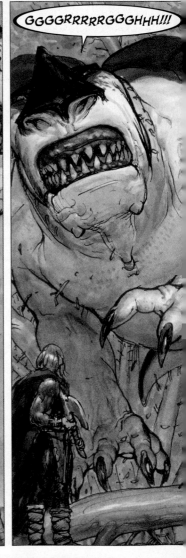

GGGGRRRRRGGGHHH!!!

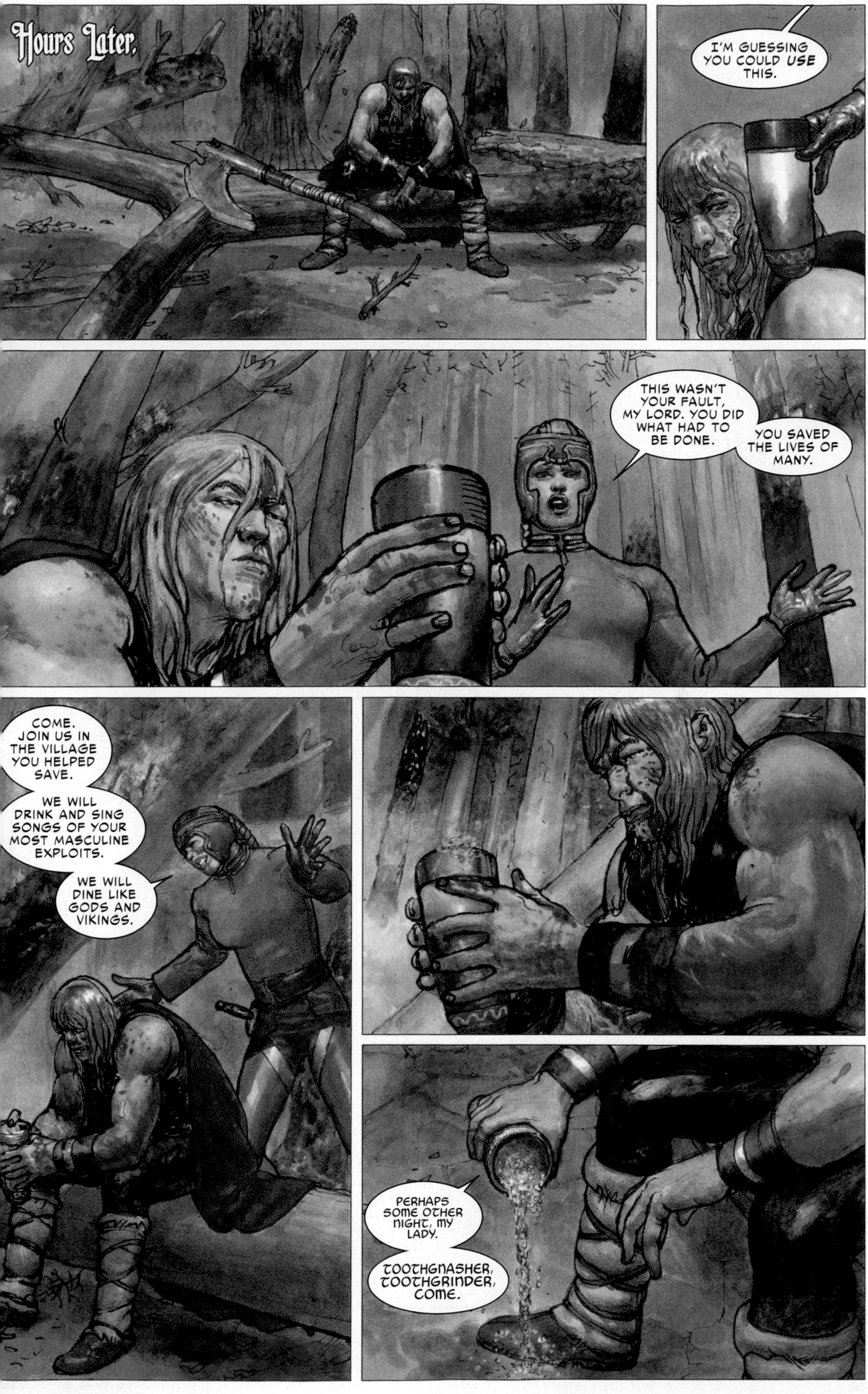
Hours Later,
I'M GUESSING YOU COULD USE THIS.
THIS WASN'T YOUR FAULT, MY LORD. YOU DID WHAT HAD TO BE DONE.
YOU SAVED THE LIVES OF MANY.
COME. JOIN US IN THE VILLAGE YOU HELPED SAVE.
WE WILL DRINK AND SING SONGS OF YOUR MOST MASCULINE EXPLOITS.
WE WILL DINE LIKE GODS AND VIKINGS.
PERHAPS SOME OTHER NIGHT, MY LADY.
TOOTHGNASHER, TOOTHGRINDER, COME.

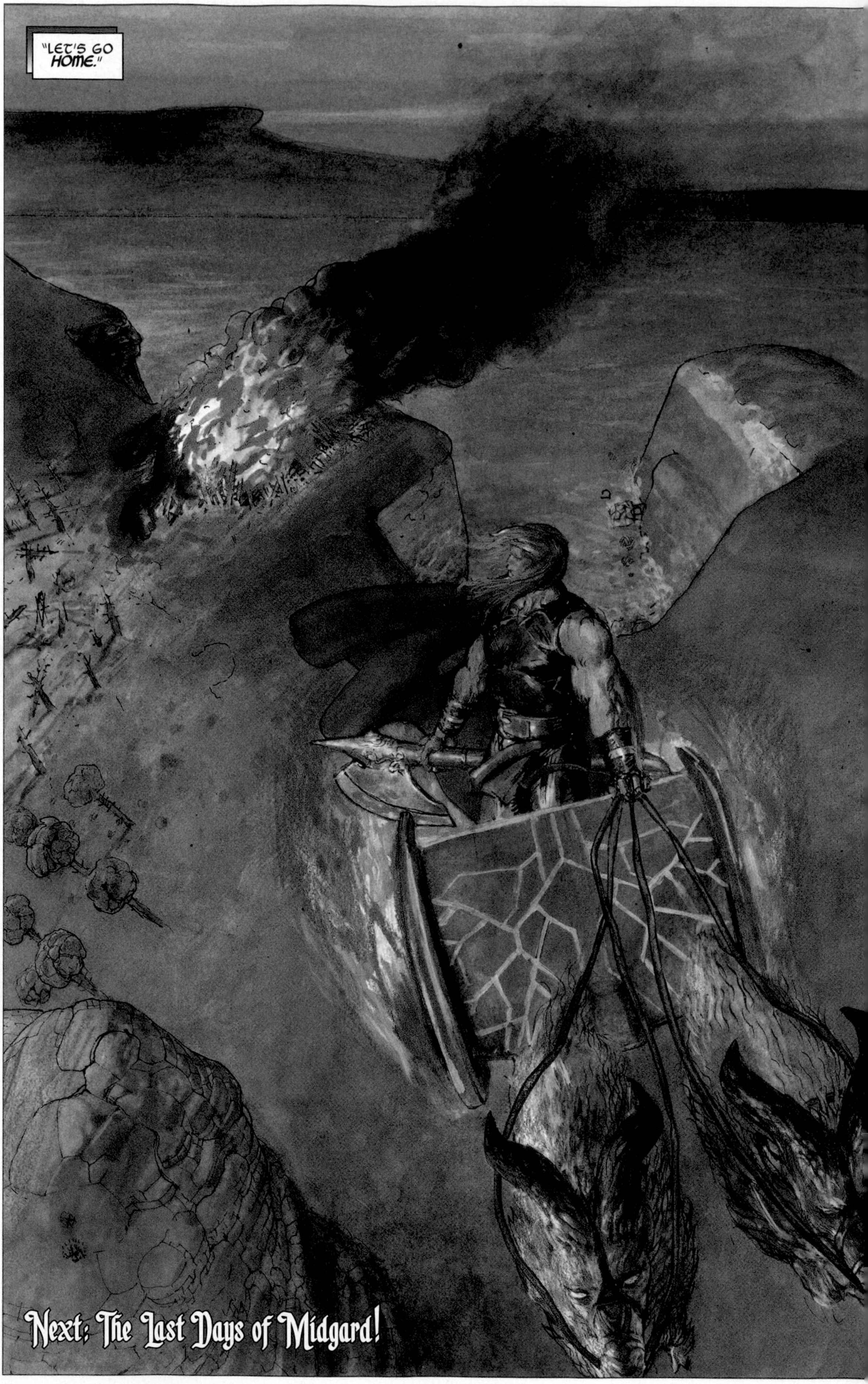
"LET'S GO HOME."
Next: The Last Days of Midgard!

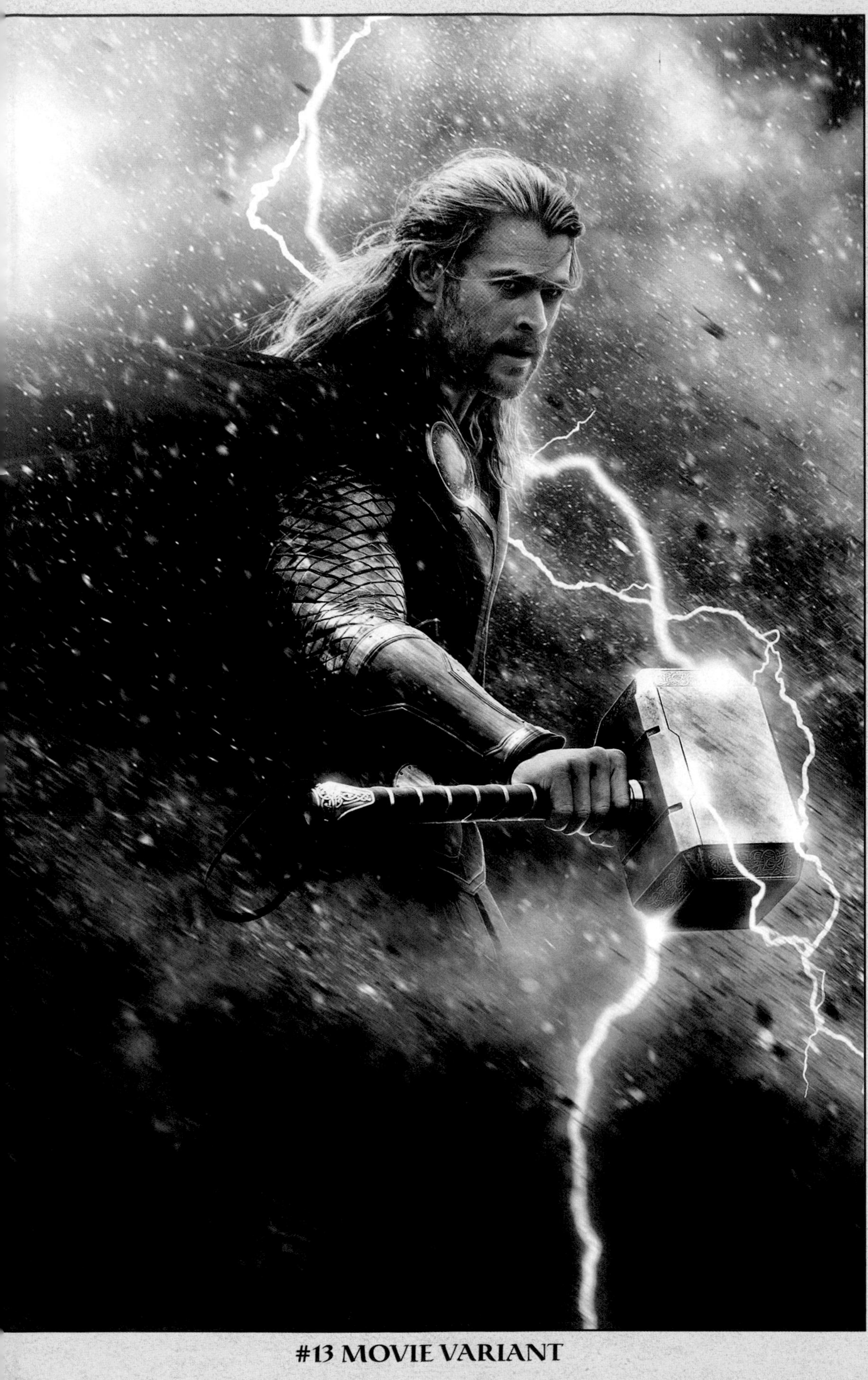

#13 MOVIE VARIANT

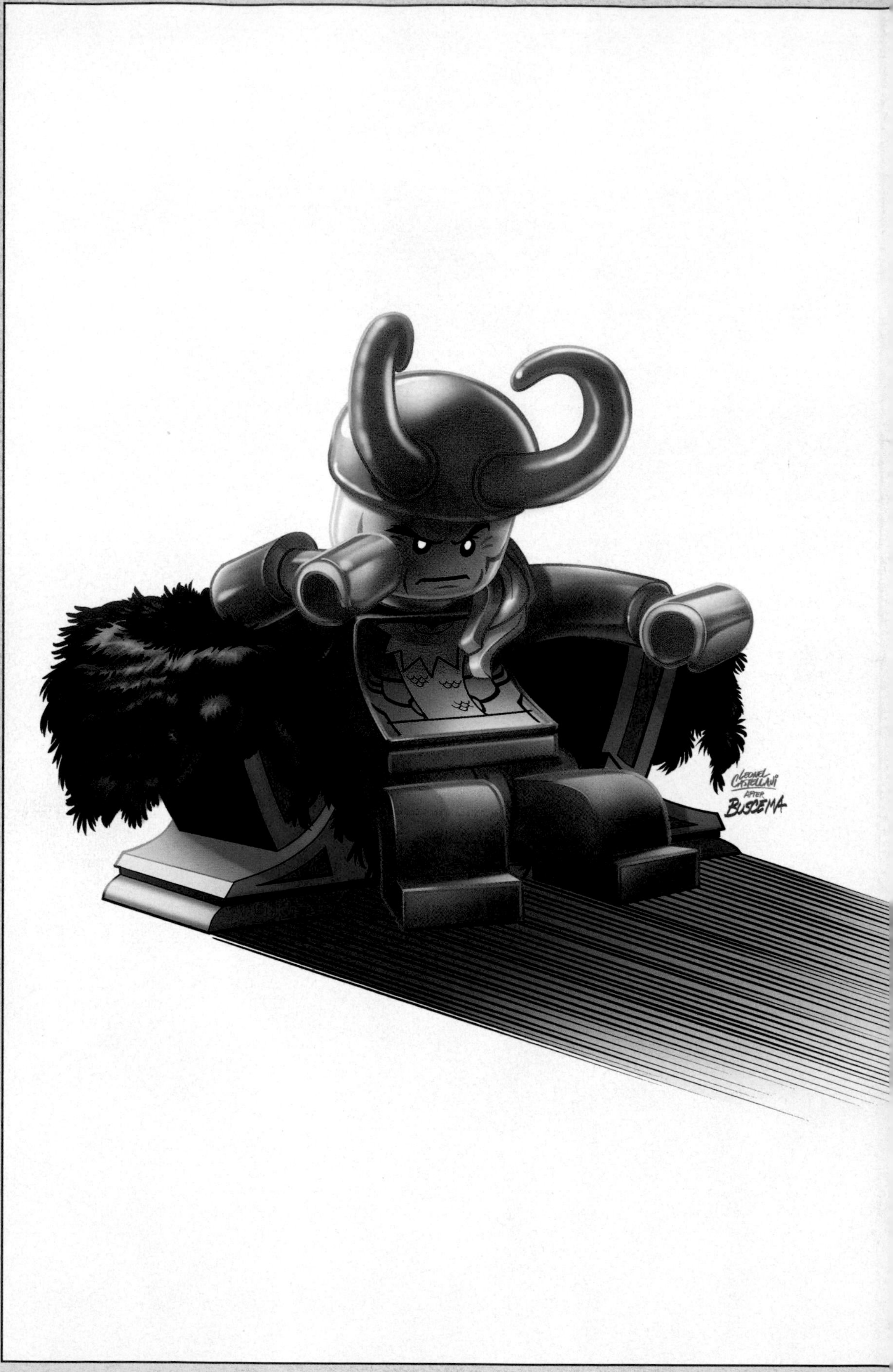
LEONEL CASTELLANI AFTER BUSCEMA

#14 LEGO VARIANT
BY LEONEL CASTELLANI

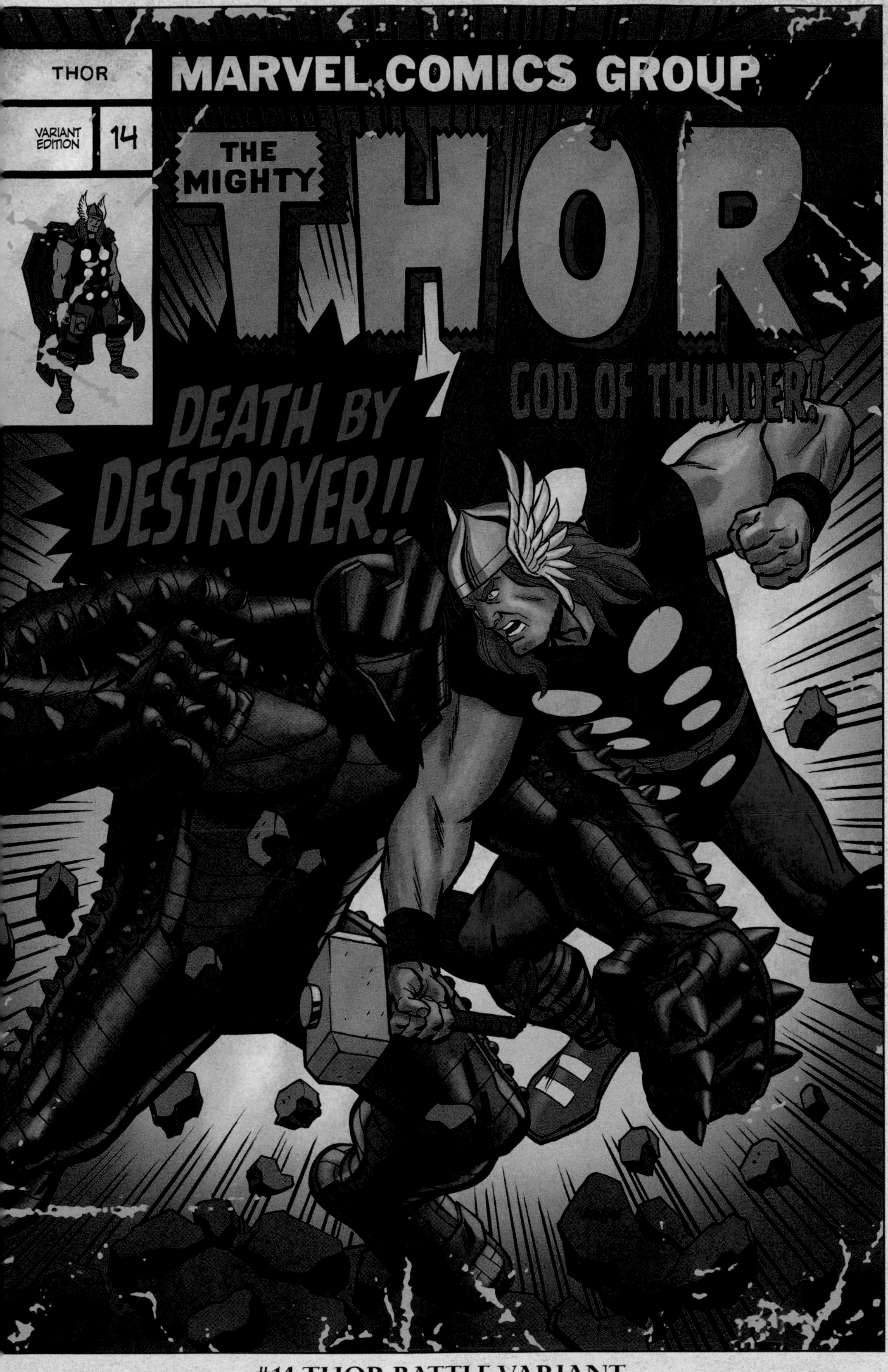
THOR
MARVEL COMICS GROUP
VARIANT EDITION
14
THE MIGHTY
THOR
GOD OF THUNDER!
DEATH BY DESTROYER!!

#14 THOR BATTLE VARIANT
BY DAVE JOHNSON

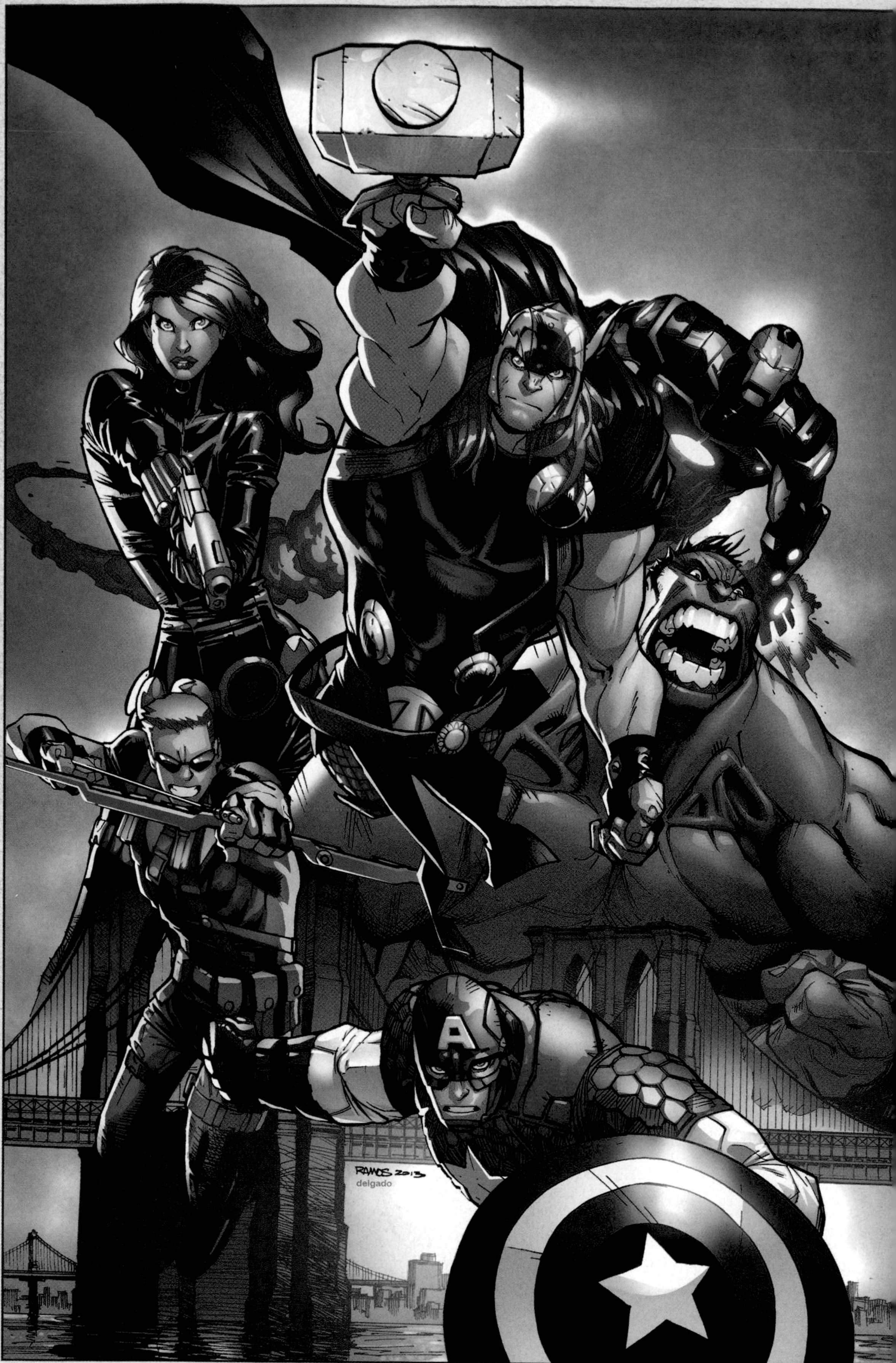
RAMOS 2013
delgado

#14 NYCC VARIANT
BY HUMERTO RAMOS & EDGAR DELGADO

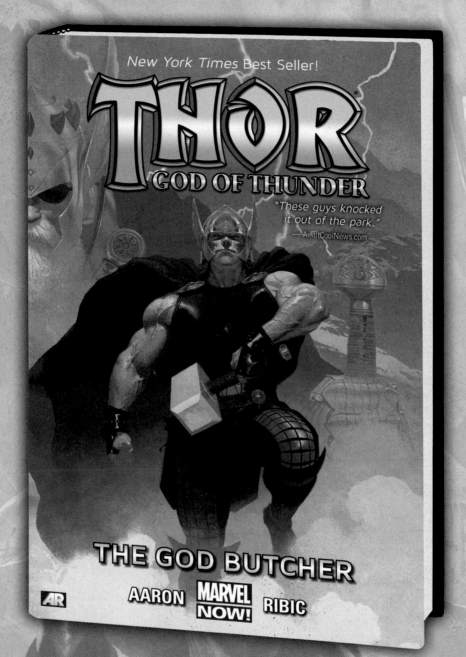

TO ACCESS THE FREE MARVEL AUGMENTED REALITY APP
THAT ENHANCES AND CHANGES THE WAY YOU EXPERIENCE COMICS

1. Download the app for free via
marvel.com/ARapp

2. Launch the app on your camera-enabled
Apple iOS® or Android™ device*

3. Hold your mobile device's camera over
any cover or panel with the  AR graph

4. Sit back and see the future of comics
in action!

*Available on most camera-enabled Apple iOS® and Android™ devices. Content subject to
change and availability.

AR
INDEX

TMAJ4MTKC9QX

TO REDEEM YOUR CODE
FOR A FREE DIGITAL COPY:

1. GO TO MARVEL.COM/REDEEM.
OFFER EXPIRES ON 3/12/16.

2. FOLLOW THE ON-SCREEN INSTRUCTIONS
TO REDEEM YOUR DIGITAL COPY.

3. LAUNCH THE MARVEL COMICS APP TO
READ YOUR COMIC NOW!

4. YOUR DIGITAL COPY WILL BE FOUND
UNDER THE *MY COMICS* TAB.

5. READ & ENJOY!

YOUR FREE DIGITAL COPY WILL BE AVAILABLE O

MARVEL COMICS APP
FOR APPLE™ iOS DEVICES

MARVEL COMICS APP
FOR ANDROID™ DEVICES